AF556891

Rodin
and the art of ancient Greece

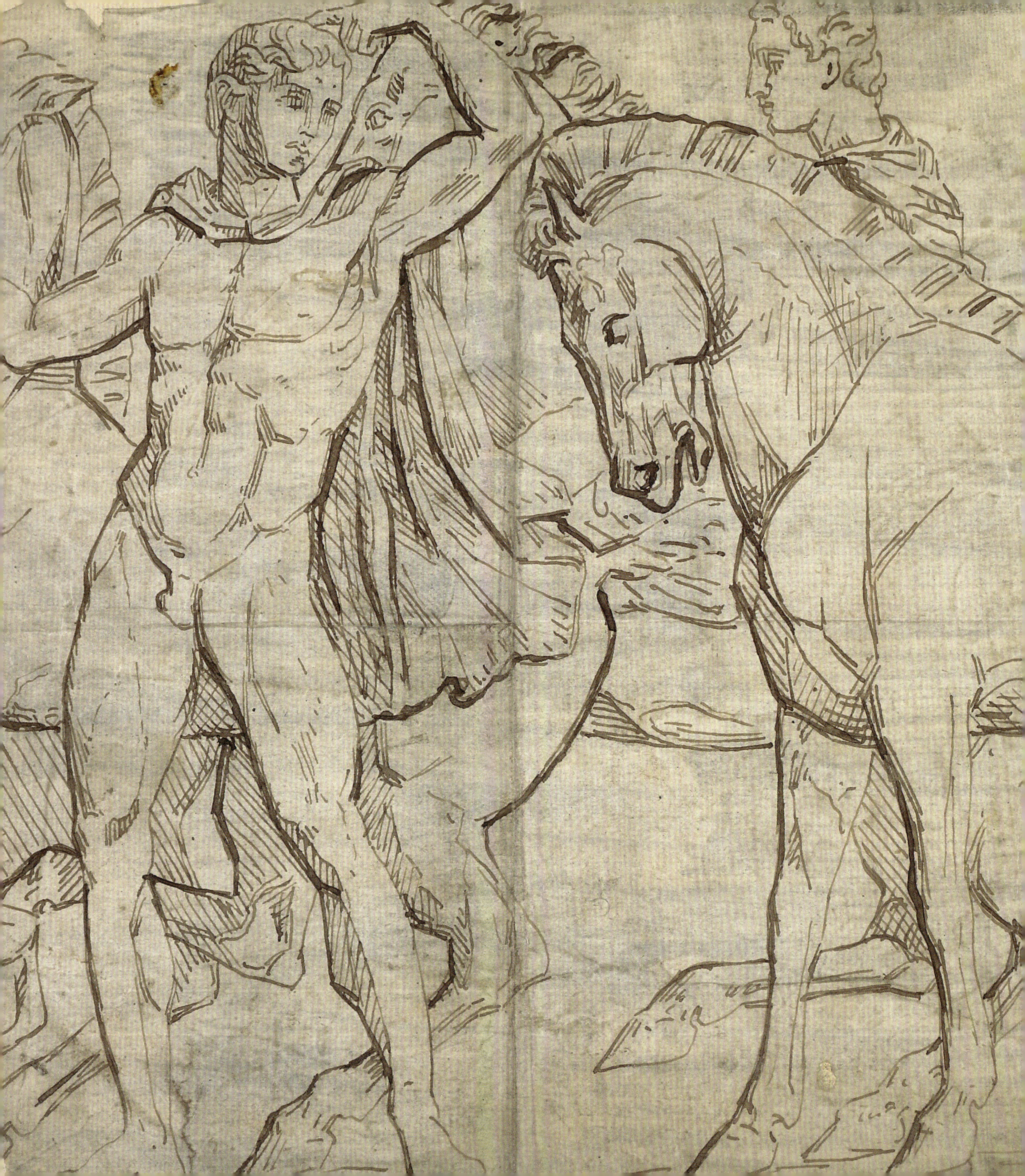

Rodin
and the art of ancient Greece

Celeste Farge, Bénédicte Garnier and Ian Jenkins

Organized with the Musée Rodin, Paris

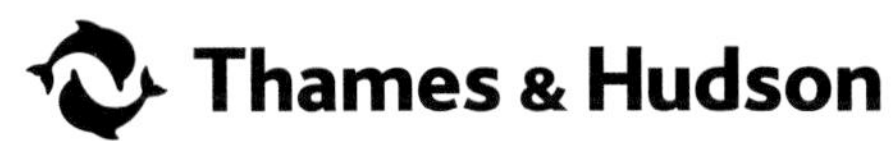

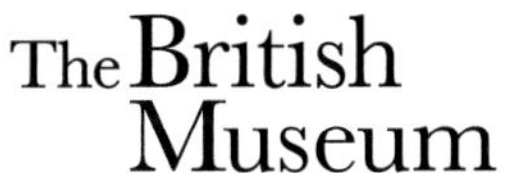

Rodin and the art of ancient Greece

Sponsored by Bank of America Merrill Lynch

Bank of America
Merrill Lynch

This publication accompanies the exhibition 'Rodin and the art of ancient Greece' at the British Museum from 26 April to 29 July 2018.

This exhibition at the British Museum has been made possible by the provision of insurance through the Government Indemnity Scheme. The British Museum would like to thank the Department for Digital, Culture, Media and Sport and Arts Council England for providing and arranging this indemnity.

Additional support for this publication has been provided by the Henry Moore Foundation.

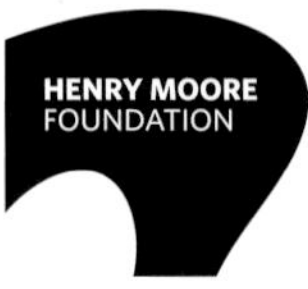

First published in the United Kingdom in 2018 by Thames & Hudson Ltd, 181a High Holborn, London WC1V 7QX in collaboration with the British Museum

Designed by Peter Dawson, gradedesign.com

British Library Cataloguing-in-Publication Data
A catalogue record for this book is available from the British Library

ISBN 978-0-500-48030-4

Printed and bound in Italy by Printer Trento SrL

To find out about all our publications, please visit **www.thamesandhudson.com**. There you can subscribe to our e-newsletter, browse or download our current catalogue, and buy any titles that are in print.

For more information about the Museum and its collection, please visit **britishmuseum.org**

Frontispiece: Auguste Rodin, Study of the Parthenon North Frieze (block XLVII, figs 132–136), before 1870 (Cat. 5; detail). Graphite and pen and ink on fine paper. Musée Rodin, D. 61, Rodin donation, 1916.

Contents

Sponsor's foreword

Bank of America Merrill Lynch is delighted to sponsor *Rodin and the art of ancient Greece*.

We have a long-standing relationship with the British Museum. Through our Art Conservation Project we proudly supported the restoration of the British Museum's impressive sixth-century Amitābha Buddha sculpture, on view in its North Staircase. Prior to that, we enabled the conservation of a group of Begram Ivories and sponsored the corresponding exhibition of these works in the British Museum's *Afghanistan: Crossroads of the Ancient World*.

We know that the arts matter. They provide education, and are the heart of a thriving public community; they inspire creativity and empathy for the human experience through the ages.

Moreover, the arts speak to us in a universal language that provides pathways to greater cultural understanding, something Rodin would have appreciated. He was inspired by the history and magnificence of the Classical antiquities which he witnessed at the British Museum.

We hope you will enjoy this unique presentation of how that experience shaped Rodin, both as an artist and as a man.

Alex Wilmot-Sitwell
President, Europe, Middle East & Africa
Bank of America Merrill Lynch

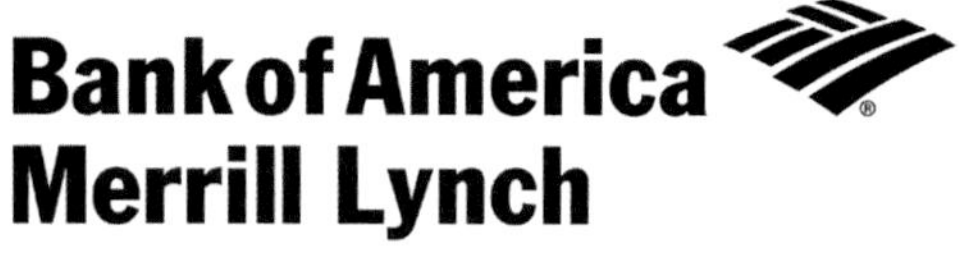

British Museum Director's foreword

This exhibition is a landmark in the history of the British Museum. The Parthenon sculptures, one of the Museum's greatest treasures from Classical Greece, are for the first time shown with the work of a modern master. Auguste Rodin admired the sculpture of Greece, and in particular that of the Parthenon, with a lifelong passion rarely surpassed by any other artist of his time. He rejoiced in the Parthenon sculptures as precious survivors of the art of Pheidias, the most famous sculptor of all antiquity. In Pheidias, Rodin found a spiritual companion and mentor.

Rodin's modernism bridged the abyss of time, and the relics of the past were brought into the present. The fragmentary status of the Parthenon sculptures, lacking heads and limbs, was to him not to be lamented. Each fragment was seen as complete in itself. Rodin's empathy for the ruined state of the Parthenon sculptures inspired him to turn the torso into a new genre of art. The headless, armless *The Walking Man* seems to stride into the twentieth century announcing a new purpose for sculpture, for art, for mankind.

If we are to understand the place of the encyclopaedic museum and its influence in world culture, we have to acknowledge the extraordinary creativity in art and thought it has engendered. With this exhibition, it is Rodin whose works are brought into focus. There are other artists we shall highlight in the future.

The unique nature of this exhibition has been made possible by a creative collaboration with the Musée Rodin. The works by Rodin shown in the exhibition are principally drawn from the collection of that museum, and they have been coupled with the Parthenon sculptures in themes chosen to help us understand the dialogue between ancient and modern. Also exhibited will be some of Rodin's own collection of ancient Classical sculpture. We are truly grateful to the director of the Musée Rodin, Catherine Chevillot, for her generous and spirited role in the making of this project. We also wish to thank her talented and dedicated staff, especially the co-curator of this exhibition, Bénédicte Garnier.

I also want to thank our sponsor Bank of America Merrill Lynch, without whose generous support nothing could have been achieved.

Hartwig Fischer
Director, British Museum, London

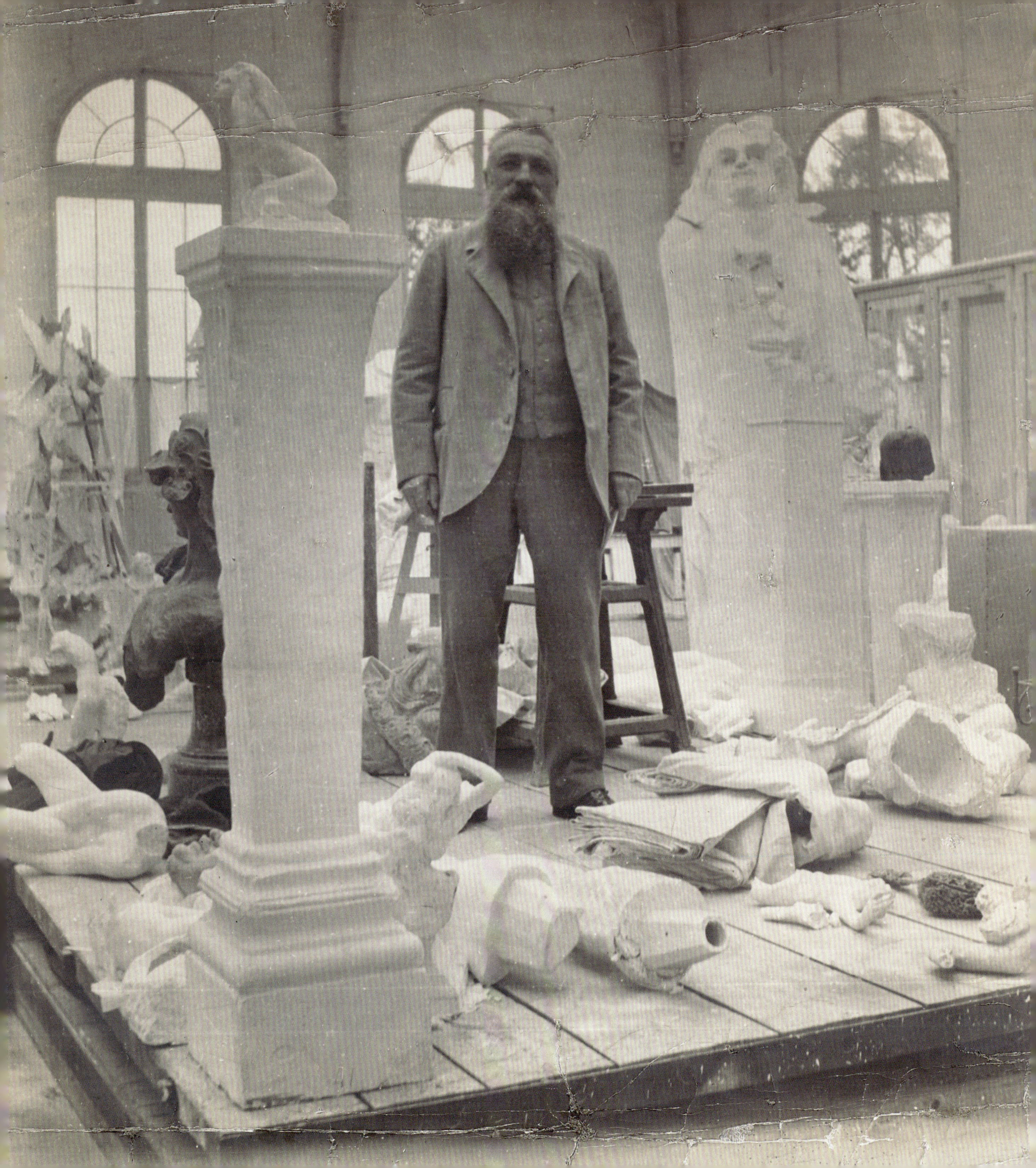

Musée Rodin Director's foreword

Rodin face to face with the Parthenon – probably the greatest sculptor of the late nineteenth century expressing his veneration for the universally revered symbol of Antiquity. But there is more to this juxtaposition than that. For Rodin there were two ultimate and undisputed references: Antiquity and Michelangelo. And when we place the scattered remains of the Parthenon and the unfinished works of Michelangelo beside the fragmentary creations of Rodin, we begin to see a unique and profound relationship. Rodin's sculptures acquire a poetic consistency and significance: that of incompletion.

The almost arbitrary nature of the Parthenon sculptures today is the result purely of the vagaries of history. And yet it is precisely this dislocated aspect that fascinated Rodin, that gave him the courage to present fragments as finished works. Through them, at the same time, he showed himself to be an artist of his age, an age in which accepted ideas were being overturned. Revolutions in thinking had led to new ways of interpreting the world and of addressing the central questions of human existence and destiny, producing a vision of a universe that was constantly changing, unpredictable and transitory.

In 1880, Rodin received the commission for *The Gates of Hell*, a personal reinterpretation of a Gothic archway, intended as the entrance to a new museum of decorative arts to be constructed on the site of a building that had burnt down in 1871, its remains since abandoned and overgrown. The challenge as Rodin saw it was to create something out of ruins, to gather up the pieces of the past and attempt to fashion them into a coherent image of the present. *The Gates of Hell* would be a polymorphic creation that would in some way symbolize humanity's position in an unstable universe. But when Rodin came to show this monumental work to the public for the first time, he presented it not complete, but in pieces – both as a representation of the incompleteness of the works on which he modelled his own and, perhaps, as the most appropriate symbol of the confusion of his time. It was also a kind of final homage – whether conscious or unconscious – to Pheidias, from whose Parthenon sculptures he had learnt so much.

This British Museum exhibition, which gives us a rare opportunity to measure Rodin's work against that of his idol, is also an opportunity to assess the extent to which these mythical reliefs still act not only as an artistic benchmark but also as a yardstick by which to judge human civilization.

Catherine Chevillot
Director, Musée Rodin, Paris

Eugène Druet (1867–1916)
Rodin among his works in the Pavillon d'Alma at Meudon
Around 1902
Gelatin silver print
H 25.6 cm, W 25.2 cm
Musée Rodin, Ph. 203
Rodin donation, 1916

Introduction

Hartwig Fischer

The most interesting part of London is the number of its antiquities. In my spare time I simply haunt the British Museum. It is a most noble institution. My one regret is that I have not the time to frequent it more.

Auguste Rodin, 'Mr Rodin in London', *The Daily Chronicle*, 2 March 1903

The ancient sculptor Pheidias is best known today for his association with the Parthenon and its architectural sculptures. This great temple stood on the Acropolis of Athens from the middle of the fifth century BC. A comparison of the Parthenon sculptures with the works of Auguste Rodin from the late nineteenth and early twentieth century AD reveals fresh insights into the mind and artistic practice of both sculptors. One was the most famous artist of all antiquity, while the other became, and arguably still is, the best-known sculptor of the modern era. Our collaboration with the Musée Rodin has given us a unique opportunity for bringing together the works of two great artists. Rodin, of course, is not alone in being inspired by the Parthenon sculptures, but few responded with his passion, which lasted a lifetime.

In antiquity Pheidias was famous not so much for the architectural sculpture on the outside of the Parthenon, as for the colossal gold and ivory (chryselephantine) statue of Athena Parthenos (Virgin) that stood inside. His other chryselephantine statue was that of Zeus at Olympia, which became one of the Seven Wonders of the Ancient World. Neither the Athena, nor the Zeus, nor any of the other works for which he was most famous have survived. However, the Parthenon sculptures are rare fifth-century BC originals from Pheidias' workshop, and he can be said to have designed them.

Pheidias was born around 480 BC, and grew up in the golden age of intellectual and artistic humanism that flourished in Athens in the fifth century BC. Perikles' statesmanship, Sokrates' philosophical discourse, Sophokles' drama, Herodotus' ethnography and Thucydides' political and military history have all contributed to the modern idea of the individual human being as someone of unique intelligence possessed of the capacity for self-determination and with personal responsibility for the welfare of his or her own soul.

In the fifth century BC, the Parthenon sculptures were conceived as a composite body of carefully chosen images that collectively positioned Athens at the centre of the cosmos. Today the sculptures of the Parthenon are even better known than they were in antiquity. Moreover, they have transcended their original focus upon Athens to become representations of humanity at large and, in the frieze that ran high up all round the building in particular, the pageant of idealized residents of ancient Athens can now serve as an image of our own best selves, members of a community that reaches around the globe.

Every day people from all over the world gather in the British Museum. In this collection of world cultures, visitors can look back on what went before the Parthenon and that inspired it, and forwards to see how the sculptures influenced later civilizations. Ever since they were rediscovered in the seventeenth century, the Parthenon sculptures have enjoyed an international appeal – at first European and subsequently around the world. A curious moment in the Enlightenment culture that surrounded the acquisition of the Parthenon sculptures in London is to be found in the response of the great German writer Johann Wolfgang von Goethe when he first became aware of them in the 1780s. He predicted the importance that the Parthenon sculptures would have for European taste, art and thought. As early as August 1787 he wrote from Rome:

> Yesterday I saw many drawings in the possession of the nobleman Worthley who has travelled to Greece and Egypt. What interested me in particular were the drawings after bas-reliefs on the frieze of the temple of Minerva in Athens, the work of Pheidias. It is impossible to imagine anything more beautiful…[1] [they] made a decisive and unforgettable impression on me.[2]

The 'nobleman Worthley' is in fact Sir Richard Worsley, who at this time was the British representative in Venice.[3] The drawings were by William Pars, who joined the Society of Dilettanti's Ionian expedition in 1764. In 1765, on their way back to England, he and his fellow travellers reached Athens. There Pars, suspended in a cradle, drew the Parthenon sculptures face-to-face for the first time. It is not known how Worsley came to possess the drawings by Pars, but he published them in his great two-volume work, *Museum Worsleyanum*.[4]

More than a century after Goethe saw the beauty of the Parthenon sculptures through a glass darkly, Rodin made his way to London in 1881 to see them for himself. Time and again Rodin, in his writings and in his art, returned to an abiding conviction that ancient Greek sculpture, whether fragment or whole, was not merely a passive survival of the past, but could be an active force in the present. In empathy with the ruination of antiquity, Rodin did not so much lament what we have lost as rejoice in what has survived. To Rodin's creative mind the Parthenon and its sculptures were objects of modernity that allowed the past to be in the present and the present to reach back to the past.

1. Goethe, *Italienische Reise*, 23.8.1787. For Goethe and the Parthenon sculptures see Grumach (1949).
2. Goethe, *Italienische Reise*, August 1787.
3. Guilding (2014), 208ff.
4. Worsley (1798–1824). Cf. Jenkins and Sloan (1996), 101–02.

The French romance for Greek marbles

Celeste Farge and Ian Jenkins

John Ruskin once remarked of the painter G. F. Watts that he was paralysed by the Parthenon sculptures. Auguste Rodin, by contrast, was somebody whose intellectual and artistic agility was enhanced and augmented by a lifelong fascination for the ancient sculptor Pheidias, whom he would evoke as his mentor and companion.

Rodin and Pheidias

Both masters of the sculptor's craft, Rodin (1840–1917) and Pheidias (about 480–430 BC)[1] pushed at the boundaries of what sculpture could be. In antiquity Pheidias was celebrated for his two colossal statues, one of Athena in the Parthenon on the Acropolis of Athens and the other of Zeus in the god's eponymous temple at Olympia. These so-called chryselephantine sculptures, constructed out of sheets of gold and ivory over a wooden armature, overwhelmed the senses and seemed to immerse the spectator in a divine presence.[2] Said to be possessed of a powerful and intuitive imagination (*phantasia*), Pheidias was able to beckon the gods from the holy mountain of Olympos and place them before the viewer in all their awe-inspiring majesty.[3] In Pheidias' colossal works, grand forms infused with close observation from nature seemed to live and breathe. Breathing vitality is also one of the salient properties of Rodin's work, nowhere more so than in *The Age of Bronze* (Cat. 39). When Rodin exhibited it in Belgium and France it provoked harsh criticism because the body type seemed excessively naturalistic and Rodin was accused of having cast it from life. This was not in itself such an extraordinary accusation. It had been a commonplace from antiquity onwards for sculptors to use casts of real bodies in order to construct the ideal body. However, the charge that was laid at the feet of *The Age of Bronze* was a deliberate attempt to deny the role of sculpture as an intervention between nature and culture.[4] Rodin had no regard for the body cast; he himself condemned such plagiarism. In the Parthenon sculptures he saw a closeness to nature greater than had hitherto been associated with the artistic establishment.

The modulated surfaces of Rodin's figures invite the eye to roam freely, unrestrained by the contemporary academic beaux-arts conventions of measured proportion, which had their origins in the architectonic system of the canons of Classical antiquity. Rodin's modelling was concerned not only with the visible outside, but also with the invisible interior on which external effects depended for success. In explaining his notion of 'interior modelling' Rodin said, 'rather than imagining the different parts of the body as flat surfaces, I pictured them as projections of interior volumes'.[5]

Rodin is sometimes seen posing for the camera with hammer and chisel in hand. His actual practice was not to carve himself, however. His preferred medium was clay, modelled into animate subjects that might then be cast in plaster or bronze. Or he would delegate to a stone-carver the task of copying the model in marble under his personal control. In this, his studio practice may not have been very different from that of Pheidias. It is most unlikely that Pheidias would have carved any part of the architectural sculpture of the Parthenon, but he very probably designed it, fashioning models (*typoi*) and making drawings for the pediment and frieze compositions. The Parthenon sculptures are thus the nearest we have to a survival of Pheidias' own work. Pheidias is reported to have been unusually versatile in his range of craft skills. He is, for example, referred to by some ancient sources as a *lithouergos* or worker-in-stone. This does not necessarily indicate that he carved stone himself, but may simply suggest that carved stone issued from his workshop. Certainly, we could apply the term to Rodin's practice. Rodin, as a modeller of clay, seemed to prefer building up the shape of his subject rather than, as in stone-carving, to take away.

A hallmark of Rodin's workshop is the contrasting finish that is given to different parts of the stone sculpture. So, for example, in the case of the portrait of Mrs Russell as Athena (Cat. 1), the high polish of the face is given a blurred (*sfumato*) treatment contrasting with the rough finishes of the hair and the dress. This *all'antica* ('after the antique') look to some of his sculptures can produce very beautiful effects of pleasingly contrasting surfaces, which retain the signs of craft

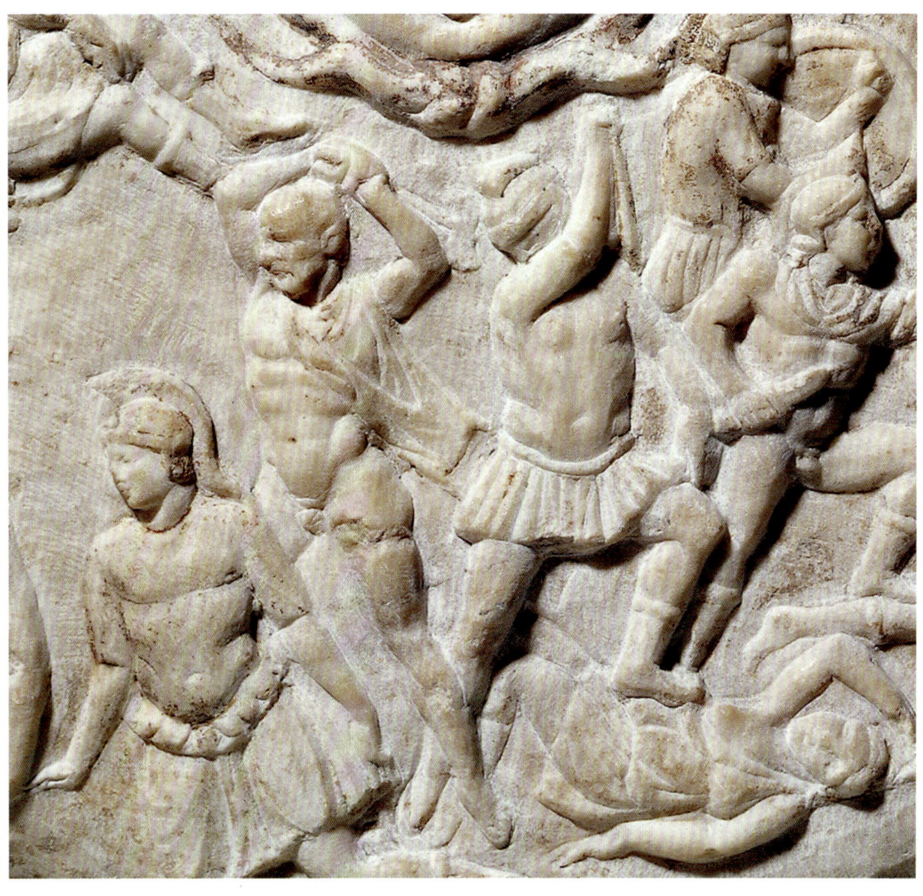

Fig. 1
The Strangford Shield (detail): Pheidias and Perikles fighting the Amazons
Roman
AD 100–150
Marble
H 41.18 cm, W 45.72 cm
British Museum, 1864,0220.18

production. The marks left by the punch or point, or the flat or claw chisel, compare with the finger impressions left in the clay model.

Both Rodin and Pheidias drew upon poetry for inspiration. Homer was to Pheidias what Dante was to Rodin. In later antiquity, mention of Pheidias' name as the greatest of all visual artists could equally bring to mind the name of Homer as the greatest of all poets. Pheidias himself is reported as saying that, in creating his colossal gold and ivory statue of Zeus at Olympia, he kept before his mind's eye the image of the god as portrayed by Homer. That statue is long lost, but we may compare the characterization of the gods shown as individual personalities on the East Frieze of the Parthenon with their description in the closing lines of Homer's Book I of the *Iliad*.

Of Pheidias' life we know next to nothing, and what we are told comes from the pen of Roman authors writing half a millennium after he lived. He is said to have trained in the making of bronze sculpture in the workshop of Ageladas of Argos. There, the great fifth-century BC sculptors Myron and Polykleitos were also said to have learnt their craft. Plutarch says of Pheidias that he was *episkopos* or overseer of the programme of architectural renewal of Perikles' Athens after the devastations of the Persian Wars.[6] As a prominent member of that great statesman's inner circle, Pheidias naturally had enemies. Before he left Athens for Olympia to make his statue of Zeus, he was charged with embezzlement of the gold that had been entrusted to him for the Athena Parthenos. He had, however, anticipated this, and made the gold drapery in such a way that it could be detached. When this was done and it was weighed, all was found to be in order.

Another charge against Pheidias in the making of the colossal statue of Athena was that he carved a portrait of himself and Perikles in the shield the goddess held at her side. The shield does not survive, like the rest of the statue, but so beautiful were its relief carvings that in the Roman period many copies were made.[7] The example in the British Museum is unique for its remarkable pairing of two figures, one bald and the other helmeted, fighting back to back (Fig. 1). The helmeted figure holds an arm across his face, as if not wanting to reveal his identity, while the other is fully visible and is a frank portrait, unusual for the period, of a man affected by obvious hair loss.

One version of the ending of Pheidias' life was that he was in fact found guilty by his Athenian accusers and died in prison. In another version he escapes prosecution and completes his great commission at Olympia. Remarkably, a building was excavated there in the last century that is generally accepted to have been the workshop of Pheidias. This is as close as we get to Pheidias the man.

Rodin, by contrast, left a legacy that documents his life perhaps more fully than that of any other artist of our time. From it emerges an indefinable genius who is as smooth and polished, or as unfinished and multifaceted, as any of his sculptures. Yet curiously we find in Rodin a figure who is in some ways as enigmatic as Pheidias.

Reflections on the Parthenon, its sculptures and their meaning

It is a paradox that while in Rodin's time the sculptures that decorated the exterior of the Parthenon came to enjoy world fame, in antiquity they barely receive a mention in the written record. Even the meticulous second-century AD guidebook to Greece compiled by Pausanias only mentions the mythical subjects of the

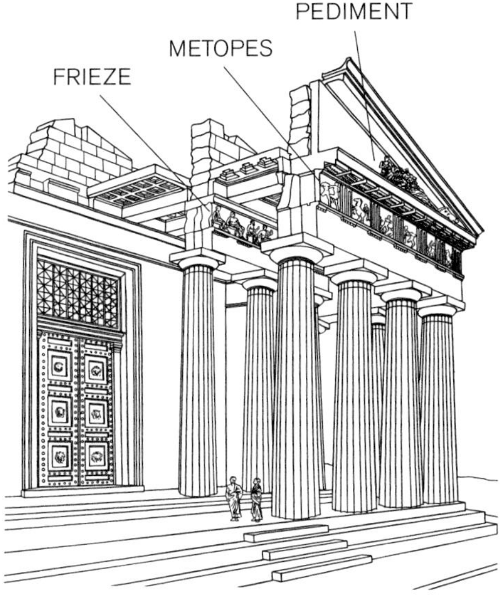

Fig. 2
Cut-away drawing to show the Parthenon's three kinds of external sculpture

pediments.[8] These two great compositions of freestanding sculptures fitting into the triangular spaces at the gable ends of the temple showed, at the east end, the birth of Athena, and, at the west end, her contest with the sea-god Poseidon to become the patron deity of Athens. The metopes and the frieze that ran around the temple on the outside and inside of the colonnades are not mentioned at all (Fig. 2). Pausanias' principal interest lay in the statue that stood within. The reason for this lack of commentary on the architectural sculptures is that the Parthenon was an Athenian monument and did not, as is often supposed, reflect the values of Greece as a whole. The ancient Greeks did not comprise a nation-state as modern Greeks do. Hellas was not a country but a collection of city-states, with their peoples scattered along the coasts of the Mediterranean, Aegean and Black seas. In antiquity you were an Athenian, a Spartan or a Boeotian first, and a Hellene second. Hellenic identity depended upon common language, a common set of gods and common values such as a tendency to democracy and to the culture of male athletics. To Rodin and his contemporaries the Parthenon was supremely an emblem of ancient Greek civilization in a way it never was in antiquity.

Another common misapprehension concerns the purpose of the Parthenon in antiquity. In Rodin's day, and even today, it is often presumed that the statue that Pheidias constructed from gold and ivory, standing forty feet high with its sculptured base, was the cult statue of Athena Parthenos. But there was no cult practised here. This is not to say that the Parthenon was a secular building. Its location on the Acropolis was, after all, within a sacred enclosure. The temple and its statue should, rather, be thought of as a grand votive offering to commemorate Athens' role in the victory over the Persians in the first two decades of the fifth century BC. In this respect the external sculptures of the Parthenon had a significant role in projecting Athens as defender of the divine order and as sharing a purpose with the gods who resided at the centre of the cosmos. The building also acted as a treasury for the wealth of the city in the form of its accumulated bullion, not least the tribute paid to Athens by the other Greek states who were members of the so-called Delian League. This had been created in the aftermath of the Persian invasion in 480 BC, and its purpose was to keep the enemy out of Greece by maintaining a fighting force in readiness. Athens usurped the federal nature of this alliance and transformed it into a maritime empire. It also appropriated the League's exchequer, transferring it to the Acropolis in 454 BC, and thereby providing the means with which to finance the Periklean building programme in Athens.

In the fifth century BC the Parthenon was constructed to commemorate Athenian greatness past and present. The subject matter of both the pediment sculptures and the metopes is taken exclusively from the exploits of gods and heroes. The ninety-two metopes in the form of panels represent in high relief scenes of battles between mythical beasts and humans, notably the Lapiths and the centaurs. The Ionic frieze, however, broke with all tradition in portraying the Athenians themselves as an ideal community of god-like men and men-like gods. These are the *kaloi kai agathoi* ('the beautiful and good'), as Plutarch refers to the citizen body of Athens.[9] The Parthenon frieze procession represents a pageant of the kind that Perikles devised in order to bring a particular class of people together and united them in a common purpose. The actual festivals of ancient Athens have long faded into oblivion, and yet the ever-youthful procession of the frieze endures. Indeed, as Rodin reflects:

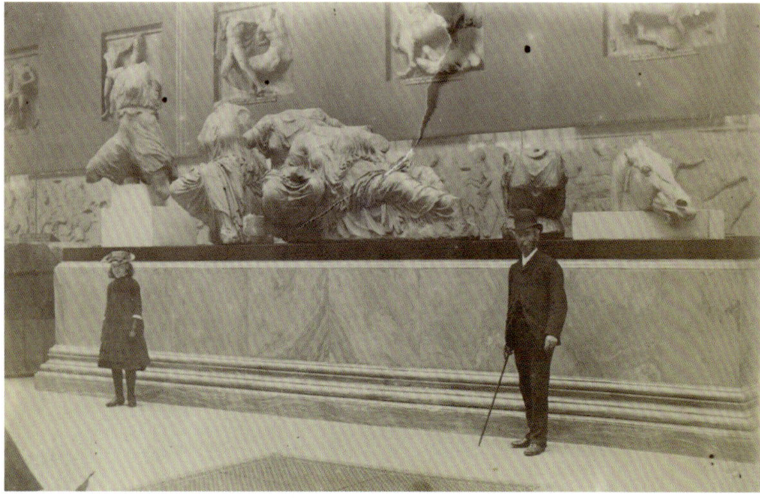

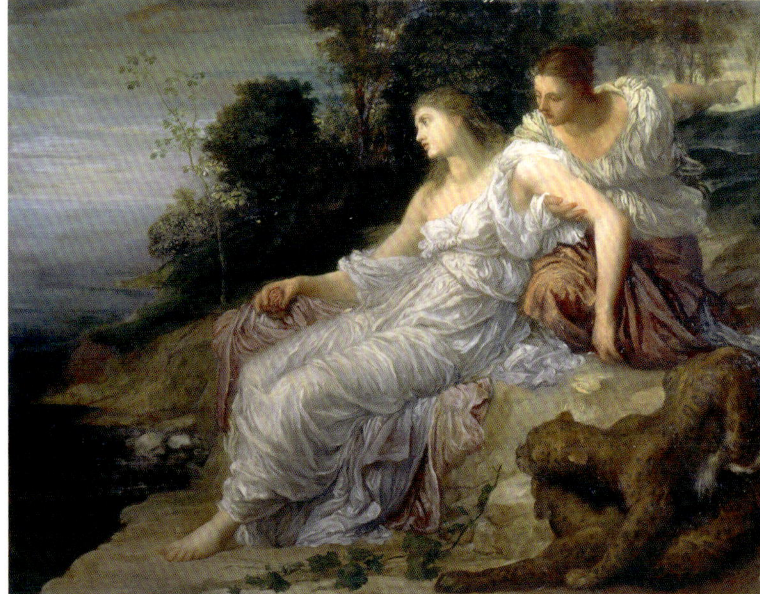

LEFT
Fig. 3
Anonymous
The Elgin Room
About 1890
Photograph
H 10.5 cm, W 15.3 cm
British Museum, Department of Greece and Rome archive

BELOW
Fig. 4
George Frederic Watts (1817–1904)
Ariadne on the Island of Naxos
1875
Oil on canvas
H 75 cm, W 94 cm
Guildhall Art Gallery and London's Roman Amphitheatre, 986

> For me the ancient masterpieces are bound up in my memory with all the joys of my teenage years: or, rather, Antiquity is my youth itself, now welling up in my heart and hiding from me the fact that I have grown old.[10]

London and Paris

When Rodin first visited the British Museum in the summer of 1881, it was a time of certainties. This temple of the Muses in London's Bloomsbury was at the heart of a late Victorian Greek revival in art and taste founded on the premise that ancient Greek culture was superior to all others. The Museum's external architecture was modelled on the ancient Athenian version of the Ionic order, while the interior was embellished with patterns of ancient architectural polychromy. A walk through the ground-floor galleries of the western wing was a journey through time that saw civilization arise first in the Nile Valley, then flourish in Mesopotamia, the land of the two rivers, and finally become established in the Mediterranean region, where it culminated in the city-state civilization of Classical Greece.

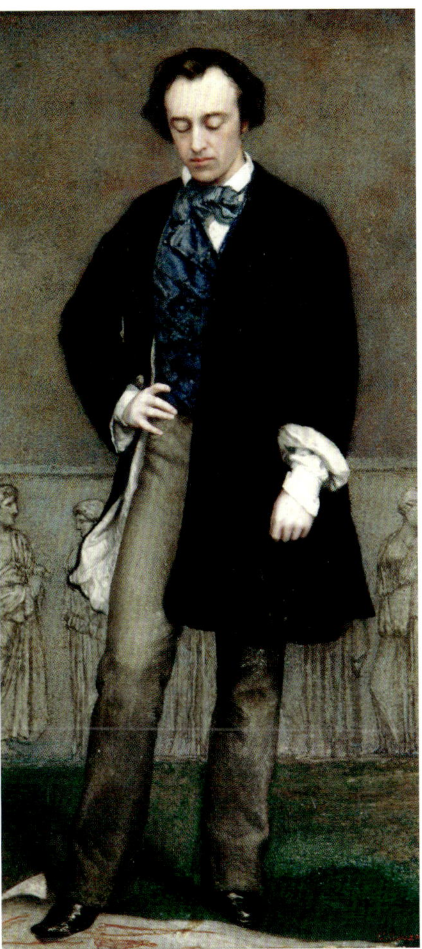

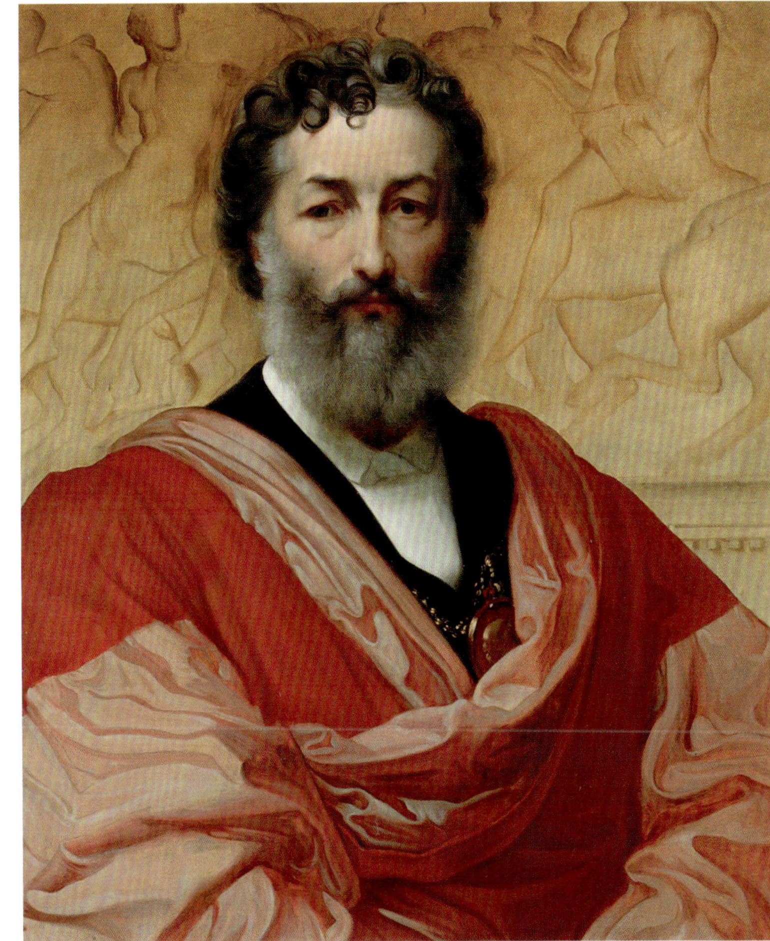

ABOVE LEFT
Fig. 5
Charles Couzens
(*c.* 1821–1889)
Portrait of G. F. Watts standing in front of a cast of block VII of the East Frieze of the Parthenon
About 1849
Tempera on ivory
H 41 cm, W 21.4 cm
Watts Gallery, Compton

ABOVE RIGHT
Fig. 6
After Frederic, Lord Leighton
(1830–1896)
Self-portrait, with a cast of the cavalcade on the North Frieze of the Parthenon
1880 (date of original)
Oil on canvas
H 76 cm, W 64 cm
Private collection

The inner sanctum of a maze of rooms was the gallery of the Elgin Marbles (Fig. 3). Here, among other pieces collected by Lord Elgin, were the sculptures from the Acropolis of Athens, made when Pheidias, Perikles and Sokrates walked the earth, which were thought to be the finest works known to humankind. The exhibition of the Parthenon sculptures, purchased for the Museum in 1816, had never been static, however, and the displays were almost constantly under review. In particular, there was ever the need to find satisfactory ways of exhibiting sculpture designed to be high up on the outside of a building but now hung on the interior walls of a gallery. At different times there was speculation that the Parthenon sculptures should be removed from Bloomsbury altogether and exhibited with the paintings in the National Gallery to create a new museum of fine arts. The proposal, however, was opposed by those who argued that the Museum was not an anthology of non-related elements, parts of which could be simply plucked out and dispersed. Rather, it was a great chain of comparative artefacts tracing the material endeavour of humanity through time and around the globe.[11]

At the time Rodin first saw the Parthenon sculptures for himself they were at the height of their fame. Contemporary painters, more than ever before, had succeeded in incorporating the natural forms of the Greek body, draped and naked, male and female, into their compositions. Not least among them was George Frederic Watts (1817–1904), whose obsession with the Parthenon sculptures was all consuming. His *Ariadne on the Island of Naxos* of 1875 is a dazzling display of diaphanous drapery adapted directly from the Parthenon sculptures (Fig. 4, and see also Cat. 41).[12] A full-length portrait of Watts by the artist Charles Couzens shows him around 1849 standing in front of a plaster cast of block VII of the East Frieze (Fig. 5); the original block was then, as now, in the Louvre. Later in the century, Frederic, Lord Leighton (1830–1896) became President of the Royal Academy and presiding genius of Victorian Olympos. The Uffizi Gallery in Florence commissioned a self-portrait in which Leighton appears Zeus-like against a backdrop of the cavalcade of the Parthenon frieze (Fig. 6).

A community of French artists had already established themselves in London when Rodin first visited. Chief among them were the sculptor Aimé-Jules Dalou (1838–1902), a political exile, and the painter, sculptor and engraver Alphonse Legros (1837–1911).[13] In 1877 Dalou was made professor of modelling at the National Art Training School in South Kensington (later the Royal College of Art). Meanwhile, Legros was Slade Professor of Fine Arts at University College London between 1876 and 1892; under the influence of Dalou, he gave lessons in sculpture and modelling. Like Rodin, Dalou was a modeller rather than a carver and he assisted Leighton in the creation of *An Athlete Wrestling with a Python*, which was shown at the Royal Academy in 1877 (Fig. 7). This work is arguably the beginning of what is known as the New Sculpture movement, which was to dominate British art in the latter part of the nineteenth century. The bronze figure was awarded the gold medal at the Exposition Universelle in Paris in 1878. Leighton was a frequent visitor to Paris, where he was particularly interested in developments in French sculpture, and he presided over a new understanding between French and British sculptors. It is significant that Leighton was the purchaser of a version of Rodin's *Man with the Broken Nose* (Cat. 97), when it was exhibited at the Grosvenor Gallery in 1882.[14]

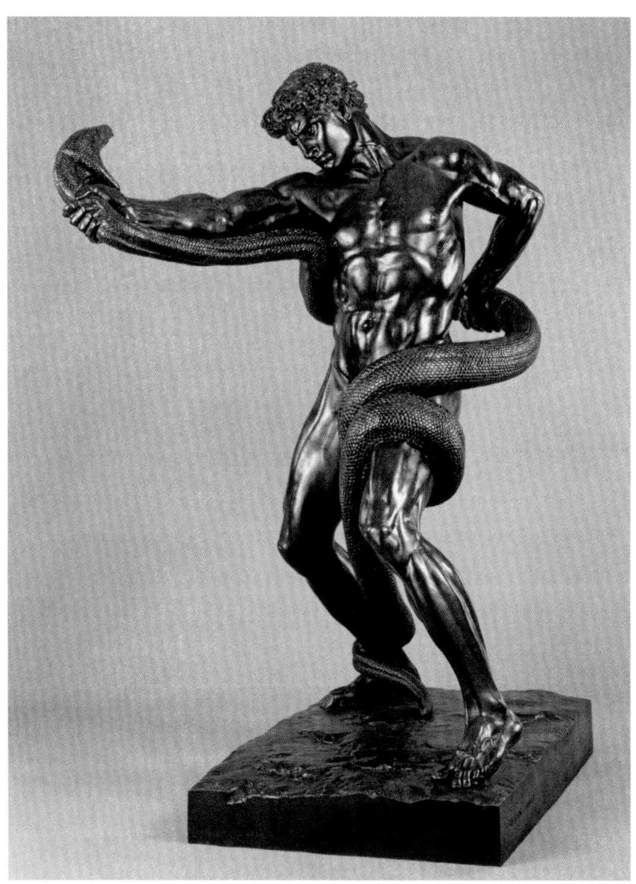

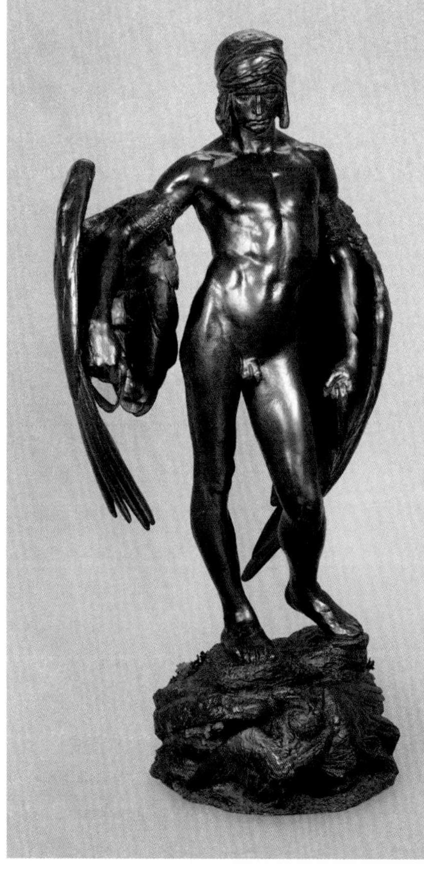

FAR LEFT
Fig. 7
Frederic, Lord Leighton (1830–1896)
An Athlete Wrestling with a Python
1877
Bronze
H 174.6 cm, W 98.4 cm, D 109.9 cm
Tate, London, NO1754

LEFT
Fig. 8
Sir Alfred Gilbert (1854–1934)
Icarus
1884
Bronze
H 100 cm
Amgueddfa Cymru – National Museum Wales, Cardiff, NMW A 116

Another genius to emerge in this decade was Alfred Gilbert (1854–1934). An Englishman, he migrated to Paris to complete his education and is associated with the stylish New Sculpture movement more than any other sculptor of his age. Gilbert's most famous works are the Eros at Piccadilly Circus, London, and the tomb of the Duke of Clarence in St George's Chapel, Windsor. The youthful male body-type of Gilbert's sculpture, *Icarus* (Fig. 8), along with other examples, calls to mind that of *The Age of Bronze* (Cat. 39).[15]

In 1903 Rodin was elected President of the International Society of Sculptors, Painters and Gravers on the death of its founder, the painter James Abbott McNeill Whistler (1834–1903). Rodin's inaugural address is an interesting reflection upon the differences between the London and Paris art scenes, and an affirmation of his feeling at home in a London that was to accept him as an 'eminent Victorian'.

Discovery and destruction of the Parthenon

Rodin's fascination with the Parthenon sculptures is part of a rich, long and sustained French tradition,[16] which begins with the arrival in Athens of the Marquis de Nointel. French involvement in this story is anticipated only by the Italian Cyriac of Ancona, who visited Athens in the 1430s and 1440s and whose notebooks contained highly fanciful and inaccurate sketches of the Parthenon and one or two of its sculptures.

Greece had been part of the Ottoman empire since the mid-fifteenth century, and in 1674 Charles-Marie-François Olier, Marquis de Nointel (1635–1685), Louis XIV's ambassador to the Ottoman court in Constantinople, arrived in Athens. Nointel was bound by that same *noblesse oblige* that later required Lord Elgin to raise the standard of art and manufacture in his native land. The French ambassador was instructed to acquire Greek manuscripts, medals and sculptures, and to collect paintings and drawings on his travels. In an official dispatch dated 17 December 1674 to a senior figure in the Ministry of Foreign Affairs in Paris, Nointel gives his impressions of the Parthenon sculptures.

> They number more than two hundred figures, fabulous as well as human, in high and low relief, some complete and others mutilated. There are men, women and centaurs, battles and victories, triumphs and sacrifices. If it were possible for me now to put into words the rich confusion that such a fine order, so animated an arrangement and an expression of so many different passions has left in my mind I should undertake it with pleasure.[17]

In Nointel's entourage was an artist called Jacques Carrey (1649–1726), who drew the monuments of the ancient city of Athens, including the sculptures of the Parthenon. Following the death of Nointel, the drawings passed through a series of hands until they entered the Bibliothèque Nationale in Paris in 1770. Carrey's drawings were to be engraved and published in *The Antiquities of Athens* by James Stuart and Nicholas Revett, as well as in other publications. Faithful copies of Carrey's drawings were commissioned by the British Museum immediately after the acquisition of the sculptures of the Parthenon in 1816 (Fig. 9).

The drawings of Jacques Carrey may not be considered great art, but they are an indispensable resource for knowing what sculptural elements survived on the

Parthenon before the explosion of 1687, when the building and many of its sculptures were blasted into fragments. Around 7 p.m. on 26 September 1687 a shot was fired from a cannon during the siege of the Ottoman garrison on the Acropolis led by the Venetian general Francesco Morosini. Gunpowder had been stored in the Parthenon and the bomb fell through the roof and ignited it, causing a great explosion. Three hundred of the village community of the Acropolis had taken refuge within its strong walls – all were killed. The heart was ripped out of the building, and substantial parts of the long walls and their colonnades were brought down. The Turks later returned, and Morosini and his European allies withdrew from the city. The Christian population, who had welcomed the Venetians, now feared reprisals and fled. The once great city of Athens was for

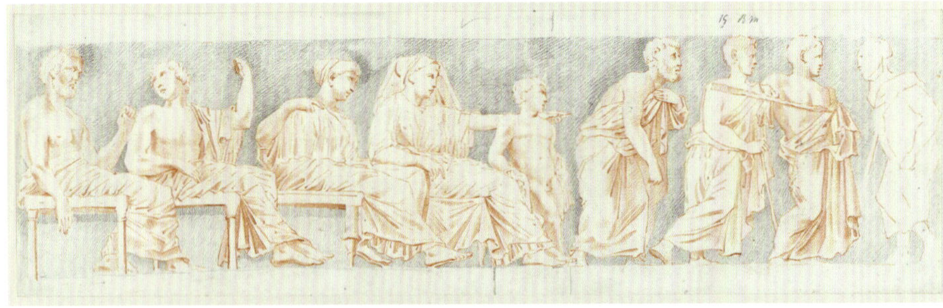

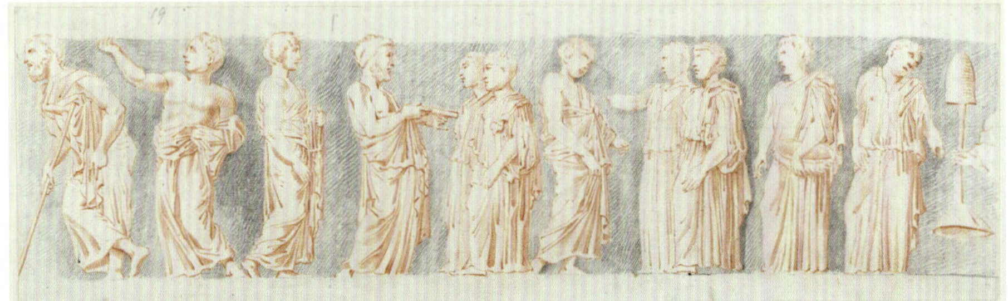

LEFT
Fig. 9
Facsimiles after Jacques Carrey (1649–1726)
Studies of the Parthenon frieze
1816
Red and black chalk
Top: H 13.2 cm, W 43.1 cm
Bottom: H 13 cm, W 42.7 cm
British Museum, Department of Greece and Rome archive

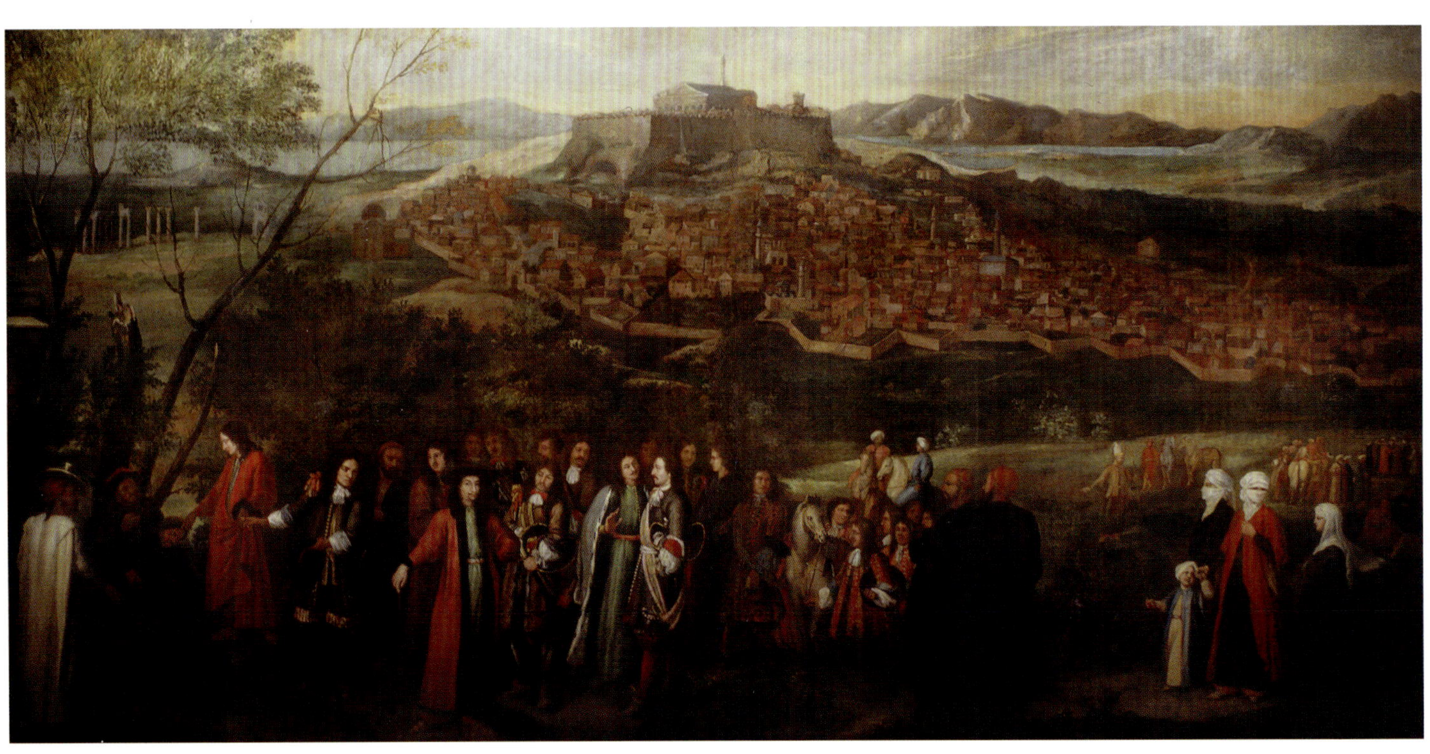

BELOW
Fig. 10
Jacques Carrey (1649–1726)
Arrival of the Marquis de Nointel in Athens on his way to take up his embassy in Constantinople
1674?
Oil on canvas
H 272 cm, W 520 cm
Musée de Chartres, Inv. 4383

a while abandoned, until the Ottomans were forced to coax the people back. Following this calamity the Parthenon was destined to be a wretched ruin, quarried for its worked stones and the bronze clamps that held them together.

A unique discovery relating to the story of French involvement in the modern cult of the Parthenon and its sculptures was made around 1890. An enormous portrait by Jacques Carrey of the Marquis and his company on their visit to Athens turned up in an antiques show in Paris (Fig. 10) and was recognized by Georges Duplessis, curator of the Cabinet des Estampes at the Bibliothèque Nationale in Paris. The painting, set against the western approach to the Acropolis, was afterwards acquired by the Musée de Chartres.[18]

In the same decade as Nointel, Jacob Spon (1647–1685), a French physician and antiquary, and George Wheler (1651–1724), an English clergyman and traveller, visited the Acropolis and in particular the Parthenon. They were the first to imagine the Acropolis without the post-antique buildings that had grown up around the Classical monuments.[19] This Neo-Classical tendency would burgeon in the following century.

A French Elgin

The late eighteenth-century reception of the Parthenon and its sculptures is given added zest by Marie-Gabriel-Florent-Auguste, Comte de Choiseul-Gouffier (1752–1817). His is a tragic tale of aspiration and determination thwarted by adverse forces beyond his control. He would have succeeded in acquiring the Parthenon sculptures had the French Revolution and its consequences not prevented him.

Choiseul-Gouffier had joined a voyage in 1776 to Ottoman Greece and the west coast of Turkey arranged by the Académie des Sciences and led by the astronomer Joseph Bernard, Marquis de Chabert (1724–1805). Choiseul-Gouffier's published account of his travels was entitled *Voyage Pittoresque de la Grèce*, and as it began to appear from 1782 in handsome folio volumes richly illustrated with engravings, his fame and good fortune rose accordingly.

In 1784 Choiseul-Gouffier was appointed ambassador to the Ottoman court in Constantinople and, like the Marquis de Nointel before him, he took with him an entourage of scholars, scientists and artists. He used his residence as a base to explore widely in the Aegean and eastern Mediterranean. The Palais de France in the Pera district of Constantinople became an international centre for travellers to the city.

The French consul in Athens at the time, Louis François Sébastien Fauvel (1753–1858), was a man of no less intellect and ambition (Fig. 11).[20] We know a great deal about Fauvel's life because of numerous letters from him now in the Bibliothèque Nationale in Paris. Fauvel served as Choiseul-Gouffier's agent in procuring antiquities, at the same time indulging his own fascination for the ancient world. So it was that Fauvel was active on the Acropolis, acquiring sculpture for Choiseul-Gouffier, some years before Lord Elgin arrived in the eastern Mediterranean.

Fragments of the Parthenon acquired by Choiseul-Gouffier included a block of the East Frieze (block VII) and two metopes (South VI and X). The frieze block shows young women (known as the Ergastinai or 'workers in wool') standing at the head of the Panathenaic procession, an Athenian festival celebrated in high

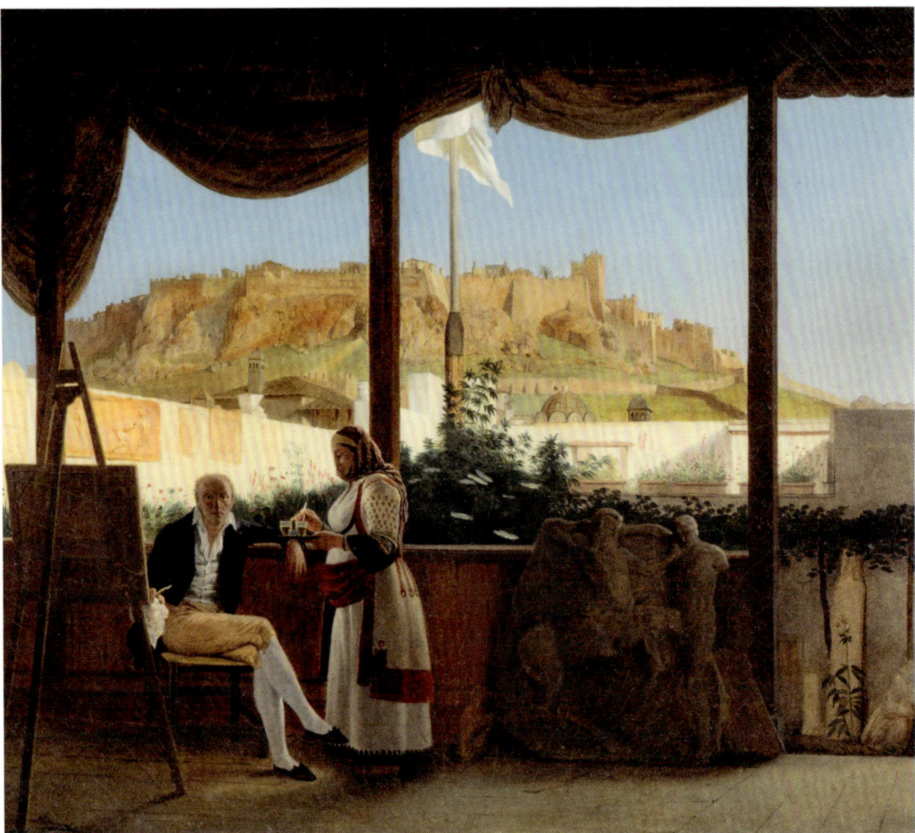

Fig. 11
Louis Dupré (1789–1837)
Portrait of Louis Fauvel, French Consul in Athens, with the Acropolis in the background and a cast of South Metope XXXI
1819
Oil on canvas
H 55 cm, W 62 cm
Private collection

summer in honour of the goddess Athena, met by marshals who face them.[21] This block entered the Louvre in 1801 while Choiseul-Gouffier was in exile in St Petersburg.[22]

One of the two metopes (South VI) is said to have fallen from the building in a storm and broken into three fragments. It was acquired by Fauvel on behalf of Choiseul-Gouffier. On the voyage back to France in 1803, the ship *L'Arabe* carrying the fragments was intercepted by a British warship, HMS *Maidstone*, commanded by none other than Horatio Nelson, as the two countries were again at war. Cases containing the metope, along with other antiquities and plaster casts owned by Choiseul-Gouffier, found their way to the Custom House in London, where unclaimed antiquities were regularly sold off. Later, in 1806, Lord Elgin purchased at auction unmarked cases that were then identified as belonging to Choiseul-Gouffier and which included the three fragments of the metope. A long correspondence regarding ownership ensued and was only brought to an end by the death of Choiseul-Gouffier in 1817, after which the metope became a permanent fixture in the Elgin Room of the British Museum.

Meanwhile, the other metope (South X) entered the Louvre when in June 1818 Choiseul-Gouffier's collection was sold in Paris. The British, unsuccessful in their bid for the metope, later acquired a cast of it for display in the Elgin Room.[23]

Writing a year before he died, Choiseul-Gouffier requested Lord Elgin's assistance in retrieving, at least, the casts that had been packed in the same consignment as the metope:

> Lord Elgin has the good fortune to possess a great number of the original marbles from which these casts were produced. It is an inappreciable treasure.

> For me I would be happy to recover my casts and to be able to complete thus the decoration of my modest sanctuary where I seek to console my losses.[24]

Choiseul-Gouffier's so-called modest sanctuary was in fact a magnificent building just outside Paris, modelled on various façades from a wide range of monuments of Athens and Palmyra in Syria, and with an interior done out in pure Greek taste to provide a sympathetic environment for displaying sculpture and casts. However, it is not known what happened to these casts.

The Parthenon sculptures become the Elgin Marbles

Lord Elgin and his embassy to Constantinople would succeed where Choiseul-Gouffier and his embassy had not. The defeat by Nelson of Napoleon's fleet at the Battle of the Nile in 1798 had substantial consequences for the cultural aspirations of both the British and the French governments. When Napoleon had invaded Egypt, along with his army he also took with him teams of draughtsmen, cast-makers and scholars. He had already conquered the Italian peninsula and had occupied Rome, where he had plundered the Vatican and the grand houses of powerful families and sent their artworks back to Paris. The Louvre became a great showcase for the proud boast that there was no longer a need for European Grand Tourists to go to Rome, since Rome had already come to Paris.[25] Napoleon was less successful in his Egyptian campaign. The loss of the fleet forced the French land army to retreat to Alexandria, and they fought on there until 1801, when the surrender was called. The antiquities that had been assembled for the Louvre, including the Rosetta Stone, were now forfeited to the British.

Thomas Bruce, 7th Earl of Elgin (1766–1841), had been appointed as British ambassador to the court of the Ottoman Sultan in Constantinople in 1799 and arrived there on a wave of pro-British feeling because of the delivery of Egypt, a dominion of the Ottoman empire, from the French. Already before his departure he had begun the process of assembling a team of scholars and draughtsmen, who made their way to Athens and, with the permission of the Ottomans, started work on the Acropolis. The expulsion of the French from Egypt in 1801 increased British standing with the Ottomans and facilitated the issuing in May of that year of a *firman* that gave Elgin permission to excavate and remove stone carvings and inscriptions from the Acropolis of Athens and elsewhere in the city.[26]

By early 1803 Lord Elgin's embassy in Constantinople was at an end. His visit to the Athenian Acropolis in the spring and early summer of the previous year had confirmed that his agents were proceeding according to his wishes. On his way home, under the protection of the Peace of Amiens, Elgin made an excursion to Paris. But hostilities were suddenly resumed, and he found himself under house arrest as a prisoner of war. The French blamed Elgin, unjustly, for the harsh treatment of French soldiers at the hands of the Turks.[27] Elgin met Choiseul-Gouffier in Paris at this time, the Frenchman having returned to France from exile in 1802. Already stripped of his titles and fortune, Choiseul-Gouffier had but one interest, namely his antiquities.

Elgin was released from captivity in 1806 and returned to London. His expenses in obtaining the sculptures and the cost of retrieving some that were in a ship that sank off Kythera on the way home meant that Elgin was now experiencing

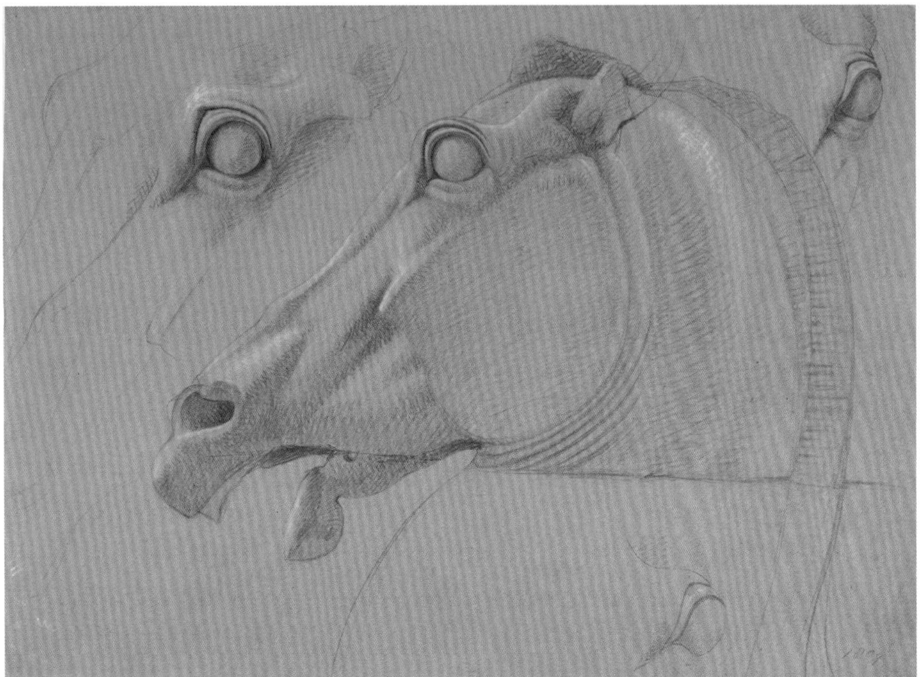

Fig. 12
Benjamin Robert Haydon
(1786–1846)
Head of the horse of Selene
1809
Chalk on paper
H 55.4 cm, W 75.9 cm
British Museum 1881,0709.346

severe financial difficulties, and he began the process of trying to sell his collection to the British government. This precipitated a lively debate as to its merits, the authority under which it was acquired and its suitability as a purchase for the nation. There was also the matter of the sculptures' public exhibition. They were first displayed in London at a site on the corner of Park Lane and Piccadilly, and afterwards removed to Burlington Gardens, where today the Royal Academy is situated. The first venue was accessible from May 1807 to persons admitted by appointment, and it was there that artists and connoisseurs went to see them. To many they were a revelation, as being the true art of Pheidias, and at a stroke they eclipsed the Roman copies of lost Greek originals that had recently been imported from Rome to Paris. Not everyone who viewed the sculptures was impressed, however. Some saw only broken, disfigured and stained ruins. The larger-than-life figure of the painter Benjamin Robert Haydon (1786–1846) was not among them. He was a determined and outspoken advocate of the sculptures, and his volatile temperament veered between joy at experiencing them and despair at their not being appreciated as they should be (Fig. 12).[28] Haydon's first visit to see the Elgin Marbles prompted exclamations of ecstatic delight, and he declared them heralds of a new age. But he was to become disillusioned at what he perceived to be the failure of the artistic establishment, in particular the collector and scholar Richard Payne Knight (1751–1824), to seize an opportunity to acquire them that would never come again. As Haydon recorded in his journal of May 1815:

> I came home from the Elgin Marbles melancholy. I almost wish the French had them. We do not deserve such productions. There they lie, covered with dust and dripping with damp, adored by the artists, admired by the people, neglected by the government, doubted by Payne Knight, because to doubt them is easier than to feel them, and reverenced and envied by foreigners, because they do not possess them.[29]

Fig. 13
William Pars (1742–1782)
Study of South Metope II
1765–1766
Pen and ink, red-brown wash
H 27 cm, W 38.1 cm
British Museum 2013,5005.1.12

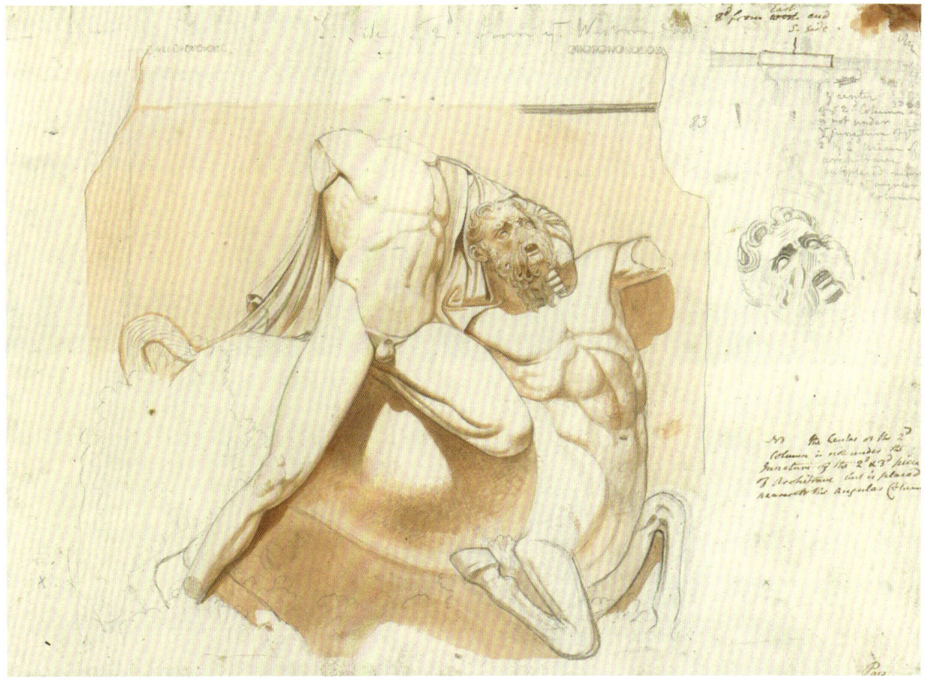

Exactly who these foreigners were is not made clear, but perhaps Haydon had in mind the succession of distinguished Europeans who came to London to view the Marbles.

'Distinguished Europeans'

One whose aesthetic sensibility was won over by the Elgin Marbles was Crown Prince Ludwig of Bavaria (1786–1868), who had acquired the Aegina Marbles – the sculptures from the pediments of the Temple of Aphaia on Aegina – when they came up for sale in 1812. On seeing the Parthenon sculptures looking as if they had just stepped on to their plinths, he could not help but compare their realism with the stiffness of the Aegina Marbles, from an earlier period, with their relatively muted modelling and strong outline. Ludwig was so impressed with what he saw in London that he instructed his bankers to make £30,000 available in case Parliament should reject Elgin's offer and the collection go back on the market.

Another distinguished visitor was the Italian Ennio Quirino Visconti (1751–1818), who had once been responsible for the papal collection of antiquities. His republican sympathies were aroused when the French invaded Rome in 1796, and he then had to leave the city in the company of the famous artworks claimed by the French occupiers, and oversaw their installation and interpretation in the Louvre.

Visconti was one of many commentators on the sculptures of the Parthenon who, while acknowledging their greatness, was nevertheless reluctant to abandon the existing canon of Classical works such as those exhibited in the Belvedere Courtyard of the Vatican. Working from engravings only, Visconti had already published extensively on the Parthenon sculptures when, at the invitation of the English politician and antiquary Richard Worsley (1751–1805), he compiled a commentary on the drawings of the sculptures by William Pars (1742–1782) (Fig. 13) and the outline engravings by Vincenzo Dolcibene after Pars.[30] Pars had spent two months drawing the sculptures close up on the Parthenon in Athens in

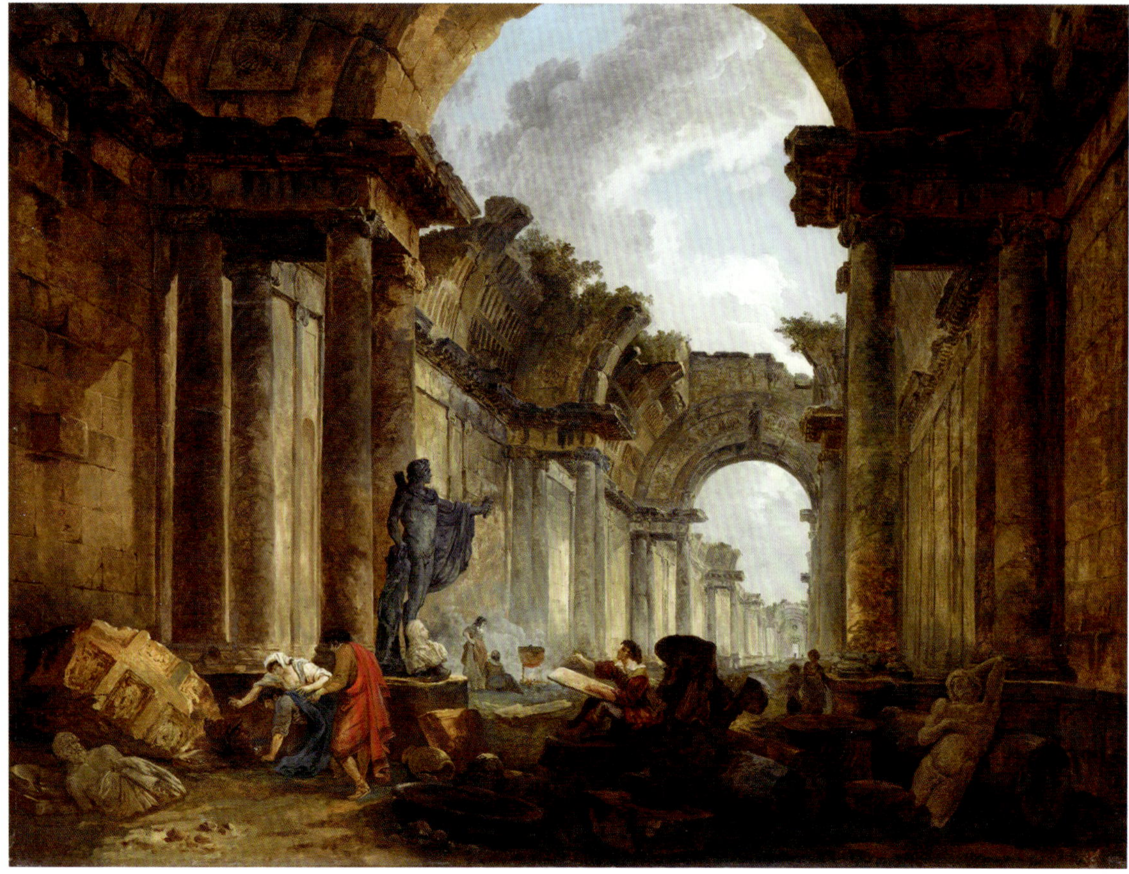

Fig. 14
Hubert Robert (1733–1808)
Caprice of the Grande Galerie of the Louvre in ruins
About 1796
Oil on canvas
H 33 cm, W 40 cm
Musée du Louvre, Département des Peintures, Paris, R.F. 1961-20

1765, when the Society of Dilettanti's Ionian expedition travelled back from Turkey through mainland Greece. On the strength of Visconti's demonstration of his sensitivity to the Parthenon sculptures, and his reputation at large, Elgin invited him to London in October 1814. There the sculptures were to be a revelation to him – he expressed an unrestrained admiration for these great works of art, even in their broken state, with their grand and imposing forms.

Visconti thought that Pheidias had not only designed the sculptures, but that he had also executed a large part of them, and he declared that they would herald a new age for the development of sculpture in Britain. All of this went obligingly into the text of his lectures at two meetings of the French Academy on 21 October and 10 November 1815.[31] Visconti's two lectures were translated and later bound together with the report from the House of Commons Select Committee Enquiry of 1816,[32] which scrutinized Elgin's behaviour in acquiring the Parthenon sculptures and interrogated a broad section of London's artistic society on their artistic merit, and also raised the question of their worthiness to be acquired by the nation. Final victory in the Napoleonic Wars in 1815 had prompted the British establishment to lay claim to the mantle of ancient democratic Athens in a narrative that would see Waterloo as the new Marathon and the Battle of the Nile as a latter day Salamis, when the ancient Athenians had been victorious over the Persians. Imperial France's claim to have established Rome in Paris was made manifest by grand squares, the boulevards that linked them, triumphal arches, and palaces and their gardens. London could not compete with Paris' Roman grandeur and chose Greek glory instead. If the Louvre was to be Napoleon's 'Trophy of Conquest' then the British Museum could be a triumph of excellence.

While negotiations for the purchase of the Elgin Marbles continued, measures were in place to dismantle and disperse the artworks of the Napoleonic Louvre. Lord Castlereagh, in his capacity as Foreign Secretary, took as his amanuensis William Richard Hamilton (1777–1859), who had been secretary to Lord Elgin and whose exceptional zeal for dismantling the Louvre was regarded by some as unseemly. Hamilton was a strong advocate for the acquisition by the state of the Elgin Marbles.

In the audience of Visconti's first lecture to the French Academy on the Elgin Marbles in October 1815 was the sculptor Antonio Canova (1757–1822). His purpose in Paris was to oversee, on behalf of the Pope, the restitution of the Vatican sculptures. At the invitation of the English sculptor John Charles Felix Rossi (1762–1839), Canova also visited London and, like Visconti before him, was greatly affected by the Parthenon sculptures. Rossi made a cast of Dionysos (East D) from the Parthenon pediment. His son Henry made the reduced-scale versions of this figure as well as the Ilissos (West A), restoring the missing parts, that are now in the Sir John Soane's Museum in London. In November 1815 Canova wrote a long letter to Lord Elgin, recounting his impressions:

> I think I can never see them often enough, and, although my stay in this great capital must be extremely short, I dedicate every moment that I can spare to the contemplation of these celebrated remains of ancient art. I admire in them the truth of nature combined with the choice of finest forms. Everything here breathes life with a veracity, with a knowledge of art which is the more exquisite for being without the least ostentation or parade of it, which is concealed by consummate and masterly skill. The nude is perfect flesh and most beautiful in its kind. I think myself happy in having been able to see with my own eyes these distinguished works and I should feel perfectly satisfied if I had come to London only to view them.[33]

Elgin would maintain to the last the possibility that his famous sculptures would be more attractive if restored. Fortunately for us, and for the Parthenon sculptures, he was advised against it by Canova's sound counsel. Canova's arguments resisting the restoration echoed those of Michelangelo in reply to Pope Julius II's pressure to restore the Belvedere Torso. *Vera Carne* – real flesh – is how Canova referred to them, and insisted that their quality placed them beyond imitation and thereby beyond restoration. He also regretted that he had not seen them earlier in his career.

In 1818 another important figure arrived in London from Paris. Antoine-Chrysostome Quatremère de Quincy (1755–1849) was a patriot and antiquary of singular intelligence. He had in 1814 produced a highly regarded study on Pheidias' colossal gold and ivory statue of Zeus created for the temple at Olympia. At first he resisted Canova's insistence that he come to London to see the Elgin Marbles for himself, giving the same answer to Canova that he had given to the committee responsible for the dispersal of the artworks looted by Napoleon from collections in Italy and elsewhere. He alone had spoken out against the spoliation of Rome by Napoleon in 1796, and published a warning to his countrymen not to endorse a chain of events that must eventually bring nemesis to Paris. His foreboding is mysteriously echoed by Hubert Robert's caprice imagining the Apollo Belvedere standing amidst the ruins of the Grande Galerie of the Louvre

(Fig. 14). Quatremère condemned the absurdity of reviving in the eighteenth century the ancient Roman right of spoils, one that was founded on the same premise as slavery. But not even in ancient Rome did such actions meet with universal approval. Quatremère invoked the Greek historian Polybius on the Roman plundering of art from Syracuse in 212 BC, and argued that such de-contextualization of cultural property was to create 'gods without altars, altars without worshippers'.[34] Some twenty years after putting forward such views, Quatremère could not have guessed that he would succumb to Canova's urging that he travel to London, where he encountered the sculptures of the Parthenon. Removed from their architectural setting on a building on the sacred rock of the Athenians and displayed in an alien, albeit elegant, gallery he should have loathed them, but to his great surprise these broken remains gave him not only aesthetic pleasure but also intellectual gratification. They appeared to be somehow unfinished, as if he were viewing them in the sculptor's workshop when they had not yet fully come into being. With characteristic originality, Quatremère anticipated Rodin's own acceptance of headless, limbless fragments and saw them as virtuous survivors.

Art practice and theory

Having debated the Select Committee's report, the House of Commons voted to purchase the Elgin Marbles in 1816 for £35,000. Immediately following their installation in the temporary gallery at the British Museum, the initial wave of Parthenomania subsided into a more sedate reverence and contemplative appreciation. John Keats's 'Ode on a Grecian Urn' (1819) brilliantly captures the spirit of the Parthenon frieze, with its 'silent form … in midst of other woe'. The Parthenon sculptures did not succeed in initiating a new 'School of Art', as some hoped they might; there was no great revolution of art practice, no renaissance of British history painting, as Benjamin Robert Haydon had proclaimed there would be. At the same time, however, the Parthenon sculptures maintained, and indeed increased, their reputation as the highest form of art. Thus we witness the separation of art theory from art practice that would cause commentators later in the century to acknowledge that the study of art history has little to do with the process of painting and sculpture itself. In American art historian Jacob Rothenberg's words, 'the Elgin Marbles were venerated by all but emulated by few'.[35]

Haydon's own drawing school, where an artist's ability was measured in relation to how well he drew first-hand from the Parthenon sculptures, was the exception. Those who attended were a renegade bunch, who disregarded the conventions of the contemporary Academy Schools. Once their numbers dwindled, the Elgin Room, the permanent gallery completed in 1832, became an island of tranquillity where, in 'calm of mind all passion spent',[36] art could be seen to have reached an inimitable perfection. It was this inimitability that had ensured that the Elgin Marbles remained unrestored, and the decision not to restore them was crucial in determining their future status. It set them apart from the Graeco-Roman sculptures of Rome and Paris, and from the Townley Marbles in the British Museum. Even the Aegina Marbles, which – next to the British Museum's sculptures from the Temple of Apollo Epikourios at Bassai in southern Greece – were the only comparable body of original Greek sculpture, had been made whole again according to the Neo-Classical taste of the Danish sculptor Bertel

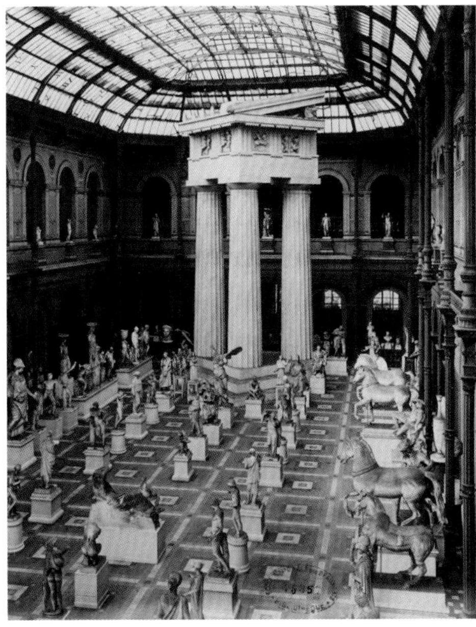

Fig. 15
Anonymous
The central atrium of the École des Beaux-Arts, with the reconstruction of the northwest corner of the Parthenon from moulds struck in Athens by Philippe Le Bas
1863–1874
Photograph
École des Beaux-Arts, Paris

Thorvaldsen (1770–1844). Elgin's Parthenon sculptures, however, were to retain an archaeological purity of form and appealed not only to the senses but also to the intellect. They came to represent a fixed standard of beauty for the nineteenth-century Hellenist, both in the concrete and abstract sense. Their physical condition as fragments made them off-putting to the mass of the people, but this served only to increase their appeal to an elite class of cognoscenti, who could see beyond the ruin to a purer truth. As the most beautiful man-made creations in existence, they came closest to an earthly paradise, a manifestation of that unseen beauty pursued in Plato's *Theory of Forms*. If in the repertoire of ancient sculptural paradigms the nineteenth century could invoke a greater model still, it would be the lost and so now invisible art from the hand of Pheidias himself, the chryselephantine Athena from the Parthenon and the Zeus from the temple at Olympia. Reverential awe for these lost originals surpassed even that felt for the fragmentary Elgin Marbles. Having part of a statue, one might say, turns out to be second best only to having no statue at all.

France in Greece

In the years that followed the dismantling of Napoleon's 'Trophy of Conquest' in Paris, there was a gradual shift in French cultural identity from Rome to Greece. The Prix de Rome was a competition for young trainee architects seeking an opportunity to travel abroad. Normally it focused upon Roman Italy, but in 1845 the medallists were granted the chance of spending four months in Athens during their last year of a three-year travel bursary. A year after this change, France was the first European country to establish an archaeological school in Greece. This would provide a base for the Prix de Rome medallists, as well as for French excavations such as those at Delphi and on the island of Delos. The travelling architects mapped the surviving archaeological remains of the great monuments of Greece, which they then reconstructed on paper, often with an unusually strident and sometimes alarming extravagance in restoring ancient architectural polychromy. The Parthenon and other Acropolis monuments were at the very heart of their mission and they set new standards in the technical drawing of ancient architecture.

The French scholar Philippe Le Bas (1794–1860) received a commission from the French government to make casts of the architecture of the Parthenon, and the British Museum was to benefit from his energy in casting the temple's northwest corner in 1844. This was erected in the École des Beaux-Arts in Paris (Fig. 15) and was partially reconstructed in the British Museum from the same moulds.[37]

Charles Newton (1816–1894), the future first Keeper of the Department of Greek and Roman Antiquities at the British Museum, was one person who was enthusiastic in his appreciation of the French contribution to the understanding of the Parthenon sculptures. In 1853 he was on the Acropolis making a list of Parthenon fragments from which the British Museum would request casts. He mentions the Marquis de Nointel and the drawings of Jacques Carrey, and also praises the efforts of Léon de Laborde (1807–1869), who had intended a series of books on the Parthenon that would have amounted to a comprehensive catalogue of the entire monument and its architectural sculpture. However, Laborde's journey to Athens in 1844 was never repeated, and his ambitious plans were to remain unrealized. His *Le Parthénon: documents pour servir à une restauration* was published in Paris in 1848 and subsequently, in 1854, appeared *Athènes aux XVe, XVIe et XVIIe siècles*.[38]

The installation of the Elgin Marbles in the permanent gallery in the British Museum strengthened a long-standing resolve to bring together all the sculptures of the Parthenon, including casts of elements not in the Museum, in one room. Newton was just one of a series of visitors to the Athenian Acropolis who sought to acquire casts for the British Museum of fragments that had been brought to light after the Greek War of Independence, which ended in 1832. One actual fragment came to London via the French curator of antiquities in the Louvre, Monsieur J. J. Dubois, who presented the fragmentary head and breast of a human figure from block XIV of the West Frieze in 1840.

Casts

In addition to the acquisition by the British Museum of fragments and casts of pieces not included among the Elgin Marbles, the Museum itself supplied many institutions, at home and abroad, with casts from its own collection. France was in the vanguard of foreign countries wanting to acquire casts of the Elgin Marbles, submitting a request for a complete set as early as 1819. The Trustees of the British Museum proposed that the French might like to exchange South Metope X, acquired for the Louvre the previous year in the sale of Choiseul-Gouffier's collection (see p. 22), for a set of casts to a value of £1,200, but nothing came of the suggestion. The request for casts was repeated in 1835, submitted now by the statesman and historian Adolphe Thiers, who wished to place an entire set in the École des Beaux-Arts.

At this time, the sculptor, and later Professor of Sculpture at the Royal Academy, Sir Richard Westmacott, was responsible for the presentation of the sculpture collections in the British Museum (from 1808 until his death in 1856). He also had a monopoly on the making and selling of casts, which he executed on an ad hoc basis. While fulfilling the wishes of the Trustees, he was not above a little private business and it was reported that by 1818, full-scale plaster casts of the Elgin Marbles were available in Paris at the private gallery of the wealthy sculptor and collector Jean-Baptiste Giraud (1752–1830). In response to an interrogation by the Museum's Trustees, Westmacott later recalled the people and institutions that had received casts from his hand:

> I find from my memoranda that in 1818 the Court of Tuscany had a complete set of casts from the Elgin Marbles paid by the Treasury; 1819, the Court of Rome, Naples and Prussia had each a complete set paid by the Treasury; 1819, The Academy at Venice a part only of the Elgin Marbles paid by the Treasury; 1819, The Academy [i.e. the Athenaeum] at Plymouth – order, the Prince Regent, paid by Sir B. Blomfield; 1821, the town of Liverpool – order His Majesty, a complete set paid through Sir B. Blomfield, but I believe by the Treasury; the Royal Academy in 1817 and the Institution at Bristol in 1823 had each part of the Phigalian frieze [from Bassai] but which were paid for by those institutions; St. Petersburg, Bavaria and Wurtemburg had each parts of the Elgin Marbles but which were paid for by their respective courts…[39]

By 1835, when the Museum received the grand request from Adolphe Thiers, the Westmacott moulds were no longer serviceable, and the Trustees faced for the first time the prospect of taking moulds from all the Parthenon sculptures and then supplying everyone who asked for them with good-quality casts in plaster. Edward Hawkins (1780–1867), Keeper of the Department of Antiquities, was dispatched to Paris to attend the sale of vases from the collection of Edmé Durand in 1836, and while there he went to consult Monsieur Jacquet, who was the *formatore* in charge of the manufactory of moulds and casts attached to the Louvre. Hawkins explained in his report to the Trustees that he did not anticipate a large demand for the Elgin Marbles since they 'are not generally objects of furniture, for any gentleman's residence, and many museums are already supplied'.[40]

The casting went ahead in 1836, and contrary to the opinion of Hawkins, requests for the casts of the Marbles flowed in. These included one from the Prussian Consul-General in Athens, Bernard Hebeler, in 1839. In 1846 *The Moor of Venice* sailed from England to Athens with 70 tonnes of plaster casts. These had been requested by the Archaeological Society of Athens, but in the event the British Museum's Trustees resolved to present a full set of casts to the King of Greece. Having been carefully preserved in Athens for over a century and a half, these casts were installed in the new Acropolis Museum in 2008.

The making of the moulds in 1836 was the first and last time that the Parthenon sculptures were officially moulded in the British Museum. All subsequent requests for casts were met by making a mould from the type-cast, rather than from the sculpture itself. This process of casting from an existing cast naturally reduces the sharpness of each successive strike, and those now in the Acropolis Museum and those supplied to France were among the first strikes from the new moulds and are therefore of the best quality.

Dreams of Hellas

Rodin never visited Greece. In this he is in the company of a number of distinguished Hellenists who did not go there either. One example is John Milton (1608–1674), whose poetic portrait of an Athens he never experienced first-hand expresses a melancholy of longing for the unattainable:

> behold
> Where on the Aegean shore a City stands,
> Built nobly, pure the air, and light the soil,
> Athens, the eye of Greece, Mother of Arts
> And Eloquence, native to famous wits.[41]

Johann Joachim Winckelmann (1717–1768), who compiled the world's first modern history of Greek art, died before he could visit the land of his passions. For Winckelmann, Greece was a world that was as yet unseen and one that he feared might after all be an illusion, a ghost-like impression that signified a false hope and nothing more.[42] The architect and collector Sir John Soane (1753–1837) contented himself, as many travellers would, with the monuments of Magna Graecia, where at Paestum in southern Italy and on Sicily the ruins of great temples testified to the one-time splendour of Greek architecture.

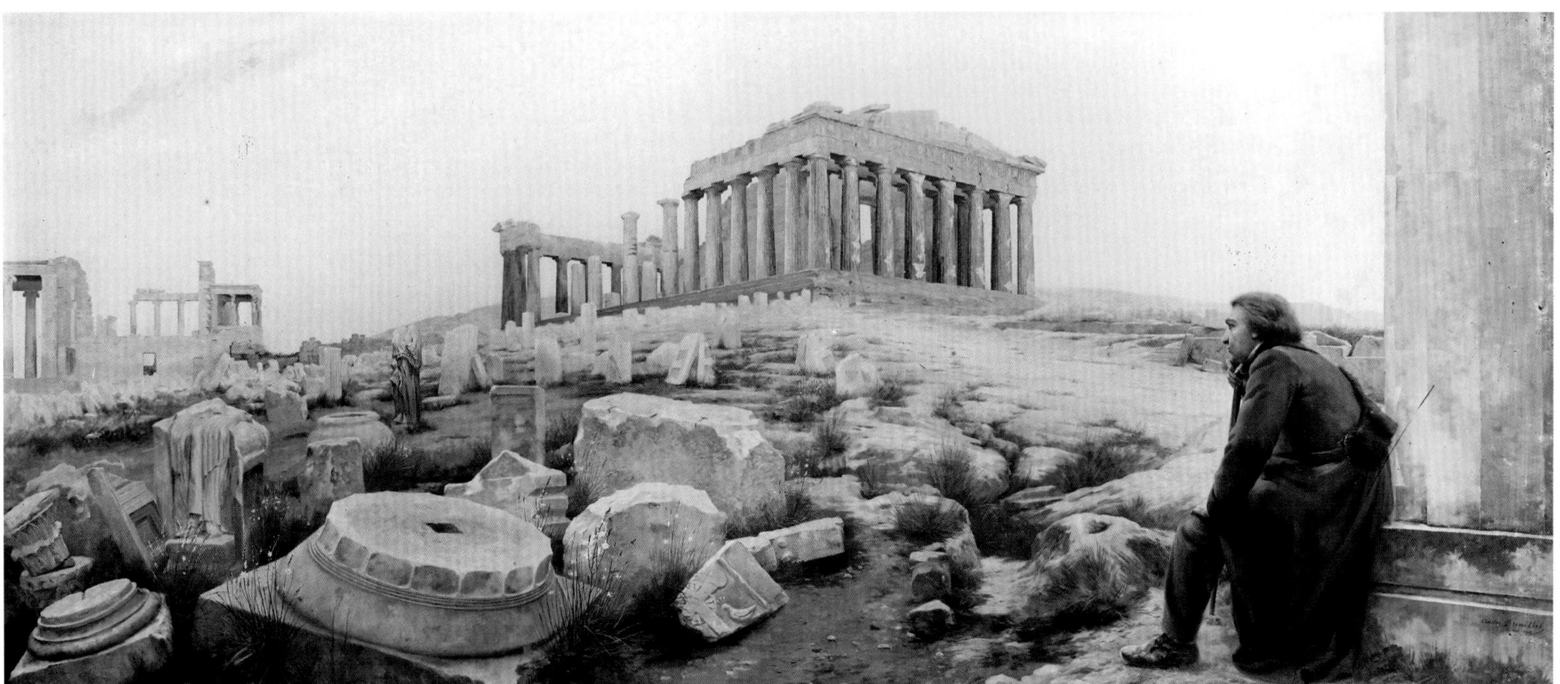

Fig. 16
André Brouillet (1857–1914)
Ernest Renan in contemplation of the Parthenon
1902
Oil on canvas
Conservation des Oeuvres d'Art Religieuses et Civiles, Paris

The fact that Rodin never saw the Parthenon itself did not deter him from joining in a controversy about its proposed restoration (see also pp. 40–41). In 1894 an earthquake had affected the Acropolis monuments and the Parthenon had suffered some structural damage. Expert advice was sought. An anxiety arose, however, that any intervention might lead to a more general restoration of the whole building. Among those who campaigned against this possibility was Rodin, who wrote a paper in highly personal and poetic language warning the reader against interfering with the ancient fabric of the Parthenon, as had already been done to the cathedrals of France. He feared the tendency of a restorer's hand to turn natural ruins into anachronistic pastiches. Rodin's anxieties were not misplaced, and a general restoration did follow, conducted by the now notorious Nikolaos Balanos, a French-trained engineer, who from 1899 to 1902 and then again from 1922 to 1933 had the freedom to restore according to his own methods, which actually did untold damage to the architecture.[43]

In spite of even these changes, the romance of the Parthenon as an inviolable and eternal monument endured. Rodin's older contemporary, the philosopher and writer Ernest Renan (1823–1892), did travel to Athens and was beguiled by the Acropolis, where he would sit for hours at a time surveying the sacred landscape (Fig. 16). Renan's meditation 'Prière sur l'Acropole' ('Prayer on the Acropolis') eloquently captures the sensibilities of the French reception of the Parthenon and its sculptures.

The romance of ruins was not exclusively the province of artists and poets, and there is a pleasing sensitivity to the Parthenon sculptures evident even in the work of academic archaeologists, not least Maxime Collignon (1849–1917). His great book on the Parthenon, *Le Parthénon; l'histoire, l'architecture et la sculpture*, appeared in 1912, and followed the 1910 account by A. H. Smith of the British Museum, *The Sculptures of the Parthenon*. Both are large-format folio books of a kind that had become increasingly rare since the eighteenth century, when they were an essential element of every gentleman's library. While Smith stays close to the sculptures and makes it his mission to record every last fragment, be it in the

British Museum, on the Acropolis or elsewhere, Collignon's stated interest is the architecture of the building as a vehicle for the sculpture. The photographic plates in his book included many by Frédéric Boissonnas (1858–1946), the celebrated Swiss photographer renowned for his captivating images of Greece, which brought a new aesthetic to the appreciation of the ancient building.

Conclusion

Rodin's contribution to the artistic and intellectual reception of the Parthenon sculptures has, until now, not been fully recognized and credited. In France, no artistic figure, whether in sculpture, poetry or painting, comes close to Rodin, with his remarkable understanding and brilliant interpretation of the Parthenon and its sculptures. Only Rodin could have thought of lopping the head and limbs from his own sculptures in order to render them closer to the archaeological ruins of the past to create a new genre of contemporary art, namely the headless, limbless torso.

Rodin's response to the Parthenon sculptures was as intuitive as it was understated. He does not appropriate the sculptures of Pheidias in order, through them, to boast of his own achievement. He is no bombast, and his aphoristic declarations of respect and admiration for the works of Pheidias were as modest as they were sincere. As Hartwig Fischer points out in his introduction to this catalogue, Rodin defies the boundary between past and present.

This essay has set Rodin's love affair with the Parthenon into a longer narrative that reaches back into the seventeenth century. In the next essay, Bénédicte Garnier, working closely with the archive at the Musée Rodin, brings together the evidence for reconstructing the depth and extent of Rodin's relationship to the Parthenon and its sculptures.

1. The literature on the works of Pheidias is vast. See Davison (2009) and for a useful summary Harrison (1996).
2. For chryselephantine statues see Lapatin (2001).
3. Cicero, Orator, II,9. For *phantasia* see Pollitt (1974), 53–55.
4. Meredith Shedd. On the closeness to nature and its effect on French art and thought see Leoussi (1998)
5. Rodin (1911) quoted in Çakmak (2014).
6. Plutarch, *Perikles*, 13,4.
7. Harrison (1981).
8. Frazer (1898).
9. Plutarch, *Perikles*, 7.3.
10. Rodin (1910), 246.
11. Jenkins (1992), 201–202.
12. Jenkins (1984).
13. For Dalou and Legros see Read (1982), 302ff.
14. On Leighton see Ormond (1975) and Jones et al. (1996).
15. For Gilbert see Dorment (1986).
16. See Leoussi (1998 and 2015).
17. Bowie and Thimme (1971), 4.
18. Bowie and Thimme (1971), XII.
19. Spon and Wheler (1678).
20. For Fauvel see Clairmont (2007).
21. The Lesser Panathenaia was an annual event, while the Greater was held every four years.
22. See Garnier in this volume.
23. Jenkins (1992), 80.
24. Smith (1916), 357.
25. Rowell (2012).
26. Williams (2001 and 2009).
27. St Clair (3rd ed., 1998), 119–131.
28. Cummings (1963 and 1964).
29. Rothenberg (1997), 362.
30. Worsley, Vol. 2 (1794).
31. Rothenberg (1977), 375.
32. The French addition appeared two years later, see Visconti (1818).
33. Rothenberg (1977), 371.
34. Jenkins (1998), 469.
35. Rothenberg (1977), 449.
36. Milton, *Samson Agonistes*, line 1758.
37. Jenkins (1990), 92 and Tournikiotis (1994), 223, note 81.
38. Jenkins (1990), 95.
39. Jenkins (1990), 102.
40. Jenkins (1990), 104; Jenkins (1992); Jenkins (2007).
41. Milton, *Paradise Regained*, Book IV, 237–240, published 1671.
42. For Winckelmann see Jenkins (1992), 19–24.
43. Bouras in Tournikiotis (1994), 322–324.

'My dream as a sculptor' – the thousand Parthenons of Auguste Rodin

Bénédicte Garnier

The Parthenon – ancient, dreamlike, multifaceted – was for Rodin a lifelong preoccupation.[1] For him, it was as if there were more than one Parthenon. No sooner had he begun to sculpt than he discovered this fragmented monument, which seemed to embody his very dreams and which became an obsession that never left him. Rodin spent his life constructing his own Parthenon, piece by piece, in various forms – in his thoughts as well as in his work (Fig. 1). Drawn or modelled, the Parthenon would emerge from Rodin's imagination. In the Parthenon Rodin discovered his favourite themes – the monument and the human body. For Rodin, Pheidias was synonymous with sculpture and, together with Michelangelo, was his master.

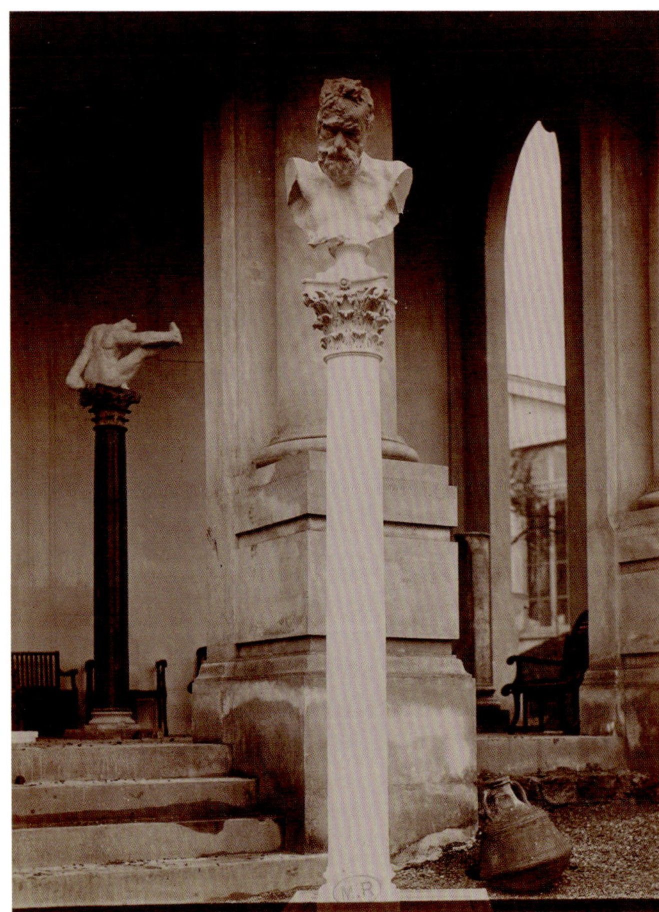

Fig. 1
Jean Limet (1855–1941)
Peristyle of the Pavillon de l'Alma, Meudon
After 1901
Aristotype
H 24.3 cm, W 18 cm
Musée Rodin, Ph. 1306

Paris – Rodin's first studies of the Parthenon

In 1854, at the age of fourteen, Rodin set out on his artistic studies at the Petite École in Paris,[2] where a cast of the Parthenon frieze was displayed 'in one of the arcades leading to the courtyard'.[3] In 1855 he was awarded a Second Prize in drawing from memory, and then in the winter term of 1856/1857 he won the First Prize in the category 'Decorative modelling inspired by Classical sculpture'. At the same time, he began making regular visits to the Louvre, and in particular the rooms dedicated to antiquities. 'How many times did I come here then, when I was barely fifteen years old … I would copy the ancient statues with just pencils and paper.'[4] The block of the Parthenon frieze (East Frieze block VII) showing young women, the so-called Ergastinai, which Rodin discovered in the Louvre during his visits in the 1850s, had been restored around 1820 to include the missing heads, in accordance with the practice of the day (Fig. 2).[5] On 12 August 1856 the apprentice sculptor was granted admission to the Print Room at the Imperial Library, where he studied the collection of drawings and engravings.[6] The impressive illustrated works by archaeologists and Classical scholars such as Adolf Michaelis (1835–1910),[7] Maxime Collignon and Salomon Reinach (1858–1932)[8] had not yet appeared, but Rodin was able to look at the engravings that were displayed in the Musée Napoléon in 1804[9] and those published by A. L. Millin (1759–1810) in 1806,[10] both of which included images of fragments of the Parthenon before restoration. The work of Comte de Clarac (1777–1847), published in 1841, showed the fragments after restoration, with the added heads.[11] Rodin would also have been able to consult books by James Stuart (1713–1788) and Nicholas Revett (1720–1804),[12] Charles Lenormant (1802–1859)[13] and Léon de Laborde,[14] with their illustrations by Jacques Carrey (see p. 19), and not least

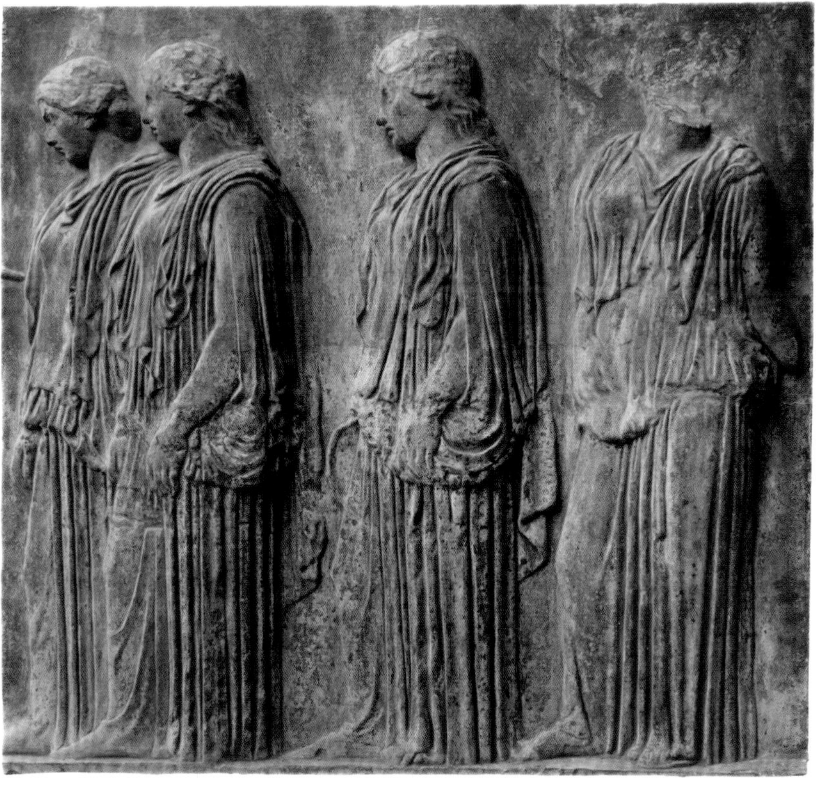

Fig. 2
Photograph of a cast, now lost, of the Parthenon East Frieze (block VII) presented to the British Museum in 1820 by F. Chantrey, showing the so-called Ergastinai with restored heads

the volumes with engraved plates in the series *A Description of the Collection of Ancient Marbles in The British Museum*. Part VI was on the Parthenon pediments (1830), Part VII on the metopes (1835) and Part VIII on the frieze (1839).

As Rodin remembered: 'In the afternoons, I would go to the Louvre to draw the ancient sculptures, or to the Print Room in the Imperial Library. As I wasn't very well dressed, they only let me see certain things, but I also looked at the books that had been left out by more highly regarded visitors. I was open to everything; I was eager to learn.'[15] We don't know if Rodin saw Jacques Carrey's original drawings of the Parthenon as it was in 1674, before it was badly damaged by an explosion (see p. 20).[16] And so the young man's eye encountered images of the Parthenon at various stages in its history, showing its sculptures in different states – fragmentary, restored and reconstructed.

Rodin's experience of the shapes and forms of the sculptures of the Parthenon also encompassed the reduced-scale models sold unofficially on the bridges over the Seine (Cats 13–15) and the life-size casts that adorned the rooms of the École des Beaux-Arts. The collection there was constantly rearranged throughout the nineteenth century and did not achieve its definitive layout until the end of that century, as can be seen from contemporary photographs and from the guidebook by art historian Eugène Müntz (1845–1902).[17] Friezes ran around three sides of the Cour du Mûrier (Fig. 3) as well as encircling the Vestibule de l'Horloge and the vestibule of the Salle de Melpomène (Figs 4 and 5). In the vestibule of the Palais des Études itself, casts of the pediments and metopes were displayed in the Greek Room, while casts of three columns supporting an entablature with four metopes

BELOW LEFT
Fig. 3
Émile Camut (1849–1905)
La cour du Mûrier et le Monument à Regnault
École des Beaux-Arts: cast of the Parthenon frieze, Cour du Mûrier
1877
Ink and watercolour
H 55.4 cm, W 38.9 cm
Paris, École nationale supérieure des beaux-arts, Pc 62741

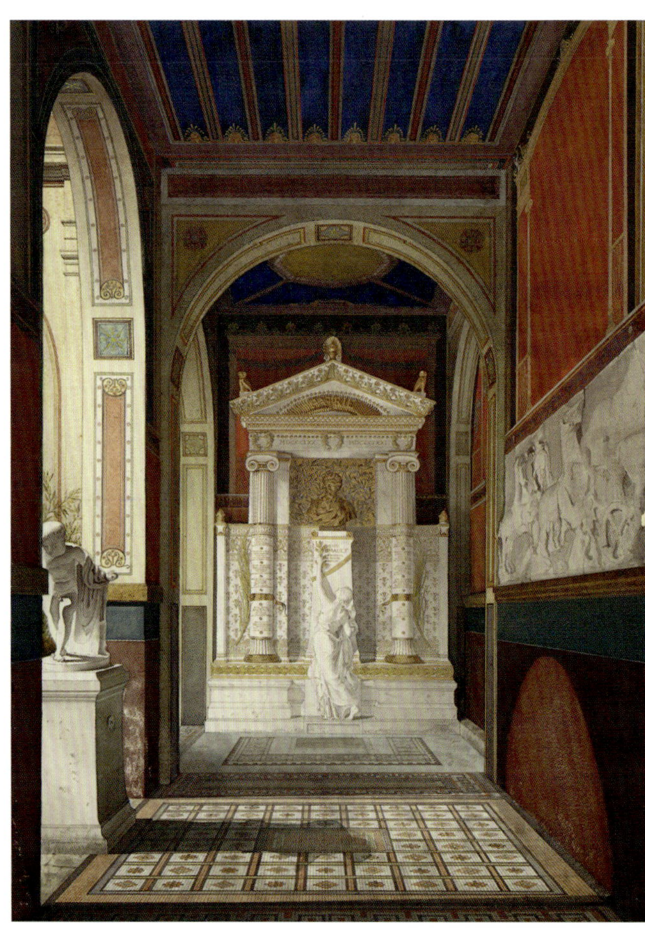

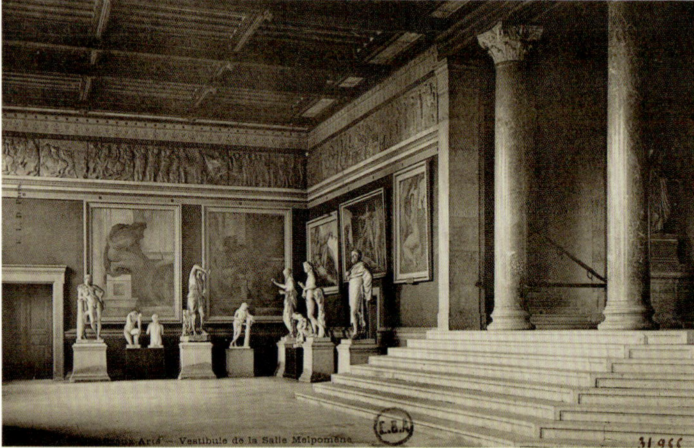

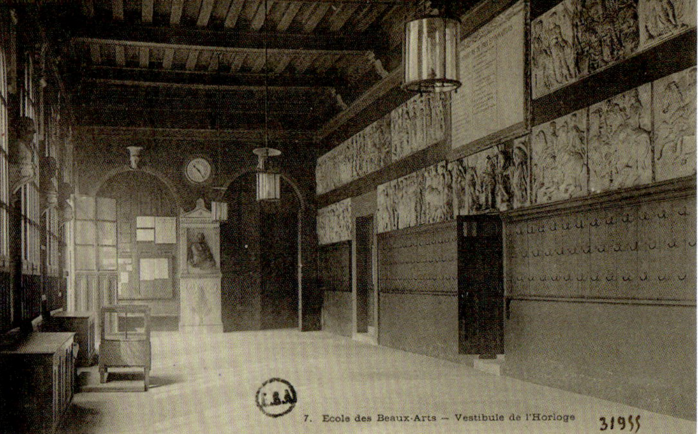

extended into the covered courtyard. Through these fragments – copies of elements in the British Museum as well as of ones remaining in Athens – Rodin was able to simulate the experience of visiting the Parthenon itself. The cast manufactory at the Louvre would have been another place to study the Parthenon sculptures[18], which as well as receiving casts from the British Museum would also have supplied them upon request, especially of the Parthenon frieze block in the Louvre.

While staying in Brussels between 1871 and 1877, Rodin continued his exploration of the Parthenon. He was again able to study copies of the fragments held in the British Museum, as well as of sculptures that were still in Athens.[19] '[Rodin] spent most Sundays at the Museum of Sculpture and Plaster Casts, which was then part of the Palace of the Academies [where] he analysed the ancient sculptures in minute detail in order to immerse his mind in their style and forms of beauty.'[20] Rodin and the sculptor Julien Dillens (1849–1904) would spend hours together, 'considering and discussing the beauties of the ancient statues, losing themselves in intense contemplation'.[21]

London – the first encounter with the Parthenon sculptures in the British Museum

In 1880 Rodin received his first commission from the French government: a monumental door for a new decorative arts museum that was to be constructed in Paris. *The Gates of Hell*, inspired by Dante's *Divine Comedy* and Baudelaire's *Les Fleurs du Mal* (published in 1857) became Rodin's magnum opus. He continued to work on it, intermittently, for the rest of his life, adding to it and abstracting from it, removing each of its numerous fragments, like an archaeologist, and reinventing them.

Rodin visited London for the first time in 1881, from 22 July until 1 September. While there, his friend Alphonse Legros introduced him to the art of drypoint printmaking, and, together with the painter Dorothy Stanley (née Tennant) (1855–1926), they visited the British Museum. Twenty-five years later, Stanley still vividly remembered her first meeting with the sculptor, to whom she wrote:

> Dear Mr Rodin, How kind of you to think of me and to propose spending a morning with me! Yes, I am completely free every day – and even if I weren't, I should ensure that I made myself available in order to have the privilege of going to the British Museum with you. I shall see you, then, on the morning of the 24th. I shall meet you there and we shall visit whichever parts of the Museum you like, as we did in the past, when you were much younger and we went there together.[22]

Rodin thus discovered the Parthenon sculptures, which had remained unrestored following the advice of Antonio Canova. He could study sculptures from the pediments and frieze juxtaposed at eye level, and, looking up, could take in the metopes that ran around the walls. We know little of Rodin's immediate impressions of the British Museum exhibits, but the experience was to remain with him for the rest of his life.

During his visits to the rooms of antiquities at the British Museum, as at the Louvre, Rodin developed a certain ritual: observing and drawing, making solitary

OPPOSITE RIGHT, ABOVE AND BELOW
Figs 4, 5
Ernest Louis Désiré le Deley (1859–1917)
École des Beaux-Arts: Vestibule de la Salle de Melpomène and the Vestibule de l'Horloge
1903
Postcards
H 9 cm, W 14 cm (both)
Paris, École nationale supérieure des beaux-arts, Pc31955.23 and Pc31955.22

visits, or sharing his responses and conversing with friends, artists, curators and archaeologists. He returned to the Museum again and again, and always with the same delight, incorporating these special moments into his timetable whenever he came to London for an exhibition or to receive an honour. Europe's museums had a special place in Rodin's heart – one could go so far as to say that each city, even each country, was valued in terms of its museum of antiquities, which was its temple to the beauty of the ancient world. For Rodin, the British Museum and the Parthenon sculptures *were* London: he would later write in his notebook, 'temple London Museum of muses' (Cat. 19).[23] By the time of his visit to the museum in 1883, his approach to antiquities had undergone a profound change. Rather than the dutiful, academic drawings of his youth, and taking his inspiration from the Assyrian reliefs, he reimagined the ancient forms with immense freedom in the busts of Victor Hugo he was working on at the time (Fig. 6).[24] It was undoubtedly no coincidence that, on his next visit, in June 1886, he presented two drypoint portraits of the famous writer with the dedication 'a Monsieur Colvin, conservateur des Estampes au British Museum/hommage cordial' ('to Mr Colvin, curator of prints at the British Museum, with kind regards').[25]

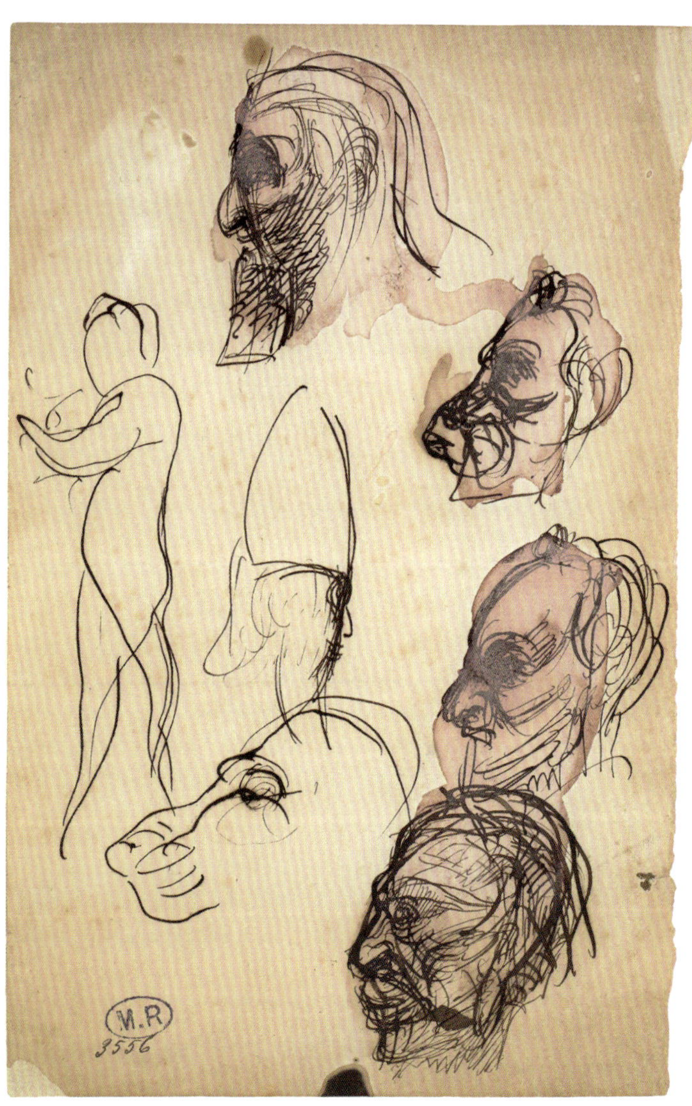

Fig. 6
Auguste Rodin
Sheet of studies: a profile figure; four profile male bearded heads; head with a mitre
1883?
Ink and gouache on laid paper
H 20.3 cm, W 13.1 cm
Musée Rodin, D. 3556

A new interest in antiquities and collecting

The 1890s saw a development in Rodin's thinking and in his creativity. He felt a powerful urge to study ancient art, but this time with a new vision. He later reflected on how the masterpieces of the ancient world were bound up with his memories of adolescent stirrings, saying 'Antiquity is my youth.... Antiquity and nature are part of the same mystery.'[26]

In 1893 Rodin moved from Paris and settled in Meudon, southwest of the city, in the heart of the countryside, where he began collecting ancient artefacts – first in the house known as the Maison du Chien-Loup and later in the Villa des Brillants. With a vision of creating an ultimate masterpiece, Rodin bought, more or less purposefully, objects that reminded him of the Parthenon, as substitutes for the famous marbles. Although inevitably of lesser quality, they rekindled his admiration for the great monument. To the collection in his imagination he now added a real one.

Rodin also rediscovered the Parthenon in Paris, in part through the fragments at the Louvre, where the collection was newly exhibited in the room of ancient Greek art with the addition of casts.[27] The frieze block (VII) showing the young women had been returned to its original condition, and was now displayed without the restored heads. A cast of four of the figures was exhibited alongside the original to show what the previous restorations had looked like (see Fig. 2 and pp. 128–29).[28] A cast of the head of Iris from the West Pediment (N), the original of which at that time belonged to Léon de Laborde, was also exhibited.[29] This new display served to reinforce Rodin's view that the frieze block was not only particularly well preserved, but was also an exceptionally fine rendering of its subject and had been one of the highlights of the frieze procession. His perception of this 'new' ancient fragment fed into his thinking about the partial body in his work. It became also a source of inspiration for objects in his own collection – albeit ones of a less outstanding quality.

A museum of casts had been created at the Sorbonne in 1891 by Maxime Collignon, to coincide with the founding of a Chair in Archaeology there on the German model.[30] Rodin visited it with the young sculptor Antoine Bourdelle (1861–1929), and was pleased to find plaster casts of more of the Parthenon sculptures. Rodin's obsession with antiquities also took him to museums across Europe in May and June 1902 – the Albertinum in Dresden, and the cast museums in Prague and Vienna. At that time his passion for the Parthenon was shared by many of his contemporaries; in Vienna, the young Croatian sculptor Ivan Meštrović (1883–1962) was taken by surprise:

> One day, while I was admiring a fragment of sculpture from the Parthenon, I noticed two other visitors standing beside me.... When I saw that the older man was sketching the outline of a statue while conversing with his companion and I heard that they were speaking in French, I knew at once that it must be Rodin.[31]

Rodin also travelled to Strasbourg in March 1907 for the opening of an exhibition of French art, and while there visited the university's museum, then under the directorship of Adolf Michaelis: 'This morning, I had the pleasure of giving a tour of my museum to Mr Rodin, who was most interested in seeing the Classical works of art.'[32] Here, too, Rodin discovered plaster casts of sculptures from the Parthenon.

Rodin's road to the Parthenon

The year 1900 marked a turning point in Rodin's career. On the Place de l'Alma, on the fringes of that year's Exposition Universelle in Paris, Rodin had a huge pavilion erected, in which he mounted a public exhibition of all his work to date for the first time, and in an innovative manner. A number of small statues and groups of statues were set on columns with ornate capitals, as was the Naxian Sphinx from Delphi (a plaster cast of which was on display at the Louvre), and others were placed on tall columns, such as those found in Greek temples, in particular the Parthenon, whose partial reconstruction Rodin had seen in the École des Beaux-Arts.

After the turn of the century, Rodin's trips to London became more frequent. He visited every year from 1902 to 1907, and then spent two long periods there in 1913 and 1914. The British press reported his reactions to his visits to the British Museum: 'Your beautiful museums, with their marvellous collections, Greek, Assyrian, and Egyptian, awakened in me a flood of sensations, which, if not new, had at any rate a rejuvenating influence; and those sensations caused me to follow Nature all the more closely in my studies.'[33] In 1903, in response to a journalist asking him 'What are your impressions of London on the whole?', his reply was unequivocal: 'The most interesting part of London is the number of its antiquities. In my spare time I simply haunt the British Museum. It is a most noble institution. My one regret is that I have not the time to frequent it more.'[34] He had already been dubbed 'the French Phidias'.[35]

Other thoughts can be found in his notebooks: 'Why go to the British [Museum] when it makes all our efforts seem inadequate … since London has the Parthenons, it seems the flavour of the marble blend with English blood [sic].'[36] But London also revealed other ancient treasures to Rodin. In addition to the British Museum, he regularly visited the Victoria and Albert Museum to see plaster casts of Greek and Roman sculptures and works by Michelangelo, as well as the Burlington Fine Arts Club, where in 1903 he fell in love with the 'Warren Head', a Classical sculpture of the head of a young woman from Chios (Fig. 7; the head is now in the Museum of Fine Arts, Boston).[37] The Swiss archaeologist Salomon Reinach commented judiciously on the difference of opinion concerning this famous sculpture between Rodin and the circumspect Cecil H. Smith (1859–1944), who was Keeper of the Department of Greek and Roman Antiquities at the British Museum between 1904 and 1909 before he took up the directorship at the Victoria and Albert Museum:

> This controversy is most interesting. As a true archaeologist, Mr Smith was irritated by the rather sickly aspect of this Chios marble, while Mr Rodin, the famous sculptor, admired it from a technical point of view. I accept Mr Rodin's opinion and I accept Mr Smith's opinion: the piece is extremely well executed and most agreeable to the eye, in spite of the careless cleaning process to which it has been subjected, but one has only to look at the Parthenon friezes to see that it could not possibly be the work of one of the great masters.[38]

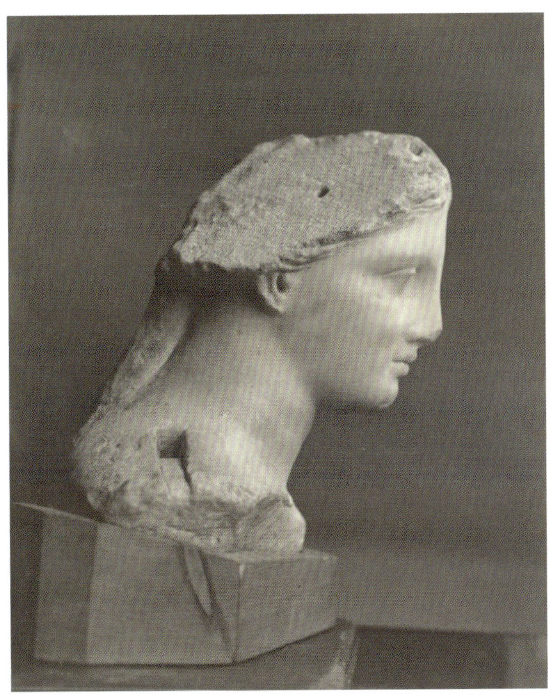

Fig. 7
Frederick Hollyer
(1837–1933)
The Warren Head
Around 1904
Gelatin silver print
H 31.4 cm, W 24.5 cm
Musée Rodin, Ph. 2489

Rodin was invited by Edward Perry Warren (1860–1928), a collector and owner of the 'Warren Head', to his home in Lewes, southern England, where Rodin saw his collection of antiquities bought with the help of his friend John Marshall. In 1907 Rodin visited the Ashmolean Museum in Oxford. He also often stayed with the Scottish sculptor John Tweed (1869–1933) and his wife Edith, who spent a great deal of time with archaeologists in London. Tweed asked Rodin to invite Ernest Gardner (1862–1939), professor of Greek archaeology at the University of London, to Meudon later that year.[39] The following year, Edith Tweed suggested to Rodin that he purchase a terracotta figure from Spink and Son, one of the antiquarian dealers he regularly visited in the area around the British Museum.[40]

In 1905, the English writer and patron of the arts Thomas Scott-Ellis, 8th Baron Howard de Walden (1880–1946), had commissioned two sculptures from Rodin: *The Benedictions*, in marble, and *The Thinker*, in bronze. In the following year, while Rodin was working on his bust, *Lord Howard de Walden*, Scott-Ellis sent him, via Robert Bosanquet (1871–1935), professor of Classical archaeology at the University of Liverpool, a plaster cast of a Greek sculpture: 'At Lord Howard de Walden's request I am sending to you a cast of the arm of the marble throne, called the Throne of High Priest of Dionysus, in the theatre at Athens. I hope that it may reach you safely.'[41] Such a gift, intended as a thank-you for the bust, must have sealed the new friendship between the two men. The part of the throne in question was not in the collection of Liverpool's Walker Art Gallery, but a cast of the whole throne was on display in the Elgin Room of the British Museum and would therefore have been well known to Rodin. Rodin had last visited London in February/March of that year, and Scott-Ellis may have seen it with him then. No doubt Robert Bosanquet, who had been Director of the British School at Athens from 1900 to 1906, was the person best placed to obtain a copy rapidly from the workshops of the British Museum, or even directly from the National Archaeological Museum in Athens.

Restoring the Parthenon?

Rodin also engaged in a debate about the restoration of the Parthenon led by Nikolaos Balanos after the earthquake of 1894 (see also p. 32). The organizers of the first International Congress of Archaeology that was to take place in April 1905 in Athens posed the question: 'How and to what extent should Greece's ancient monuments, and particularly the Parthenon, be restored?' The debate was not a new one, but in France a group of artists and scholars, opposed to the prevailing policy of 'filling in the gaps', was raising objections to the very idea of restoration. Several periodicals joined in the debate,[42] one of which, *Le Musée: revue d'art antique*, collected various statements by artists and writers in order to raise a petition against the proposal.[43] This, together with a message to the King of Greece, was sent to the President of the Congress.

A statement by Antoine Bourdelle was not included,[44] but the artist wrote to Rodin: 'I am entirely at one with your excellent letter on the Parthenon and the cathedrals.'[45] Rodin was the most famous name on the list. A contributor to *Le Musée* since 1904, he had naturally been asked for his support. The subject was close to his heart and he submitted a specially written article in which he stated his position unequivocally: 'I would like to widen the question', he wrote, going on to compare the Parthenon with the great cathedrals of France, which he thought had been over-restored, seeing it as a symbol both of the Greek nation and of the venerated ancient world:

> Chartres is what Olympia once was, Beauvais has the harmonious splendour of the Parthenon.… Yes, we must demand with all our energy and vigour that the ruins of the Parthenon be left to the breezes that play among its broken columns; let our admiration rise towards it and let that same admiration be directed at our own Parthenons, sullied as they may sadly be.[46]

Rodin had been in London in February 1904 – and, of course, at the British Museum – and he continued his article with these words:

> In fact, I have just been to London (how passionately I love the days I spend there!) to see again the statues of The Fates [Parthenon East Pediment figures K, L and M] and of Theseus [or Dionysos; figure D], and was glad to find these great blocks of stone unchanged, with only wooden supports to prevent them from falling. This, then, is what I ask: that any structure supporting a temple or statue be of wood or stone and that, whichever it is, it be left in its natural state. Let us never allow these vulgar carvings that are appearing everywhere as if we had entrusted our monuments to children – or, alas, had become children ourselves![47]

Was Rodin never tempted to go to Athens and climb the rock on which the Parthenon stood, to study at first hand the sculptures that were still in situ? On 3 November 1906, at a dinner at the Élysée Palace, he received an invitation from the King of Greece, as was reported in the press: 'Soon he will gain still greater insight, among the ruins of the Acropolis and the Parthenon, into the secret of the eternal beauty of these ancient monuments, which have for so long been his models. The master is going to Greece. He is delighted.'[48] Rodin intended to go in March 1907, but the pressure of work, poor health and the prospect of a long sea journey on which he was likely to be seasick combined to make him abandon the idea. 'No, I have not yet made the journey to Greece. It has been delayed by an urgent commission that has arrived just at the time I thought I would be able to go. Nevertheless, I hope it is only postponed, rather than cancelled.'[49] But he would never get there. And so we cannot picture him climbing up to the Parthenon and gasping in amazement as he came face to face with the actual monument, as he had when he first encountered the fragments of it at the British Museum. For Rodin, as for Antoine Bourdelle, the Greek temple would always remain a myth, an inaccessible dream.

The Parthenon in articles, letters and postcards

Rodin never again succumbed to the temptation to visit Greece. As he wrote to the French writer Ernest Renan (see also p. 32): 'Ah, Renan! You have left Brittany to prostrate yourself before the Parthenon, as a sculptor brought up in Greece might come from the Parthenon to admire our cathedrals!'[50] But the Parthenon continued to fire the artist's imagination through images and descriptions sent to him or published by friends, such as the account by the art historian Élie Faure (1873–1937) that appeared in the journal *Le Musée* in 1906: 'I climbed the sacred rock and saw the golden skeleton of the Parthenon spring from the stony plateau on to which the Propylaea opens majestically like a great floodgate.'[51] In 1908 Rodin's partner, Rose Beuret (1844–1917), was sent a photograph of the Parthenon by their friend Mary Marshall, to whom Rodin wrote: 'Though this magnificent Parthenon was a gift to Rose, it also gives me great pleasure. I had not imagined it to be so majestic. Its grandeur is even grander than I thought. It is an absolutely beautiful photograph to have such a spiritual and terrifying effect on me.'[52] And again later: 'I am still delighted by this image of the Parthenon.'[53] The architecture of the temple, standing like a human body on the rock of the Acropolis, impressed him as much as the fragments of sculptures that belonged to it.

The Parthenon was also an icon for many of Rodin's contemporaries. Antoine Bourdelle often referred to it in his letters to Rodin: 'You have made me think again of Plato's idea that beauty is the splendour of truth, but truth is composed of many things.… Only today, I was telling two young painters that learning to draw is about learning to think. Think of the Parthenon and you have an answer to Plato's conundrum.'[54] It had a profound emotional effect on everyone who went to see it. In 1915, the sculptor Serge Youriévitch[55] sent Rodin an idyllic description of Greece, enlivened with reflections on Classical sculpture:

> For me, it was a revelation. Only here, in this limpid air, in this monumental light amid these arid mountains with their unexpectedly harmonious outlines, only here, it seems to me, can one fully understand and absorb Greek art.… The Acropolis, the Parthenon, the home of Athena, dominates the city, Attica, Greece and is the ideal of pure and immortal beauty that, even today, shines out across the world. This small corner of the modern city takes you back to ancient Greece.… Every time I go to France, I shall travel via Greece. *Athens and Greece should be a place of pilgrimage for all sculptors.…* It is above all the immensity and grandeur of the light that makes Greece uniquely delightful.[56]

Helene von Nostitz (1878–1944), who posed for Rodin, also wrote to him from Greece, including this note on the back of a photograph of an ancient Kore (a votive female statue) she had seen at the Acropolis:

> Athens, 1st April 1912. Dear friend, I often think of you here, where imposing outlines are an object of worship. You are the only living artist I can imagine forever contemplating the ancients.… As I stood on the Acropolis in the moonlight, a sad song floated up from the city and brought its majestic columns to life. Yes, such sensations should be expressed through music.[57]

Another friend who modelled for him, the American Kate Simpson (d. 1943), gave Rodin a photograph of one of the three Fates from the East Pediment in 1902, when she came to pose for her bust. The note she wrote on it, 'My bust /

group of the Parthenon',[58] was no doubt intended to describe Rodin's sculpture retrospectively rather than to inspire him (Figs 8 and 9).

The Parthenons of Meudon – perpetuating an ancient practice

Rodin transformed the Villa des Brillants into his own mythical setting – on the hill above Meudon he was like Pheidias on the sacred rock of the Acropolis (Figs 10 and 11). Visitors explicitly compared its setting to that of the Parthenon: 'I shall be very happy to see Meudon again, and your Acropolis',[59] said Antoine Bourdelle in 1906, while Count Harry Kessler (1868–1937), on a trip to Greece with the artist Aristide Maillol (1861–1944) in 1908 wrote 'We are surrounded by masterpieces and thinking of the sacred rock of Meudon.'[60]

At Meudon, Rodin was not only a sculptor but also an architect. In 1900, he designed a building to house his collection of Greek and Roman statues with a façade and colonnade in the style of a Classical temple, and the following year he extended it by dismantling the pavilion he had created on the Place d'Alma for the Exposition Universelle, reconstructing it next to the Villa des Brillants. He modified the curved entrance to create a rectangular peristyle, in which he put the larger Roman statues, along with the great columns, complete with capitals. The columns also spread into the interior of the pavilion, as they had at the exhibition, when several of his own sculptures had been placed on top of them.

BELOW LEFT
Fig. 8
Anonymous
Figure K from the Parthenon East Pediment; annotated by Kate Simpson, sent to Rodin
1902 or after
Photomechanical print
H 9 cm, W 7 cm
Musée Rodin, Ph. 2565

Fig. 9
Jacques Ernest Bulloz (1858–1942)
Bust of Kate Simpson in marble; 'à Monsieur Rodin/mon sculpteur/Paris le 20/septembre 1904'
Carbon print
H 35 cm, W 26.8 cm
Musée Rodin, Ph. 971

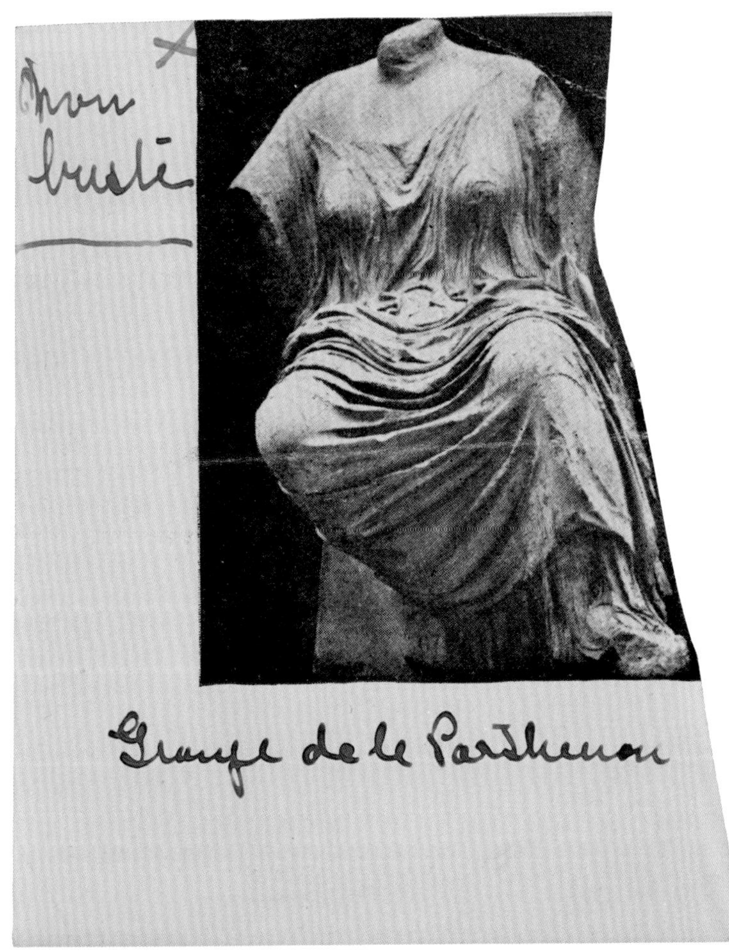

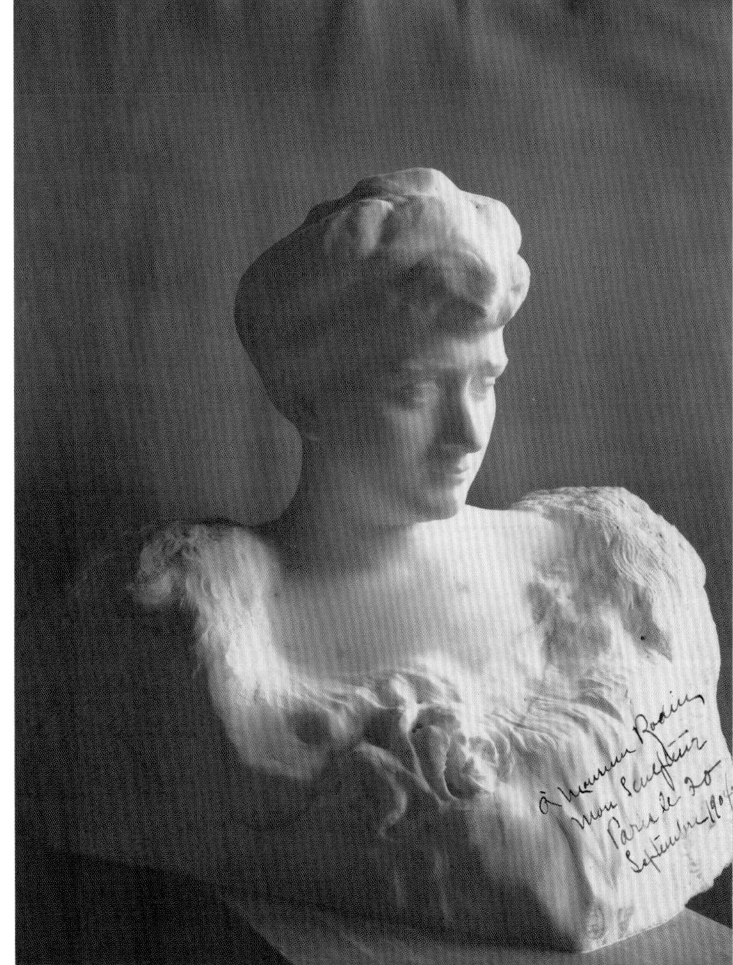

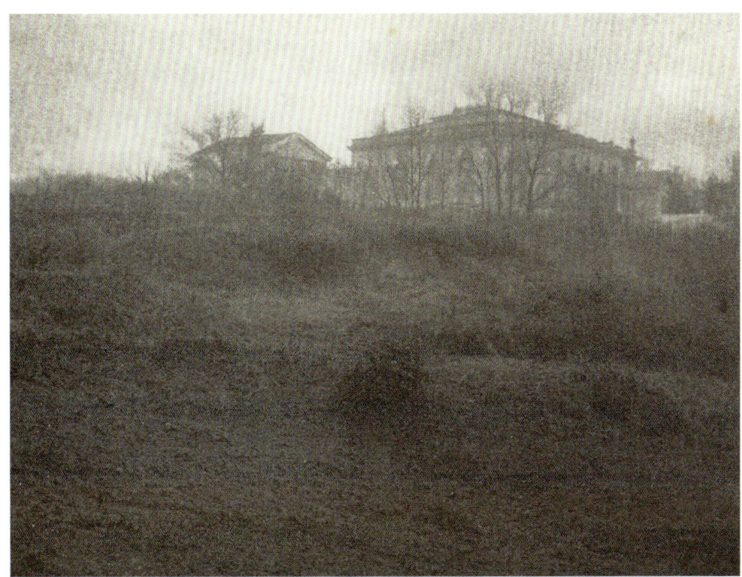

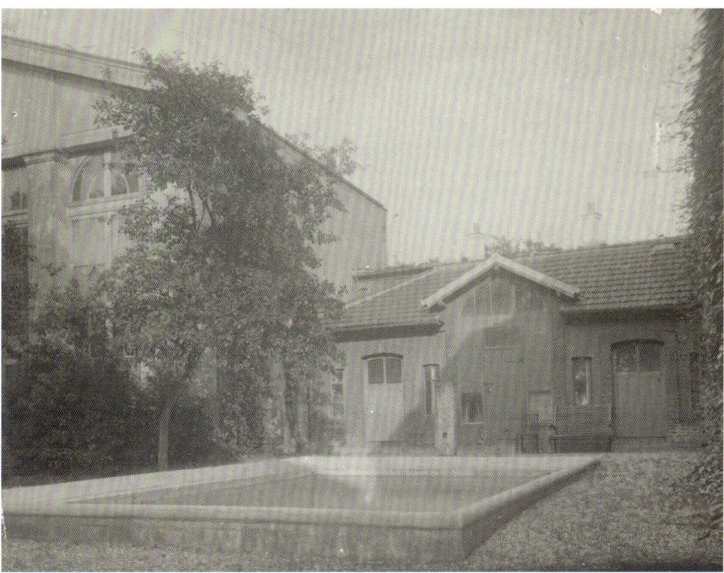

ABOVE LEFT
Fig. 10
Stephen Haweis (1878–1969)
and Henry Coles (1875–?)
The Pavillon de l'Alma
and the Museum of
Antiquities, Meudon
1903–1904
Carbon print
H 16.3 cm, W 22.5 cm
Musée Rodin, Ph. 1984

ABOVE RIGHT
Fig. 11
Anonymous
The Museum of Antiquities,
Meudon
Around 1913
Gelatin silver print
H 12.7 cm, W 17.2 cm
Musée Rodin, Ph. 9014

> A column standing as if in prayer has a particular beauty; it seems to have come from the Underworld. Now, like us, it stands in the sun and is part of the landscape, as if the sculptor of Pluto's Palace has brought his genius, his mind's secret thoughts, into the daylight to ennoble our vision.[61]

As soon as spring arrived, Rodin would move his collection, together with his own sculptures, out into the grounds of the Villa, transforming them into a fusion of Italian garden and open-air studio: 'As I'm sure you know, statues lose their potency when viewed indoors; they need to be outside – especially in that marvellous Hellenic setting among the ruins of the Acropolis and the Parthenon.'[62]

Rodin was very much of his time, stimulated by the same passion for ancient Greece that gripped all of Europe's intelligentsia right up to the First World War. In 1913 his friend Isadora Duncan (1877–1927), who was similarly inspired by both nature and Hellenism, established a dance school in Bellevue, above Meudon, which she called the 'Dyonision', echoing Rodin's self-styled Acropolis (Fig. 12).

For Rodin, Greek art was paramount – Roman art was also intrinsically Greek – and emanated directly from the sculptor's chisel, such as that of Pheidias or Praxiteles. In his view it was not an anonymous art, but a celebration of the amazing skill of the human hand in capturing nature and humanity, in manipulating shapes, material, light and shade. The word Greek became synonymous with beauty and excellence. The source of inspiration, the creator's energy, was Greek. Rodin himself was thus Greek:

> I love the ancient Greek statues; they always have been and will always remain my models. I have studied the sculptors' amazing techniques in museums in Paris and London. In a further attempt to grasp what it is that makes their work timeless, I have even made my own small collection of rare and beautiful items recovered by archaeologists from Greek soil.... But such artists knew that realism should not preclude idealism, for in art there should be no separation between the real and the imaginary. For

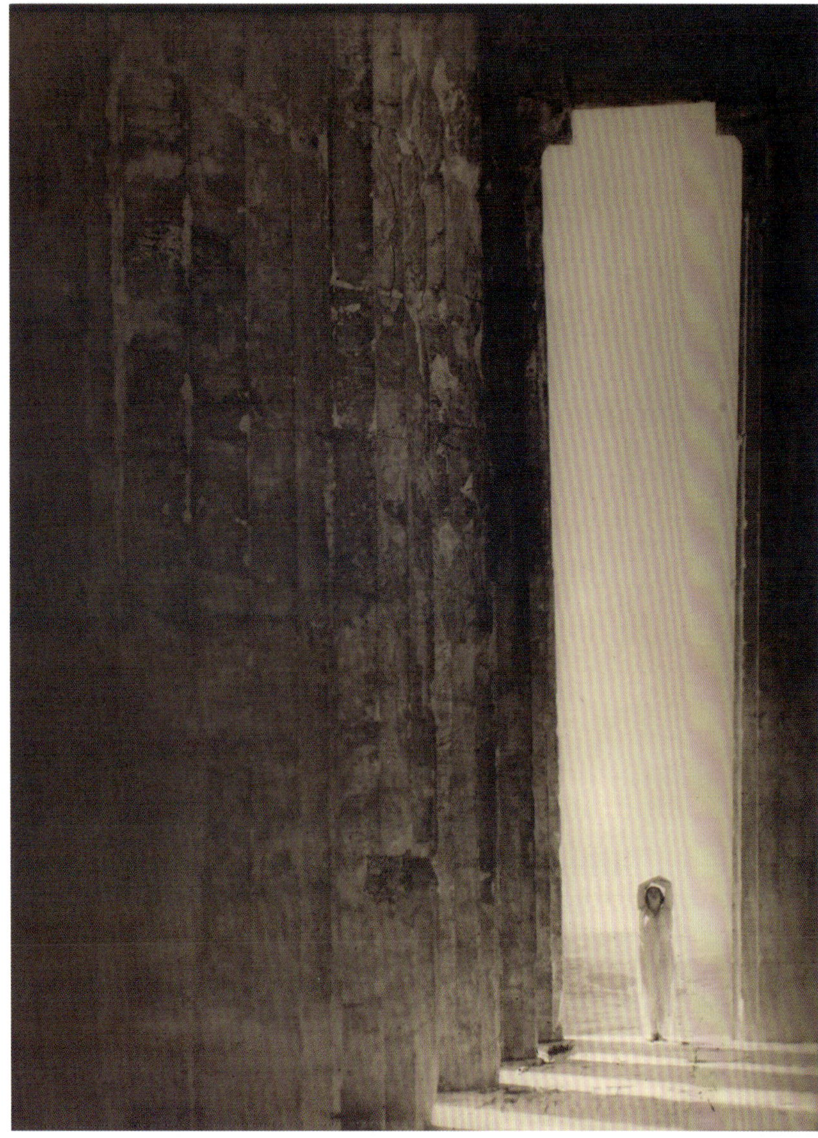

Fig. 12
Edward Steichen
(1879–1973)
Isadora Duncan under the portico of the Parthenon in Athens
1921
Gelatin silver chloro-bromide print
H 50.2 cm, W 36 cm
Toledo Museum of Art, Gift of the Apollo Society, 2002.13

> them, indeed, art was above all a matter of *honesty*. Honesty is what they saw in nature and what they strove to realize. And nature herself, being honest, lent them her strength, without weakening their spirit. Thus were they enabled to create works of absolute, faultless beauty. This is why they are great and why, across the centuries, they remain great.[63]

Rodin's art was compared by his contemporaries with that of Pheidias – as much to distinguish it as to dignify it. The comparison with Pheidias is also of relevance to Rodin's collection of ancient sculptures and his conception of it. According to him, everything he acquired was not only from the finest period in Greek art, but was also made by Pheidias himself, who was his ultimate reference (provided the sculpture was sufficiently beautiful). 'Among the many ancient fragments in Rodin's collection is a wonderful hand, part of a statue made by Pheidias.… His signature, Rodin tells me, is visible only to other artists.'[64] Around 1908–1909, one of Rodin's secretaries, Maurice Baud (1866–1915),[65] drew up a list of outstanding works from the collection, with their estimated values.[66] According to this document, which Rodin himself had almost certainly requested, they all had impressive provenance, and the words 'Parthenon', 'Michelangelo' and 'Pheidias' often appeared alongside the names of the works. In photographs of Rodin, we see him manipulating his own image and presenting himself as an ancient sage (Fig. 13).

Consciously or unconsciously, Rodin also created his own myth and immortality by perpetuating the traditional practice of 'The Sculptor', adopting the intuitive, sensory approach of Classical sculptors, which focused on looking, listening and touching. His writings from 1900 onwards placed him in a direct line with the great analysts of Classical sculpture of the eighteenth and nineteenth centuries, such as Denis Diderot (1713–1784), Johann Joachim Winckelmann and Johann Gottfried von Herder (1744–1803), as well as his contemporary, the philosopher Henri Bergson (1859–1941).

Without leaving home, Rodin could literally come into daily contact with the eight hundred or so Greek and Roman statues in his collection. It is hard to imagine him resisting the temptation to run his hands over the Parthenon statues in the Louvre or the British Museum, as he did in the National Museum in Rome in 1915, when he was seen trying to discover through touch how the *Venus of Cyrene* had been sculpted[67] – a practice that went back to the earliest days of sculpting, when the artist would attempt to internalize the shape of an object by feeling it. In so doing, Rodin would get to grips with the life within it, decipher the mysteries of what had come to resemble a familiar human body. 'At certain times, he simply stands before his relics, meditating.… How his fingers tremble when he touches these old stones with their polished, golden or occasionally grey patina!'[68] And '"It's like real flesh!" he would say.… It was as if it had been petrified by kisses and caresses.…. Touching this torso, one half expected it to feel warm.'[69]

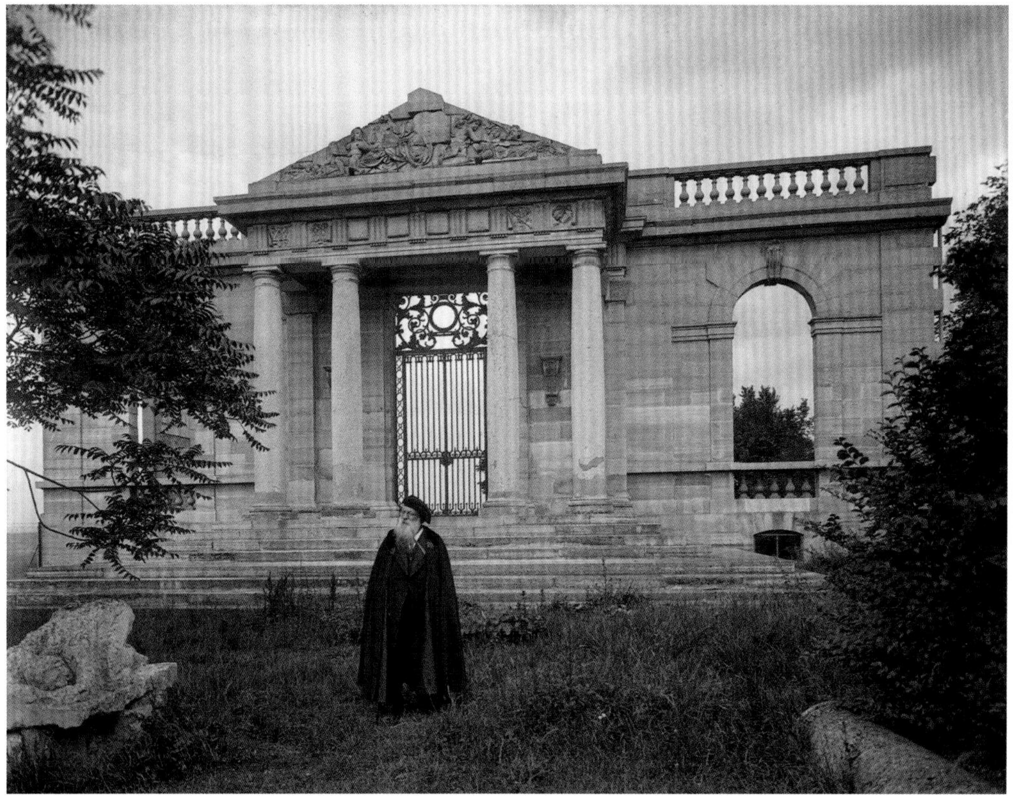

Fig. 13
Harry C. Ellis (1857–1928)
Rodin in front of the façade of the Château d'Issy, Meudon
After 1909
Gelatin silver negative on glass
H 18 cm, W 24 cm
Musée Rodin, Ph. 7756

Rodin also spent time just looking at the sculptures and would take visitors into his studio to study them by the light of a lamp or a candle, discovering first their 'skin', brought to life by the unevenness of the surface, then their shape, which revealed the 'skeleton' of these ancient marble statues:

> If I move the lamp to and fro over the marble, it seems to throb as fleeting shadows dance across it; when I hold it still, they come to rest.... Then they create other effects, refining and exploring its contours; and suddenly my admiration for this momentous work grows and pierces my heart with joy. But I pull myself together and force myself to learn from this wonderful lesson.[70]

Rodin would then refocus his attention, using a cloth or simply shielding his eyes to block out the weakest parts of the sculpture, concentrating only on the fragment that interested him. Like Pygmalion, Rodin wanted to create something new from even the most humble items in his collection.

The poet Rainer Maria Rilke (1875–1926), who came to Paris to write a monograph on Rodin and was for a time his secretary, wrote: 'Of an evening, when we entered the rooms by lamplight and roused these objects, one by one, they came back to life, hesitantly, like animals after a heavy dream – to something larger than life, as [Rodin] gives to all things, with his blessed hands.'[71] The ancient world, and particularly the Parthenon, was always alive in Rodin's imagination when he contemplated the contemporary world around him. The sculptor spoke to the ancient fragments and listened to what they had to say. And in his studio, he associated the timeless poses of life models with the ancient sculptures of an imaginary museum.

The qualities of marble

Rodin's love of Greek marble took various forms. It was this marble, after all, that had enabled Pheidias to create the Parthenon sculptures. And it was no doubt the Parthenon sculptures to which Rodin was referring when he wrote:

> There is nothing hard about Greek marble, which is the ideal medium. The Greek artists created timeless works that modern artists see and think they have discovered, but it is only after twenty years of patient study that they finally understand them and are able to defy the nature of the marble and themselves produce works that will inspire poets.[72]

Rodin did not subscribe to Winckelmann's view that antique marble statues should be pure white, preferring intermediate colours that, to the artist's eye, perfectly complemented the form of the modelling according to the interaction between the marble (preferably Greek) and the areas of light and shade. Looking at these ancient bodies in this way, they are never dull, they come to life and appear inherently natural. And marble reproduced the human body more vividly than bronze, terracotta or plaster. 'I always prefer to use Greek marble' wrote Rodin. 'It is warmer. It looks as though blood is running just below the surface. Parian or Pentelic marble is golden, as if it has been warmed by the sun.'[73]

Contrary to popular belief, however, he used Greek marble infrequently. Two examples are *Sleep* and the bust of Victor Hugo, both in the Musée Rodin,[74] which are made of Pentelic marble, like the sculptures of the Parthenon.

According to Rodin, neither Pentelic nor Parian marble could ever have been painted, even though this notion already seemed to be generally accepted in the worlds of art and archaeology in the second half of the nineteenth century. The realization came as a devastating blow to Rodin and turned his artistic vision upside-down. In 1902 the British Museum was still at the nexus of passionate arguments on this subject. The critic and watercolourist Dugald Sutherland MacColl (1859–1948), not yet daring to contradict Rodin directly, wrote to John Tweed, who showed the letter to Rodin:

> As for its *colour*, there is something we should take care to clarify. We know from contemporary accounts that Greek sculptors used a process of patinization to reduce the brilliance of the freshly cut marble. Apparently, it was rubbed with oil and wax. But they also relied heavily on the assistance of a painter called Nicias. Praxiteles, too, evidently had a knack for rendering human flesh that rivalled that of Correggio. Pheidias himself was a painter. I believe there must have been all types among the ancient Greeks: 'classicists' and 'snobs' as well as 'Rodins'. Show him these notes if he is not too busy.[75]

The following year, Rodin was still firm in his denial of the idea in his reported response to Georg Treu (1843–1921), the excavator of Olympia and curator of sculpture at the Albertinum in Dresden[76]: '"I truly wish I had not heard what he said. These archaeologists," he added jokingly, "they always judge sculpture from their point of view and not from the point of view of the subject."'[77]

The Parthenon sculptures, as well as Rodin's own antiquities, occasionally revealed the perfect surface of the original marble, both its smoothness and its appearance – its original 'skin' before this had been lost to the ravages of time. Such fragments – broken pieces of statue – no longer bore a resemblance to their original subject, but revealed normally unseen details of the composition of the marble. It all made sense: a fragment of the Parthenon became a mannequin which the artist's imagination could turn into many different things:

> I now have a collection of mutilated gods, in pieces, some of them masterpieces, and I spend a good deal of time with them. I learn from them. I love engaging with them across a space of two or three thousand years. They are closer to their natural origins than any other sculptures. I seem to understand them and I go back to them continually. Their scale reassures me. They relate to all the things I have loved in my life. And, though broken, they are not dead; they are vibrant, and I make them all the more vibrant simply by completing them in my mind. They are my eleventh-hour friends, and all from the pinnacle of the Greek Classical period, all from Greece. I am like Faust in Heaven, though less desperate. I do not have his terrible dreams, nor the dreadful visions that are conjured up *merely by reading* about them – perhaps more poetic to hear than to see on the stage. I am quite happy here between the earth and the sky – the forced happiness of being in Limbo.[78]

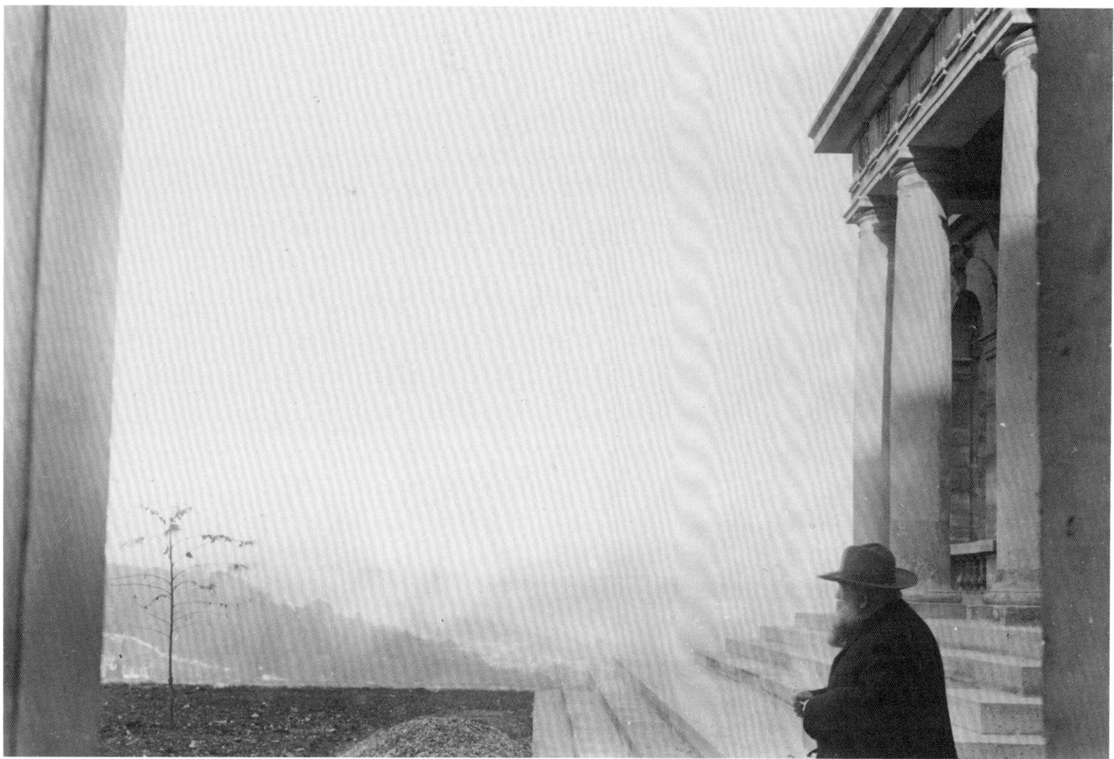

Fig. 14
Albert Harlingue (1879–1963)
Rodin in front of the façade of the Château d'Issy, Meudon, looking at the landscape
After 1908
Aristotype print
H 13 cm, W 18 cm
Musée Rodin, Ph. 6

Rodin's thinking and writing about his Parthenon

Rodin's continual dialogue with the ancient world took shape in his writings, which were permeated by the Parthenon, both as the ultimate standard and also as a means of expression.[79] His notebooks are filled with reflections on the Parthenon, and it is probably these that most clearly reveal Rodin's intimate relationship with the ancient world, a relationship that deepened year by year (Fig. 14).

'A Parthenon', 'Parthenons': Rodin referred to it in the plural as well as the singular, often omitting the definite article. A Parthenon of fragments – singular because they were all part of the same monument; Parthenons because the proper noun had become a collective noun, a familiar reference, a sort of leitmotif that could be inflected in any way he liked. For Rodin, the Parthenon was a pillar that stood firm against the onslaughts of doubt and mediocrity. The Parthenon invaded not only his thoughts and his notebooks, which he kept from around 1900, but also his published writing, right up to the final works: *L'Art*, a series of interviews collected by Paul Gsell (1870–1947) and published in 1911, and *Les cathédrales de France*, which appeared in 1914, three years before Rodin's death.

The word 'Parthenon' also appears repeatedly in the notebooks, sometimes in strange haiku-like poems. For Rodin, it was primarily a temple, which imparted its cool silence and serenity to the appearance of churches and cathedrals: 'this church lost / in silence shares / that quality with the / parthenons',[80] and writing about Amiens: 'this bas-relief is among the most beautiful things ever created; it is as wise as a Parthenon.'[81] Rodin even anthropomorphized the temple, highlighting its influence on his work: 'The Parthenon makes / me wonder / it is the dimensions / the figures of the pediment are / slender [and] dusted black / they will impose on me / like my sculpture / no more dust / metope.'[82]

Analysing the metope sculptures obsessively, and the mythology of the conflicts they depicted, particulary the fight between the Lapiths and the half-human centaurs, Rodin blended their themes imperceptibly with his own symbolic view of the world: 'Bull / Kaiser resistance / metope / man struggles against barbarians.'[83]

Rodin's worship of all that was fragmentary expressed itself through the Parthenon, and his idea that the whole could be expressed through a part: 'To drape my dream as a sculptor / like a fragment of the Parthenon.'[84] Every sculptor should measure himself against the Parthenon: 'What perfect unity there is in this fragment! … Is not the entire Acropolis here? … Greece was the land of sculpture, the only country without impurities, without legends. The subject of sculpture is life.'[85]

Focusing on the Panathenaiac procession depicted in the frieze, he wrote: 'but the dry parthenon / the glories of my whole life the / suppleness I have / studied for so long / but these panathenaia / slight from a distance.'[86] He also recalled the Fates from the East Pediment (K, L and M, now thought to be three goddesses) – or rather Fate, which he regarded as singular and unique: 'and yet under / her gaze, … / mephisto I have / never seen the breast / of the fate / pain / This belly draped in her / fine tunic / How such powerful / sensuality could be conveyed by such a severe man such as Pheidias.'[87]

Like Rodin, the Parthenon sculptors borrowed shapes and patterns from nature, such as trees and leaves. In the countryside around Meudon, Rodin would see the outlines of the Parthenon: 'Greece! Another sky intoxicated by the spring! And those two white shapes over there, on the hill – is it the Parthenon?'[88] Was the Parthenon as Rodin described it important in itself, or in terms of its associations? We cannot be certain. He used the word as a starting point for various trains of thought, making a chain of analogies, most often with the cathedrals of France: 'every projection / is striated / capitals draperies / plinths supporting chairs / saints / all broken and / yet another similarity with the Parthenon.'[89]

Rodin saw the Parthenon as a refuge for the artist, a sacred space for meditation, joy and beauty. Its sculptures made him see more clearly and more deeply:

I am not seeing things I have / just seen the parthenons / the assyrians their / lions / I have seen the connections / between the assyrians and the / chinese / I am seeing this / church after amiens its / here that I see intelligence / equal to that / which remains / in the Parthenon.'[90] It was the idealized symbol of the purity of Classical art:

> what have you done with the bleeding / heart of these ancient / people who gave their lives / to teach us / how to show suffering / cry for their genius / that is what I mean by / relics / the still more ancient Parthenon still exists / and what about yours? how / are you preserving it? / do you know more than the arab knows of the / Turk who leaves everything / alone?[91]

Even if he does not name it directly, the Parthenon is always implied: 'the hardest and softest [stone] loves man. Sculpture has elevated it. The column has made stone into a tree, a simplified tree, and given it a thousand branches and a thousand leaves, like the plants that creep over it. The sculptor has turned it into a sphinx to keep his secrets, into a temple, the home of the gods. In its shade are we exalted.'[92]

Omnipresent throughout Rodin's life, the Parthenon and its sculptures eventually dissolved into invisibility and inexpressibility. Symbolizing his thought processes, the monument and its decorative elements became no more than a part of the language he needed to construct his own myth.

1. I should like to warmly thank Ian Jenkins and Celeste Farge for teaching me about the Parthenon, and for their help reading through my text. My particular thanks go to the people who helped me in my research: Elisabeth Lebreton, Soline Morinière, Agnès Scherer and Marine Roux.
2. Paz (2013).
3. Quoted by Maxime Paz: Cochain (1997), Vol. 1, p. 176, in the caption to Figure 151.
4. Rodin (1911).
5. Marcadé and Pinatel (1984), pp. 338–342.
6. Paz (2013).
7. Michaelis (1870–1871).
8. Reinach (1909).
9. Filhol (1804).
10. Millin (1806).
11. Clarac (1841).
12. Stuart and Revett (1762–1816).
13. Lenormant (1834).
14. Laborde (1848).
15. Dujardin-Beaumetz (1913), p. 112.
16. *Temple de Minerve, à Athènes. Dessiné par ordre de Mr. Nointel Ambassadeur à la Porte. Avant que ce Temple ne fut renversé par une Bombe des Vénitiens, 1674*, Paris, BNF.
17. Müntz (n.d.).
18. Rionnet (1996).
19. Rousseau (1913), pp. 31–34.
20. Pierron (1903), p. 31.
21. Matthij (1955), p. 29.
22. Letter from Dorothy Stanley to Rodin, 16 February 1906, Musée Rodin archive, STA.5941.
23. Notebook 47, D. 6995, Musée Rodin.
24. Sheet of studies: a profile figure; four profile male bearded heads; head with a mitre, 1883, Musée Rodin, D. 3556.
25. A. Rodin, *Victor Hugo: Three-quarters View*, 1884–1885, The British Museum, 1886,0820.1; *Victor Hugo: Full Face and Three-Quarters View*, 1886, The British Museum, 1886,0820.2. Letter from Sidney Colvin to Rodin, 20 August 1886; letter from Edward A. Bond to Rodin,2 September 1886, Musée Rodin archive, ROY. 5468. Sidney Colvin (1845–1927) was Keeper of Prints and Drawings from 1883 to 1912.
26. Rodin (1910), p. 248.
27. Villefosse and Michon (1891–1901).
28. Musée du Louvre, GY.725.
29. The original head was bought by the Louvre Museum in 1928, Ma 740.
30. Martinez (2005), pp. 93–104.
31. Meštrović (2012), pp. 53–54.
32. Letter from Adolf Michaelis to Salomon Reinach, Aix-en-Provence, Bibliothèque Méjanès, fonds Salomon Reinach. I am grateful to Soline Morinière for this information.
33. Extract from a toast proposed by Rodin at a banquet in his honour at the Café Royal on 15 May 1902, in Anonymous, 'A great French sculptor in London. M. Rodin's confession of faith', *The St James's Gazette*, 16 May 1902.
34. Anonymous, 'Mr Rodin in London', *The Daily Chronicle*, 2 March 1903.
35. Anonymous, 'A French Phidias, Rodin's impressions of London', *The Tribune*, London, 2 March 1906.
36. Notebook 49, second front cover and folio 2 recto, Musée Rodin.
37. Garnier (2004).
38. Reinach (1910), p. 84.
39. Letter from John Tweed to Rodin, 21 May 1907, Musée Rodin archive, TWE.6239.
40. Letters from John Tweed to Rodin, 13 and 24 March 1908, Musée Rodin archive, TWE.6239.
41. Letter from Robert Bosanquet to Rodin, 15 November 1906, Musée Rodin archive. ROY. 5462. The cast is no longer extant.
42. See Hippolyte-Boussac (1905).
43. Among those quoted were the painter Albert Besnard (1849–1934), the writer Jules Claretie (1840–1913), the author Théodore Duret (1838–1927), the architect Frantz Jourdain (1847–1935), the sculptor Jean-Paul Laurens (1838–1921), the journalist Octave Mirbeau (1848–1917) and the poet Henri de Régnier (1864–1936).
44. Musée Bourdelle archive.
45. Letter from Antoine Bourdelle to Rodin, spring 1898, AMR BOU. 843-108, in Lemoine and Mattiussi (2003), p. 180, no. 151, p. 162.
46. Rodin (1905).
47. Rodin (1905), p. 68.
48. Anonymous, *Le Courrier du Soir*, 8 November 1906.
49. Letter from Rodin to Bigand-Kaire (Pierre-Antide Edmond), 15 November 1907, Musée Rodin archive, L. 496. See also letters from Rodin to Bigand-Kaire of 18 January, L. 492, and 22 February, L. 494.
50. Rodin (1914), p. 48.
51. Faure (1906).
52. Letter from Rodin to Mary Marshall,

14 January 1908, courtesy of Ashmolean Library, University of Oxford.
53. Letter from Rodin to Mary Marshall, 4 March 1908, courtesy of Ashmolean Library, University of Oxford.
54. Letter from Antoine Bourdelle to Rodin, spring 1898, AMR BOU. 843-19, in Lemoine and Mattiussi (2003), p. 180, no. 21, p. 32.
55. Russian-born Serge Youriévitch (1876–1969) studied with Rodin in 1903.
56. Letter from Serge Youriévitch to Rodin, 19 July 1915, Musée Rodin archive, YOU.6580 (emphasis in original).
57. Letter from Helene von Nostitz to Rodin, 1 April 1912, Musée Rodin archive, NOS.4657.
58. Musée Rodin archive.
59. Letter from Antoine Bourdelle to Rodin, 4 November 1906, AMR BOU. 845-115, in Lemoine and Mattiussi (2003), p. 180, no. 164, p. 180.
60. Letter from Aristide Maillol to Rodin annotated by Harry Kessler, 8 May 1908, Musée Rodin archive, MAI.4073.
61. Rodin (1912).
62. René de Valfori, 'Rodin en Grèce', *La Liberté*, 25 December 1906.
63. Quote by Rodin in René de Valfori, 'Rodin en Grèce', *La Liberté*, 25 December 1906 (emphasis in original).
64. Anonymous, 'Les Arts–Le musée Rodin', *Le Cri de Paris*, 7 May 1916.
65. Baud was Rodin's secretary from 7 July 1908 to 5 July 1909; he also substituted for René Chéruy in April 1907.
66. Musée Rodin archive.
67. Cladel (1936), p. 314.
68. Coquiot (1917), p. 31.
69. Rodin (1986), pp. 60–61.
70. Manuscripts and sketches, Musée Rodin.
71. Rainer Maria Rilke, letter to his wife, the sculptor Clara Westhoff, 29 September 1905.
72. Rodin (1914), pp. 222–223.
73. Roger de Chateleux, '"Hard work makes the artist" says Rodin, greatest sculptor since Michelangelo', *The World Magazine*, 26 May 1907.
74. Musée Rodin, S. 1004 and S. 464.
75. Letter from Dugald Sutherland MacColl to John Tweed, 19 May 1902 (emphasis in original). Tweed did indeed show the letter to Rodin, and it is now in the museum's archive, Musée Rodin archive, MAC.4020.
76. Garnier (2002), p. 72. In 1883, Georg Treu organized two exhibitions in Dresden on the subject of colour variation in ancient and modern sculpture. Cf. *The Colour of Sculpture, 1840–1910*, Amsterdam, Van Gogh Museum, 1996.
77. Handwritten notes by René Cheruy, Musée Rodin archive.
78. Letter from Rodin to Helene von Nostitz, 10 October 1905, Musée Rodin archive; in Beausire (1986), no. 215, p. 169 (emphasis in original).
79. I would like to thank Véronique Mattiussi and the students at the École du Louvre who undertook a Master's degree on the notebooks, under the tutelage of Claire Barbillon, for allowing me to see their transcriptions.
80. Auguste Rodin, Notebook 85, folio 20 recto, Musée Rodin archive.
81. Rodin (1914), p. 111.
82. Auguste Rodin, Notebook 84, folio 17 recto, Musée Rodin archive.
83. Musée Rodin, D. 6017.
84. Musée Rodin, D. 6016.
85. Rodin (1912).
86. Auguste Rodin, Notebook 84, folio 19 verso, Musée Rodin archive.
87. Auguste Rodin, Notebook 84, folio 23 recto, Musée Rodin archive.
88. Rodin (1914), pp. 222–223.
89. Auguste Rodin, Notebook 81, folio 19 recto, Musée Rodin archive.
90. Auguste Rodin, Notebook 85, folio 49 recto, Musée Rodin archive.
91. Auguste Rodin, Notebook 81, folio 8 recto, Musée Rodin archive.
92. Rodin (1912).

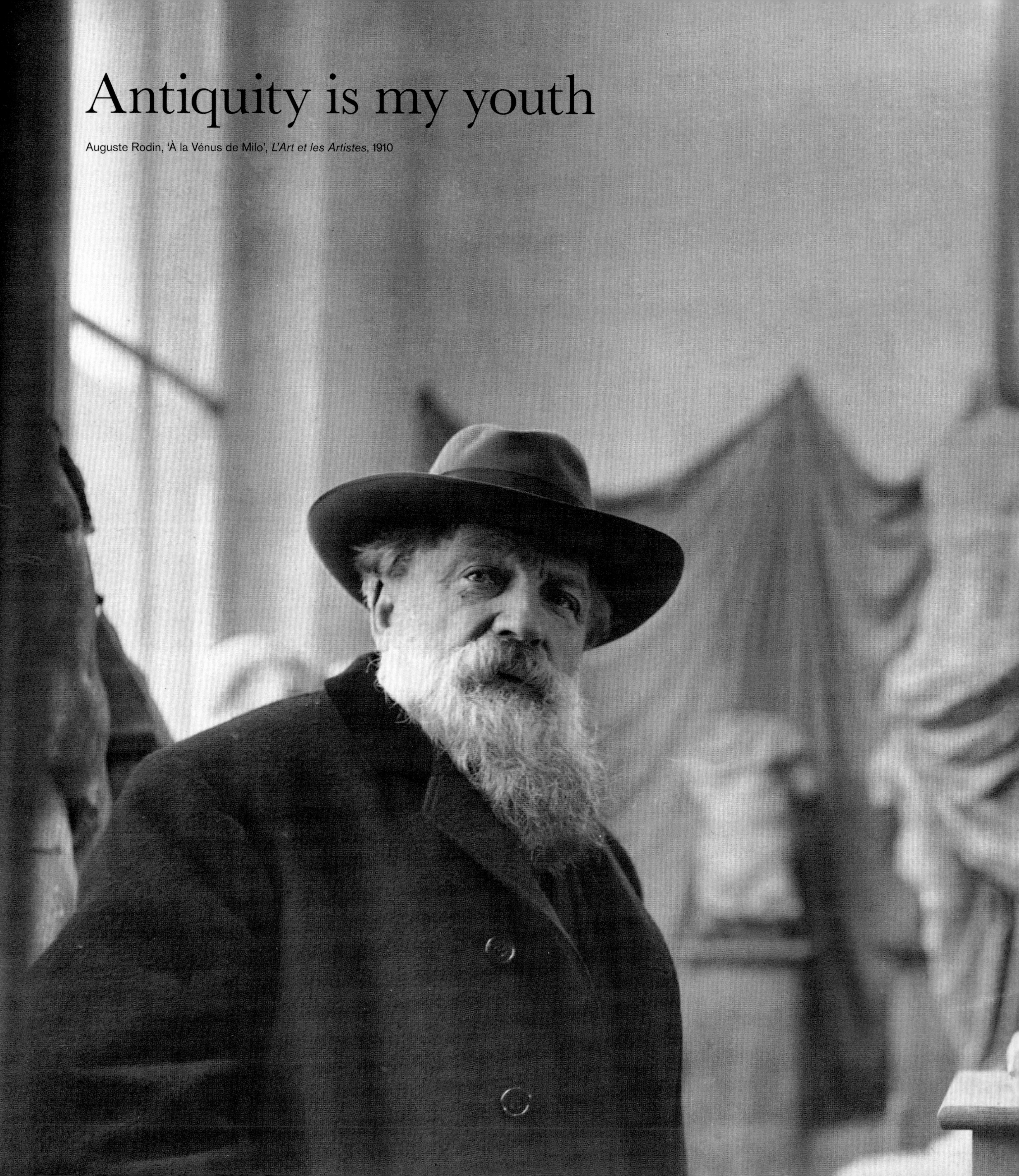

Antiquity is my youth

Auguste Rodin, 'À la Vénus de Milo', *L'Art et les Artistes*, 1910

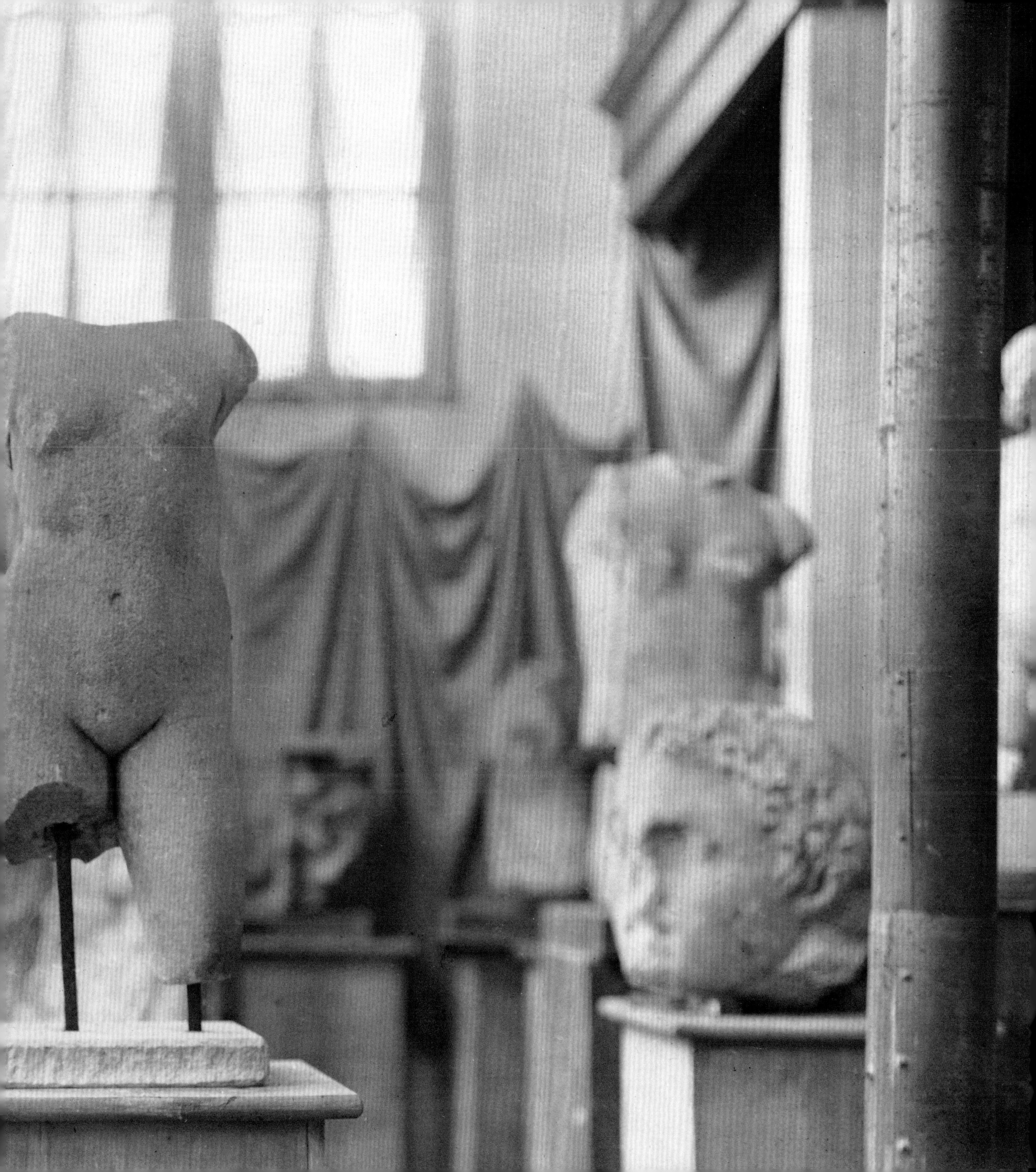

The British Museum: a temple of the Muses

Your beautiful museums, with their marvellous collections, Greek, Assyrian, and Egyptian, awakened in me a flood of sensations, which, if not new, had at any rate a rejuvenating influence; and those sensations caused me to follow Nature all the more closely in my studies.

Auguste Rodin, 'A great French sculptor in London. M. Rodin's confession of faith', *The St James's Gazette*, 16 May 1902

One of the most radical artists of the modern era, Auguste Rodin drew energy and inspiration from the art of ancient Greece. He never visited Greece, but London became his substitute for Athens, and the temple-like British Museum was to become his spiritual home, where he developed a lasting passion for the Parthenon sculptures.

In 1881, aged 40, Rodin made the first of many visits to the Museum. Bloomsbury's temple of the Muses, then at the heart of a revival of interest in ancient Greek art and architecture, attracted many thousands of artists. At a time when ancient Greek culture was thought superior to all others, the Parthenon sculptures were at the height of their fame. Although Rodin had already studied the sculptures from books, plaster casts in the École des Beaux-Arts and some originals in the Louvre, the encounter with them in the British Museum had a profound and enduring effect on him.

Pheidias was revered in antiquity as the greatest of all artists, although today we know very little about him, in contrast to the life and works of Rodin. Once celebrated artworks credited to Pheidias, including the colossal statue of Zeus at Olympia, one of the Seven Wonders of the Ancient World, and that of Athena, which stood inside the Parthenon, have not survived. The architectural sculptures of the Parthenon, which were probably carved to his designs, do survive, however. Like Rodin, Pheidias must have first modelled his sculptures in clay for assistants to carve in marble or cast in bronze. Rodin developed a personal relationship with Pheidias, one in which the ancient sculptor took on the role of mentor.

PREVIOUS
Fig. 1
Albert Harlingue (1879–1963)
Rodin in his Museum of Antiquities
Between 1908 and 1912
Gelatin silver print
H 11.9 cm, W 17.5 cm
Musée Rodin, Ph. 210
Rodin donation, 1916

OPPOSITE
Fig. 2
Leonard William Collmann (1816–1881)
Entrance Hall of the British Museum
1847
Watercolour
H 51.2 cm, W 68.4 cm
British Museum, 1902,0129.1
Donated by Herbert Collmann

No artist will ever surpass Pheidias.... The greatest of the sculptors, who appeared at the time when the entire human dream could be contained in the pediment of a temple, will never be equalled.

Auguste Rodin, *Art: Conversations with Paul Gsell*, 1911

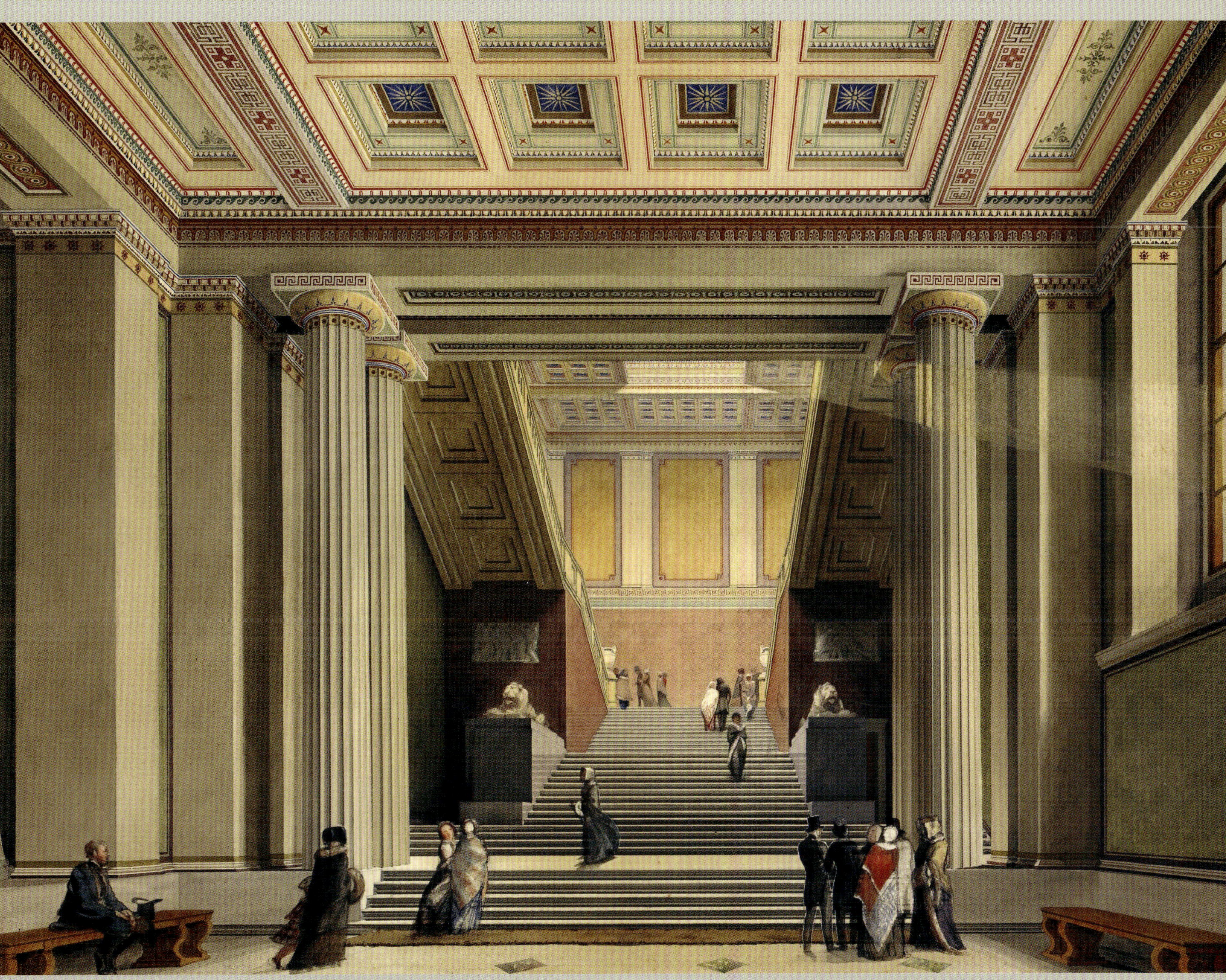

1
Auguste Rodin
Pallas (Athena) with the Parthenon
1896
Marble and plaster
H 47 cm, W 38.7 cm, D 31 cm
Musée Rodin, S. 1197
Rodin donation, 1916

Impossible to pass by without remarking upon its apparent eccentricity and asking who is represented – and why she has a Greek temple on her head – this marble and plaster bust immediately provokes interest and demands explanation. The work brings together the principal threads of Rodin's engagement with the past and the present; it references his lifelong fascination for the Parthenon and its sculptures and at the same time records one of his many friendships in contemporary artistic society. The model is Mariana Russell, the Italian wife of the Australian impressionist painter John Russell, whose classical beauty Rodin especially admired, and it is one of several representations of her as Athena. Rodin exhibited this version in 1913 in the only exhibition in which he mixed his sculptures with his antiquities.

Athena, goddess of wisdom and craft, was the patron deity of ancient sculptors as well as of the city of Athens. In Greek myth Zeus swallows her mother, Metis, displacing the unborn child from the goddess's womb to his head, from which Athena is then born. She is shown here seemingly wearing the Parthenon as if it were a crown. Comparison has been made with the mural crowns worn by Tyche, the goddess who governed the fortune and prosperity of a city, but is it so? Another explanation could be that Athena is giving birth to the Parthenon as her own brainchild. In Rodin's day, the Parthenon represented the summit of intellectual and artistic achievement.

In imitation of ancient sculpture, the facial features are polished and blurred (*sfumato*), in contrast with the hair and body that are rough-hewn.

There is marvellous work in some of these portraits, pure as antique cameos which it would seem sacrilege to touch. There are faces whose smile is nowhere defined but which plays over the features with so veil-like a softness that it seems to rise with every taking of the breath. Enigmatically closed lips and wide, dreaming eyes which gaze past everything into an eternal moonlit night.

Rainer Maria Rilke, *Auguste Rodin*, 1902

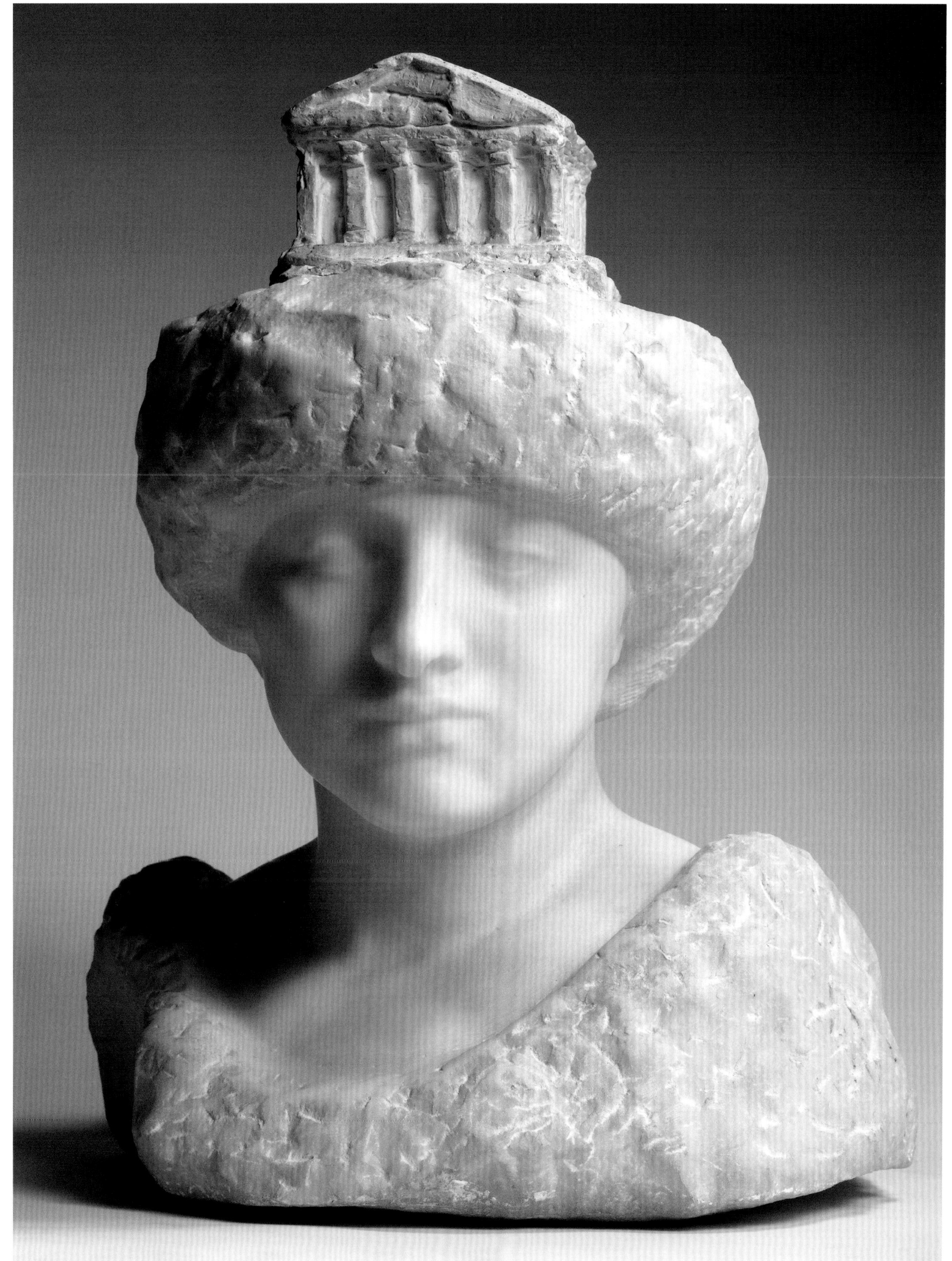

Rodin's Parthenon

For if, at this period, he ever received encouragement and confirmation of his aim and of his quest, it came from the works of the ancients.… Men did not speak to him. Stones spoke.

Rainer Maria Rilke, *Auguste Rodin*, 1902

The Parthenon has long held a fascination for the French, who were the first to study it in a scholarly way. Rodin's artistic schooling naturally introduced him to the temple. His first drawings were faithful copies of the sculptures, consistent with the academic principles of the artistic establishment of his day. Later, he began to collect images of the Parthenon and its sculptures. He assembled his early drawings and photographs in albums and bought reduced-scale casts of the Parthenon frieze, as well as original ancient Greek fragments. By 1900, by which time Rodin had seen and drawn the sculptures at the British Museum, he was interested in capturing only the essence of his subject, and transcended the lessons of his youth.

Fig. 3
Edward Steichen (1879–1973)
West porch of the Parthenon
looking south
1921
Carbon print
H 60.4 cm, W 48 cm
Musée Rodin, Ph. 234

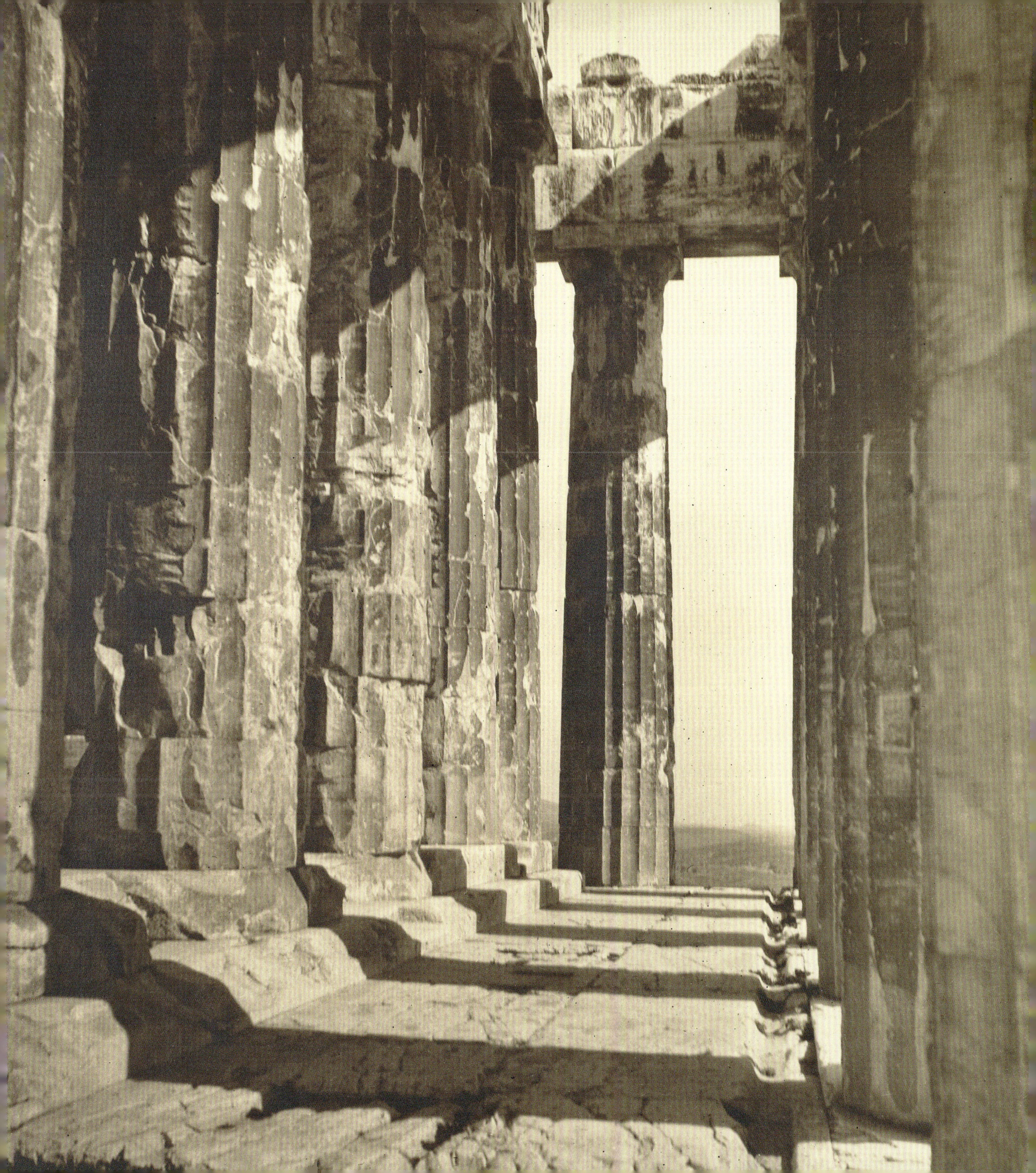

1850–1880 Drawings of the Parthenon sculptures

Rodin's earliest drawings and paintings devoted to the Parthenon sculptures pre-date his first visit to London (in 1881) by a considerable time. These studies conform to the academic criteria and scientific vision of the period and reproduce or take their inspiration from earlier sources. Judging from his surviving works, Rodin appears to have taken a greater interest in the reliefs of the frieze and the metopes, rather than the pediment sculptures carved in the round. He was probably looking at groups of casts or engravings showing the whole monument, as he drew not only the sculptures in London and Paris, but also those that were still in situ in Athens.

By looking closely at the technique of Rodin's drawings we can understand something of their history. A first group of eight drawings executed in pen and ink (Cats 2–7 and 11) were probably all produced at around the same time. Annotations or pencil additions were no doubt added later, perhaps when, as a more mature artist, Rodin was looking back over the work of his youth and pasted the sheets into an album (Album I, which was disassembled in 1930). The drawings are not exact copies of any known engraving or cast, but Rodin's graphic style is not dissimilar to, for example, engravings after the drawings by Jules-Antoine Vauthier and Pierre Lacour in *Monuments de sculpture anciens et modernes* (1820–1839). At this period, archaeologists attempted to demonstrate through casts and engravings how the Parthenon sculptures were coloured, but in Rodin's drawings they are strikingly free of any suggestion that they were once painted.

In each drawing Rodin chose to represent the sculpture in a particular state, either as it was actually preserved or as completed by a draughtsman or restorer. For instance, his drawing of the block of the Panathenaic frieze (block VII, Cat. 2) in the Louvre shows it in its condition prior to 1820, without the restored heads. He can only have drawn this from an old cast or from the engraving in the 1806 publication by Aubin-Louis Millin, after a drawing by Jules-Antoine Vauthier of around 1800, which would have depicted the work before restoration. Rodin's early drawing, in pen and brown ink, is the only one to represent the depth of the relief, as would be visible in a cast or in the engraving in Millin's publication. Block VII was acquired by the Comte Choiseul-Gouffier, the French ambassador to the Ottoman empire (see pp. 21–23), and entered the Louvre in 1801, the first major sculpture from the Parthenon to go on public display in a European museum.

Rodin sometimes follows the example of other draughtsmen (Stuart and Revett, for instance) or eighteenth- and nineteenth-century restorers by completing the missing elements of the sculptures with a lighter brushstroke or stippling in order to make this apparent, and uses a bolder line to show the surviving parts. In Cat. 3, he adds the heads of the figures in this way, as Stuart and Revett had done in their publication, though without copying them, as well as the horse on the left.

In drawing Cat. 11, which is framed with a border, reminiscent of the composition of early engravings, Rodin reinstates not only the heads, but also the right and left sections of the scene. Similarly, he restores the heads of the figures in drawing Cat. 4, D. 136, but turns that of the figure on the right the wrong way round; in D. 137 he adds the missing left arm of the Lapith and one of the centaur's rear hooves. In Cat. 5, Rodin reinstates the head of the horse on the left and the feet of the figures, while in Cat. 6, he draws the faces of Zeus and Hera, as did Stuart and Revett, but sketches in his version of the head of Iris, which was subsequently discovered and fitted to a cast of the block in Athens. On the drawing Cat 5, he wrote 'No' twice on the left side of the drawing, to indicate where his drawing of the horse was incorrect.

When Rodin assembled the drawings into Album I, Cats 3 and 11 were both glued on the same page, and Cats 2 and 5 have the same backing board. Only Cat. 6 was not pasted into the album, but was combined on a loose sheet with a drawing of an ecclesiastical figure.

OPPOSITE ABOVE

2
Auguste Rodin
Study of the Parthenon East Frieze (block VII, figs 49–54), in the Louvre
Before 1870
Graphite and pen and ink on tracing paper
H 14.7 cm, W 21.2 cm
Musée Rodin, D. 62
Rodin donation, 1916

OPPOSITE BELOW

3
Auguste Rodin
Study of the Parthenon South Frieze (block III, figs 8–9)
Before 1870
Graphite and pen and ink on tracing paper
H 12 cm, W 14 cm
Musée Rodin, D. 50
Rodin donation, 1916

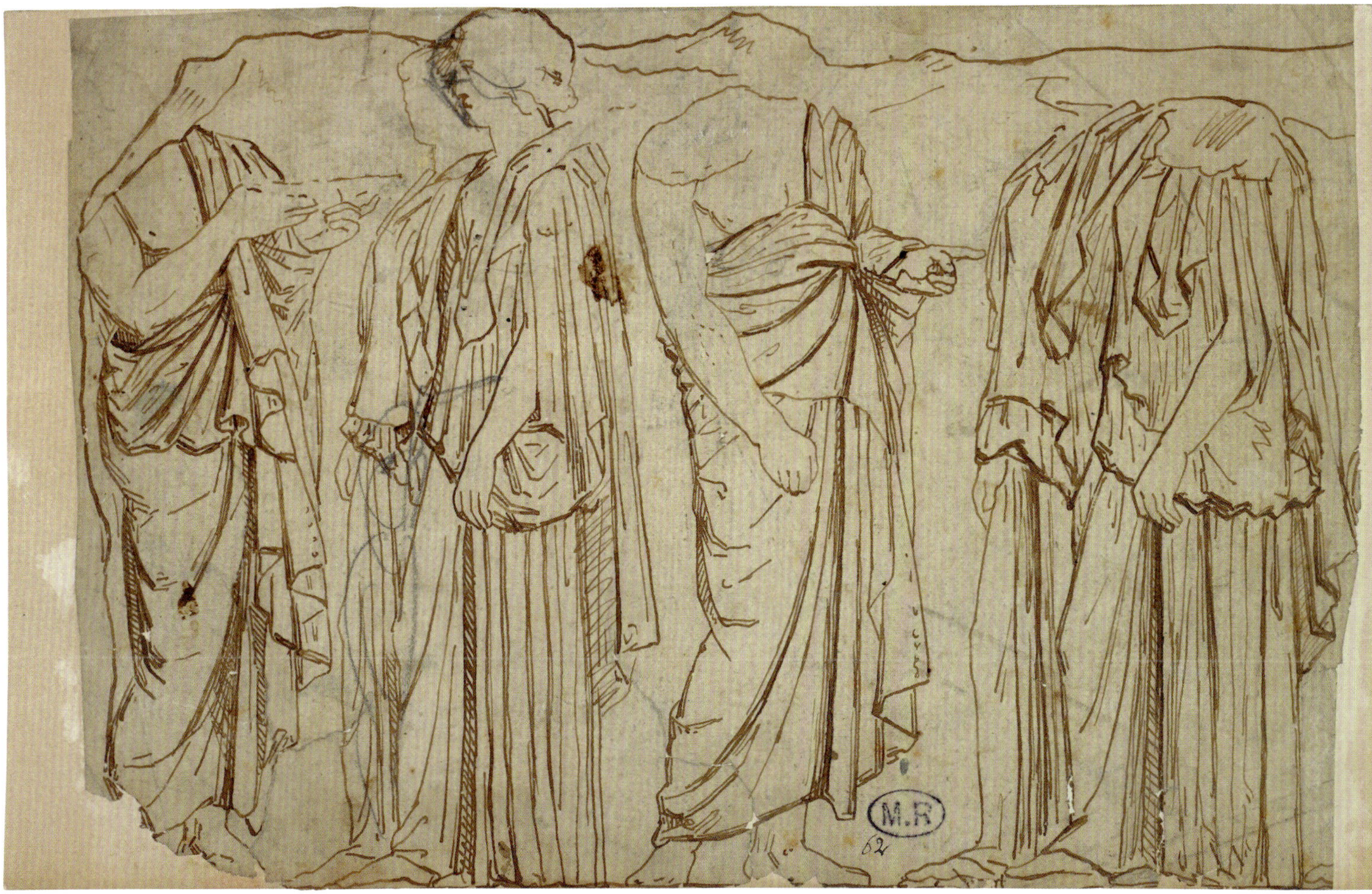

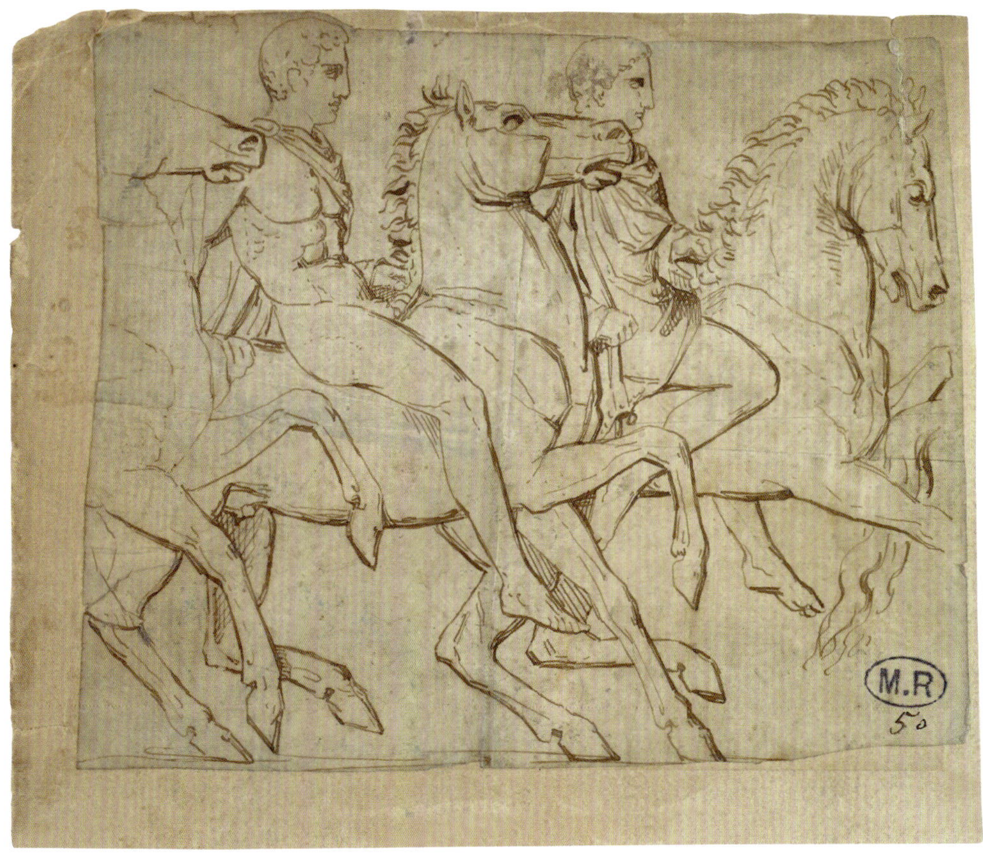
M.R

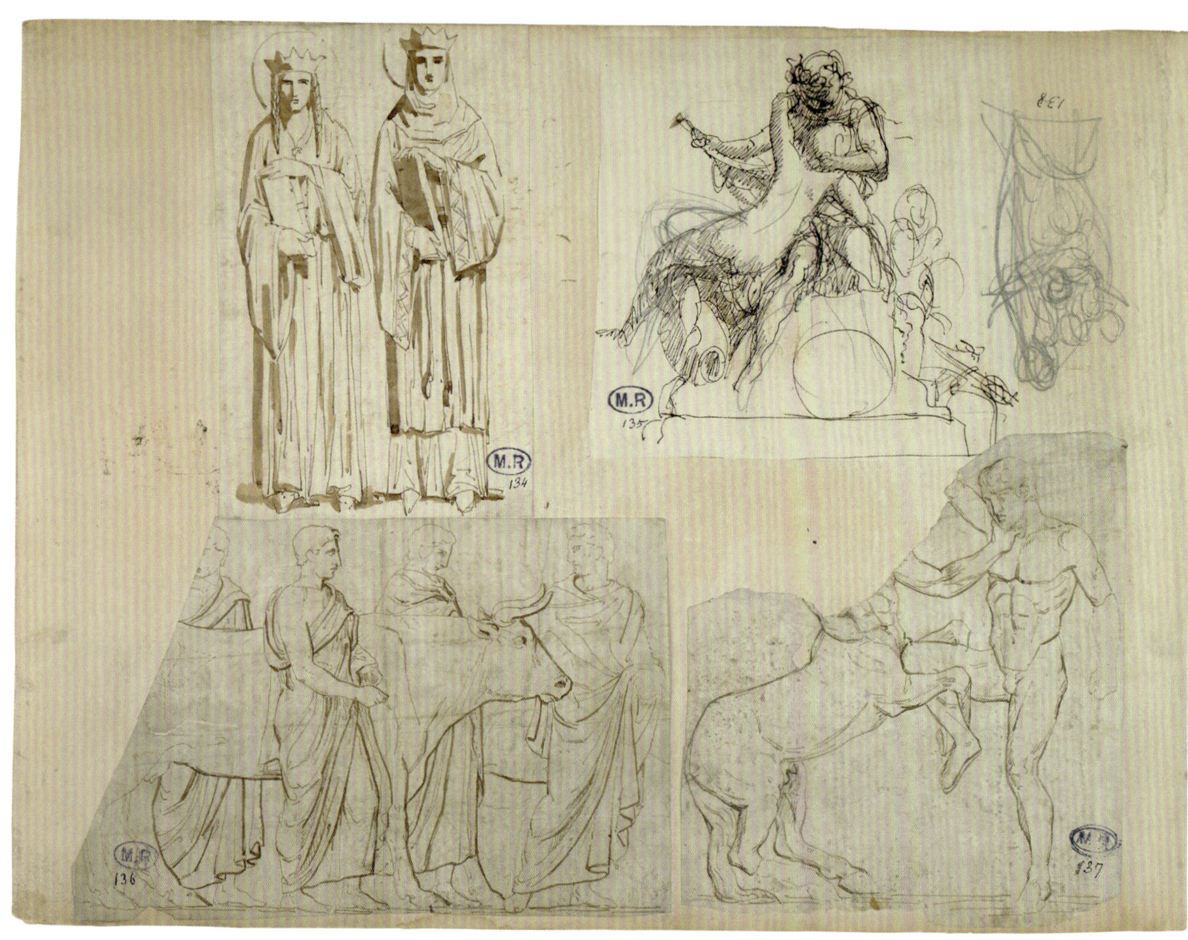

4 LEFT
Auguste Rodin
Sketches including of the Parthenon South Frieze (block XLI, figs 122–125; lower left) and South Metope (XXXI; lower right)
Before 1870
Graphite and pen and ink with wash on fine paper cut-outs stuck down on to card
H 26.2 cm, W 34 cm
Musée Rodin, D. 134–137
Rodin donation, 1916

5 BELOW
Auguste Rodin
Study of the Parthenon North Frieze (block XLVII, figs 132–136)
Before 1870
Graphite and pen and ink on fine paper
H 11.2 cm, W 19.5 cm
Musée Rodin, D. 61
Rodin donation, 1916

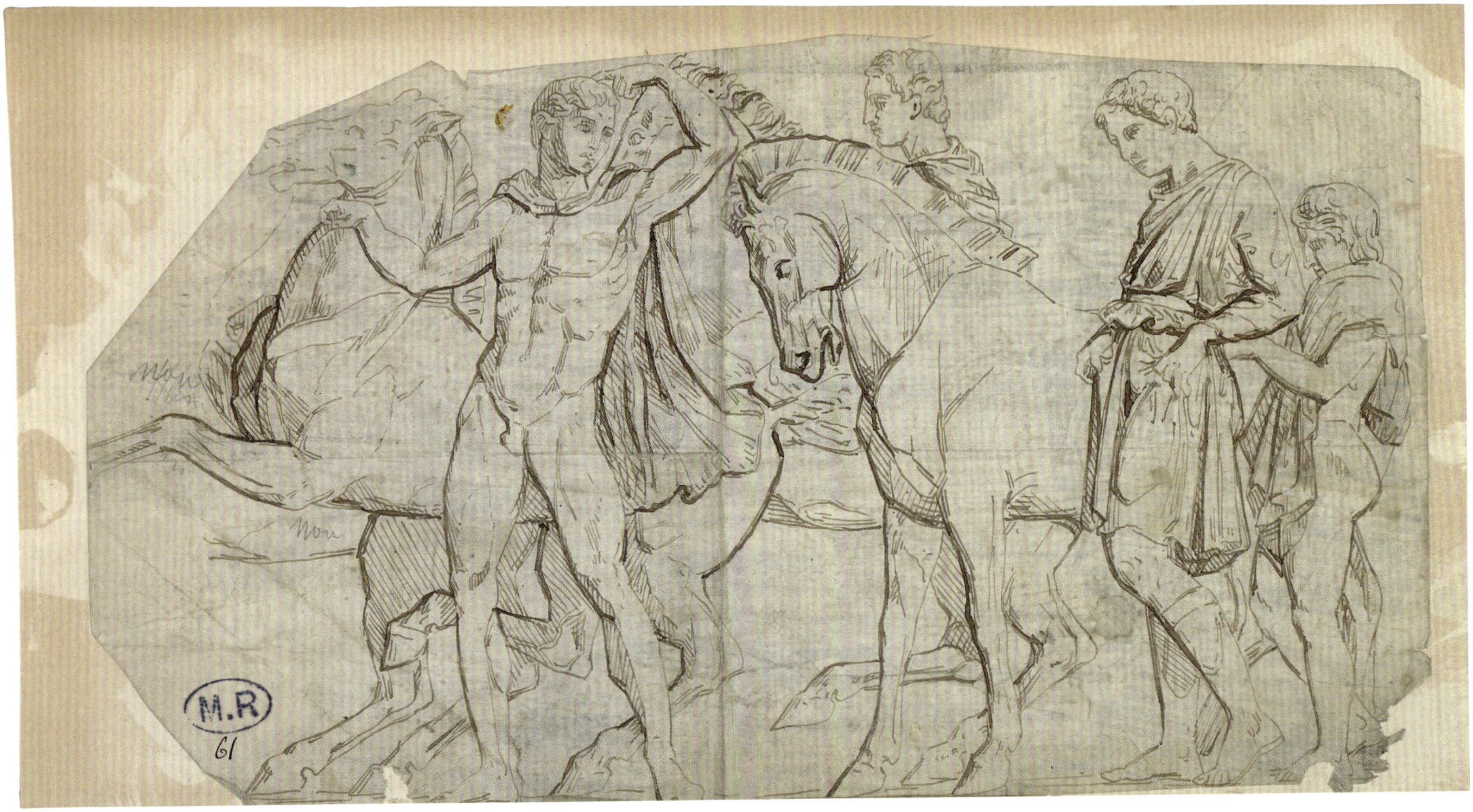

6 RIGHT
Auguste Rodin
Study of the Parthenon East Frieze (block V, figs 28–30) and an ecclesiastical figure
Before 1870
Graphite, pen and ink and watercolour on paper cut-outs stuck down on to card
H 12.4 cm, W 19.3 cm
Musée Rodin, D. 1992
Rodin donation, 1916

7 BELOW
Auguste Rodin
Study of the Parthenon East Frieze (block III, figs 7–13)
Before 1870
Graphite and pen and ink on fine paper
H 13 cm, W 20.8 cm
Musée Rodin, D. 52
Rodin donation, 1916

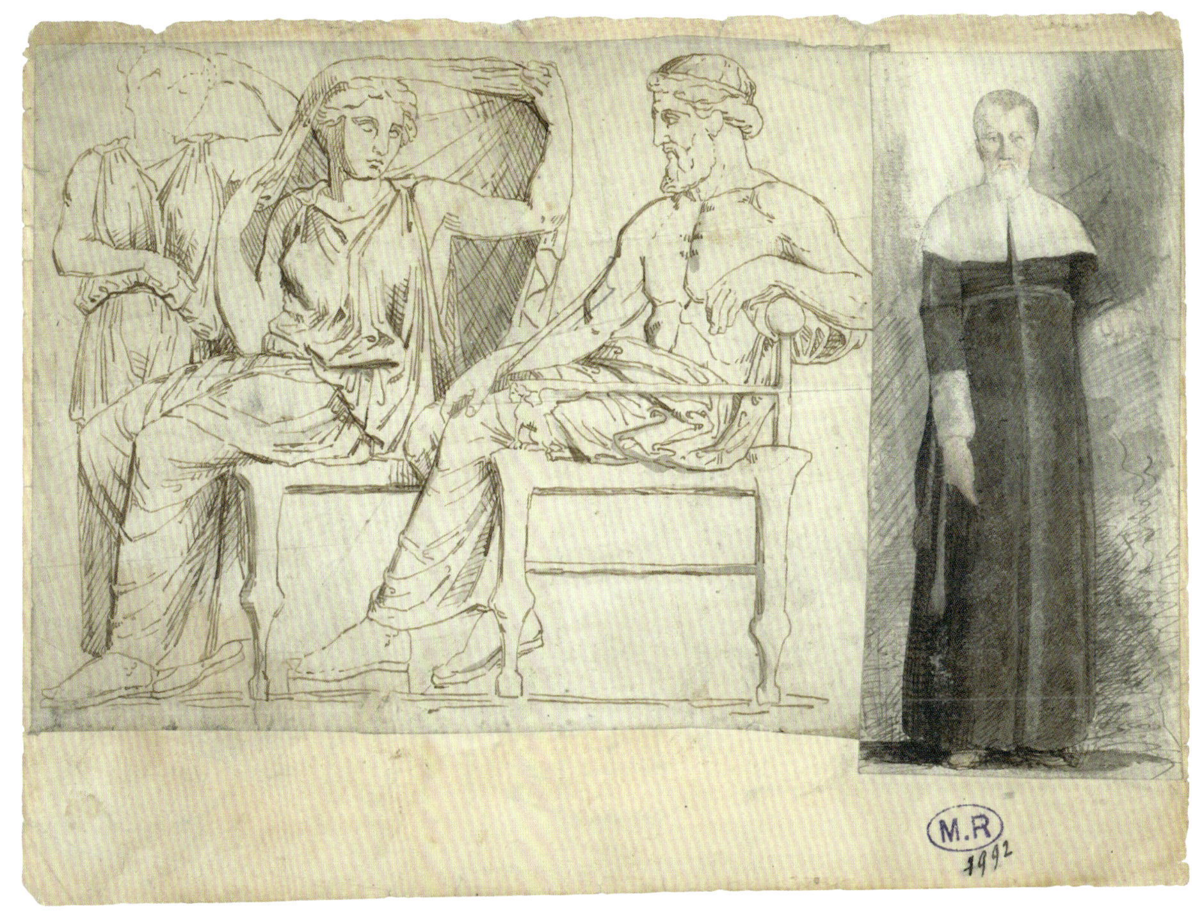

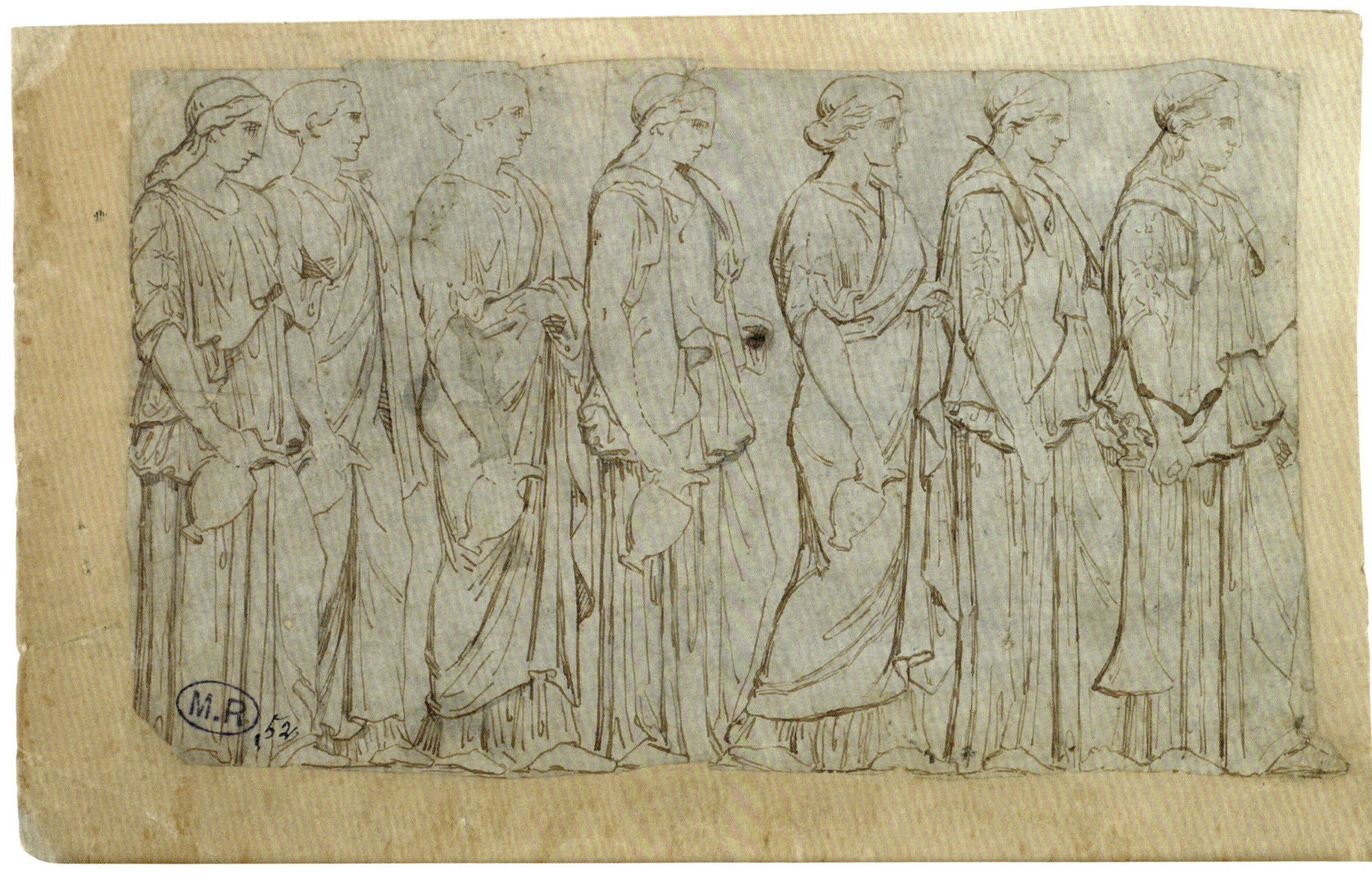

Two of these early drawings (Cats 5 and 7) are unusual in showing signs in the form of pencil traces on the reverse of having been transferred to another sheet (Cats 8 and 9), where they were reworked in places in pencil to refine the line and then partly finished in watercolour. At first glance it may seem that Rodin is experimenting with colour in order to engage with the contemporary interest in ancient polychromy. But that is not the subject here. Rather, Rodin seems to be breathing life into the marble figures in a dramatic way, adding colour to their drapery and exposed bodies and, in so doing, reaches into the past as if to resurrect the people of ancient Athens.

8
Auguste Rodin
Study of the Parthenon East Frieze (block III, figs 7–13)
Before 1870
Graphite and watercolour on paper vellum
H 21.3 cm, W 28.3 cm
Musée Rodin, D. 87
Rodin donation, 1916

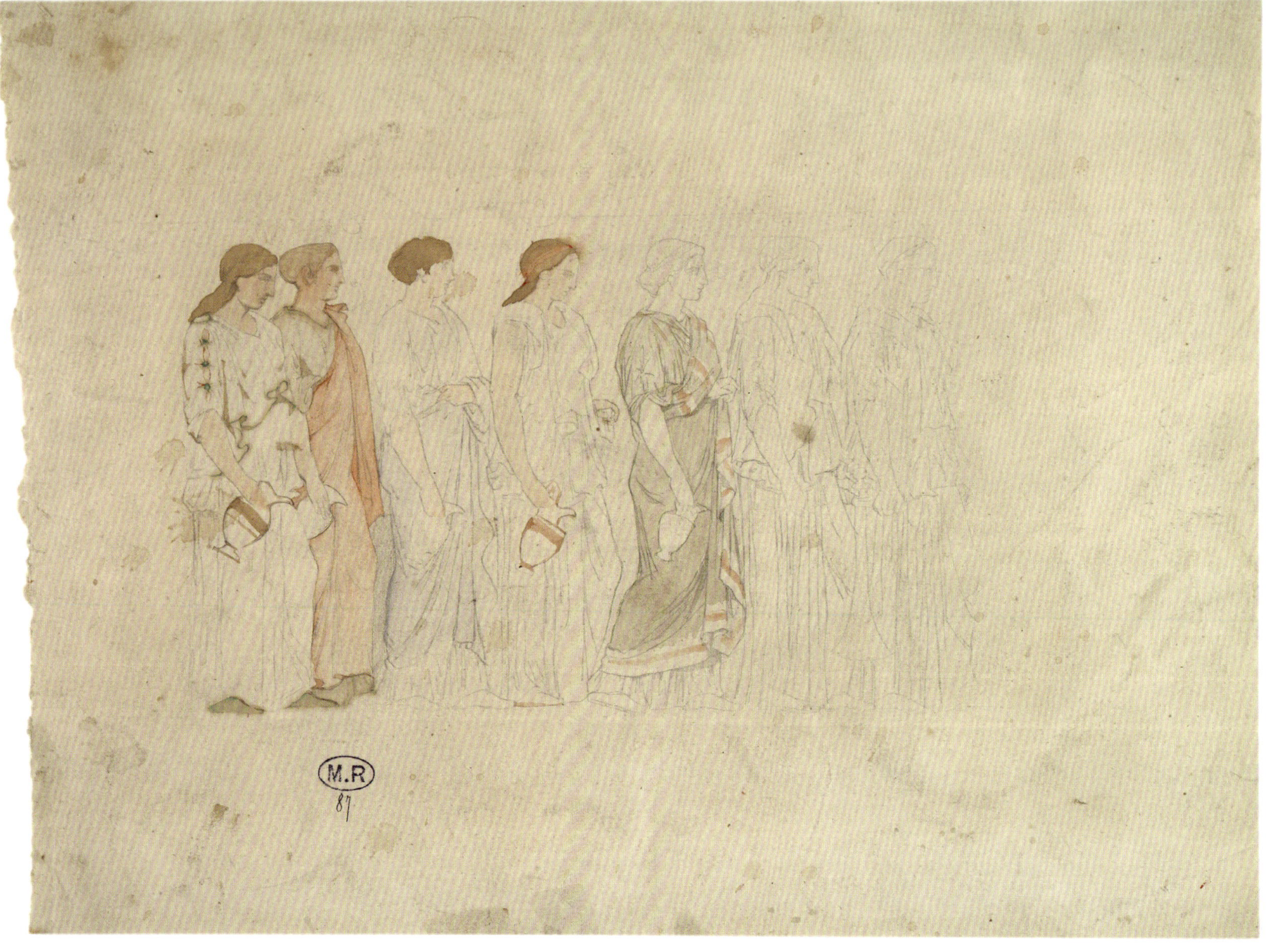

9
Auguste Rodin
Study of the Parthenon North Frieze (block XLVII, figs 132–136)
Before 1870
Graphite and watercolour on paper
H 17.4 cm, W 25.6 cm
Musée Rodin, D. 88
Rodin donation, 1916

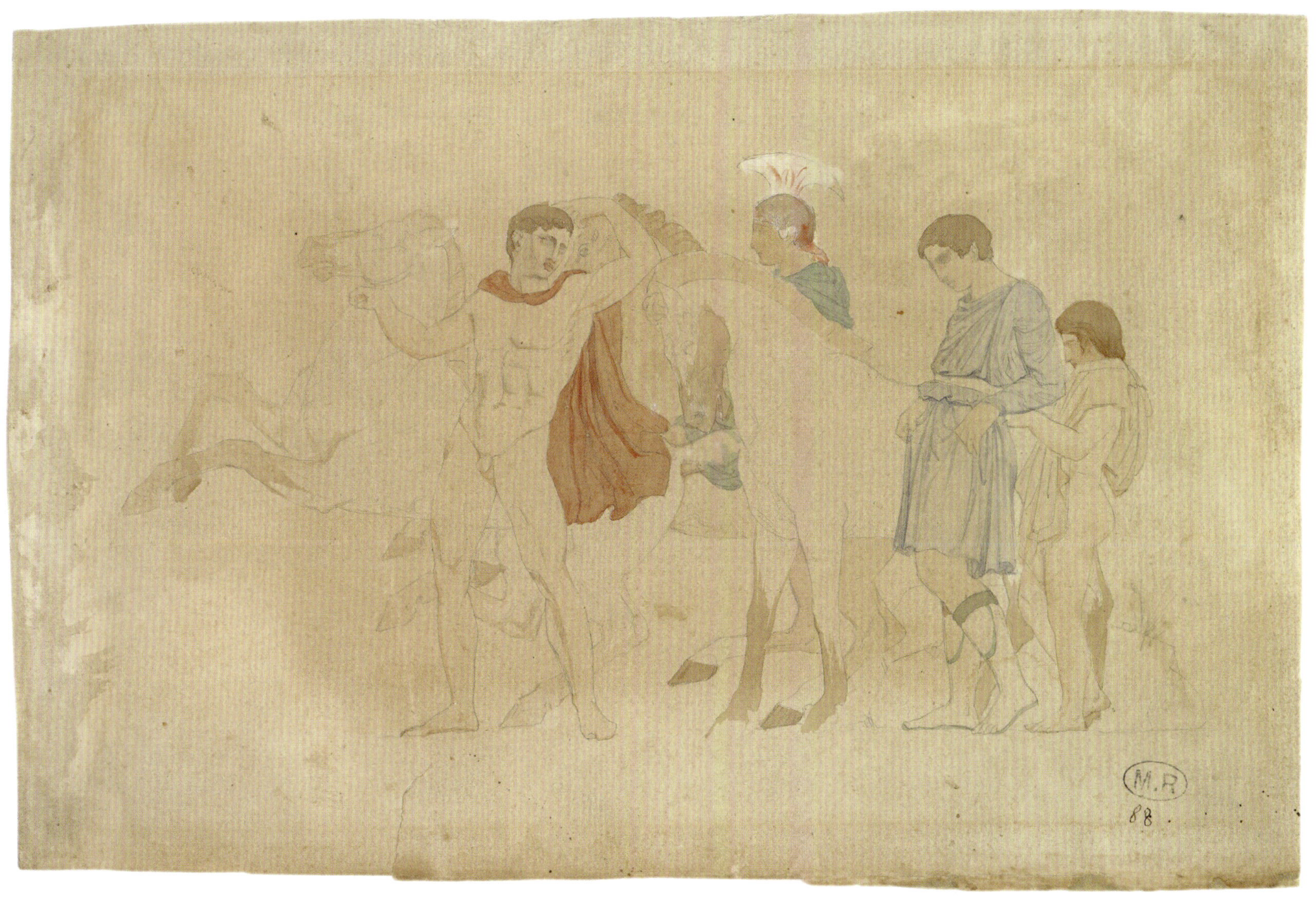

Rodin's painting of an ancient scene is an assemblage of copies from engravings, which he then placed in a landscape reminiscent of those he painted in the Forêt de Soignes, near Brussels, during the 1870s. In the centre, three horses from the North Frieze of the Parthenon (block XXIV) gallop towards a pair of figures – Dionysos and Ariadne – while a warrior appears to guard the entrance to a temple. Cat. 11, the only drawing in this early series that was squared for transfer, was used to enlarge the motif of the three horses and the chariot wheel, which were reversed in the painting.

The figure of Dionysos was copied (and also reversed) from a line engraving of a Greek vase which was published by Johann Heinrich Wilhelm Tischbein (1751–1829) (Fig. 6), which appeared as the first plate of Volume I of William Hamilton's second collection of Greek vases published in 1793 (*Collection of engravings from ancient vases mostly of pure Greek workmanship discovered in sepulchres in the Kingdom of the two Sicilies…*). Two preparatory drawings for this figure are found in the Musée Rodin collection. One, in the form of a cut-out (Fig. 4), is an exact, full-scale copy of the original engraving, which has then been enhanced by colour. Did Rodin use the cut-out technique simply to reverse the form or to serve as a pattern to transfer the design to the painting in the assemblage with the female figure? It has not been possible to formally identify the source of the drawing of Ariadne, half hidden by the body of Dionysos, but it too reflects the style of Tischbein's engravings. Rodin reworks the same composition of the couple in a large drawing (Fig. 5), on the same scale as in the painting. Rodin allows himself poetic licence and reworks the face of Dionysos to accentuate its expressiveness and modifies his clothing. The pencil work on the back of this drawing shows that it was used to transfer the lines to the canvas.

Although not a faithful copy, the temple in the background of the painting evokes the temple of Empedocles at Selinunte in Sicily, drawn and coloured by Jacques Hittorff (1792–1867) in his 1851 publication about the temple and Greek architectural polychromy, a copy of which Rodin had in his library, though perhaps acquired after he made the drawing. It is also possible to see here the freely interpreted influence of the papyriform columns of the temple at Philae in Egypt, as drawn by David Roberts (1796–1864) in the 1840s.

10
Auguste Rodin
Ancient Scene
Before 1870
Oil on canvas
H 81.2 cm, W 126 cm
Musée Rodin, P. 7219
Rodin donation, 1916

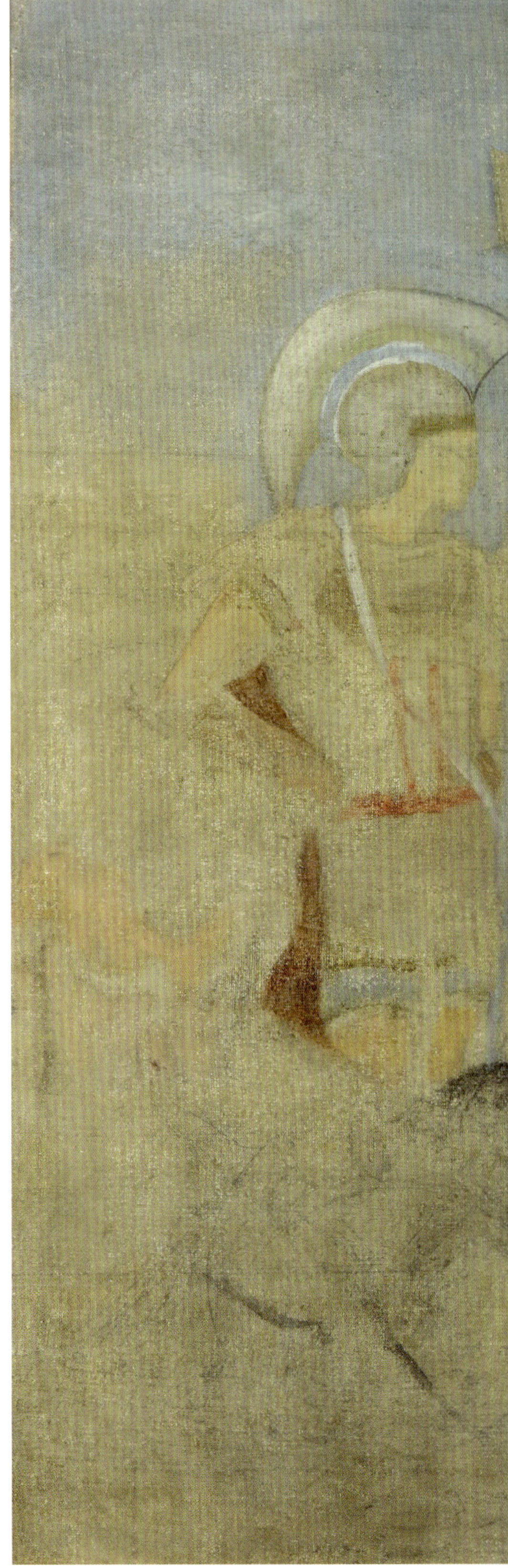

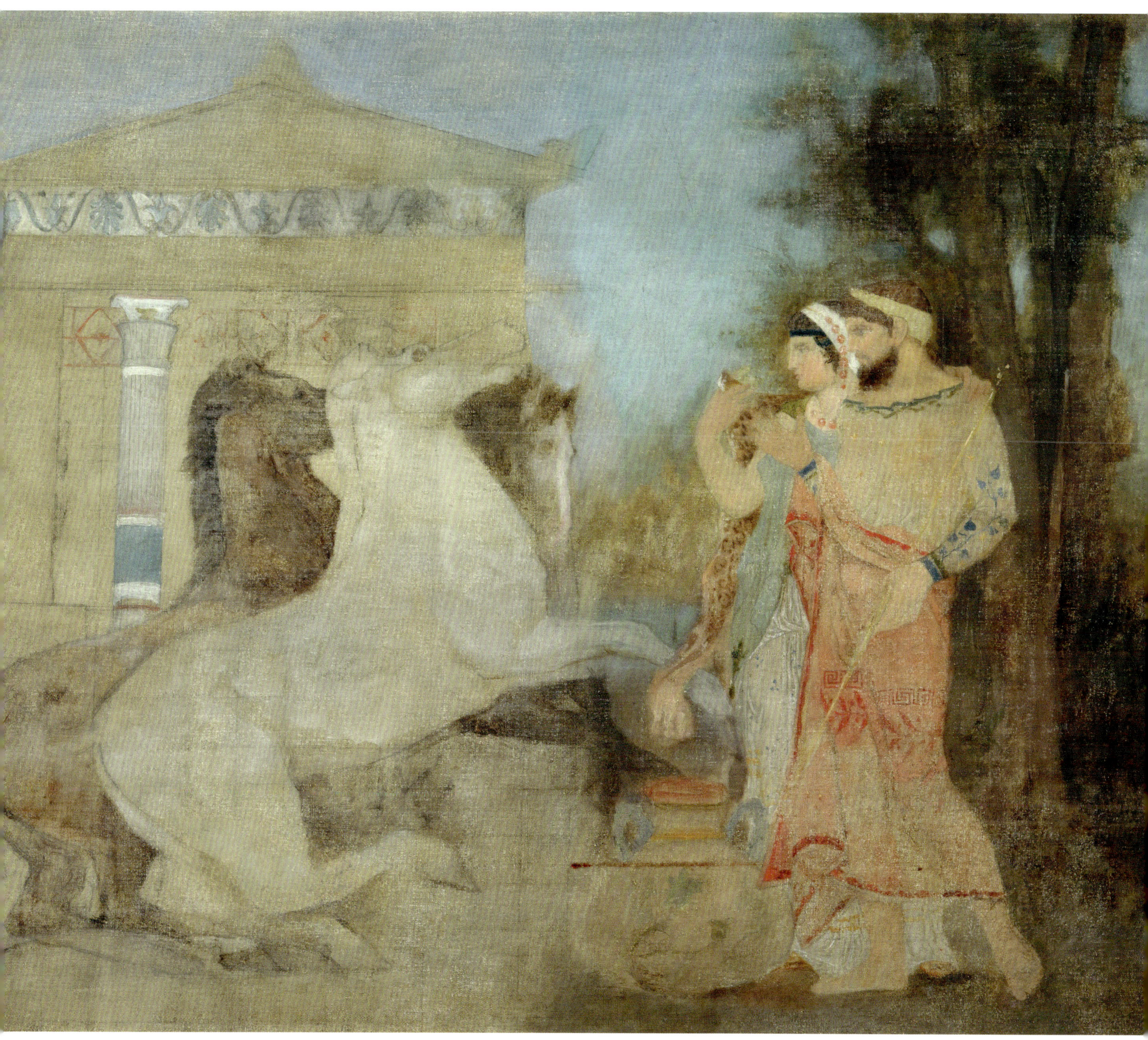

BELOW

11

Auguste Rodin

Study of the Parthenon North Frieze (block XXIV, figs 66–68)

Before 1870

Graphite and pen and ink, squared for transfer, on paper

H 12.3 cm, W 17.7 cm

Musée Rodin, D. 51

Rodin donation, 1916

OPPOSITE ABOVE LEFT

Fig. 4

Auguste Rodin

Study of the figure of Dionysos from Plate I of Sir William Hamilton, *Collection of engravings from ancient vases mostly of pure Greek workmanship discovered in sepulchres in the Kingdom of the two Sicilies…*, 1793

Before 1870

Graphite and watercolour on paper vellum cut-out stuck down on to card

H 16.8 cm, W 6.5 cm

Musée Rodin, D. 70

Rodin donation, 1916

OPPOSITE ABOVE RIGHT

Fig. 5

Auguste Rodin

Study of the figure of Dionysos from Plate I of Sir William Hamilton, *Collection of engravings from ancient vases mostly of pure Greek workmanship discovered in sepulchres in the Kingdom of the two Sicilies…*, 1793, with Ariadne inspired by the same book

Before 1870

Graphite and pen and brown ink on paper

H 60.6 cm, W 46 cm

Musée Rodin, D. 5103

Rodin donation, 1916

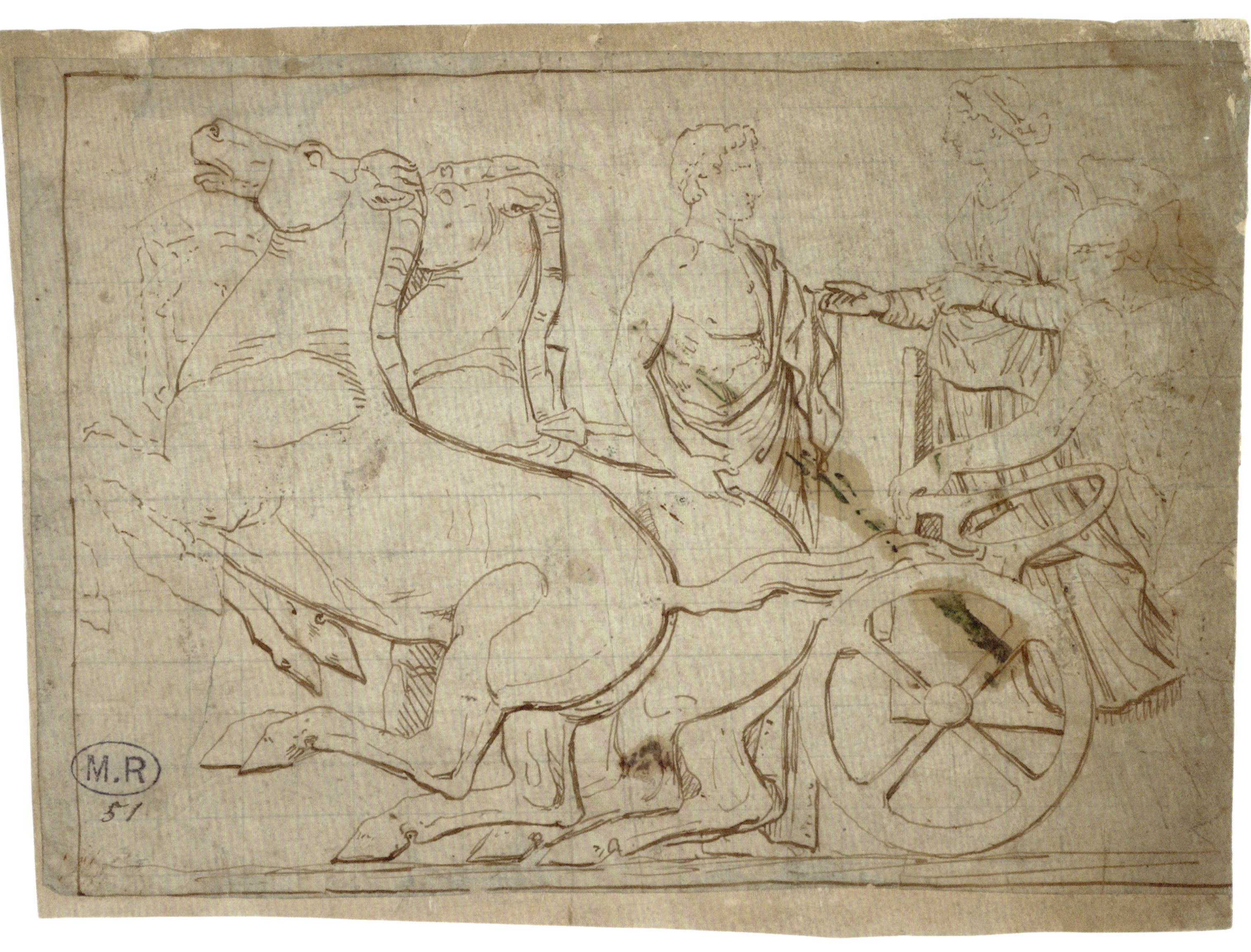

BELOW

Fig. 6

Engraving showing the decorated scene on an ancient vase

Sir William Hamilton, *Collection of engravings from ancient vases mostly of pure Greek workmanship discovered in sepulchres in the Kingdom of the two Sicilies…*, 1793, Plate I

British Museum, Department of Greece and Rome Library

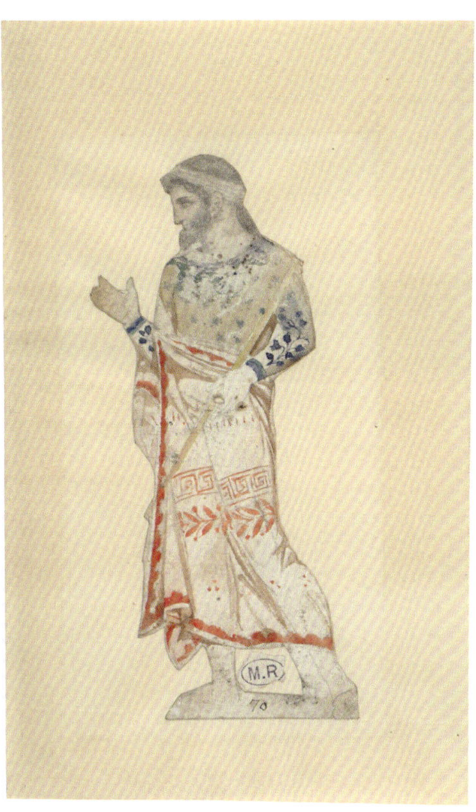

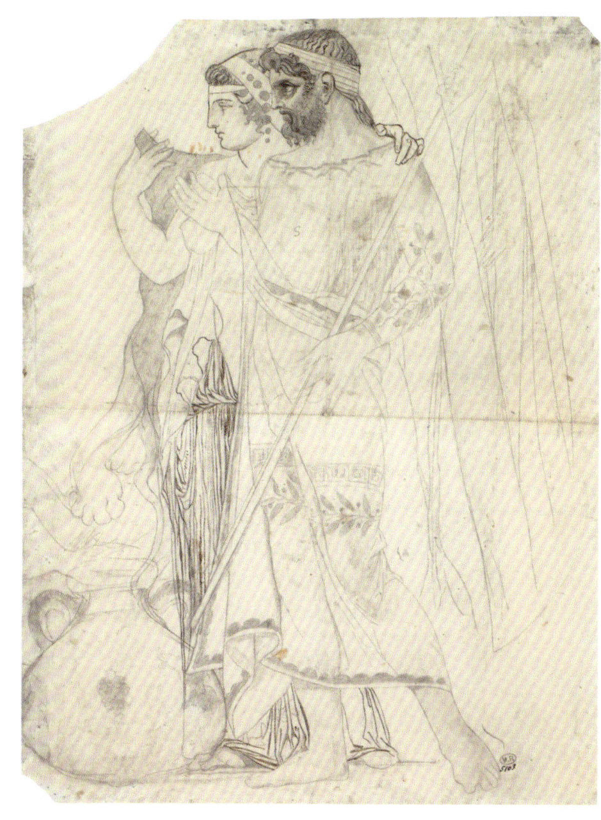

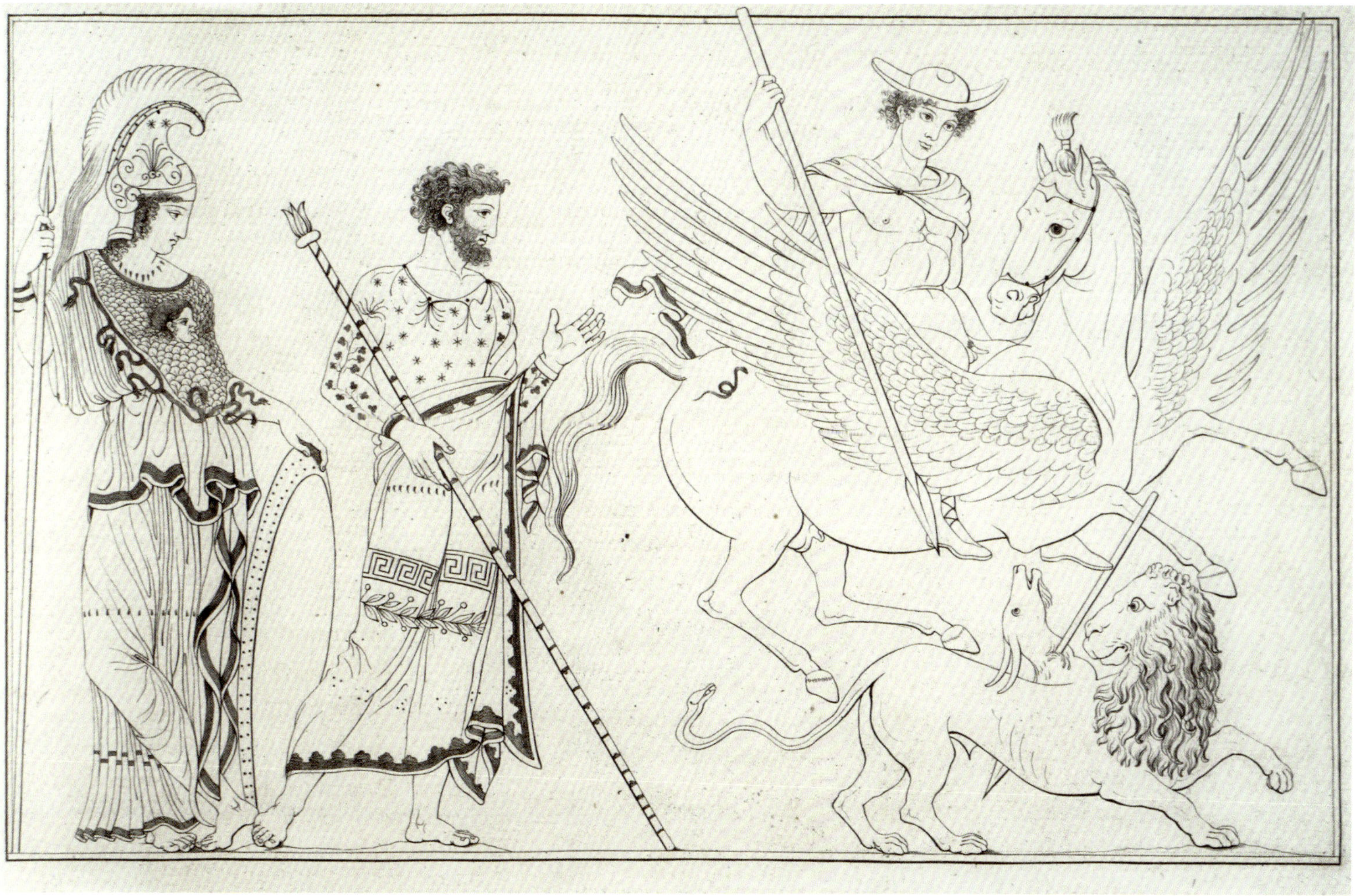

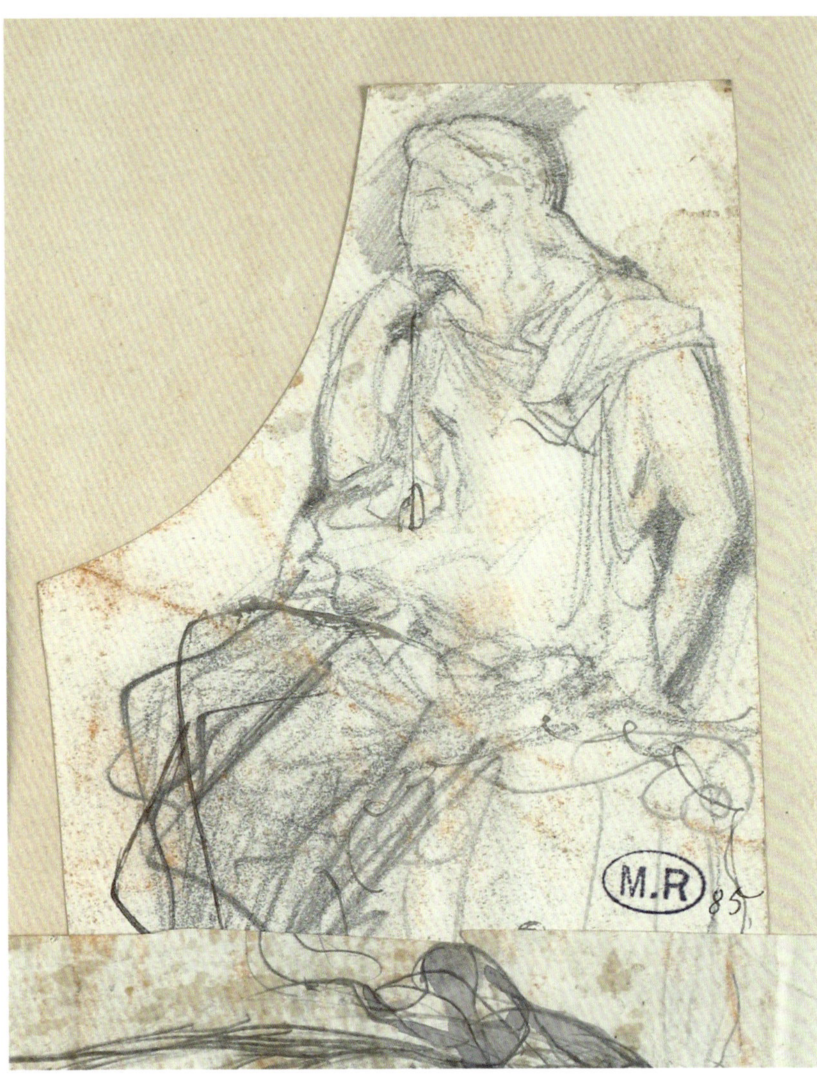

12
Auguste Rodin
Sketches including the figure of Demeter from the Parthenon East Frieze (block IV, fig. 26), and a draped running woman, three naked children and a woman with drapery with left upraised arm
Before 1874
Graphite and pen and ink with wash on paper cut-outs stuck down on to card
H 25.8 cm, W 34.3 cm
Musée Rodin, D. 80–86
Rodin donation, 1916

On the East Frieze of the Parthenon (block IV) the goddess Demeter rests her chin on the back of her hand as she mourns for her daughter Persephone, carried off by Hades to be his bride in the Underworld. Rodin's drawing in graphite of Demeter (D. 85), with the missing head restored, appears to be in a different, freer and more mature style than those in the previous series and is probably later. This cut-out pasted into Album I is partly concealed by the drawing attached at the bottom of the page depicting a draped woman, which Rodin might have associated with the Parthenon, particularly with figure G from the East Pediment. He highlighted in pencil the outline of the restored head of Demeter and added a hatched background to create volume, as a painter might. Did he perhaps rework the drawing when he placed it in the album, as with other drawings? In the lower area of the drapery, a vigorous pencil stroke isolates this figure from her neighbour, Dionysos, on the frieze. Rodin was to reproduce the gesture of the chin resting on the back of the hand when he came to create *The Thinker* (see Cat. 48).

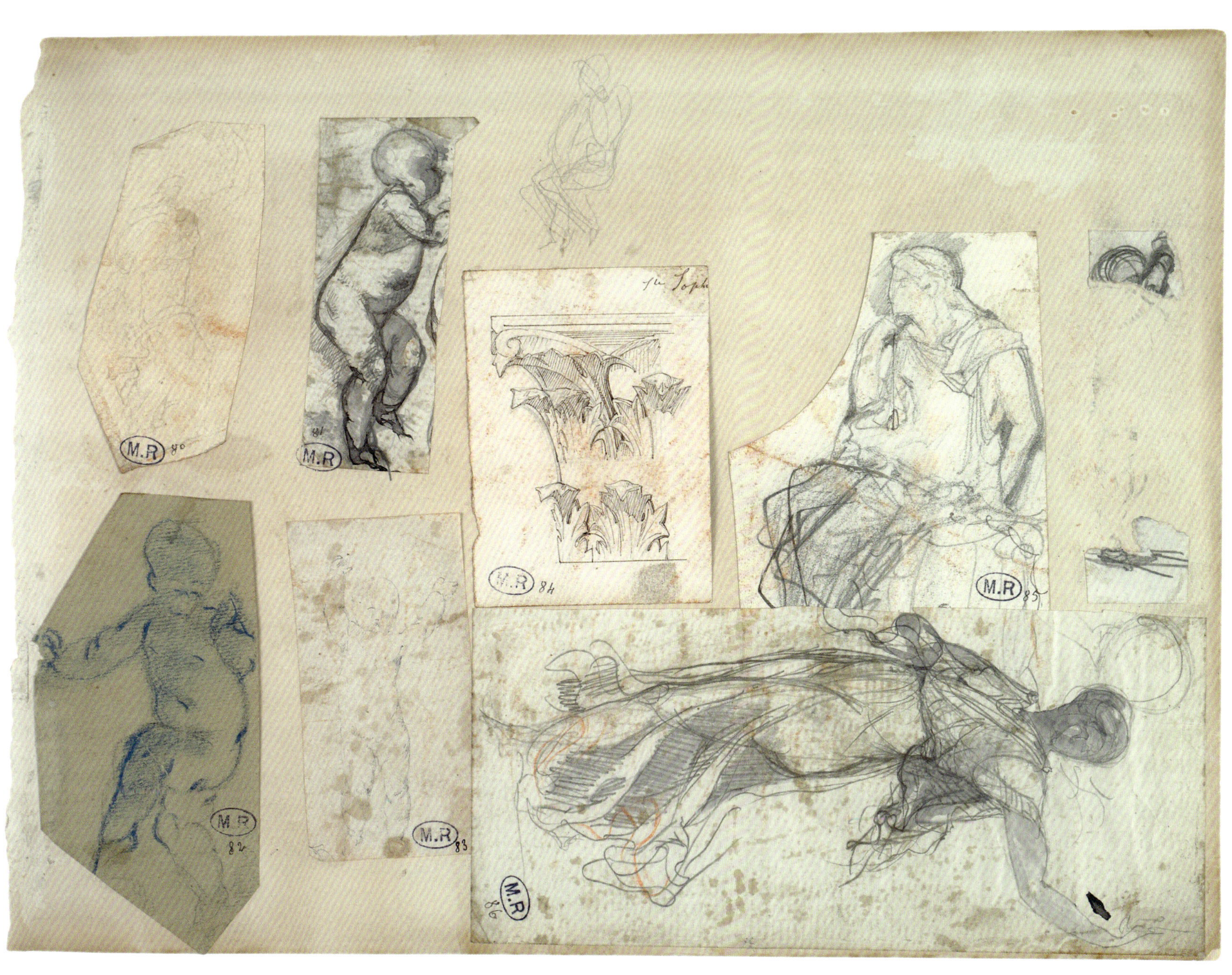

In the nineteenth century, as the fame of the Parthenon sculptures increased, it became commonplace for public buildings to exhibit casts of the Parthenon frieze as a sign of the virtuous intentions of the people who commissioned and used the building. The size and damaged state of the sculptures, however, made them unsuitable for all but the grandest houses. In 1836 Achille Collas (1795–1859) invented a method for reducing the scale of large sculptures. Reduced-scale casts of antiquities were then widely sold in France by hawkers:

> The little mould-makers who still run the streets, and who in my youth stood under the bridges, sold me many casts which were always before my eyes, and gave me instruction and an intense joy which I shall always remember. There were many antiques, bas-reliefs of the Parthenon, Venus de Milo etc.... In Paris, in the studios of young people making [industrial art] mould makers came and brought this schooling, this limited museum of plasters … and like leafing through the boxes of drawings still found on the banks of the Seine, spending time in these mould makers' shops reinforces and provides on a smaller scale the education to be gained in the rooms of museums and the casting rooms of the School of Fine Arts.
>
> Letter from Rodin to Camille Mauclair, 1900 (Musée Rodin, L. 1054)

The Musée Rodin has nine miniature casts of the Parthenon frieze, but it is not known whether the sculptor acquired them early on in his life or after 1893, when he began his collection of antiquities. These reduced-scale casts made it possible for Rodin to experience on a daily basis in his own studio the Parthenon sculptures that were in the Louvre, the British Museum or even in Athens. One of them (Cat. 14), unfortunately damaged, is of part of the block of the Parthenon frieze in the Louvre in its restored state, as it was between 1820 and 1896, complete with the heads.

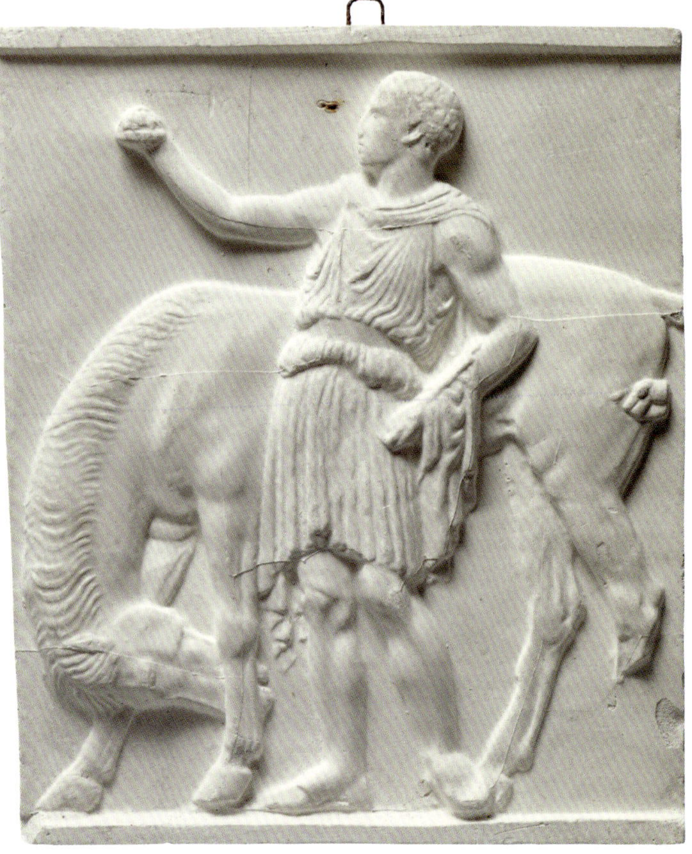

13
Reduced-scale cast of part of the Parthenon West Frieze (block XII, fig. 23)
Nineteenth century–early twentieth century
Plaster
H 27.5 cm, W 22.5 cm, D 2.5 cm
Musée Rodin, Co. 3188
Rodin donation, 1916

14
Reduced-scale cast of part of the Parthenon East Frieze (block VII, figs 55 and 56) in the Louvre
Nineteenth century–early twentieth century
Plaster
H 27.5 cm, W 16 cm, D 2 cm
Musée Rodin, Co. 3193
Rodin donation, 1916

15
Reduced-scale cast of part of the Parthenon North Frieze (block XLVII, figs 132–136)
Nineteenth century–early twentieth century
Plaster
H 27.5 cm, W 38 cm, D 2.5 cm
Musée Rodin, Co. 3191
Rodin donation, 1916

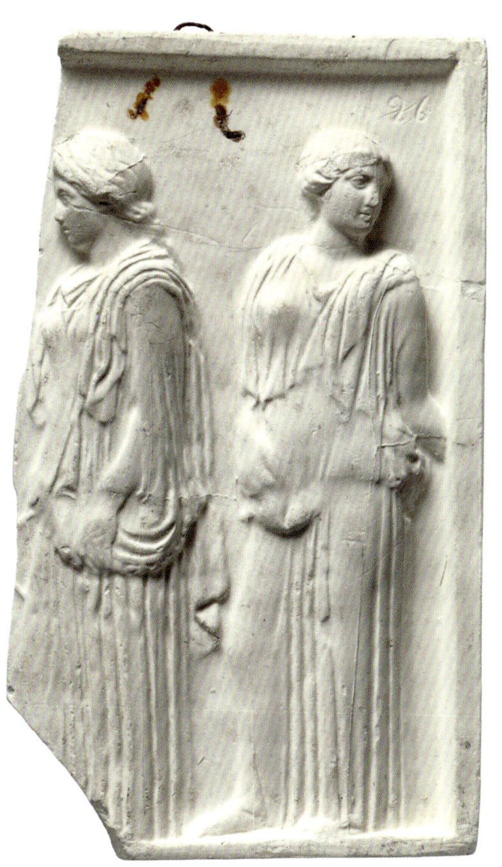

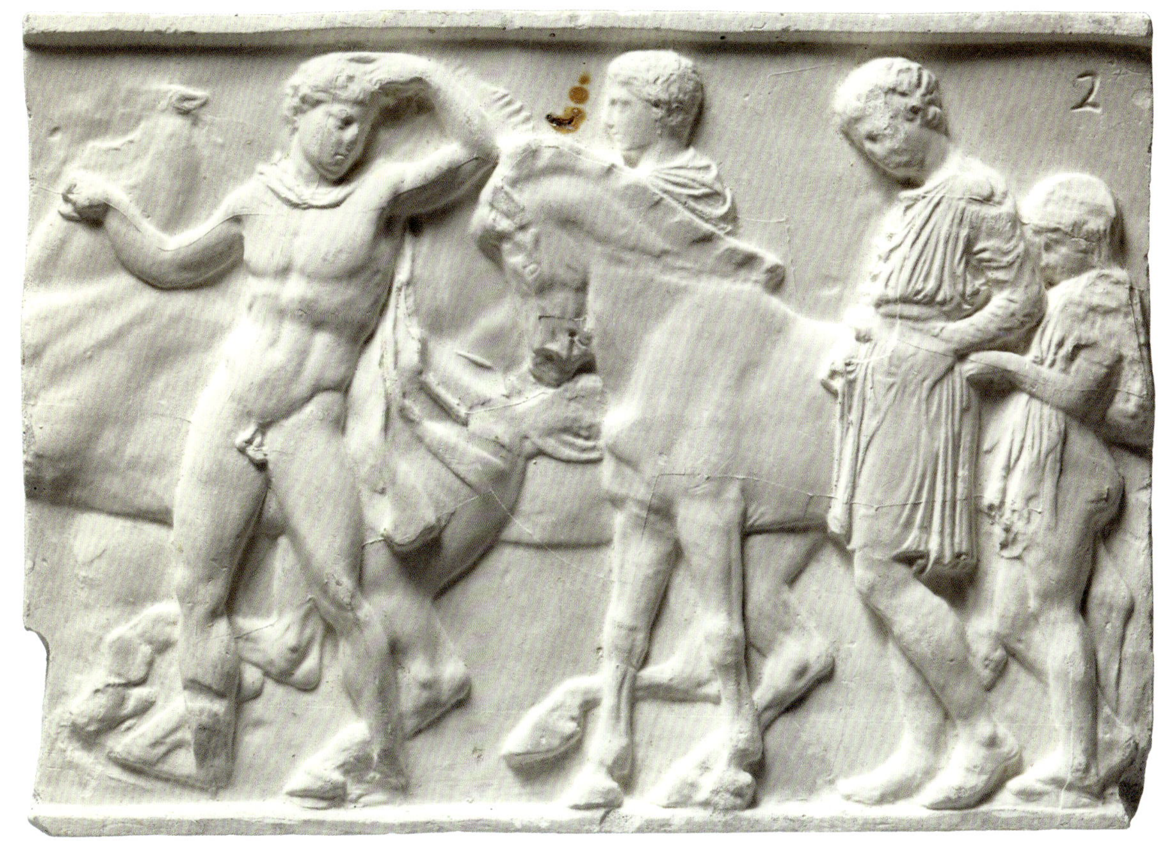

1880 Rodin and Legros: centaurs and the technique of drypoint printmaking

Rodin and Alphonse Legros both studied at the Petite École in the 1850s. Legros left Paris for London in 1863, but renewed contact with Rodin around 1880 through the sculptor Aimé-Jules Dalou (see p. 18) and the painter Jean-Charles Cazin (1840–1901). During Rodin's first visit to London in the summer of 1881, Legros introduced Rodin to drypoint, an intaglio technique of printing in which the image is incised directly into the plate. Of all the weird and wonderful creatures that inhabit Greek mythology, the centaurs are an obvious choice for Rodin's narrative because they, more than any other, combine the bodies of contrasting beings, human and equine, in what might be called an assemblage. In antiquity, just as in *fin de siècle* Europe, the centaur signified a darker aspect of human experience. More specifically it could stand for the irrational side of the human psyche.

The theme of the centaur first appeared in Rodin's drypoint engraving of 1881, *Love Conducting the World* (V&A CAI.870), and was revived by him sometime later with *Dying Centaur*. The composition of the engraving, as well as the motif of the centaur, conjures up the metopes of the Parthenon. The subject was also taken up in numerous drawings related to *The Gates of Hell*. Cat. 17, depicting a centaur abducting a woman, recalls designs by Rodin while working at the Sèvres porcelain factory from 1879 to 1882, and adopts the tight framing of the metopes of the Parthenon. But not all the centaurs of Rodin are of the same character: the centaur in the engraving and the drawing personify the creature's bestiality and combative nature, which are absent from the centaur lovers of *The Gates of Hell*. Rodin was interested in the theme of the centaur until the end of his life, and although the Parthenon was not his only source of inspiration, it was one of the first and marked him deeply.

In the years 1881–1882 the friendship between Legros and Rodin was particularly fertile. In 1881, after their summer meeting, Legros drew a portrait of Rodin (Musée Rodin, D. 9052) and then engraved it in drypoint (Fig. 8). He also painted Rodin's portrait the following year (Musée Rodin, P. 7316). Rodin in turn paid homage to his friend by modelling his portrait at the beginning of 1882 (Fig. 7). Legros' interest in the Parthenon horses resulted in a series of silver-point drawings of which Rodin bought an example from the dealer Charles Hersèle (Musée Rodin, D. 9050) in 1904, presumably in memory of his first introduction to the reliefs in London in 1881.

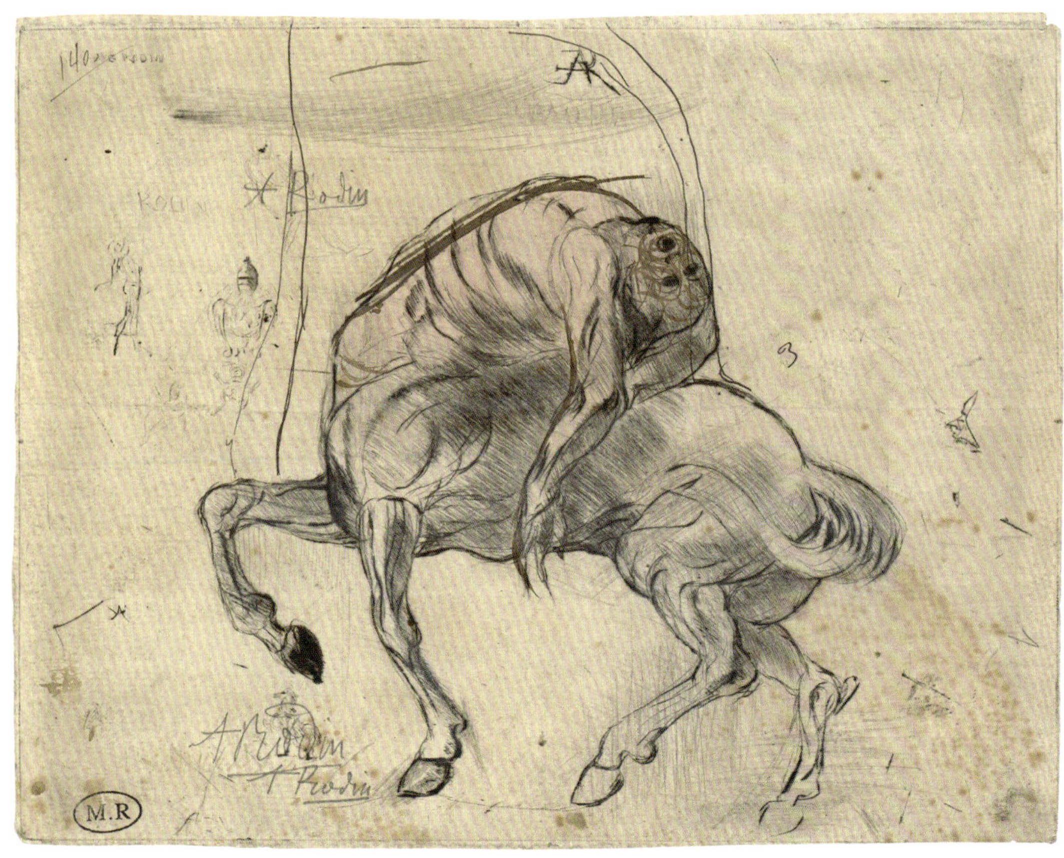

16
Auguste Rodin
Dying Centaur
1881–1900
Drypoint engraving
H 17.7 cm, W 22.5 cm (print);
H 18.1 cm, W 22.7 cm (paper)
Musée Rodin, G. 7757
Acquired in 1992

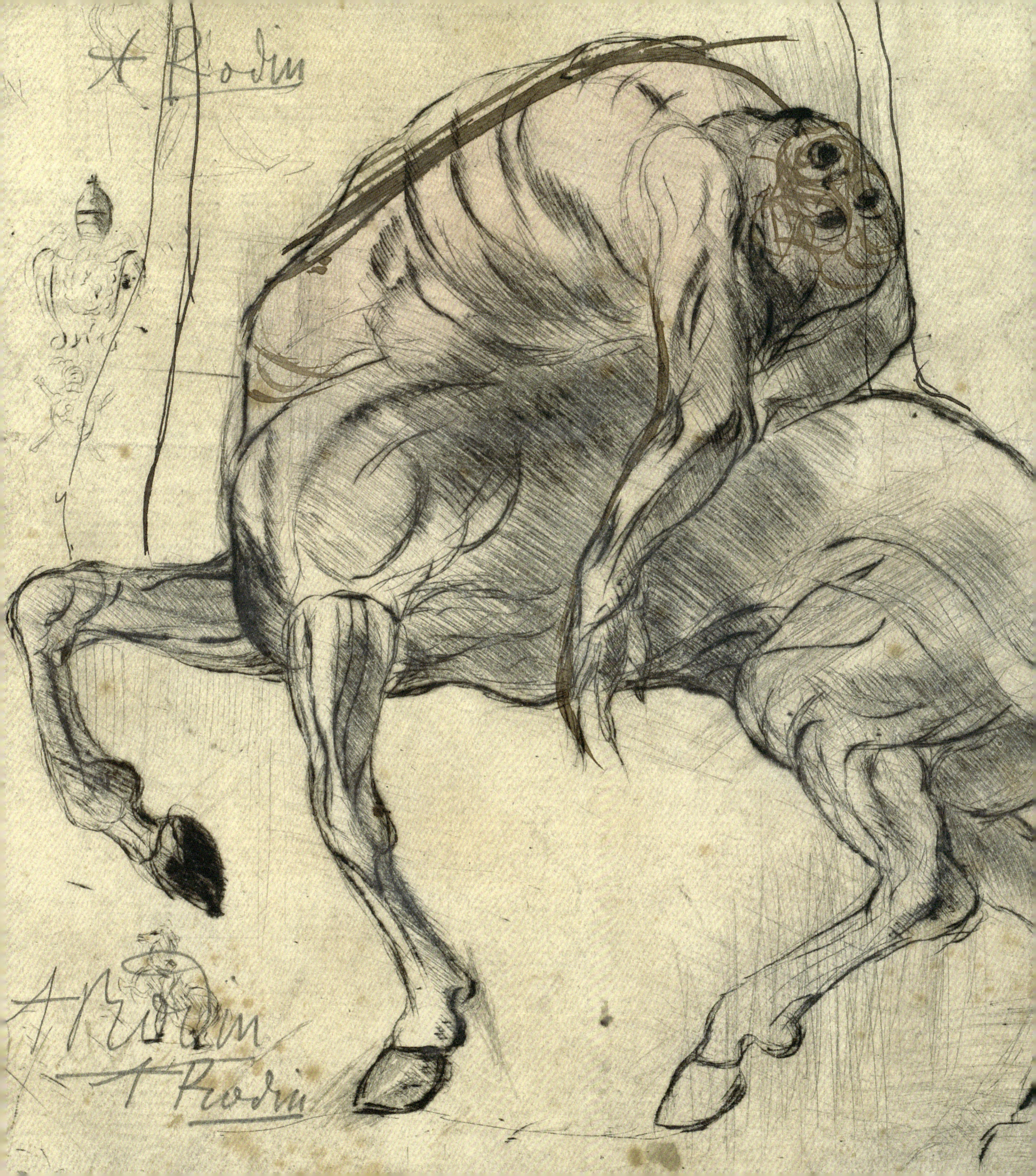
A Rodin
A Rodin

17
Auguste Rodin
Galloping Centaur Abducting a Woman
About 1880
Ink wash, graphite, bodycolour and pen and ink on paper vellum
H 15.2 cm, W 19.4 cm
Musée Rodin, D. 5087
Rodin donation, 1916

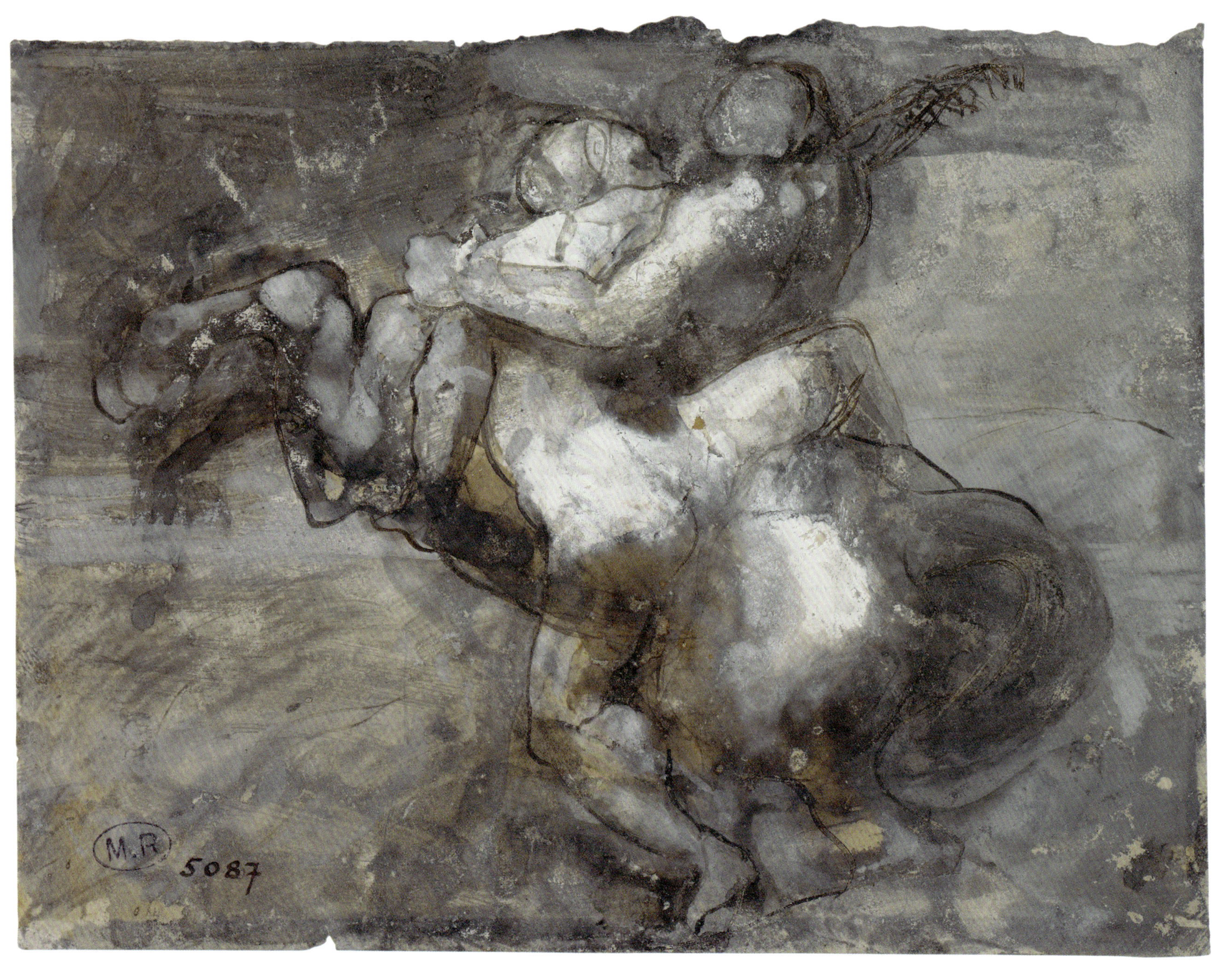

Fig. 7
Auguste Rodin
Portrait of Legros
1881–1882
Bronze; sand cast by Alexis Rudier, before 1916
H 33 cm, W 21 cm, D 24 cm
Musée Rodin, S. 1060
Rodin donation, 1916

Fig. 8
Alphonse Legros (1837–1911)
Portrait of Rodin
1882–1890?
Drypoint engraving
H 25.2 cm, W 17.4 cm
British Museum, 1949,0411.2176
Bequeathed by Campbell Dodgson

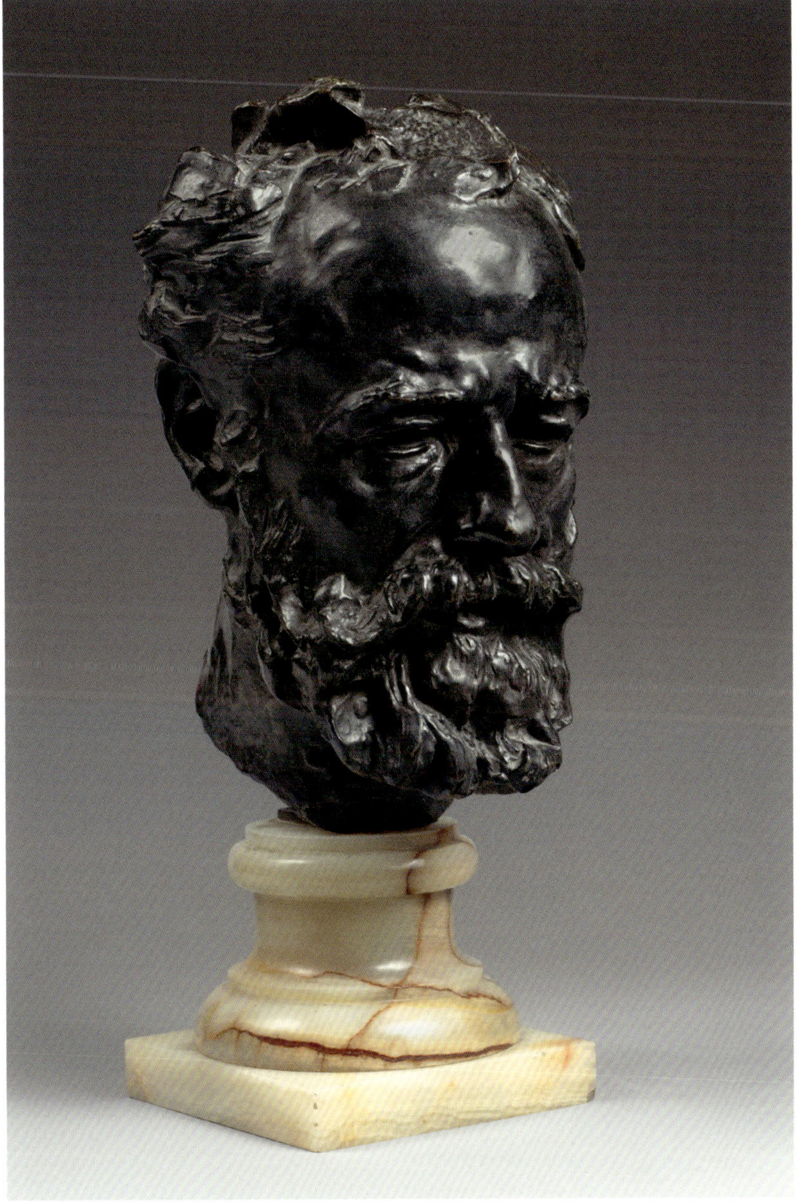

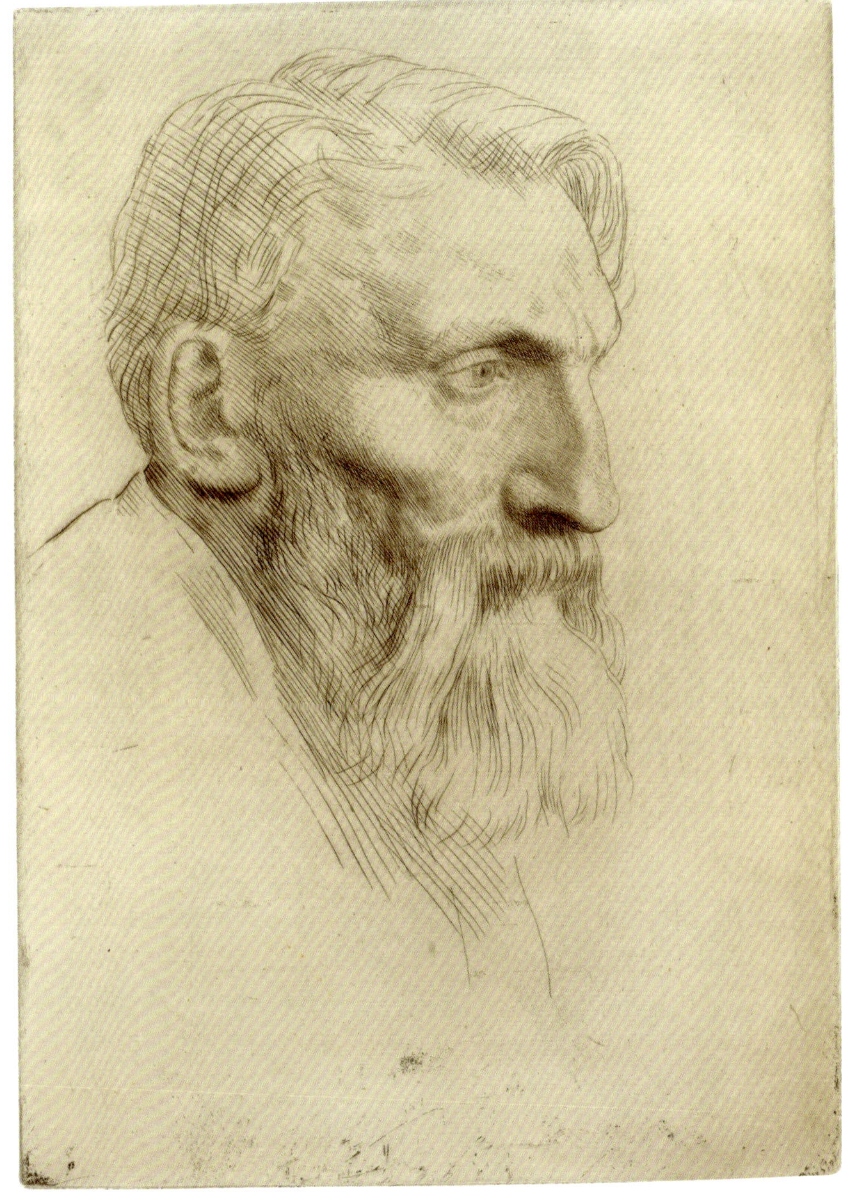

1900–1910 Breaking free from the model

After 1900, Rodin produced further drawings of the Parthenon sculptures, probably at the British Museum in front of the originals or working from casts exhibited at the Louvre. In these graphite sketches, rather than faithfully copying the model he endeavoured to capture the force lines of the sculpture and to translate the modelling. While in London, Rodin used headed notepaper from his hotel and small notebooks. In Cat. 18 we can recognize on the left a figure from the East Pediment (figure K), and on the right South Metope III showing the battle between a centaur and a Lapith. The sheet also has some rather mysterious annotations: 'drape like the Parthenon fragment my sculptor's dream–the Belgian and the Kaiser / Kaiser / Savonarola'. On the reverse is a sketch recalling a horseman from the North Frieze of the Parthenon. The annotation gives us some insight into the artist's vision of the subject, though it is still obscure: 'Bull / Kaiser resistance / metope / man struggles against barbarians / the Parthenon-Kaiser metope the centaur / the procession B.A.F.R. carrying the host? / ?agony-low-relief-Belgian-English-crouching.'

In Notebook 47, devoted mainly to architecture, Rodin makes an association between the Parthenon and the French cathedrals of Auxerre and Sens: 'temple London Museum / of muses / Sens / Auxerre' (Cat. 19). And in Notebook 49, produced in London before July 1913, and mainly featuring animals in the friezes from Nineveh and other Assyrian works, the architecture of the Parthenon takes him back once again to that of cathedrals. Above the drawing of a small column (Cat. 20) Rodin adds in pencil: 'The fluting on the columns of the Parthenon in the Gothic style the small columns together resemble fluting in reverse.' In Notebook 55 (Cat. 21), Rodin sketches casts of the Parthenon sculptures in the Louvre; here we can identify figures K and G from the East Pediment as well as a palmette: 'I started out on this fine journey with a visit to the Louvre and there I was once again struck by how intent the Greeks were on colour as well as on form; and it should also be said that well executed form gives colour and vice versa; thus the ancient palmette that I see alongside the Fates or a Victory share the same principle as the planes of beautiful sculpture, make it powerful, but taste is awakened by a dark accent and by force, what moderation in this force. In our time the effects are so widespread that moderation is actually the effect.' Rodin was not here expressing an argument for the application of actual colour to the surface of sculpture. Rather, he perceived colour as something that was produced by the transient effects of light playing on the variations in the tooled surfaces of stone and the subtly modelled shapes of bronze.

The artist's interest in the palmette motif is also evident from a cast in his collection of an antefix (the decorative element punctuating the end of a run of cover tiles on a roof) in the form of a palmette from the Parthenon (Co. 1677).

In a drawing he made from a model posing in the studio (Cat. 22; from Album XLI, dismantled in 1933), Rodin discovers in the woman's pose a timelessness that he freely associates in his annotation, 'the Fate', with figure K (one of the so-called Fates) from the East Pediment of the Parthenon. He drew this figure on three occasions, once in London (discussed above, Cat. 18), once from a cast in the Louvre (Cat. 21) and the third time in this drawing, where the annotation reflects a fleeting thought. Here Rodin reworks the face by changing the position of the eyes.

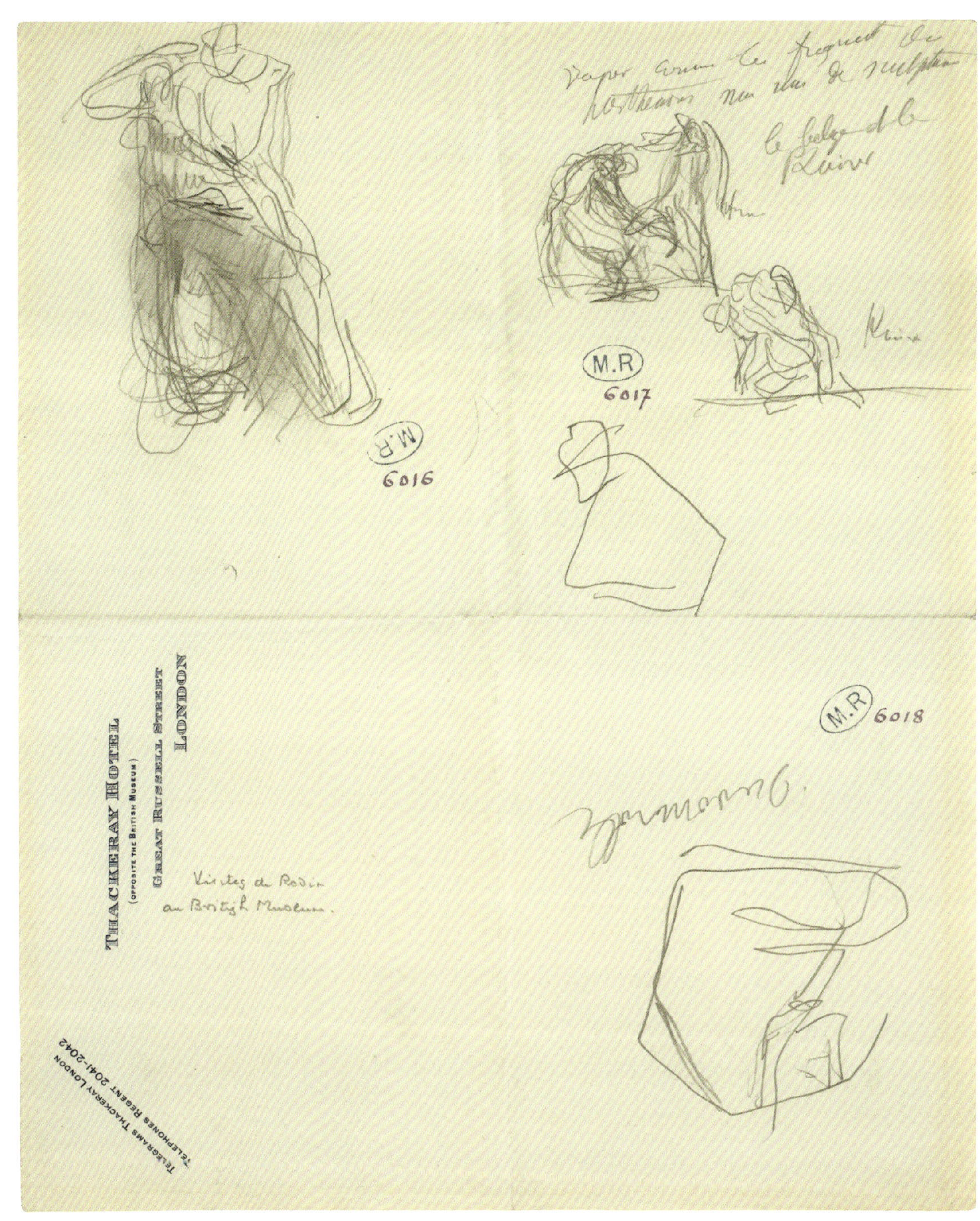

18
Auguste Rodin
Sketches including figure K from the East Pediment of the Parthenon and South Metope III
20 February 1905
Graphite with stump on paper
H 25.2 cm, W 20.3 cm
Musée Rodin, D. 6016–6018
Rodin donation, 1916

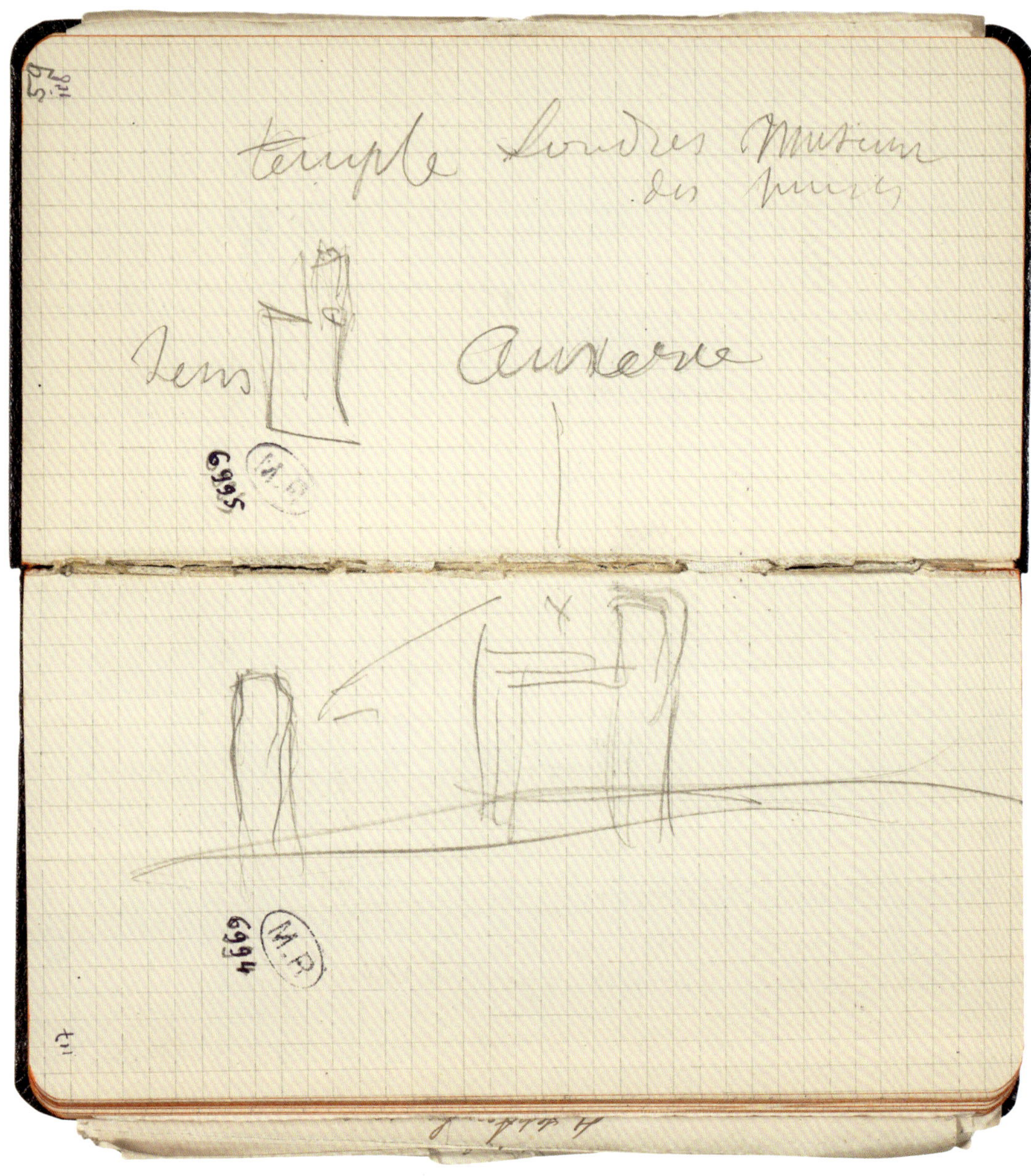

19
Auguste Rodin
Notebook with annotation:
'temple London Museum of muses'
About 1912
Graphite on paper
H 8 cm, W 15 cm
Musée Rodin, D. 6995,
Notebook 47, folio 59 recto
Rodin donation, 1916

20
Auguste Rodin
Notebook with sketch and notes about the columns of the Parthenon
Before July 1913
Graphite on paper
H 14.1 cm, W 8.3 cm
Musée Rodin, D. 7028,
Notebook 49, folio 10 verso
Rodin donation, 1916

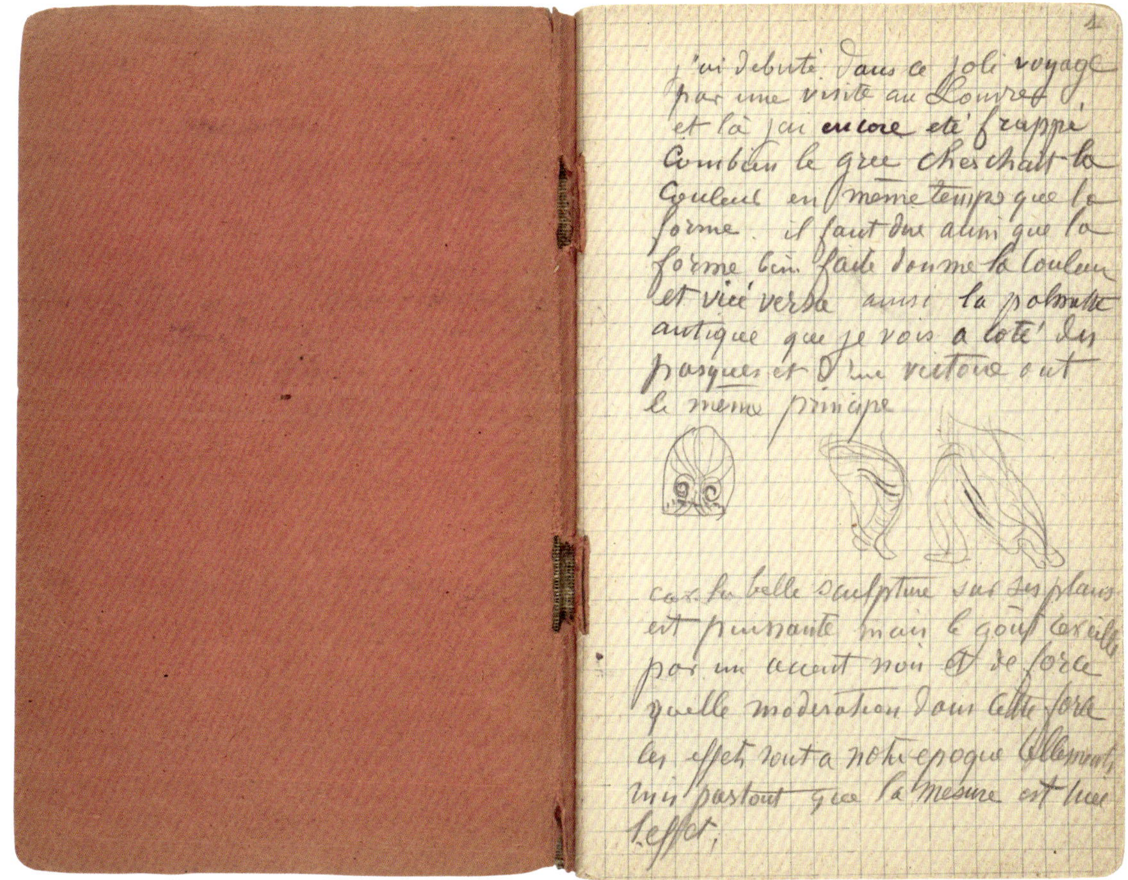

21
Auguste Rodin
Notebook with sketches of figures K and G from the Parthenon East Pediment and an antefix in the form of a palmette
After 1900
Graphite on paper
H 14.9 cm, W 9 cm
Musée Rodin, D. 7717,
Notebook 55, 1 recto
Acquired in 1962

22
Auguste Rodin
The Fate
After 1898?
Graphite with stump and
watercolour on paper vellum
H 32.6 cm, W 20.5 cm
Musée Rodin, D. 1541
Rodin donation, 1916

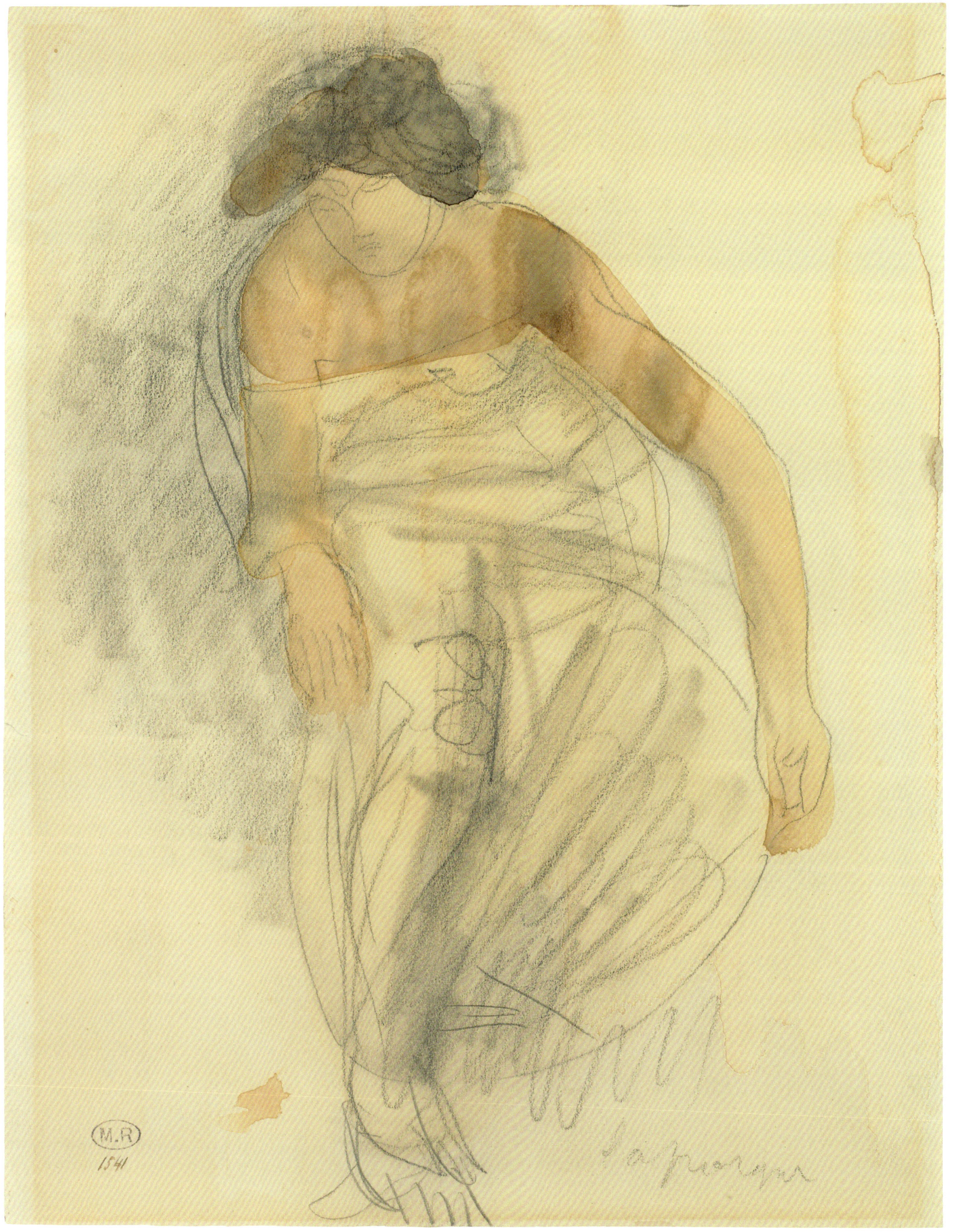
M.R
1541

Photographs as an aide-memoire

In his archives, Rodin had a large number of photographs of monuments and works of art ranging in date from antiquity to the nineteenth century, and he chose from them a selection of images that he would annotate in pencil or ink. This allowed him to place next to each other in albums different arts of the past in a system of connections – antiquity and the Middle Ages were often juxtaposed with his own sculptures. These albums formed a counterpart to those containing his drawings, in which Rodin brought together sketches he had made of works of the past. Ten or twenty years earlier, the sculptor had anticipated this system, using it at Meudon, and then later at the Hôtel Biron (where Rodin rented rooms as studios from 1908, and later exhibited his sculptures and drawings and his collection, having been told about the building by the poet Rainer Maria Rilke; now the Musée Rodin), in a collection of antiques arranged in proximity with his own work, in the style of the museum of comparative sculpture set up by Eugène Viollet-le-Duc (1814–1879). In one album Rodin slipped a photograph of figures E and F (Fig. 9) and one of two of the so-called Fates (figures L and M; Cat. 23) from the East Pediment of the Parthenon in between the Château de Chambord, the Raphael Room at the Vatican, sculptures by Mino da Fiesole and the *Venus de Milo*.

Rodin also owned a series of seven photographs of fragments of the North and East friezes of the Parthenon taken by Eugène Druet (1867–1916) at the British Museum (Cats 24–25 and Fig. 10). The photographer began collaborating with Rodin in 1896 and produced a large number of photographs, both portraits of the artist and of sculptures. Druet probably took the latter around 1904 in London, since on 8 March 1905, he also sent 'photographs of the Parthenon' to Count Harry Kessler. This documentary series made it possible for Rodin to admire the monument in the studio and the house, while at work or in meditation, as an indispensable standard of excellence.

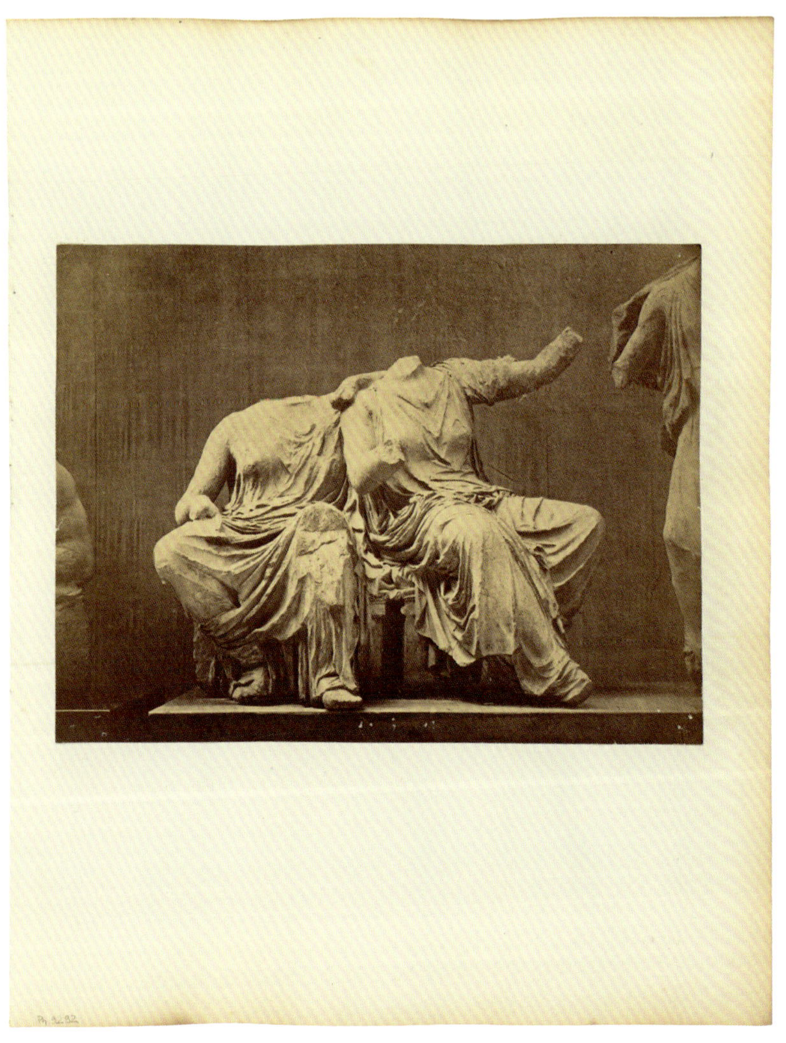

Fig. 9
Anonymous
Photograph of figures E and F from the Parthenon East Pediment, Album
About 1880
Albumen print
H 19.25 cm, W 25 cm
Musée Rodin Ph. 9292, Album I
Rodin donation, 1916

23
Anonymous
Photograph of figures L and M from the Parthenon East Pediment, Album
About 1880
Albumen print
H 17.9 cm, W 26 cm
Musée Rodin, Ph. 9293, Album I
Rodin donation, 1916

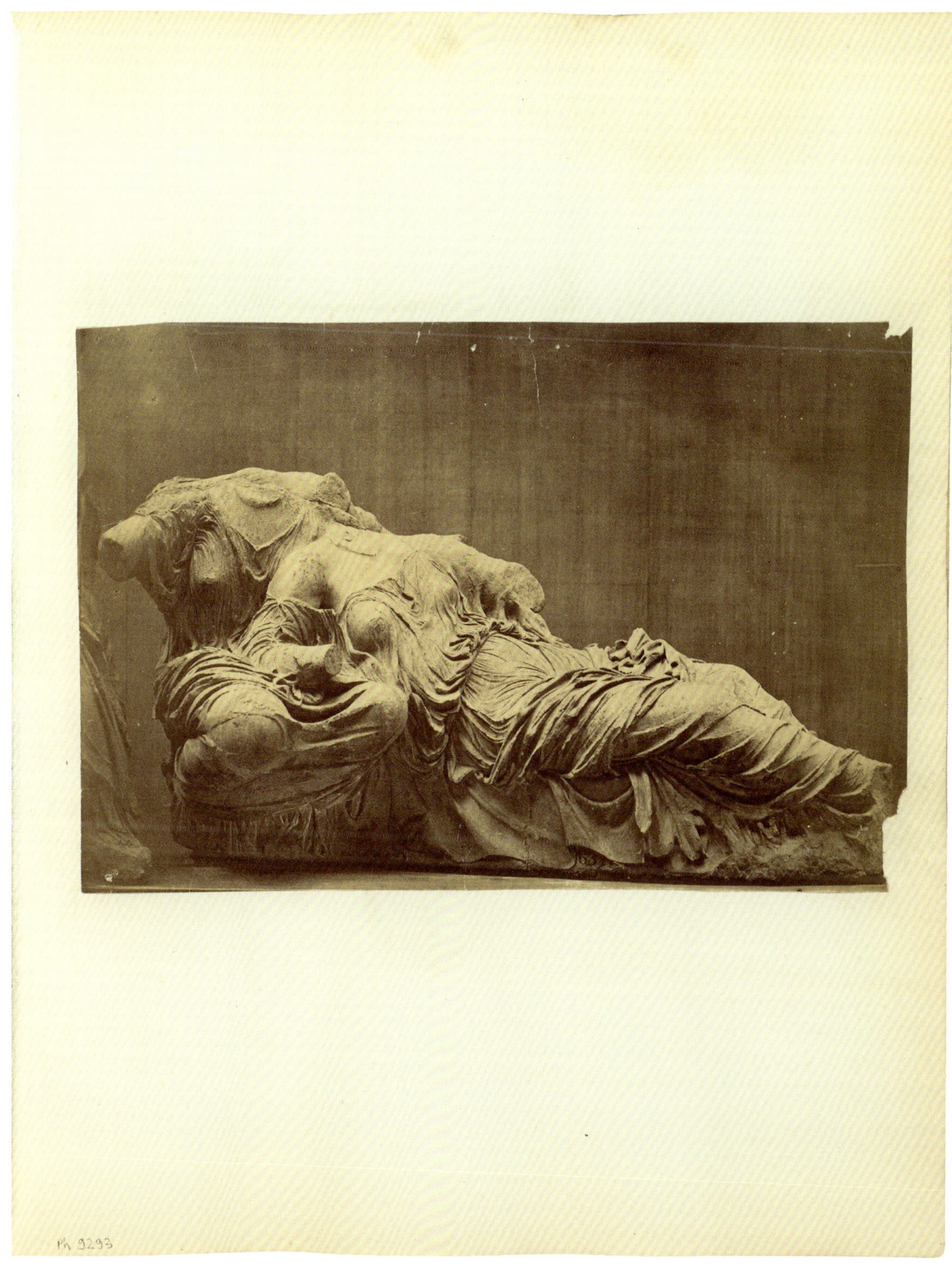

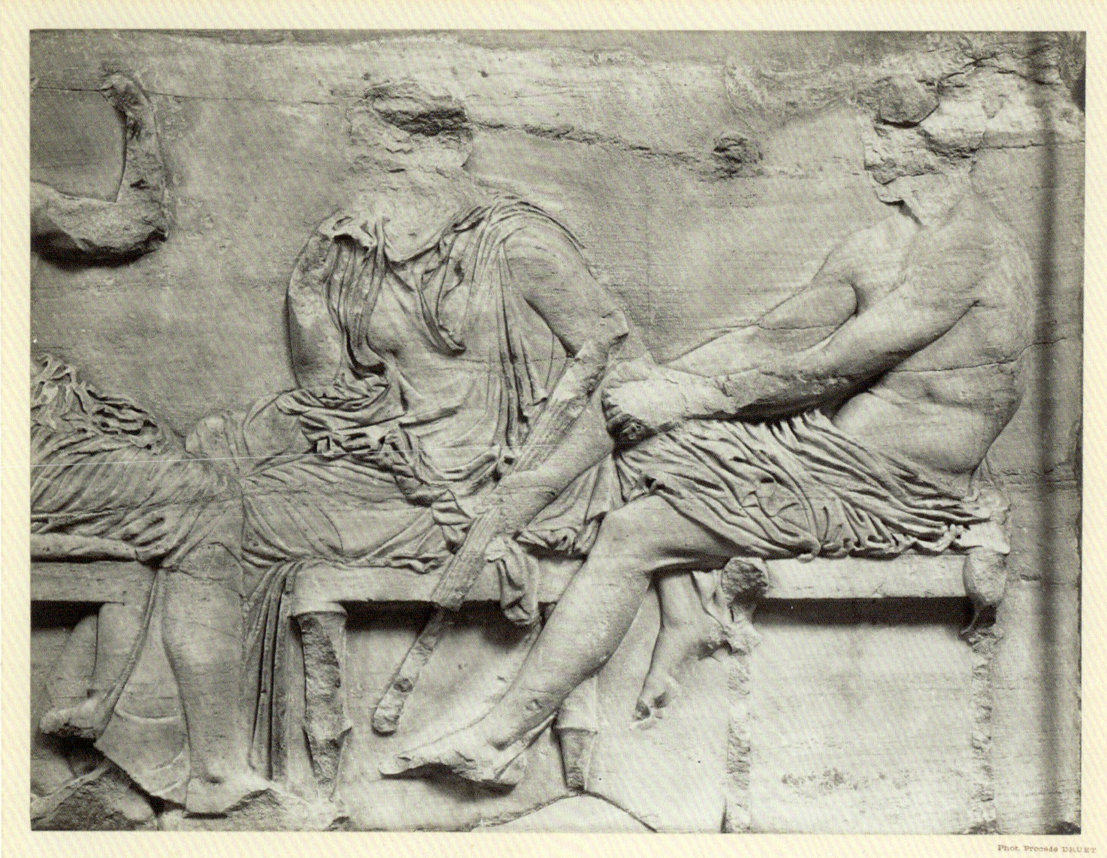

24
Eugène Druet (1867–1916)
Photograph of the Parthenon East Frieze (block IV, figs 26 and 27), showing Demeter and Ares
1903–1908
Gelatin silver print
H 27.5 cm, W 35.9 cm
Musée Rodin, Ph. 17797
Rodin donation, 1916

25
Eugène Druet (1867–1916)
Photograph of the Parthenon North Frieze (block XXIV, figs 66–68) showing a marshal and chariot
1903–1908
Gelatin silver print
H 28 cm, W 33.8 cm
Musée Rodin, Ph. 17802
Rodin donation, 1916

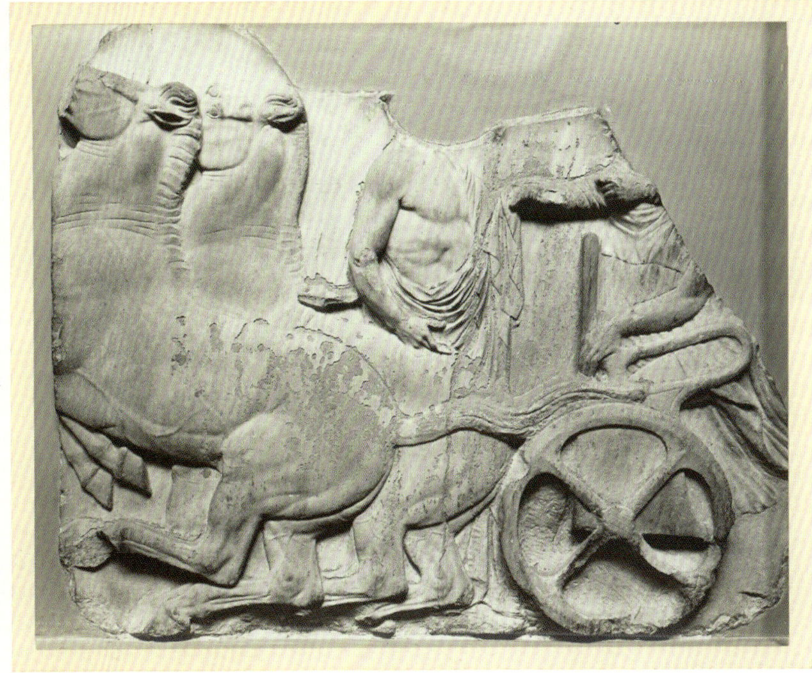

Fig. 10
Eugène Druet (1867–1916)
Photograph of the Parthenon North Frieze (block XXXVIII, figs 103–105) showing the cavalcade
1903–1908
Gelatin silver print
H 26.4 cm, W 36.4 cm
Musée Rodin, Ph. 17798
Rodin donation, 1916

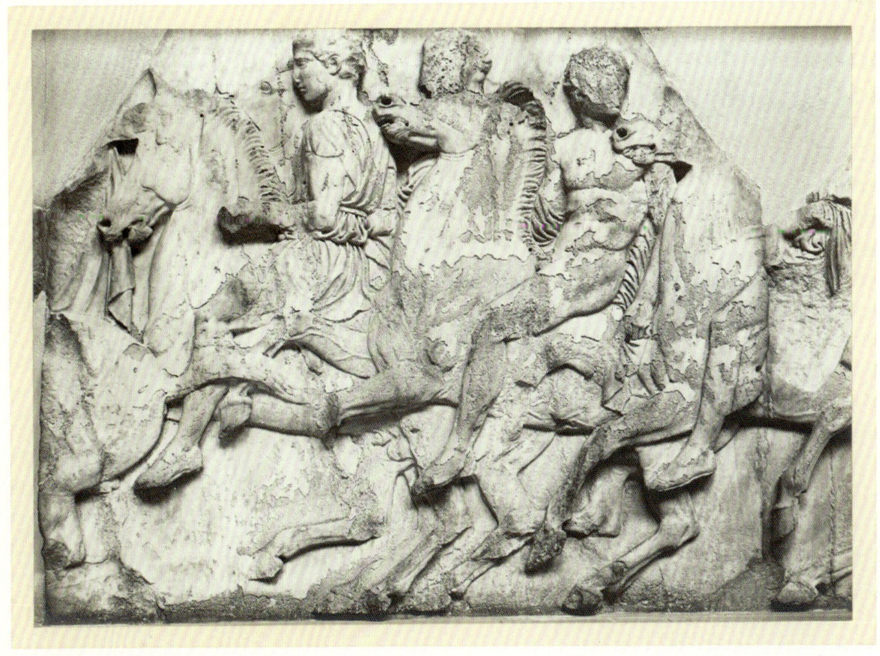

What perfect unity there is in this fragment! … Is not the entire Acropolis here?

Auguste Rodin, 'Pierre et marbre', *Paris Journal*, 1 January 1912

Rodin could not of course compete with the British Museum or the Louvre in the acquisition of ancient sculptures, and such was not his purpose. He bought his objects predominantly from Parisian antiquaries, who had acquired them in Greece and Italy or in auction houses across Europe. Rodin was well aware of the modesty of the fragments he accumulated following his own taste, with the help of a few antique dealers, but this modesty, rather than crushing his creativity allowed him greater freedom.

However, Rodin did often compare his antiquities to the great works of art he admired in museums. In the heart of his workshop his treasures – his gods as he called them – resonated with the prestigious fragments of the Parthenon. The pieces here have been selected for their similarity to themes in the Parthenon frieze, which Rodin admired in the British Museum – falling drapery, seated gods and the sacrifice of cattle.

In his transitional drawings of the early 1890s Rodin returns to the motif of ancient drapery, in particular the drawing of a woman (Cat. 27) annotated on the reverse 'C. II Beatrice'. He may have been studying the drapery on Greek terracotta figurines even before he began to collect them. Rodin's taste for reducing a figure to a detail led him to choose countless fragments of heads, hands, feet and torsos for his collection, as can be seen today displayed on the walls in a room at the Hôtel Biron, and which echo the three small Parthenon fragments chosen here (Cats 33–35).

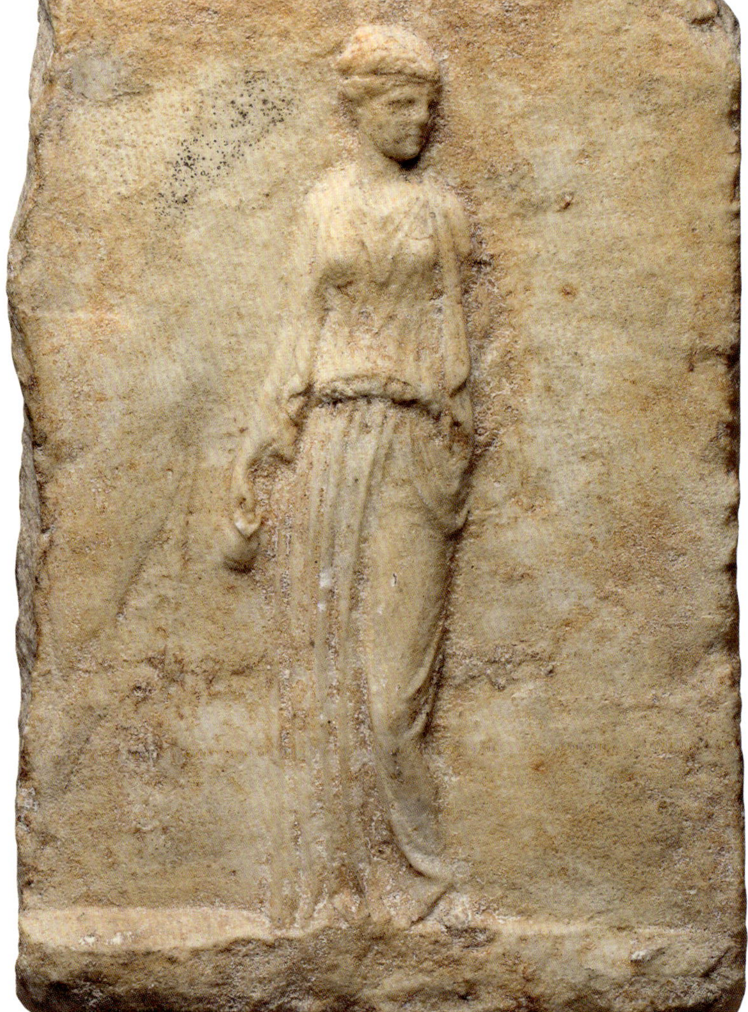

26
Fragment of a relief with a girl carrying a ritual vessel, possibly inspired by the maidens of the Parthenon East Frieze
Probably nineteenth century
Marble
H 27.6 cm, W 19.3 cm, D 3 cm
Musée Rodin, Co. 496
Rodin donation, 1916

27
Auguste Rodin
Study of a draped female figure
About 1890
Graphite, pen and ink, and ink wash on watermarked paper
H 17.6 cm, W 5.7 cm
Musée Rodin, D. 4344
Rodin donation, 1916

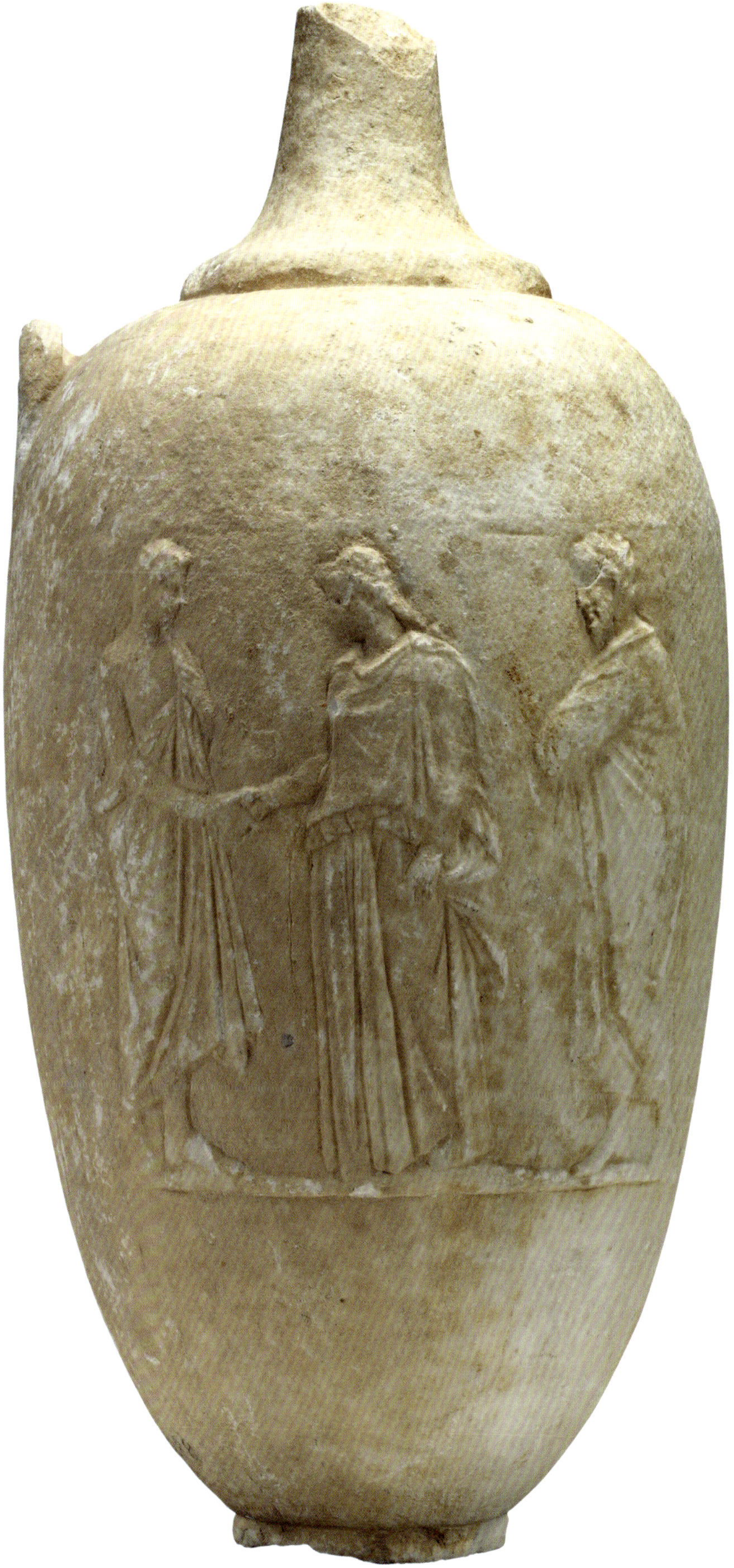

28
Funerary vessel (*lekythos*) carved in relief with a scene of a youth bidding his mother and father farewell
Greek
375–350 BC
Marble
H 71 cm, D 33 cm
Musée Rodin, Co. 1698
Rodin donation, 1916

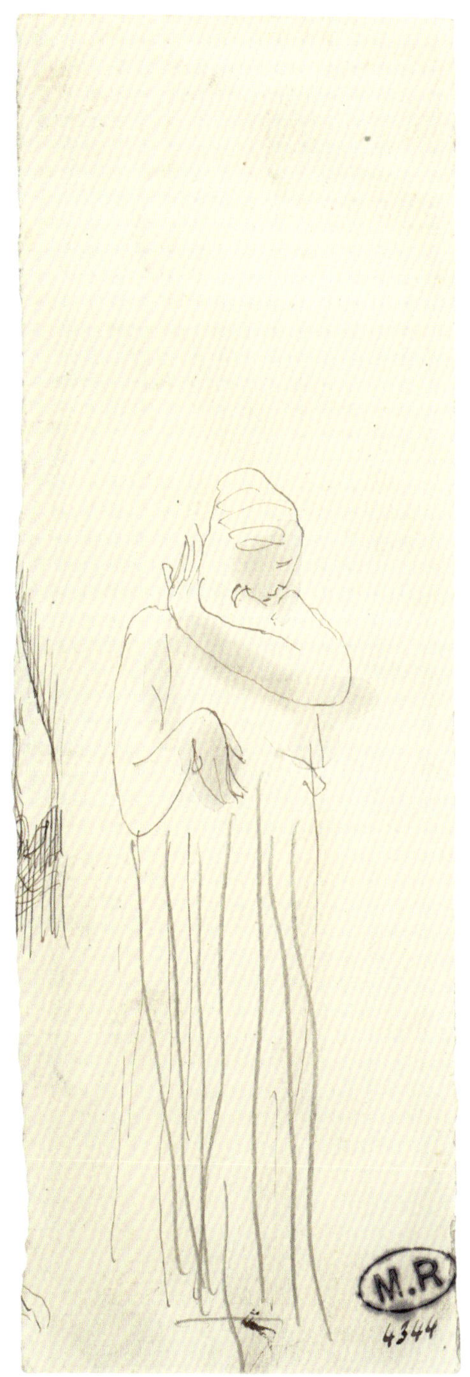

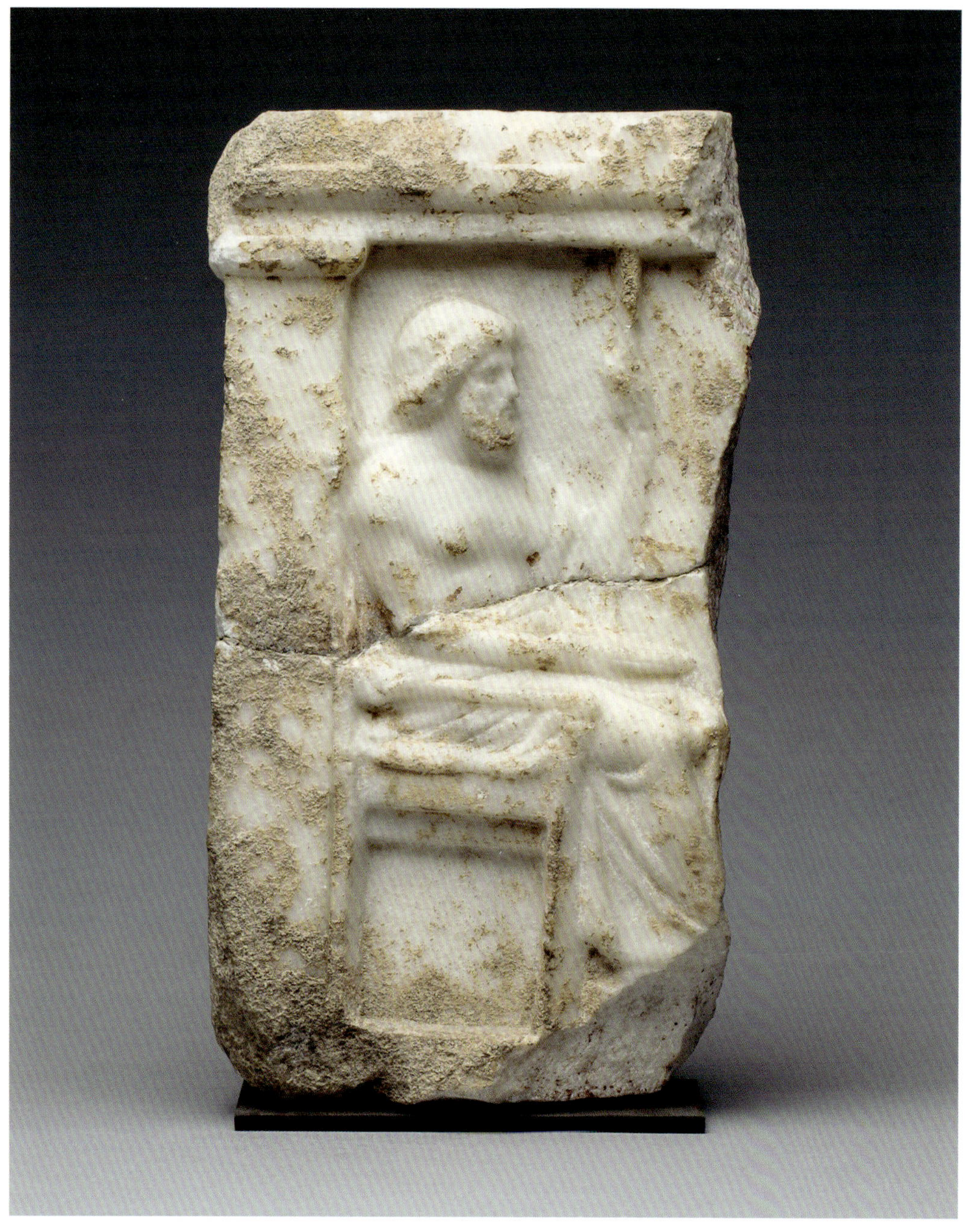

29
Attic votive relief showing
Zeus seated on a throne
Greek
350–300 BC
Marble
H 25.8 cm, W 14.2 cm, D 6.3 cm
Musée Rodin, Co. 497
Rodin donation, 1916

30
Funerary stele showing a scene of domestic life featuring a seated woman, a maid and a child
Greek
400–375 BC
Marble
H 153 cm, W 72 cm, D 22 cm
Musée Rodin, Co. 469
Rodin donation, 1916

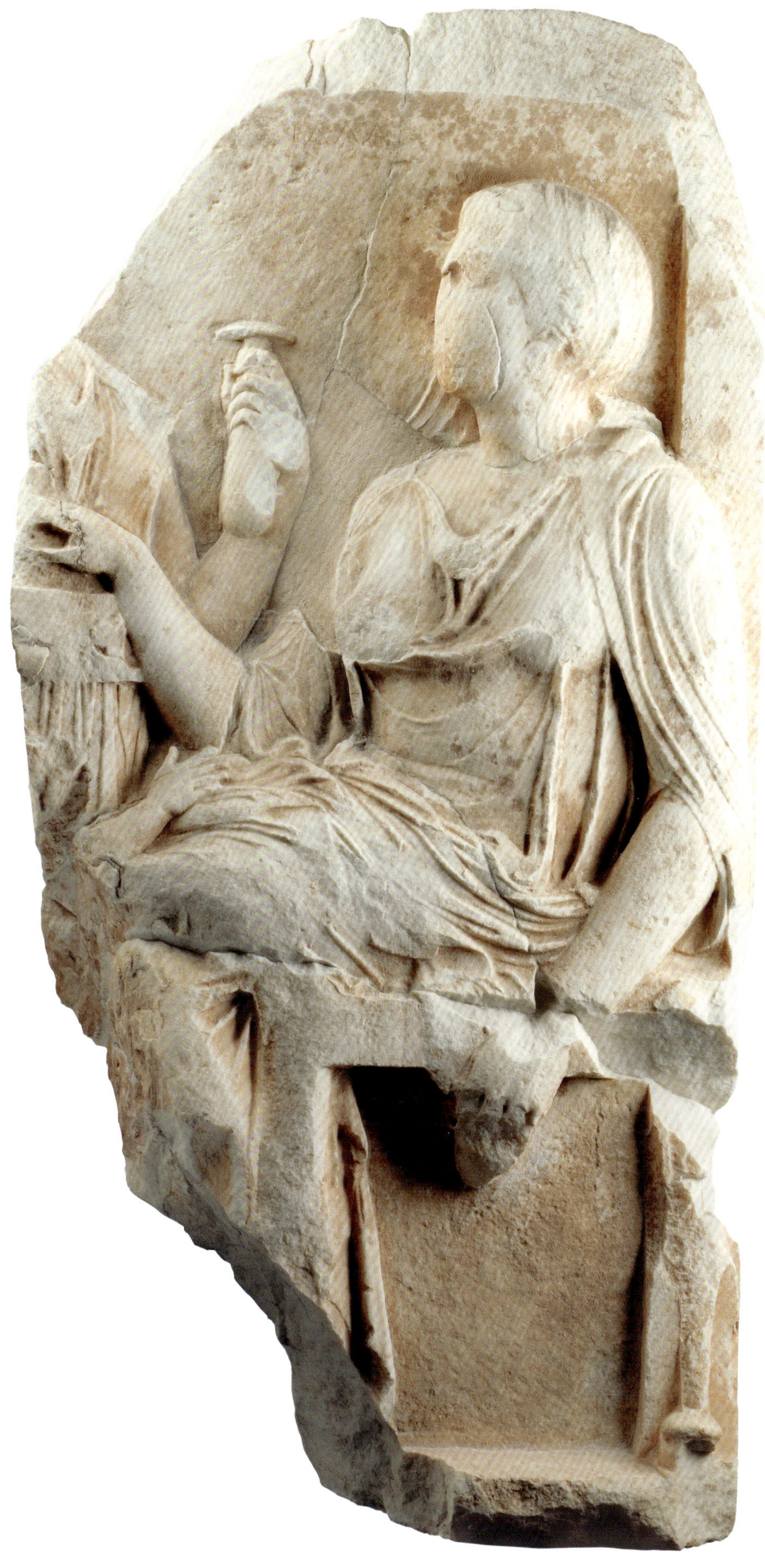

31
Head of a youth
Greek
470–460 BC
Marble
H 22 cm, W 15.7 cm, D 17.6 cm
Musée Rodin, Co. 704
Rodin donation, 1916

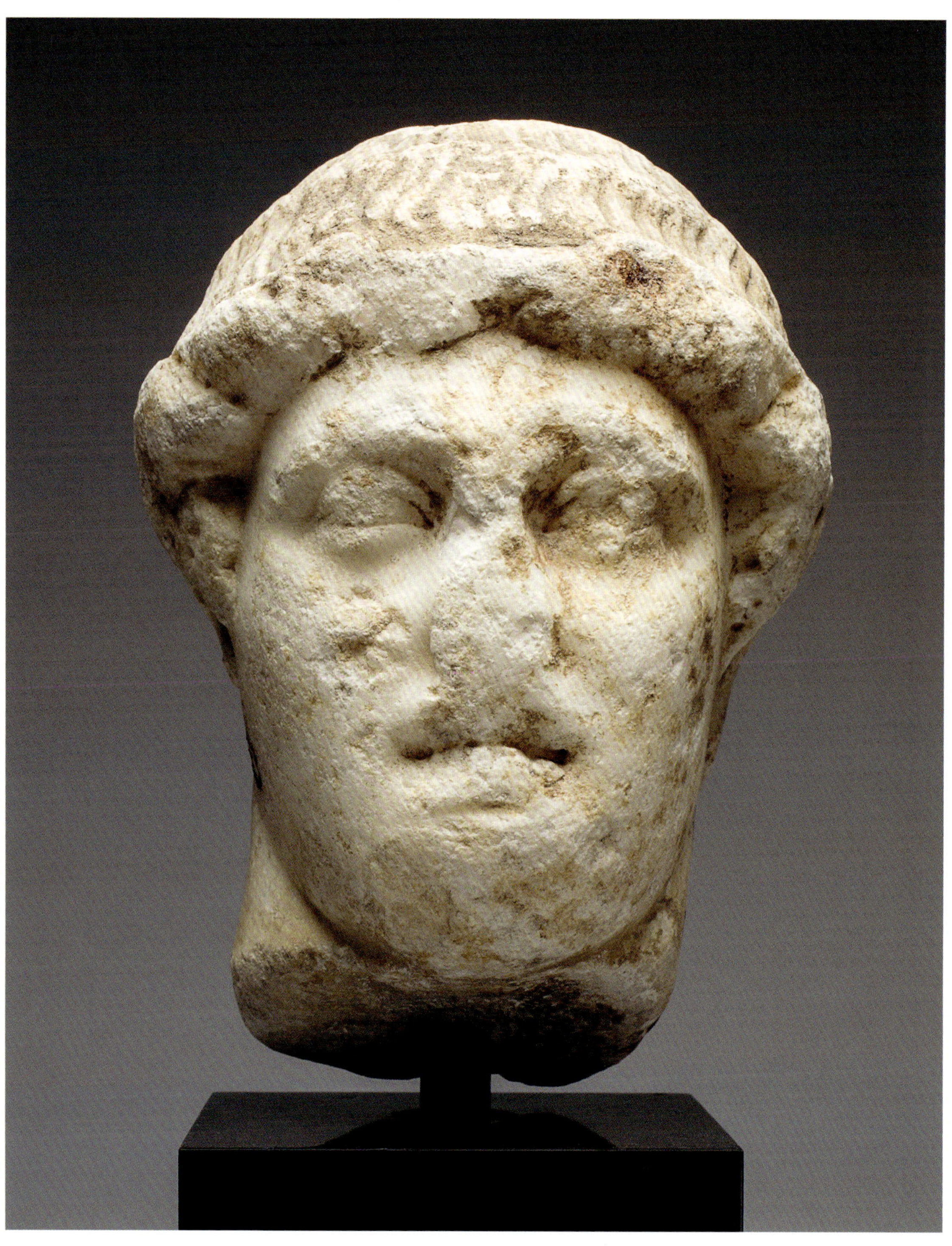

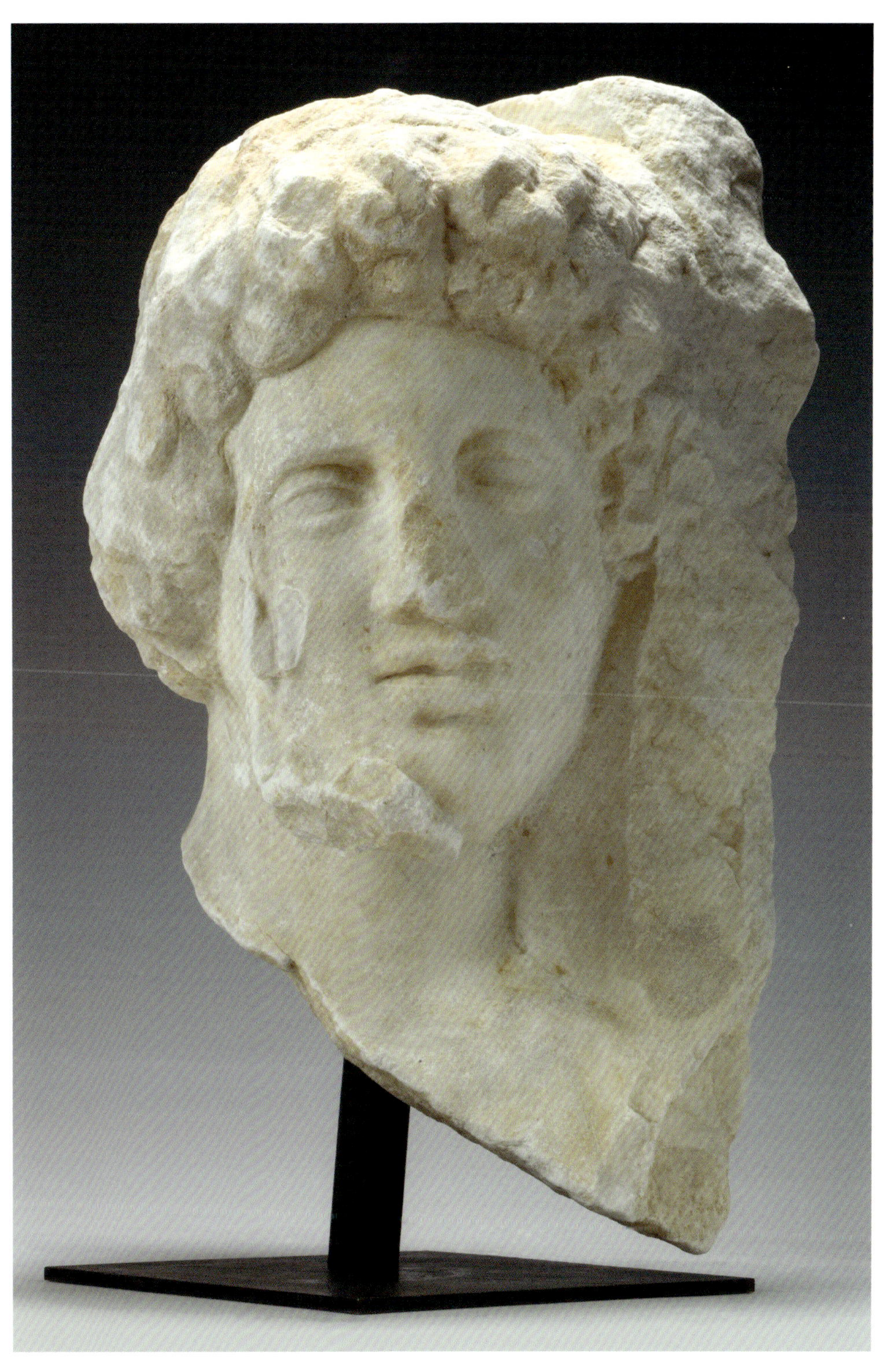

32
Fragment of a stele with the head of a male figure
Greek
325–300 BC
Marble
H 35.5 cm, W 25 cm, D 20.5 cm
Musée Rodin, Co. 463
Rodin donation, 1916

Rodin's passion for the sculptures of the Parthenon extended to the smallest fragment, each of which he saw as a work of art in itself, complete and requiring no restoration. The dispersal of the Parthenon sculptures had scattered many fragments into private collections throughout Europe. The British Museum's long-standing mission was to bring all these fragments together, whether in the original or in the form of a cast. This process of collecting continued long after the acquisition of the main body of the sculptures in 1816. For example, shortly before Rodin's first visit to the Museum, this head of a youth (Cat. 33) and the fragment of two feet (Cat. 34) had been acquired from a private collection in Karlsruhe, Germany. Rodin did not himself possess any fragments of the Parthenon sculptures, but he acquired pieces which reminded him of them and he did not hesitate to say that some were Pheidian.

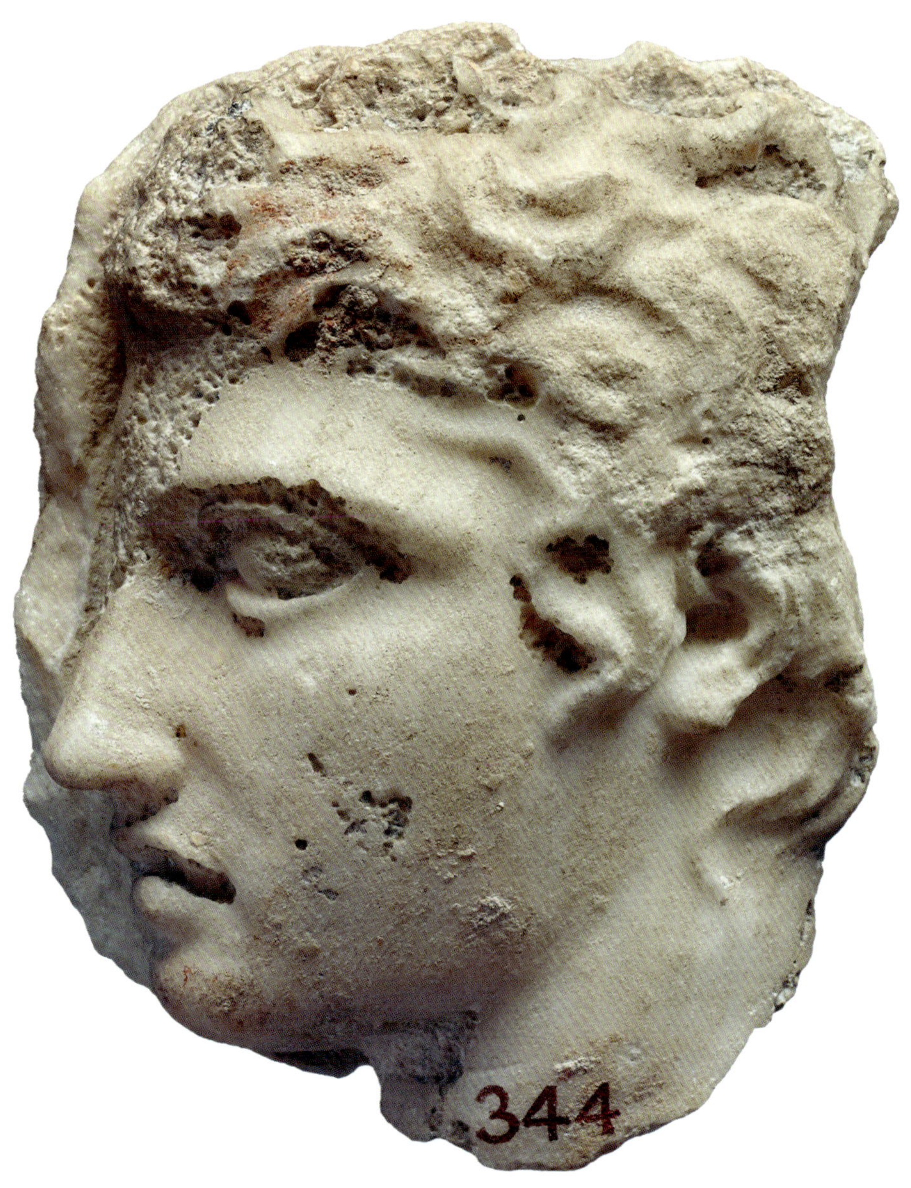

33
Fragment of a head of a youth
from the Parthenon frieze
Greek
About 438–432 BC
Marble
H 15.2 cm, W 11 cm, D 5 cm
British Museum, 1880,0117.1

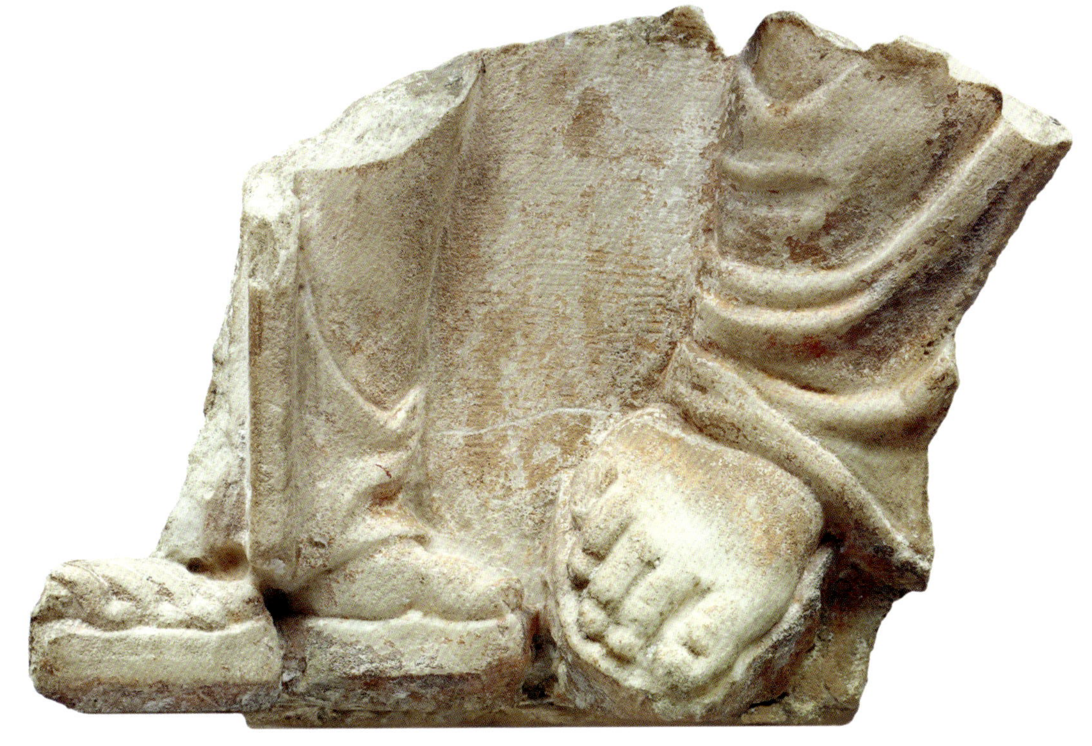

34
Fragment of feet from the Parthenon East Frieze (block II, figs 2 and 3)
Greek
About 438–432 BC
Marble
H 16 cm, W 22 cm, D 6 cm
British Museum, 1880,0117.2

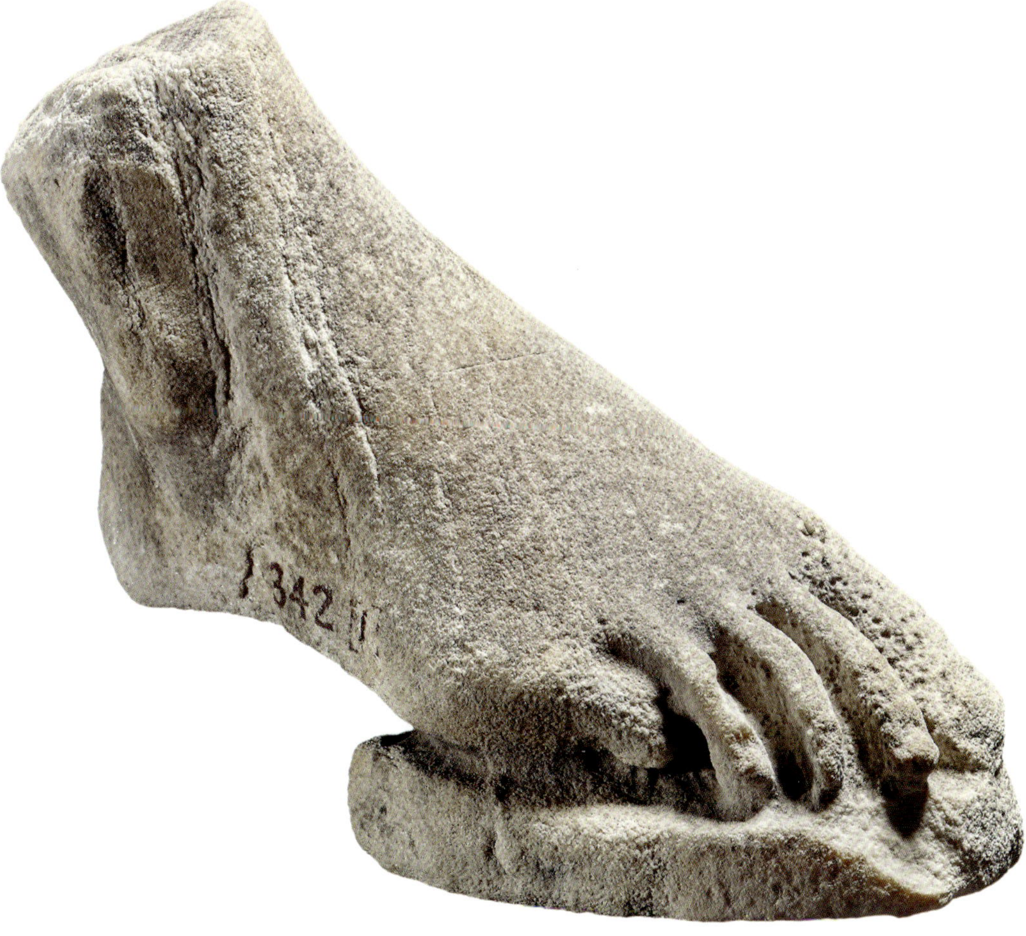

35
Fragment of a foot from South Metope XII of the Parthenon
Greek
About 447–438 BC
Marble
H 16 cm, W 18 cm, D 9 cm
British Museum, 1816,0610.403

At the end of his life, Rodin modelled these clay figures to illustrate the two major lessons he had learnt from tradition – from antiquity in his formative years, then from Michelangelo in the 1870s, and once more from antiquity in the 1890s. In this exercise he wanted to demonstrate the importance of planes in the execution of sculpture, something he used in his own work. The Michelangelo figure (Cat. 37), constructed on just two planes for the upper and lower parts of the body, with one arm hanging downwards, the other held out horizontally, head bowed, reflects a world of shadow and introspection. The figure of antiquity (Cat. 36) presents on four 'alternately opposed' planes the soft undulation of an exposed body, a happy vision of an antiquity of light and joy. This understanding would illuminate the last twenty years of the sculptor's life.

These two figures also illustrate his passion for working in clay and his modelling technique.

OPPOSITE LEFT
36
Auguste Rodin
Greek Sculpture
1912
Terracotta
H 38.8 cm, W 16 cm, D 14.5 cm
Musée Rodin, S. 222
Inscribed 'A mon illustre ami Hanotaux A. Rodin'
Made at Gabriel Hanotaux's house in Roquebrune-Cap-Martin on 22 January 1912 and purchased by the Musée Rodin from Gabriel Hanotaux in 1949

OPPOSITE RIGHT
37
Auguste Rodin
Sculpture of the Renaissance
1912
Terracotta
H 33.5 cm, W 17.5 cm, D 14.5 cm
Musée Rodin, S. 223
Inscribed 'Che mon ami Hanotaux A. Rodin'
Made at Gabriel Hanotaux's house in Roquebrune-Cap-Martin on 22 January 1912 and purchased by the Musée Rodin from Gabriel Hanotaux in 1949

The clay figure was taking shape. Rodin's hands were moving to and fro, superimposing bits of clay, moulding them in his large palms without any loss of movement. Then his thumb and his fingers played their part, forming a thigh with a single squeeze, making a hip stick out, tilting a shoulder, turning the head.... I have never seen anyone work so fast. Evidently sureness of mind and eye endow the hands of great artists with an ease comparable to the skill of the most marvellous jugglers.

Auguste Rodin, *Art: Conversations with Paul Gsell*, 1911

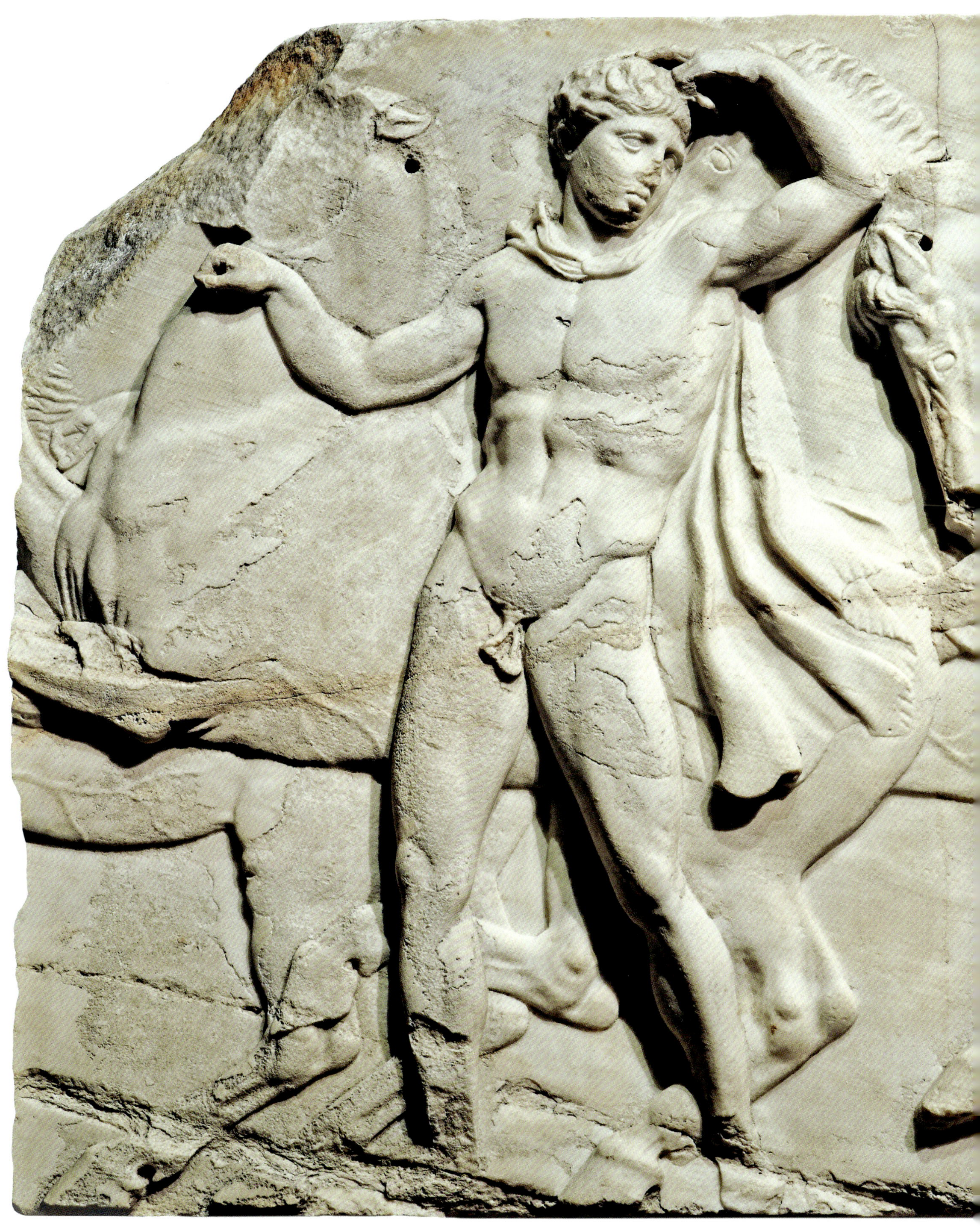

The Kiss is inspired by an episode in Dante's *Divine Comedy*, in which an adulterous couple, Paolo and Francesca, lost in a moment of reckless passion, are about to be discovered and killed by the woman's husband, Paolo's brother. However, it soon shed its literary reference to become an image of an archetypal kiss. The two figures melt into one another – anonymous and passionate. Their whole bodies express an irresistible attraction to each other. The privacy of the moment, the nakedness of their mutual desire, their disregard for the danger of being found out, cast the viewer into the role of voyeur. The emotional charge of Rodin's *The Kiss* is intensified by virtue of the fact that both figures shown in this plaster cast had been carved from the same block of stone (*ex uno lapide*).

The closeness of the two figures from the Parthenon (Cat. 41) is similarly heightened by their being cut from one block of pentelic marble. Warm flesh and flowing drapery are conjured from cold, hard marble. The figures seem to melt into each other in a remarkable study of intimacy. They may be divine sisters or mother and daughter, but their bodies are eroticized by the clinging drapery.

Looking at them through Rodin's eyes, the loss of the heads intensifies the power of the body to express emotion and narrative. Besides, to judge from the pedimental heads that do survive, there was no great variety of facial expression from one figure to the next. In Rodin's *The Kiss* similarly it is the body that gives expression to the figures while the composition does not make the faces easily visible to the spectator, and in any case the features are not fully defined.

Plaster, a compound of gypsum and water, has been used since Graeco-Roman times for the production and reproduction of sculpture. The Parthenon sculptures themselves were probably first modelled in clay (*typos*), which was cast in plaster in order to preserve the form and then copied in marble. White plaster is often regarded today as an inferior material associated with mere replicas of a sculptor's work. In the nineteenth century, however, it was common for sculptors to exhibit new work as white plaster casts. If the work was successful and attracted a buyer it might then be copied in marble or cast in bronze.

This large-scale plaster version of *The Kiss* has been chosen here because it is the one that Rodin kept by him throughout his life. It is a cast of the first marble version of *The Kiss*, which had been commissioned by the French state in 1888 and which had been carved after a smaller model. It therefore became the version from which others were copied, and which Rodin would display in exhibitions.

40
Auguste Rodin
The Kiss, large version
1888–1898
Plaster; cast from marble
after 1898
H 184 cm, W 112 cm, D 110 cm
Musée Rodin, S. 174
Rodin donation, 1916

… their [the Fates] pose is so serene, so majestic, that they seem to participate in something grand that we do not see. Over them reigns, in effect, the great mystery: immaterial, eternal Reason obeyed by all Nature.

Auguste Rodin, *Art: Conversations with Paul Gsell*, 1911

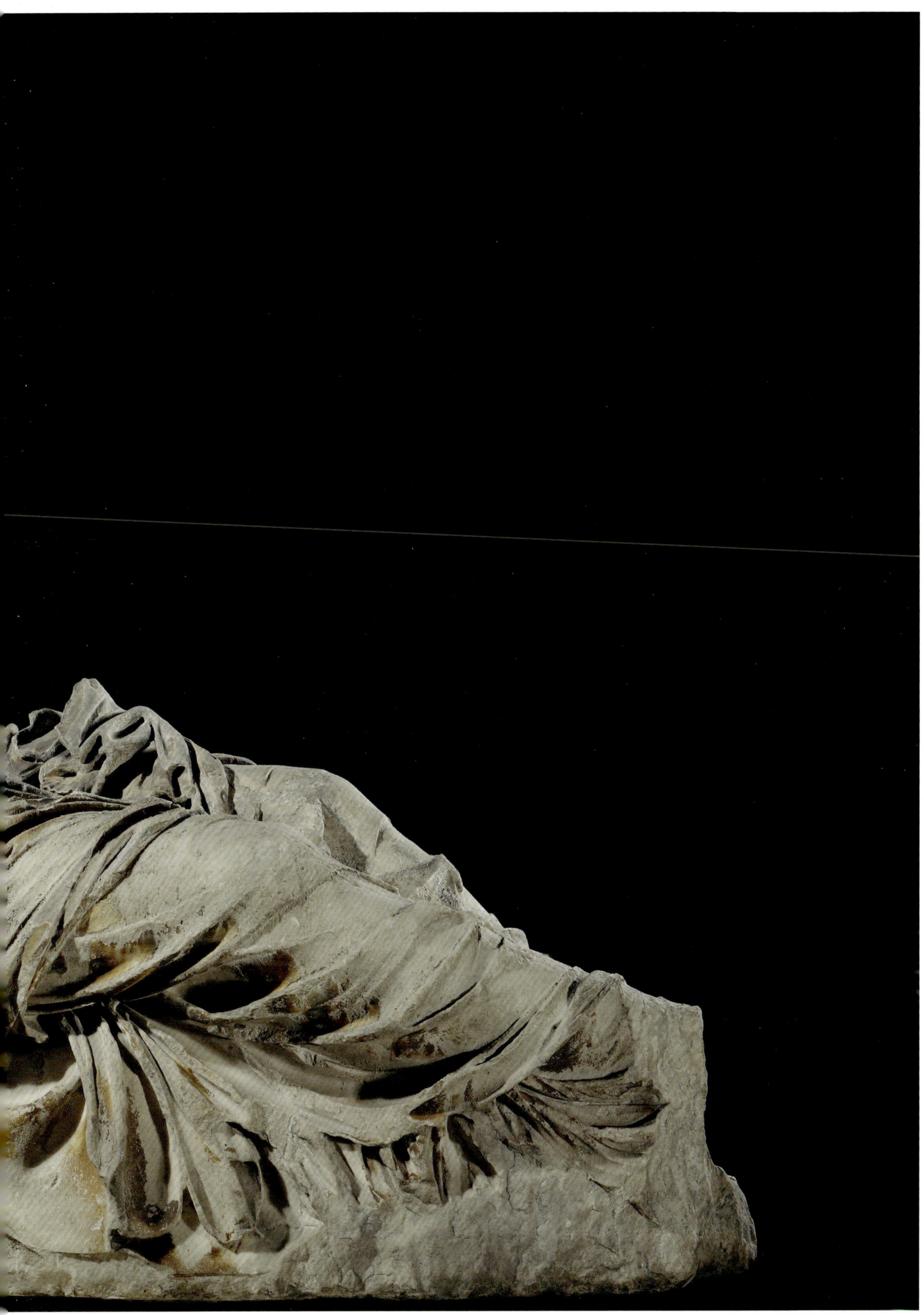

41
Goddesses in diaphanous drapery
Figures L and M from the East Pediment of the Parthenon
Greek
About 438–432 BC
Marble
H 123 cm, W 233 cm, D 98 cm
British Museum, 1816,0610.97

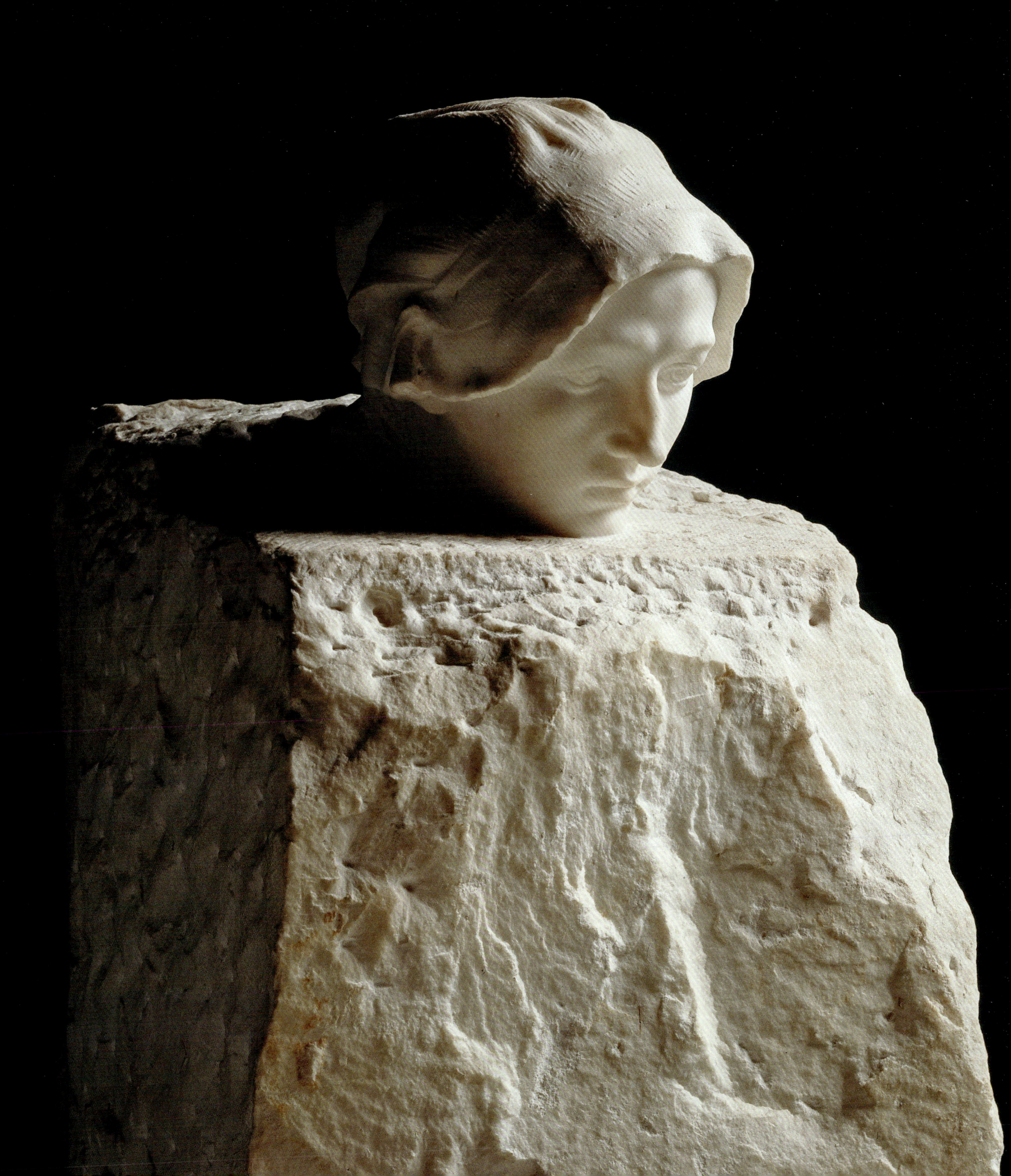

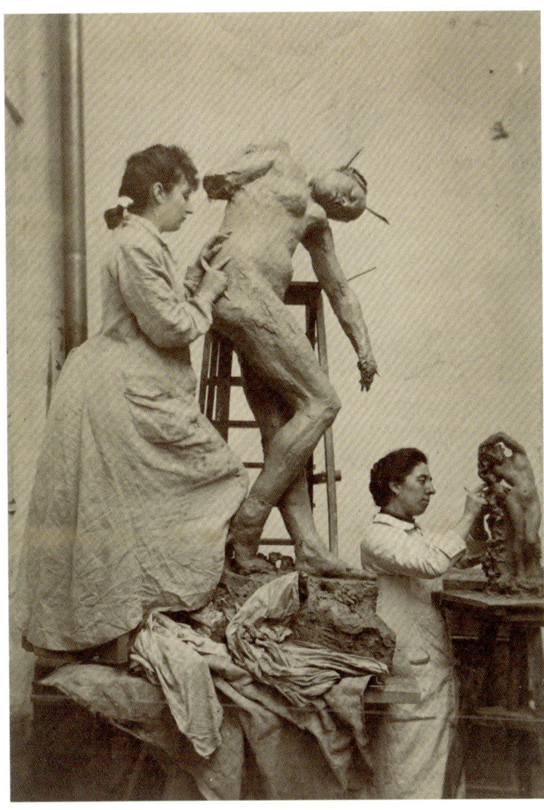
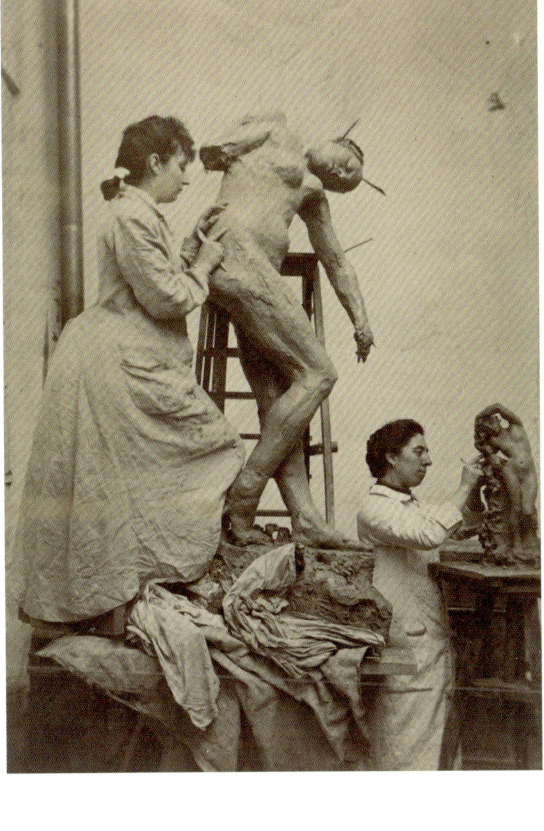

Fig. 13
William Elborne (1858–1952)
Camille Claudel and Jessie Lipscomb sculpting
1887
Albumen print
H 15.2 cm, W 9.8 cm
Musée Rodin, Ph. 1773
Rodin Donation, 1916

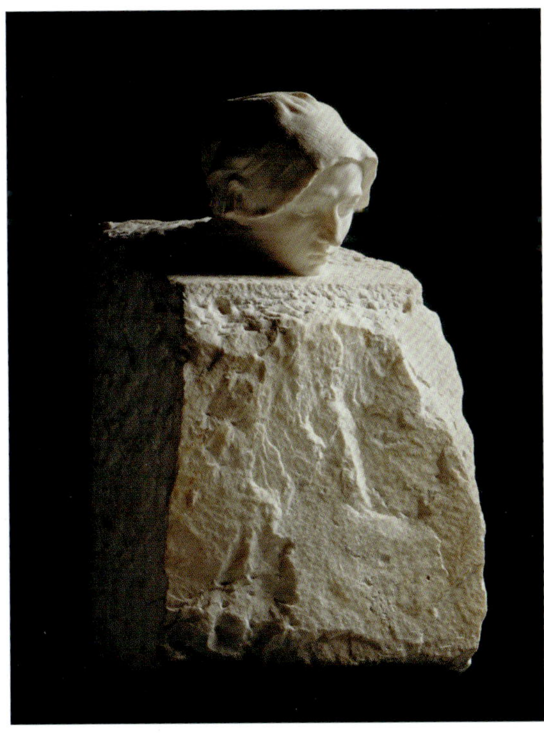

42
Auguste Rodin
Thought
About 1895
Marble; carved by Victor Peter
H 74.2 cm, W 43.5 cm, D 46.1 cm
Musée d'Orsay, RF 4065, LUX 155, S 1003

The head emerging from a rough-worked block of stone is modelled on that of the sculptor Camille Claudel (1864–1943), who was also Rodin's protégée, studio assistant and lover. In a post-Freudian age, it would be tempting to see the work as a symbolic commentary on the increasingly stormy nature of their relationship. The meaning of Rodin's title is obscure. When first carved, this portrait was called *Thought Emerging from Matter*. It could perhaps be a reference to the ancient idea that the subject of a sculpture was locked into the raw, unworked stone and that artists were intuitively possessed of an inner vision of it, so that the process of creation was one of copying what was already in their mind. In this context we can think of the unfinished slaves of Michelangelo, and further back still of the reputation of Pheidias for the force of his imagination.

Interestingly, *Thought* is one of the sculptures on which Rodin instructed his carver to show the series of tool marks used to achieve the final surface. As in *The Kiss*, so with *Thought*, we see the stone riven, then roughly tooled with a hammer and point, and then chiselled with a claw or flat chisel, then rasped and finally polished. Whatever the interpretation of this and other comparable works, it demonstrates the unique daring of Rodin and places him in the vanguard of the origins of modernism.

The monument

None of the drama of Life remained unexplored by this earnest, concentrated worker.... Here [*The Gates of Hell*] was life, a thousand-fold in every moment, in longing and sorrow, in madness and fear, in loss and gain. Here was desire immeasurable, thirst so great that all the waters of the world dried in it like a single drop...

Rainer Maria Rilke, *Auguste Rodin*, 1902

When Rodin arrived in London in 1881 he had just received his first major commission from the French state: monumental gates for a new decorative arts museum in Paris. Rodin's ambitious *The Gates of Hell*, over six metres high, stand in a great French tradition of monumentality in art, architecture and cityscape. Exploring the darker realms of his psyche, Rodin found his subjects in Dante's *Divine Comedy* and Baudelaire's *The Flowers of Evil* (*Les Fleurs du Mal*). The project for the new museum failed to materialize, but *The Gates* became a source of inspiration for Rodin for the rest of his life.

From an early stage Rodin began to remove many of the figures from *The Gates* and constantly re-invented them, changing their scale and view point, to make new monuments, fragments and assemblages. Just as the Parthenon sculptures began life as architectural ornament and were subsequently converted into art objects by their removal, so *The Gates* shed many of its sculptures. Rodin became the archaeologist of his own creation, turning figures such as *The Kiss* (Cat. 40) and *The Thinker* (Cat. 48) into monumental independent works of art.

The process of enlargement increased the evocative power of Rodin's works. They gained in force what they lost in acuteness and vigour of the modelling and became 'ancient', like Greek sculptures eroded by time. Plutarch, writing around AD 100, said of the works of Perikles' day that they had about them a bloom of youth and yet they were at the same time venerable (*archaios*).

To Rodin, a building was comparable to a living body – it came into being, it grew, it flourished and then the processes of decay set in, and eventually it melted back into the landscape. This lifecycle, Rodin thought, should be allowed to take its course without interruption by would-be restorers. This was true both of the cathedrals of France, about which he wrote, and the Parthenon – he campaigned against the general restoration of the Parthenon after an earthquake in 1894 had made parts of the building unstable. Although he never saw the original, for Rodin the Parthenon was an eternal and inviolable monument. It was the product of his imagination as much as it was a part of reality.

Fig. 14
Pierre Choumoff (1872–1936)
Rodin with his cousin Henriette Coltat in front of *The Gates of Hell*
1917
Gelatin silver print
H 22.3 cm, W 17.3 cm
Musée Rodin, Ph. 823

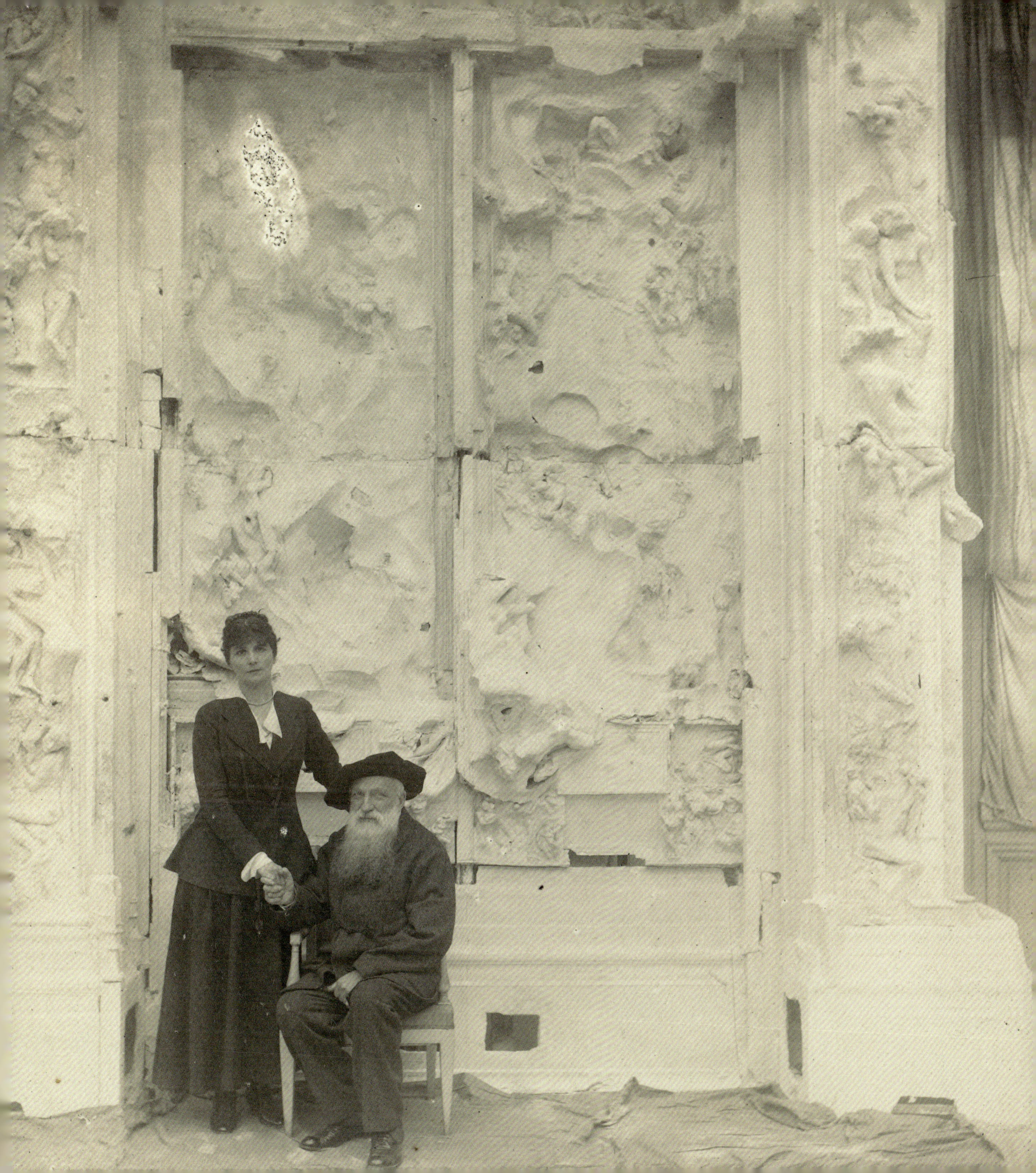

Fig. 15
Auguste Rodin
The Gates of Hell
1917
Plaster
H 635 cm, W 400 cm, D 94 cm
Musée d'Orsay, DO 1986 4, S 2450

On *The Gates of Hell* the figures, ranging from very low relief to very high relief, appear to emerge from the profiles of the mouldings and the framework of the architecture. *The Gates of Hell* is equivalent to the temple of the Parthenon in providing form and meaning to relief and freestanding sculpture alike.

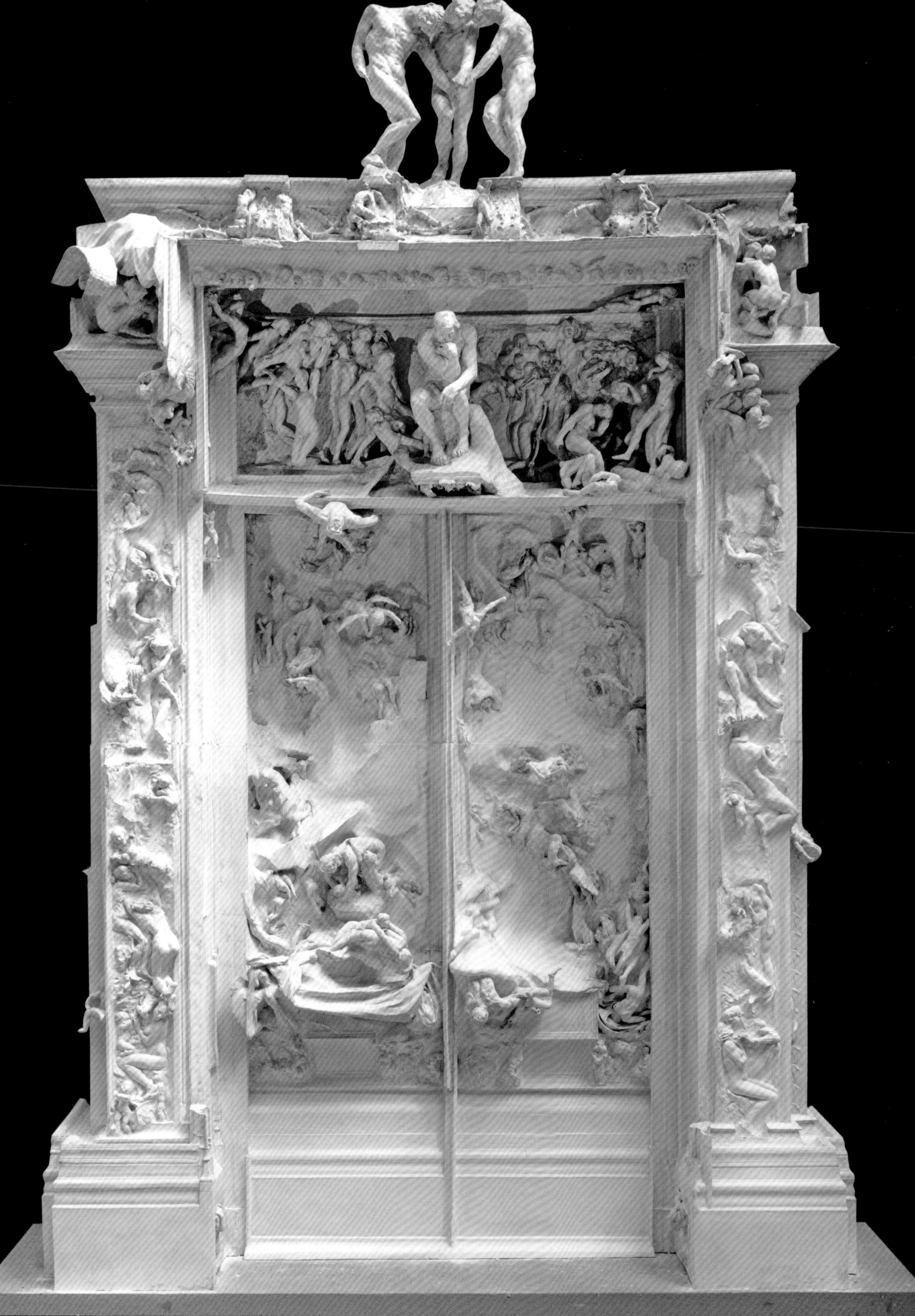

The relief *The Arrival in Hell*, so named by the critic and writer Octave Mirbeau, records one of the early states of part of the tympanum of *The Gates of Hell*, known from photographs taken in April 1887. Rodin returned to the composition of the tympanum in 1888–1889 (Cat. 43), using the existing relief background, with, on the left, the arrival in hell and, on the right, the judgment of the damned, adding figures such as *Kneeling Female Faun*, *Crouching Woman* and *Standing Female Faun*. With *The Gates* Rodin explored scenic composition within a limited architectural framework, playing with the succession of figures from left to right and in depth with increasingly projecting superimposed bodies. This interaction between bodies and architectural framing could be compared with that of the Parthenon. There, for example, the central scene of the East Frieze, with its handling of the *peplos* (the sacred robe of Athena), was cleverly framed by the pair of gods seated on either side. At the same time, the outer columns served to frame the composition, isolating and promoting the importance of this culminating episode of the frieze.

Fig. 16
Auguste Rodin
The Arrival in Hell, fragment of the tympanum of *The Gates of Hell*
1882–1885
Plaster (around 1917)
H 79.5 cm, W 89.5 cm, D 27 cm
Musée Rodin, S. 2733
Rodin donation, 1916

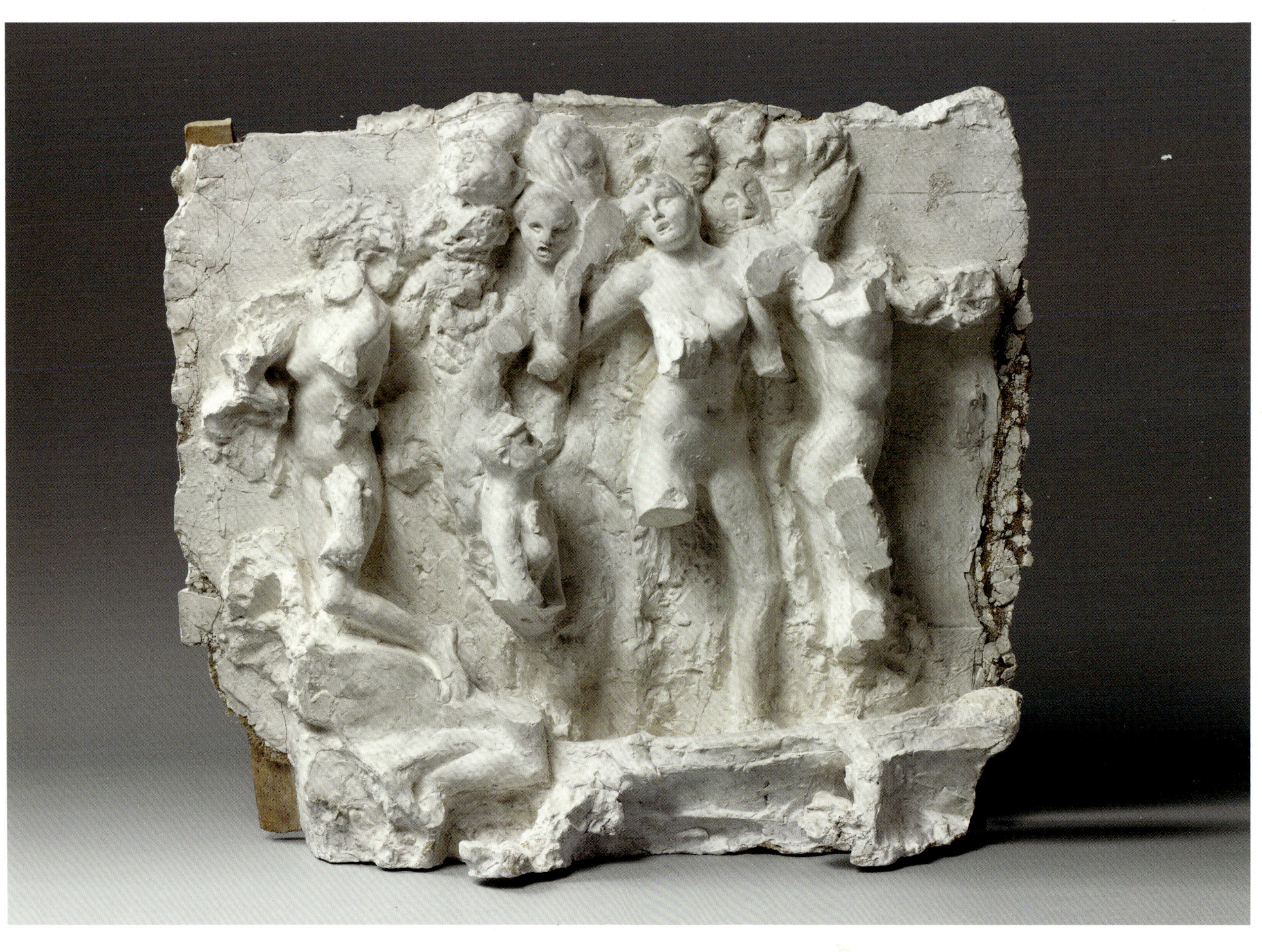

43
Auguste Rodin
Fragment of the tympanum
of *The Gates of Hell*
1887–1889
Plaster (around 1917)
H 128.5 cm, W 258 cm, D 86 cm
Musée Rodin, S. 5729

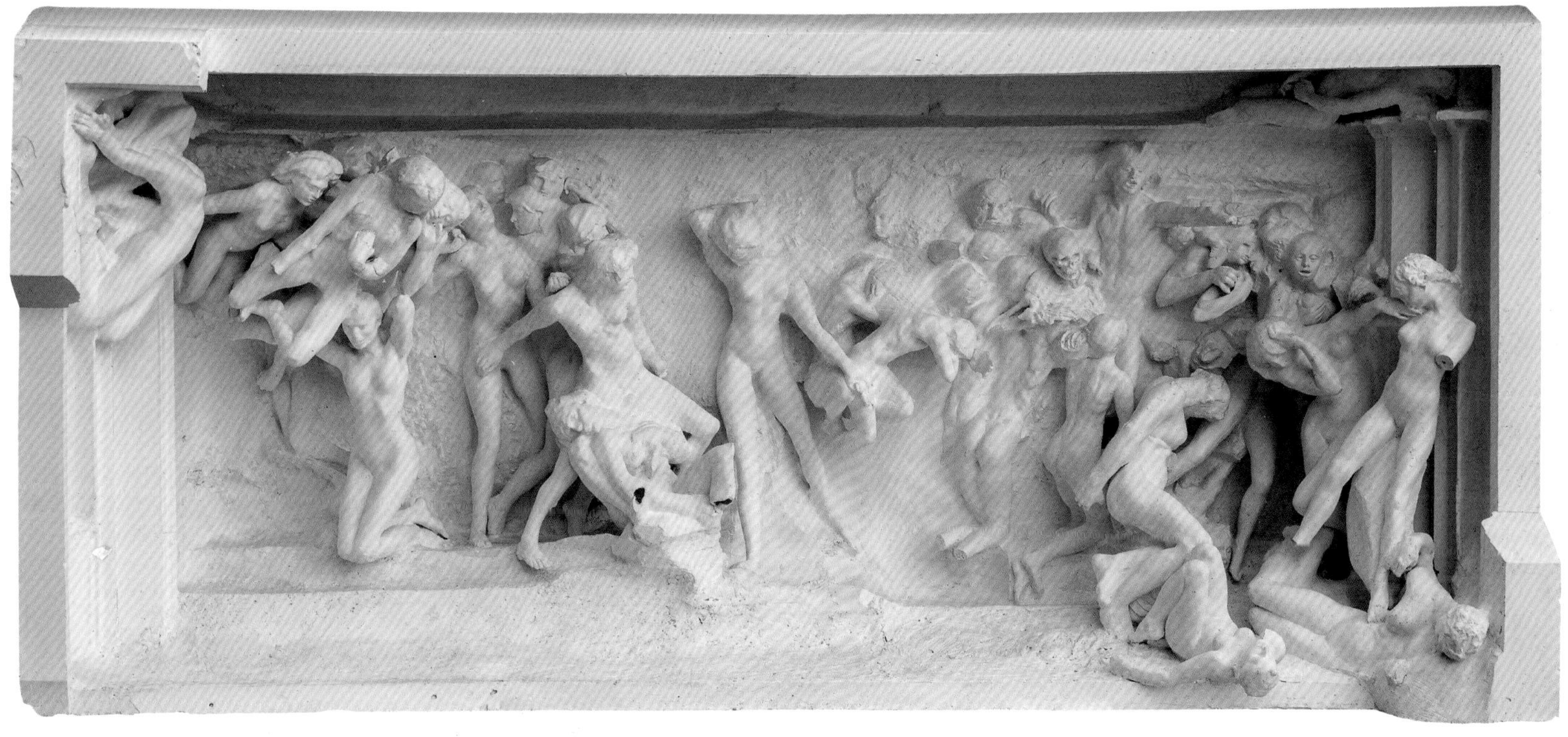

Rodin believed that a cast of an individual element could express *The Gates of Hell* in its entirety, just as a single fragment of the Parthenon had the power to evoke the whole temple. These two plaster casts from *The Gates* were made around 1917 for display in the future Rodin museum at eye level, in the same way that the Parthenon fragments were exhibited in the British Museum. This would enable visitors to see close up figures designed to be incorporated in the upper section of the work. In the first group we can recognize *I Am Beautiful*, composed of a combination of *Crouching Woman* and *Falling Man*, illustrating Baudelaire's poem 'Beauty' from *The Flowers of Evil*:

I am beautiful, O mortals, as a dream carved in stone,
And my breast, on which every man has bruised himself in his turn,
Is designed to inspire in the poet a love
As eternal and silent as matter itself

To each figure, Rodin added a few decorative elements that served to combine and thus integrate the bodies into the architecture of the moulding. We cannot now tell whether the moulding engendered the figure or vice versa. For *Falling Winged Spirit*, Rodin adapted Andromeda's body from *The Gates*, adding wings and foliage to attach the body to the projecting elements.

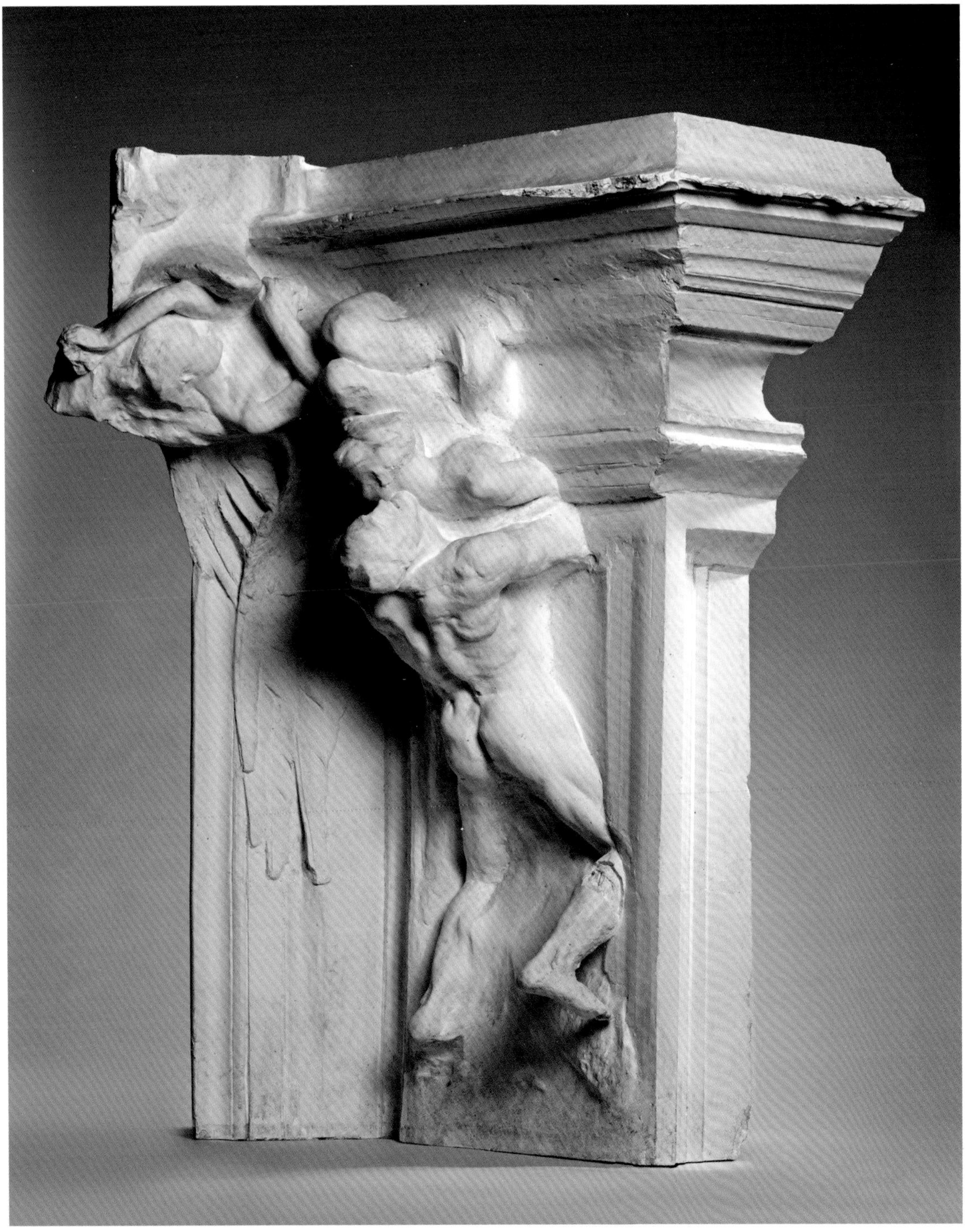

44
Auguste Rodin
I Am Beautiful, fragment of the right pilaster of *The Gates of Hell*
About 1888–1889
Plaster (around 1917)
H 100.4 cm, W 69.8 cm, D 61.5 cm
Musée Rodin, S. 5779
Rodin donation, 1916

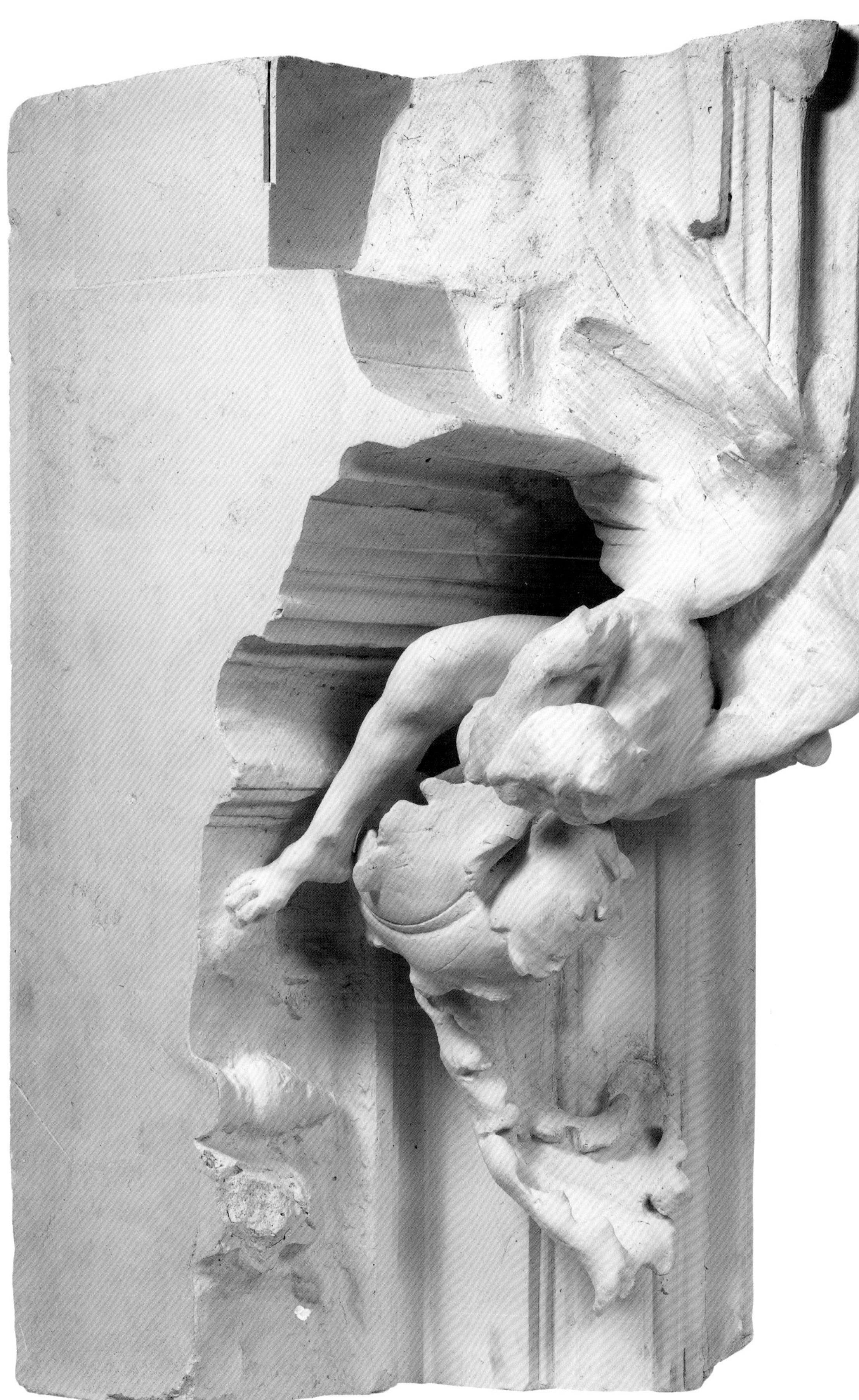

45
Auguste Rodin
Falling Winged Spirit, part above the left pilaster of *The Gates of Hell*
1887–1890
Plaster (around 1917)
H 87 cm, W 33.5 cm, D 58 cm
Musée Rodin, S. 5789
Rodin donation, 1916

Alongside his sculpted work, Rodin continually explored motifs of moulding in his drawings, from his early work on *The Gates of Hell* right to the end of his life, through countless sketches of cathedrals in France. As with his modelled fragments, the human body – in particular the female body – melds into the lines of the moulding, consisting of curves and counter-curves. A legacy of the Gothic and of the Renaissance, the motif of moulding becomes a unit of measure for the sculptor.

The five drawings shown here were collected by Rodin into different albums: Album XXII for Figs 18 and 19, Album XXIV for Figs 17 and 20, and Album XXVI for Cat. 46; these albums were dismantled in February 1933. Close examination of technique is enlightening about the artist's intentions. In Fig. 17, the outline of the figure drawn from life is repeated in pencil slightly to the left, in a schematic way, and with lines added to integrate it into the moulding. This schematization is repeated in pen in drawing Fig. 18, particularly the feet. In another drawing, Fig. 19, Rodin added horizontal lines across the sheet and hatching on the right, as well as strengthening the lines of the initial sketch, to bring out the volume of the figure.

In Cat. 46, the figure drawn freely on the reverse of the sheet is then traced through the transparency of the paper on to the front using a bold line that omits the interior details and the perspective. Lines that echo contours of the body and decorative elements suggestive of architecture are then added. The annotation 'higher up' and the repeated detail of the left arm of the female body seen in foreshortened perspective in Fig. 20 reveal clear signs of changes of mind by Rodin and his further exploration of details that occurred to him during the course of the drawing.

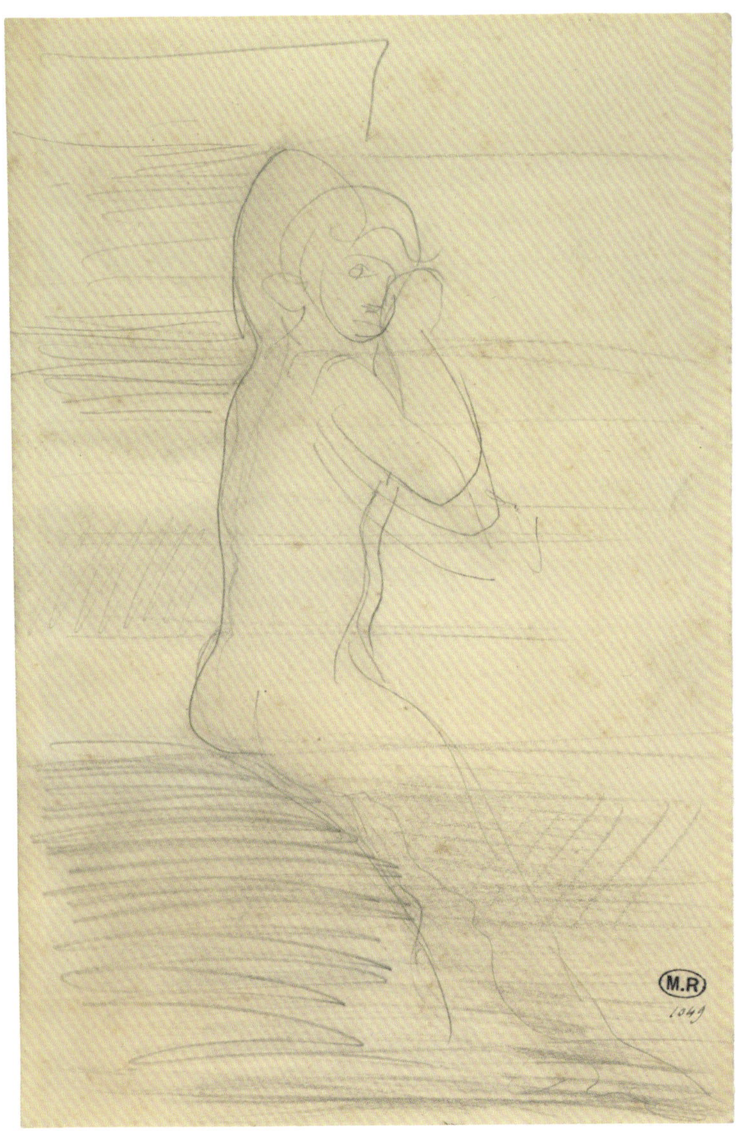

Fig. 17
Auguste Rodin
Study of a seated female nude, with vertical lines
About 1900
Graphite with stump on paper vellum
H 31 cm, W 20 cm
Musée Rodin, D. 1049
Rodin donation, 1916

Fig. 18
Auguste Rodin
Study of a standing female nude, in profile to the right
About 1900
Pen and ink, and graphite with stump on paper vellum
H 31 cm, W 19.9 cm
Musée Rodin, D. 981
Rodin donation, 1916

Fig. 19
Auguste Rodin
Nude woman standing with hands on shoulders
About 1900
Graphite on paper vellum
H 31.5 cm, W 20 cm
Musée Rodin, D. 986
Rodin donation, 1916

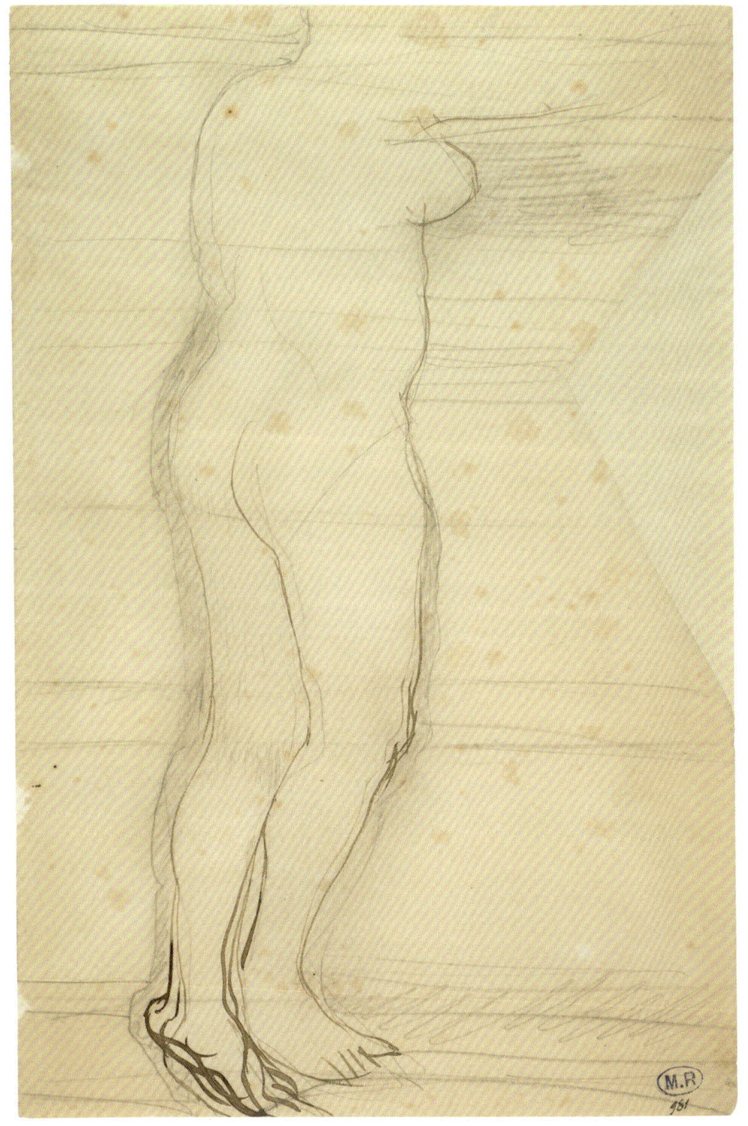

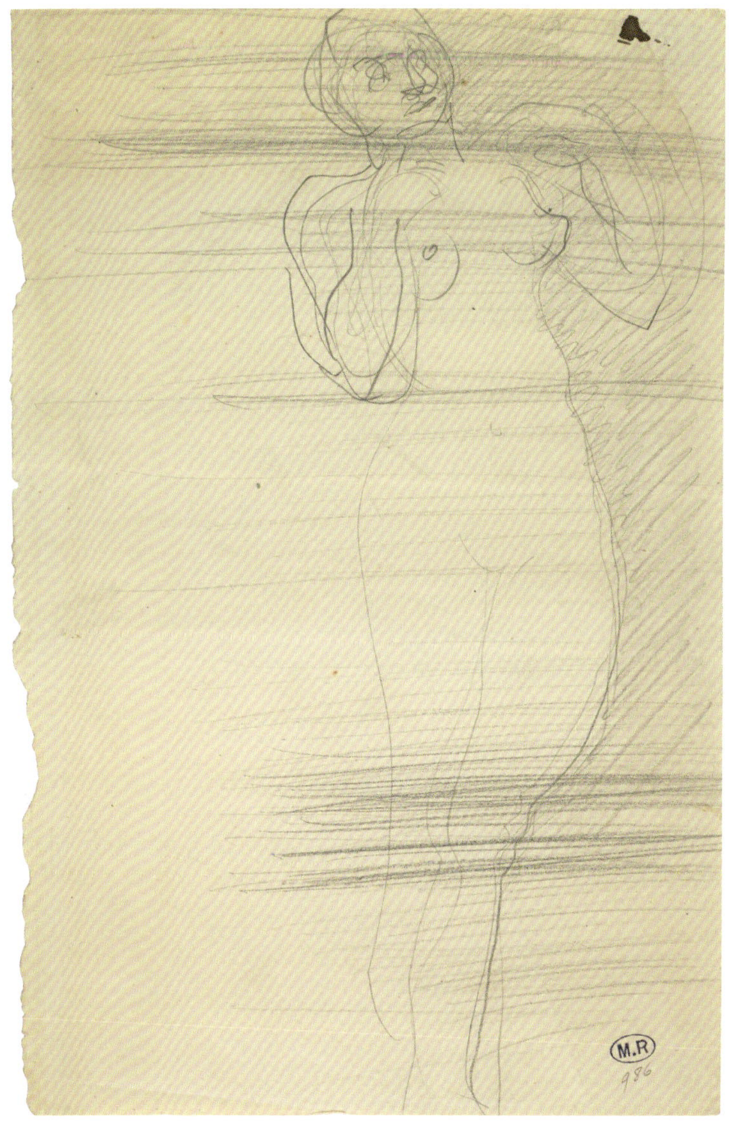

46
Auguste Rodin
Nude woman, in the shape
of an architectural moulding
About 1900
Graphite on paper vellum
H 31.2 cm, W 20.2 cm
Musée Rodin, D. 1401
Rodin donation, 1916

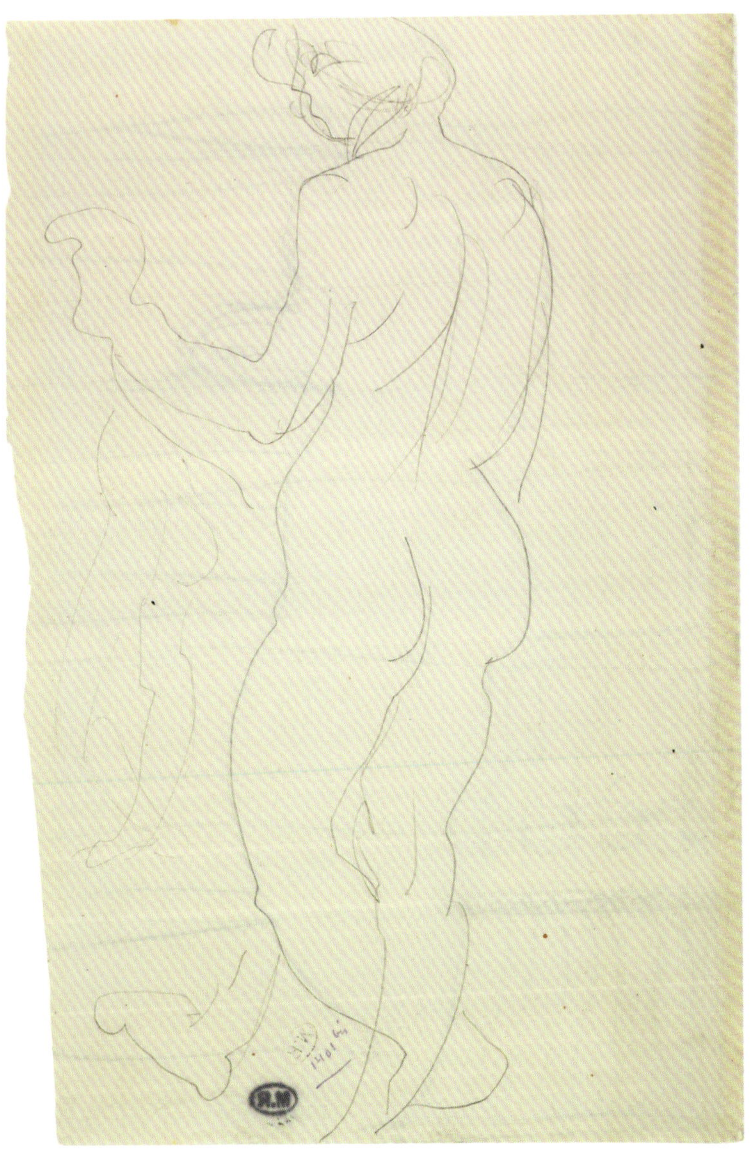

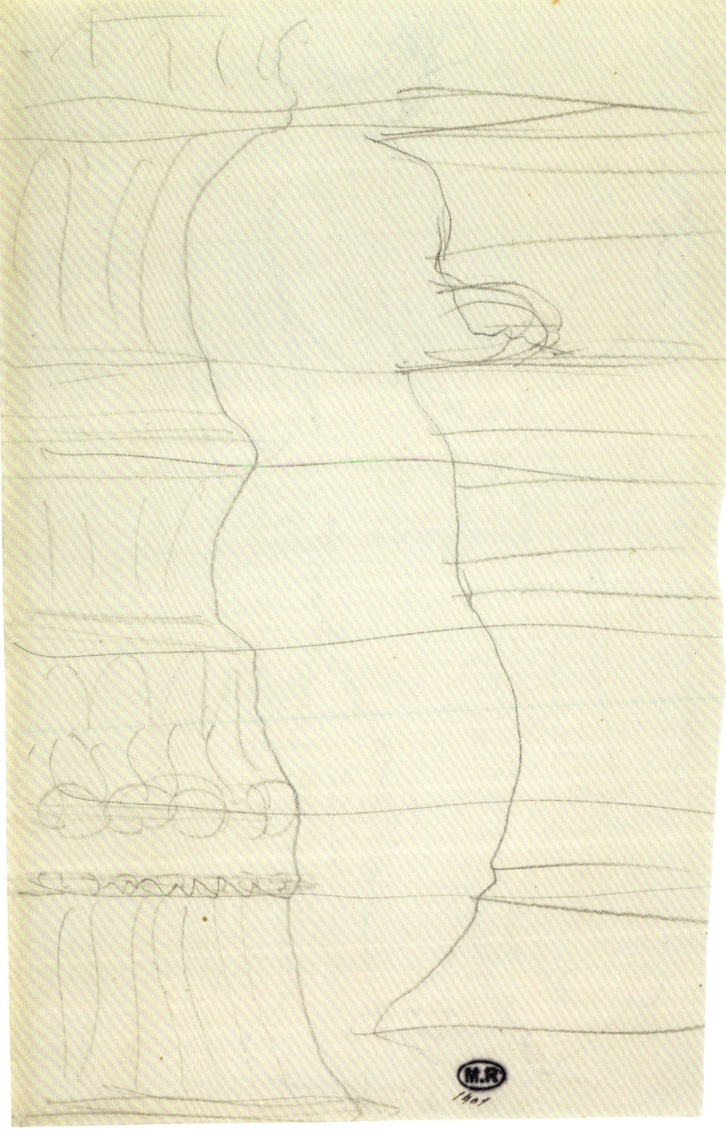

Fig. 20
Auguste Rodin
Nude woman with feet crossed, stretching
About 1900
Graphite on paper vellum
H 31 cm, W 20.3 cm
Musée Rodin, D. 1055
Rodin donation, 1916

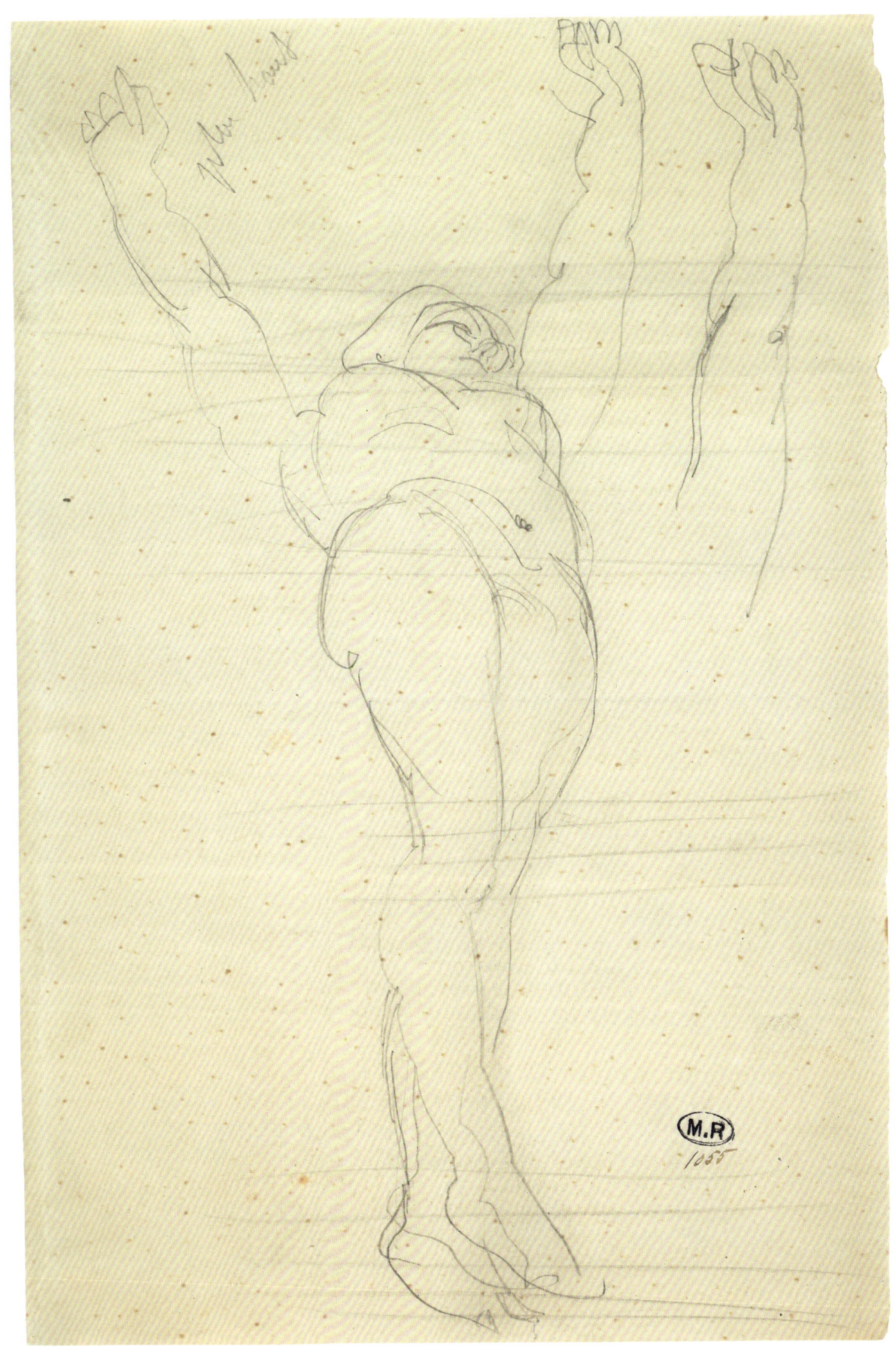

… set within the quiet, enclosed space, is the figure of the *Thinker*, the man who sees the whole immensity and all the terrors of this spectacle because he thinks it. He sits silent and lost in meditation, heavy with visions and thoughts, and, with his whole strength (the strength of a man of action), he thinks. His whole body has become a skull and all the blood in his veins has become brain.

Rainer Maria Rilke, *Auguste Rodin*, 1902

47
Auguste Rodin
The Thinker, on a capital
1881–1882
Plaster
H 87 cm, W 59 cm, D 56 cm
Musée Rodin, S. 2521
Rodin donation, 1916

This first version of *The Thinker*, sitting on a capital, was intended to be placed high up in the middle of the tympanum of *The Gates of Hell*. The figure initially represented Minos, the judge of the damned as described by Dante, then an image of Dante himself contemplating the Underworld, and finally became a portrait of the artist, Rodin, as creator. In 1903 Rodin enlarged the figure to create a monumental work, removing the capital and its association with *The Gates of Hell* to transform it into a universal symbol of a thinking man.

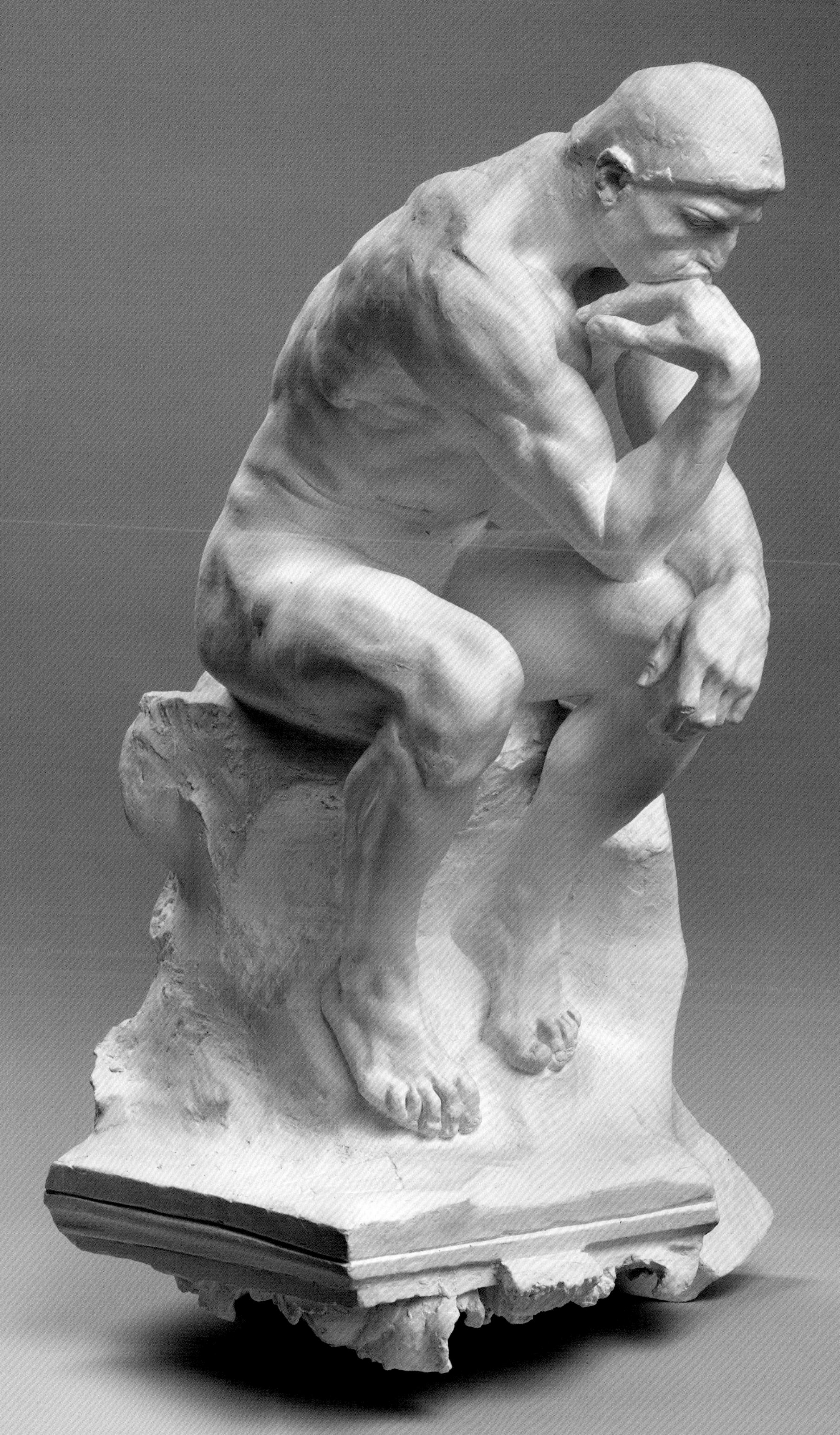

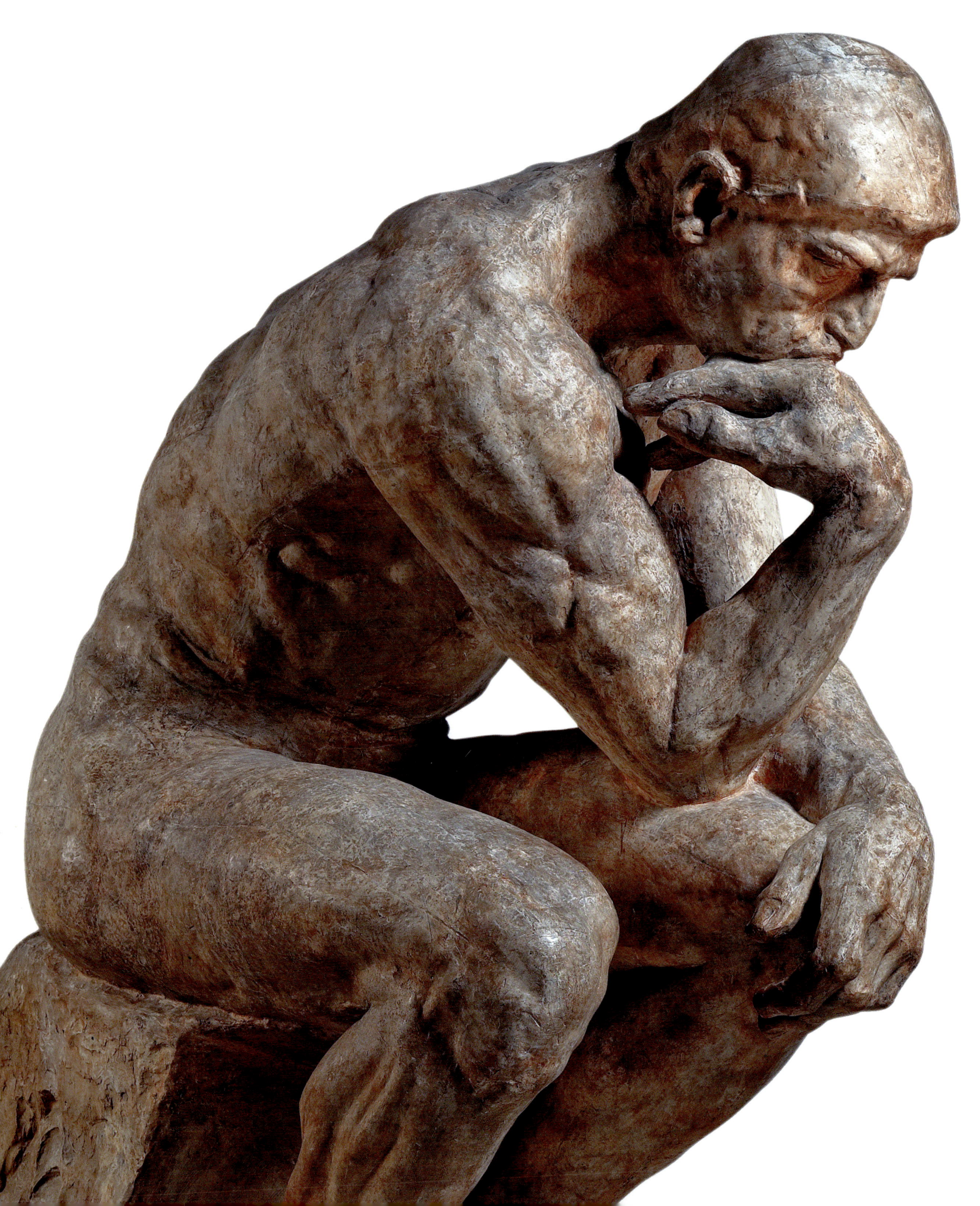

48
Auguste Rodin
The Thinker
1903
Plaster
H 182 cm, W 108 cm, D 141 cm
Musée Rodin, S. 161
Rodin donation, 1916

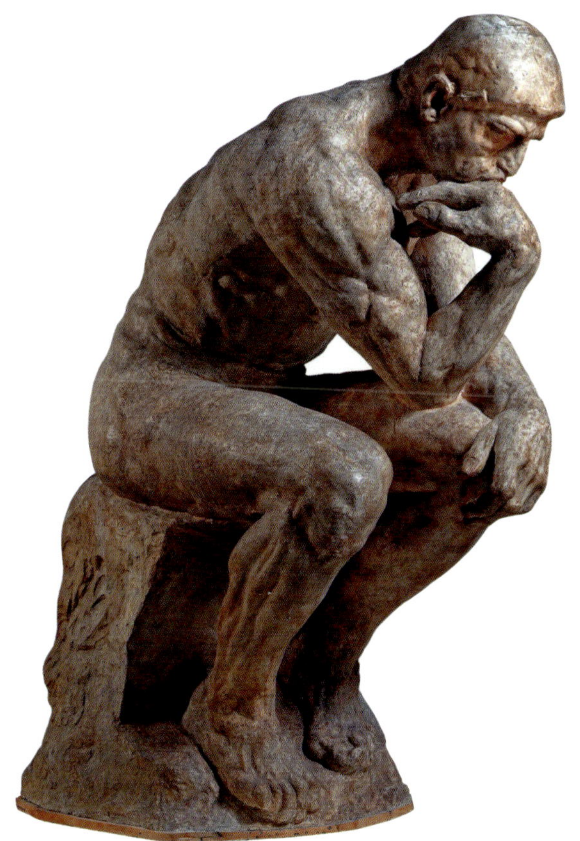

The nudity of the figure gives this sculpture a distinctively Greek appearance. It evokes the idea of an ancient philosopher cultivated in both body and mind, in a culture which regarded athletics and intellectual pursuits as part of the same set of values. But *The Thinker* sits not in quiet reflection; rather, the body is animated by the right elbow resting on the left thigh, which breaks the symmetry and creates a torsion that seems to set the figure in motion. The apparent energy of projected thought concentrated in the head supported on the back of the hand suggests that wisdom does not come as a consequence of mild reflection, but is something that must be striven for. As Rilke said of *The Thinker* 'He sits silent and lost in meditation, heavy with visions and thoughts, and, with his whole strength (the strength of a man of action), he thinks. His whole body has become a skull and all the blood in his veins has become brain.'

This striving is also captured in the forward lean of *The Thinker*, which gives him a greater dynamic than a more sedentary pose would convey. Leaning out and looking down on *The Gates* positions him as a spectator surveying the swirling mass of tortured souls. At the same time, the spectator on the ground looking up would have a better view than if the figure had been seated in a more upright pose.

How should we interpret the gesture of the head resting on the back of the hand rather than on the palm? Is it a representation of *The Thinker* as an active pursuer of truth, or is this a man of sorrows reflecting upon the tragic nature of the human condition, where the head is supported on the back of hand as in a gesture of mourning frequently seen in ancient Athenian grave reliefs – not least in the representation of Demeter mourning the loss of her daughter Persephone in the Parthenon frieze (see Cat. 12)?

The Walking Man was an assemblage combining a torso study modelled in clay in 1880 for *Saint John the Baptist*, which Rodin then found fractured in his studio sometime before 1887, and two legs from the same figure. *The Walking Man* on a column in plaster was shown for the first time at Rodin's exhibition in the Pavillon de l'Alma in 1900 under the name *Study for Saint John the Baptist*. He presented it, like many pieces in this exhibition, perched on a tall column surmounted by a Corinthian capital. It was common practice in antiquity to raise sculptures off the ground and place them on a high plinth to enhance their monumentality. This sometimes took the form of a decorative column, and Rodin would have been familiar with, for example, the Archaic Naxian Sphinx at Delphi, a cast of which he would have seen in the Louvre.

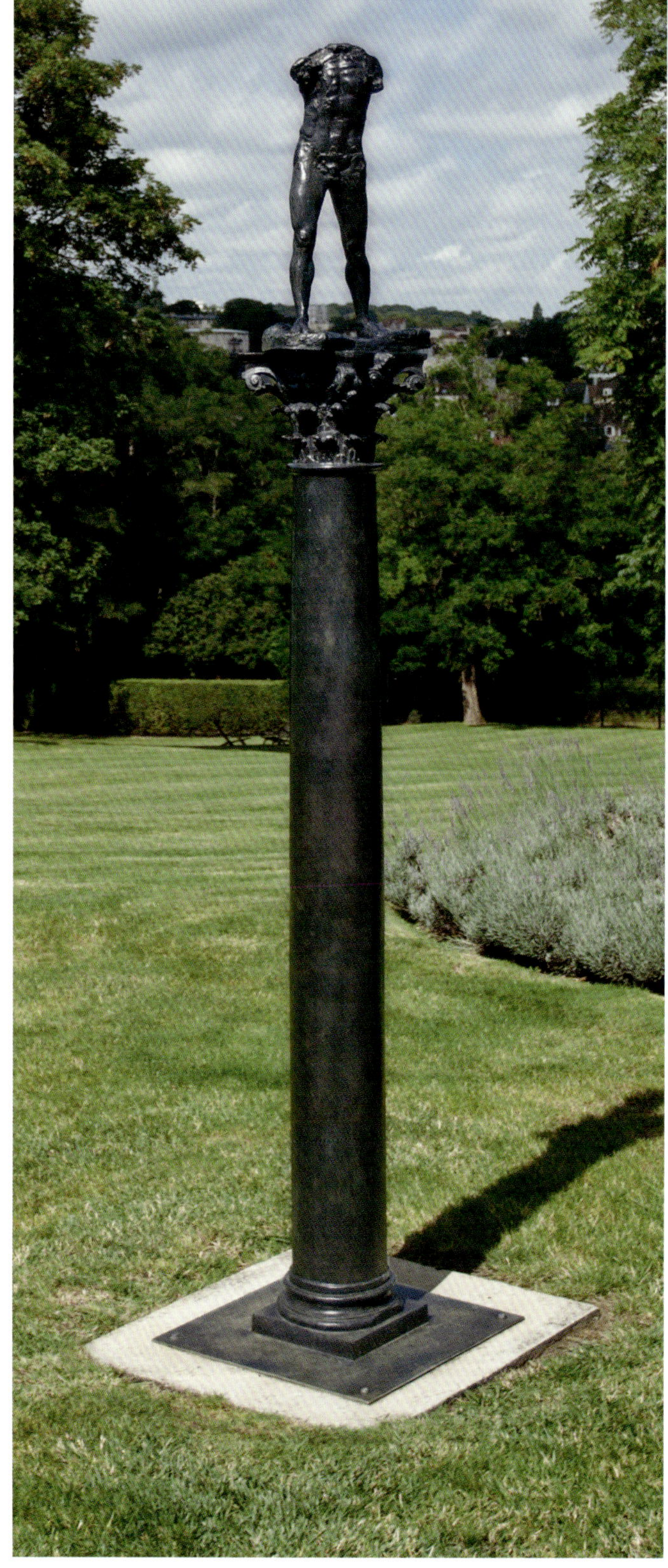

49
Auguste Rodin
The Walking Man, on a column
1900
Bronze; lost-wax cast by Fonderie Coubertin, 1999
H 354 cm, W 60 cm, D 39 cm
Musée Rodin, S. 6719

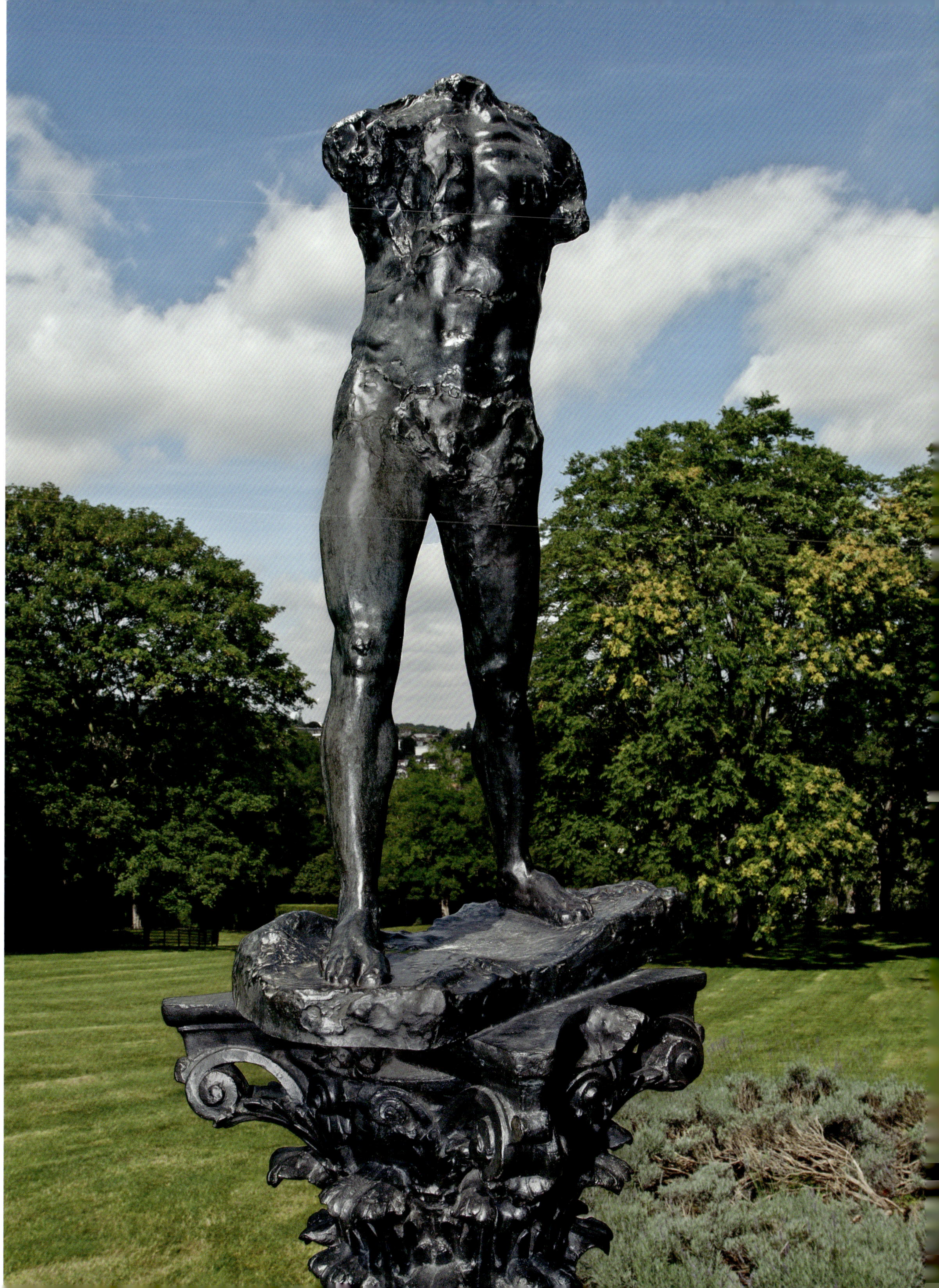

Fig. 21
The so-called Ergastinai
Block VII (figs 49–56) from
the Parthenon East Frieze
Greek
About 438–432 BC
Marble
H 96 cm, W 207 cm, D 12 cm
Louvre MR 825 (Ma 738)

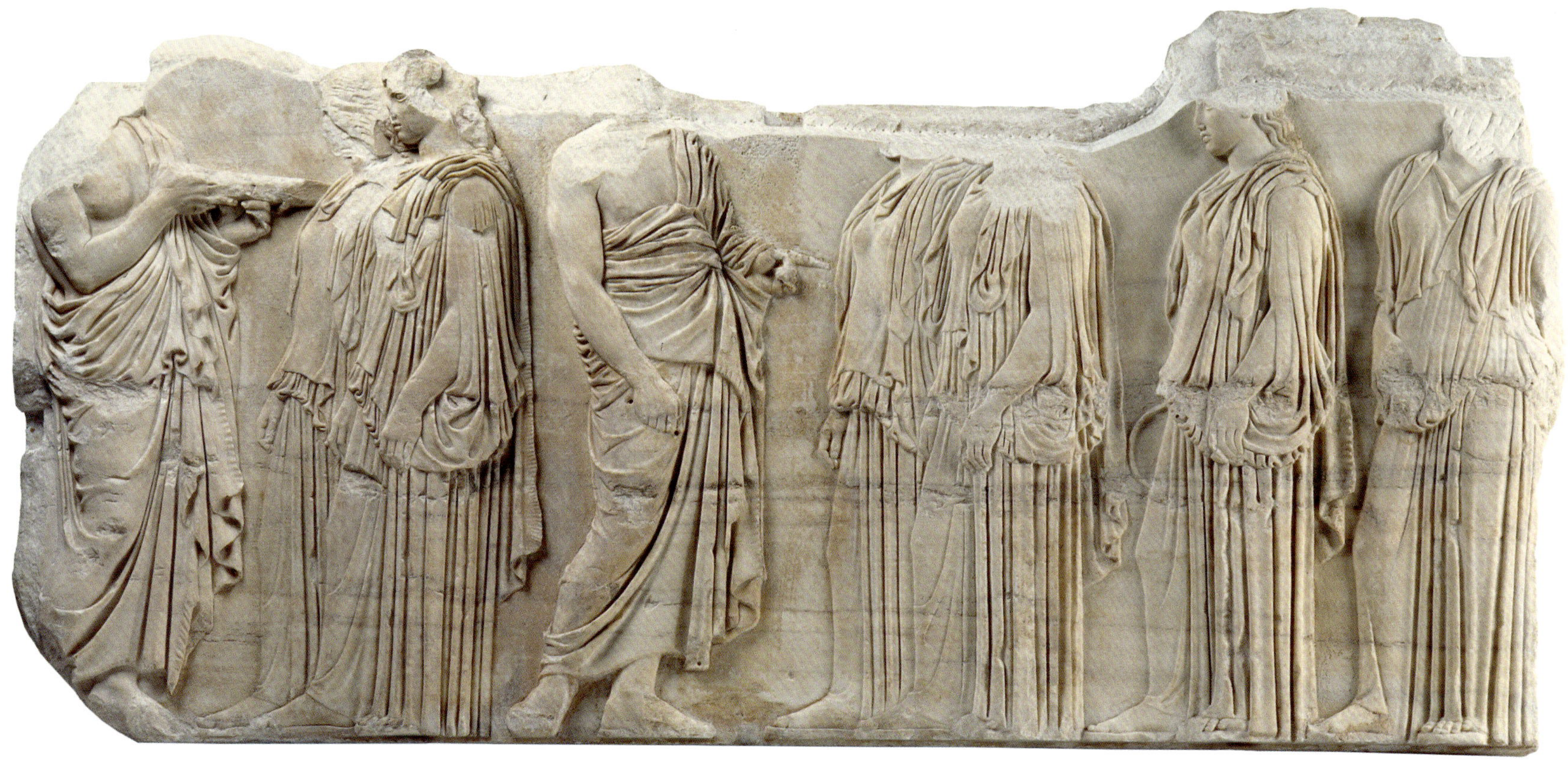

Rodin's tendency to see architecture as a living, organic bodily form calls to mind the treatise by the Roman architect Vitruvius (*c.* 80–70–*c.* 15 BC) in which the ancient Greek orders are gendered, male and female. The elegant shafts of Ionic columns, with their decorative capitals, are represented by slender girls, while the stocky understatement of Doric columns and their capitals are male.

Conversely, instead of architecture becoming body, the body in architectural sculpture could become architecture. An example of this is found in the block of the Parthenon frieze in the Louvre well known to Rodin, since it was acquired in 1801 (Figs 21–22). Here, the girls stand draped in long folds falling to their feet, which seem to echo the fluting of the columns themselves. These tectonic bodies find their fullest expression in the Erechtheion on the north side of the Acropolis, where the roof of the porch is supported by girls who actually serve as columns, or caryatids, with their drapery directly inspired by the girls of the Parthenon frieze.

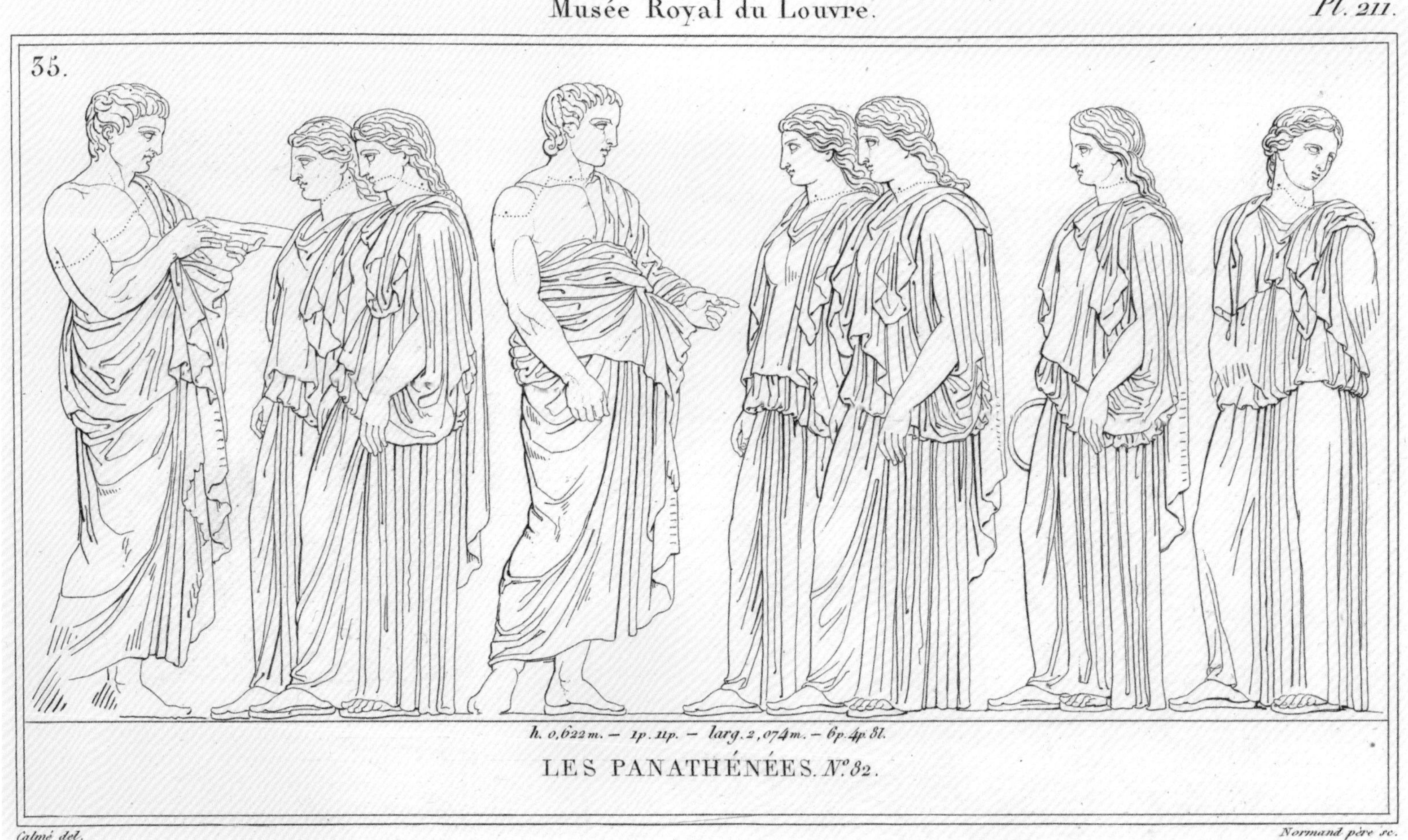

Fig. 22
Outline engraving of the Parthenon East Frieze block VII in the Louvre, showing the so-called Ergastinai with heads restored
Engraved in Comte de Clarac, *Musée de sculpture antique et moderne*, 1828–30, Vol. II, pl. 211

50
The river god Ilissos
Figure A from the West Pediment
of the Parthenon
Greek
About 438–432 BC
Marble
H 81.3 cm, W 189 cm, D 56 cm
British Museum, 1816,0610.99

Rodin would have been fascinated by the original setting of this figure in one corner of the West Pediment of the Parthenon. He himself experimented with modelling comparable figures that might be called pseudo-pedimental. In particular, this reclining figure, thought to have represented the river god Ilissos pulling himself up on to a bank, might have impressed Rodin not only as part of a much larger composition, but also for its truth to nature in rendering a languid, lissom youth and showing an extraordinary understanding of a body in movement. Although no longer complete, the river god appears to move before our gaze and is one of the great miracles of the Parthenon sculptors' ability to transform cold, hard marble into warm, living flesh and then to transform it again from body to an element in nature – water.

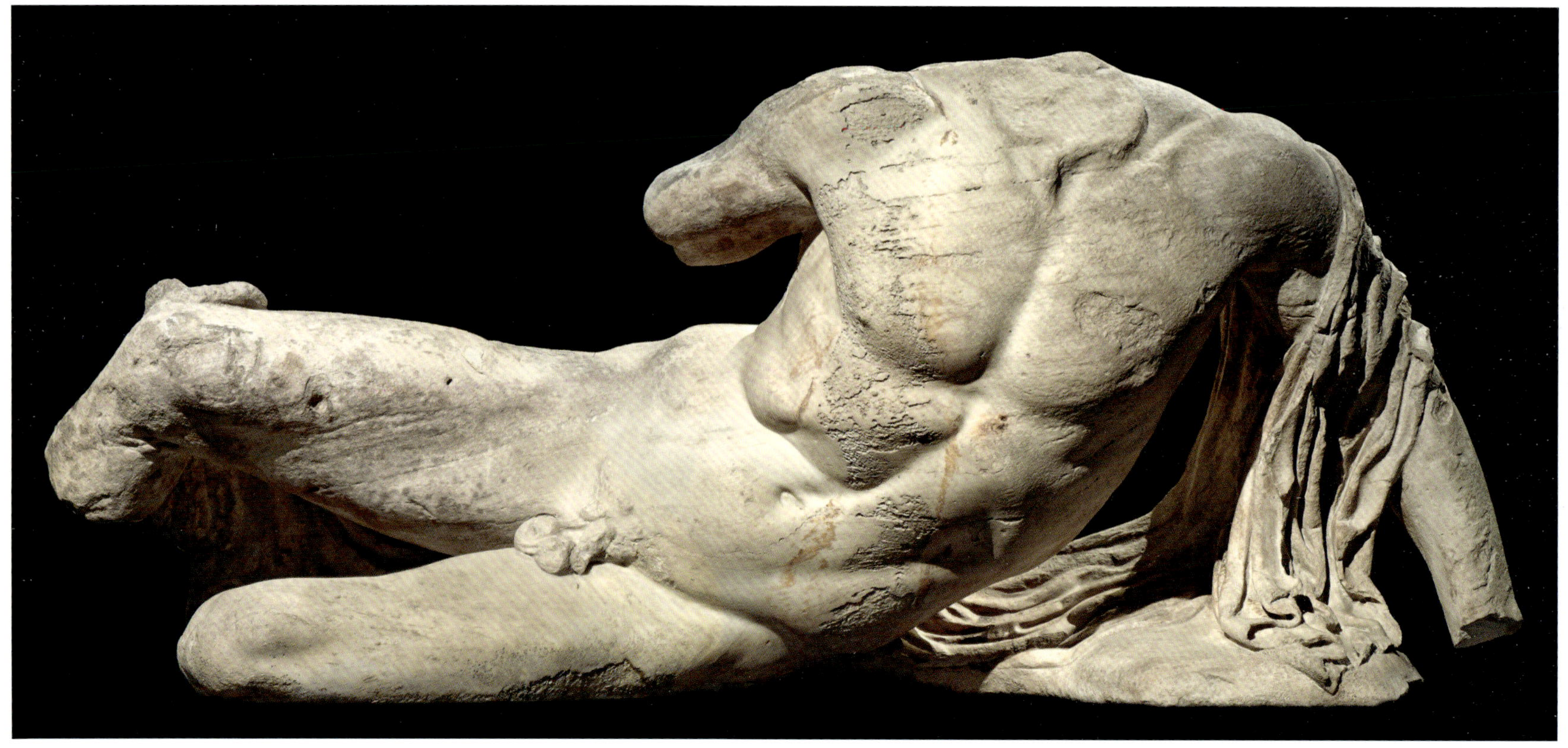

55
Auguste Rodin
The Death of Athens
1902?
Marble; carved by Lucien
or Gaston Schnegg
H 40 cm, W 77 cm, D 40 cm
National Museums, Liverpool,
Walker Art Gallery, Bequeathed
by James Smith, 1923

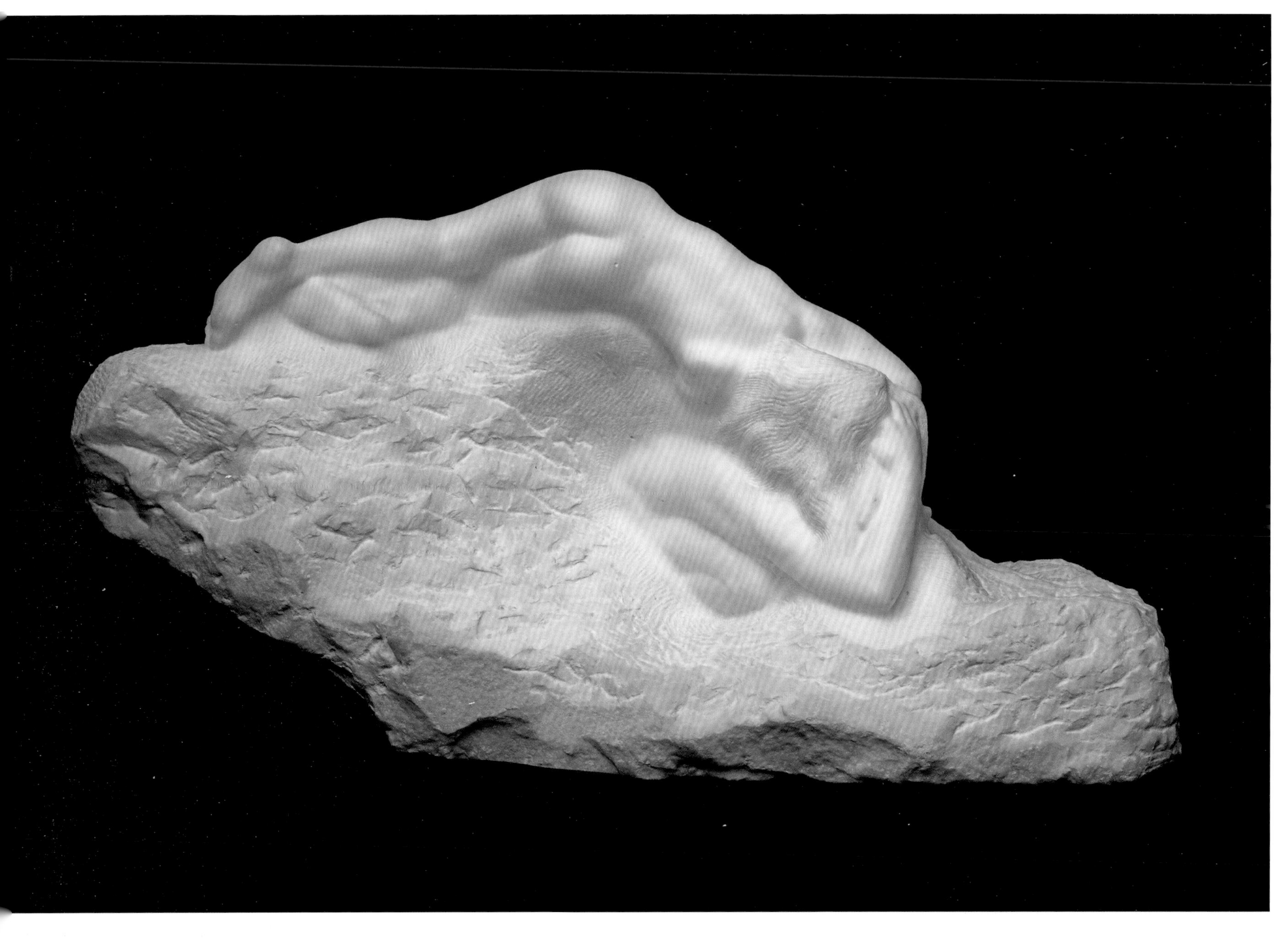

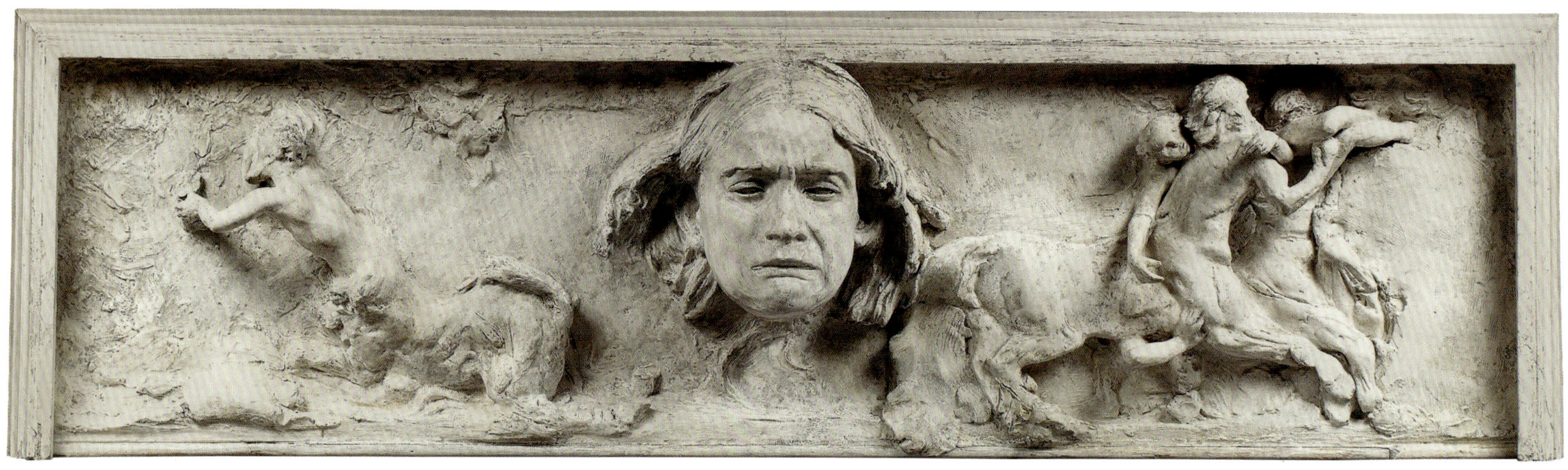

These two reliefs were designed to be placed in the lower section of *The Gates of Hell* before 1885. They had disappeared in the photographs taken in 1887, but were reintroduced before 1904, though not retained in the definitive version. Rodin constructed each of the reliefs around the central mask of his *Crying Woman* – the viewer is left to wonder at the source of their tears while at the same time being repelled by their sinister appearance. They perhaps have their origins in the apotropaic face of the Gorgon, thought to ward off the evil eye, a popular subject in the symbolism of the *fin de siècle* world of the end of the nineteenth century.

The two faces are not identical and one is more elaborately coiffed than the other. They are flanked by centaurs thrusting outwards and carrying off women. Freely interpreted on the two reliefs, the centaurs serve to amplify the other-worldliness of the mask-like faces. The centaurs were also found in *Night*, a vase that Rodin decorated for the Sèvres porcelain factory in 1882–1883.

56
Auguste Rodin
The Gates of Hell: bas-relief mask of the mourner and centaurs
Before 1885
Plaster
H 31.7 cm, W 111 cm, D 18 cm
Musée Rodin, S. 67
Rodin donation, 1916

RIGHT
58
Auguste Rodin
The Earth and the Moon
1898–1899
Marble
H 122.5 cm, W 72.5 cm, D 65 cm
Amgueddfa Cymru – National Museum Wales, Cardiff, NMW A 2509
The Davies Sisters Collection

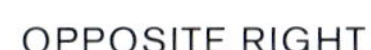

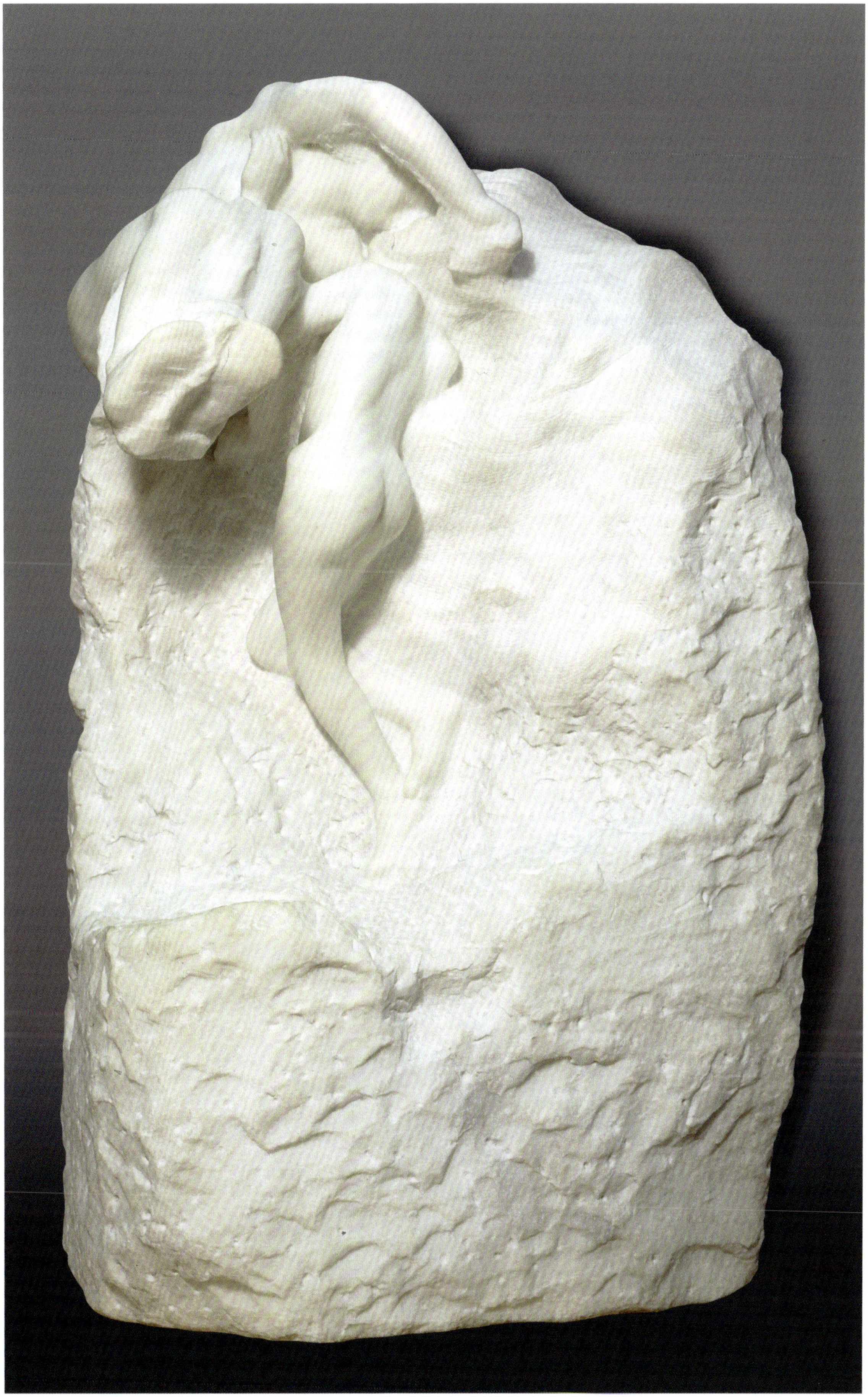

OPPOSITE RIGHT
Fig. 24
Auguste Rodin
Constellation
Before 1900
Graphite and watercolour on watermarked paper
H 49.5 cm, W 31.8 cm
Musée Rodin, D. 4671
Rodin donation, 1916

Rodin, in his drawings, gives us the delight of seeing him work. Visible are the moments when he pauses, the emotion.

Antoine Bourdelle, 'Les dessins du sculpteur Rodin', *La Grande Revue*, 1908

After 1895 Rodin changed his way of drawing. He chose to work on larger-format paper and to draw from life. His figures are then enhanced by watercolour and often annotated in pencil. This system of annotating as he worked was like an association of ideas, taking the work to another, mythological, poetic or natural dimension. As Rodin confided to the writer Judith Cladel (1903): 'Indeed, when one follows nature one has everything. When I have the beautiful body of a woman as a model, the drawings that I make from her give me images of insects, birds, fish. It seems improbable to me and I was unaware of it myself.... A woman, a mountain, a horse – all the same thing.'

Fellow sculptor Antoine Bourdelle was witness to this cosmogony, writing in *La Grande Revue* in 1908: 'This crowd today who seem to want to tear themselves free from mother earth, you take them out to sea, you deliver them vast sky-filled horizons, in your drawings you assimilate them to the rocks, to the trees, to the soil, to fire, to fine beasts; the whole of life comes into play in all the assembling of your work, which is quite dazzling.'

Observation of Rodin's technique sheds light on the stages of his creation. In the five drawings illustrated here, he began by drawing a figure in graphite, then applied watercolour after the model had left, which had the effect of dissolving the model's body and melding it into nature. In *The Calm Sea* (Fig. 25), the colour blurs the lines, giving rise to the annotation: 'the sea stretches forth'. The brown of the hair calls to mind a rock, while another brown patch suggests the shore. The faint sketch of two sailing boats, added later in the upper left part of the drawing, accentuates the new direction his drawing was taking. In another drawing (Cat. 59), annotated 'Cloud', the initial pencil line is later repeated more forcefully, though with changes of mind around the eyes. The added watercolour appears to be the reflection of the reclining person, looking at their image in the water. This is in the same style as the drawing with the annotation 'Night' (Fig. 26). In Fig. 27 Rodin adds the rays of the sun emerging from the figure and corrects his own annotation: 'the good planet / afternoon setting sun [crossed out] – flower bent over'.

These were not preparatory drawings for sculpture in the strict sense, but they did underpin his modelling and assemblage work in the first decade of the century, as the annotation 'make as sculpture' on the drawing labelled 'Comet' (Cat. 60) reveals.

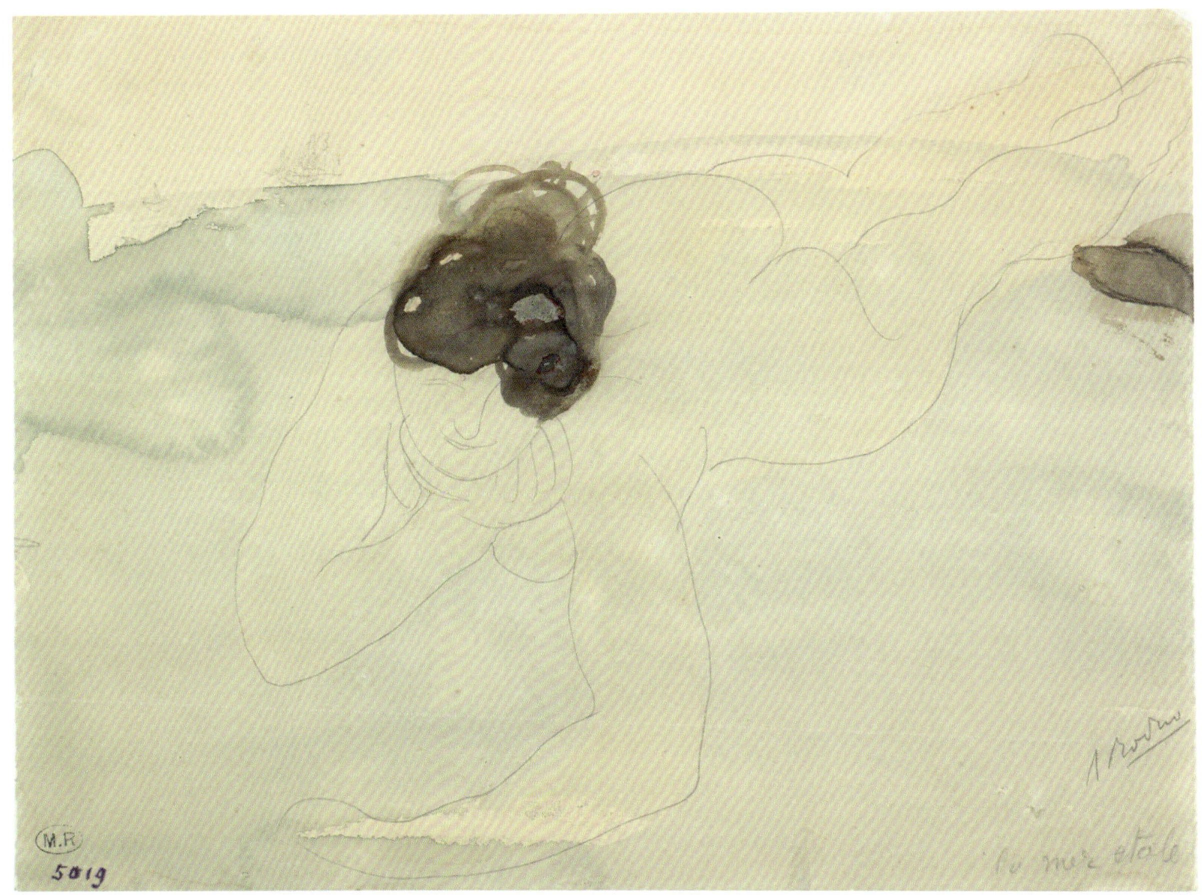

Fig. 25
Auguste Rodin
The Calm Sea
After 1898?
Watercolour and graphite
on paper vellum
H 23.8 cm, W 31.8 cm
Musée Rodin, D. 5019
Rodin donation, 1916

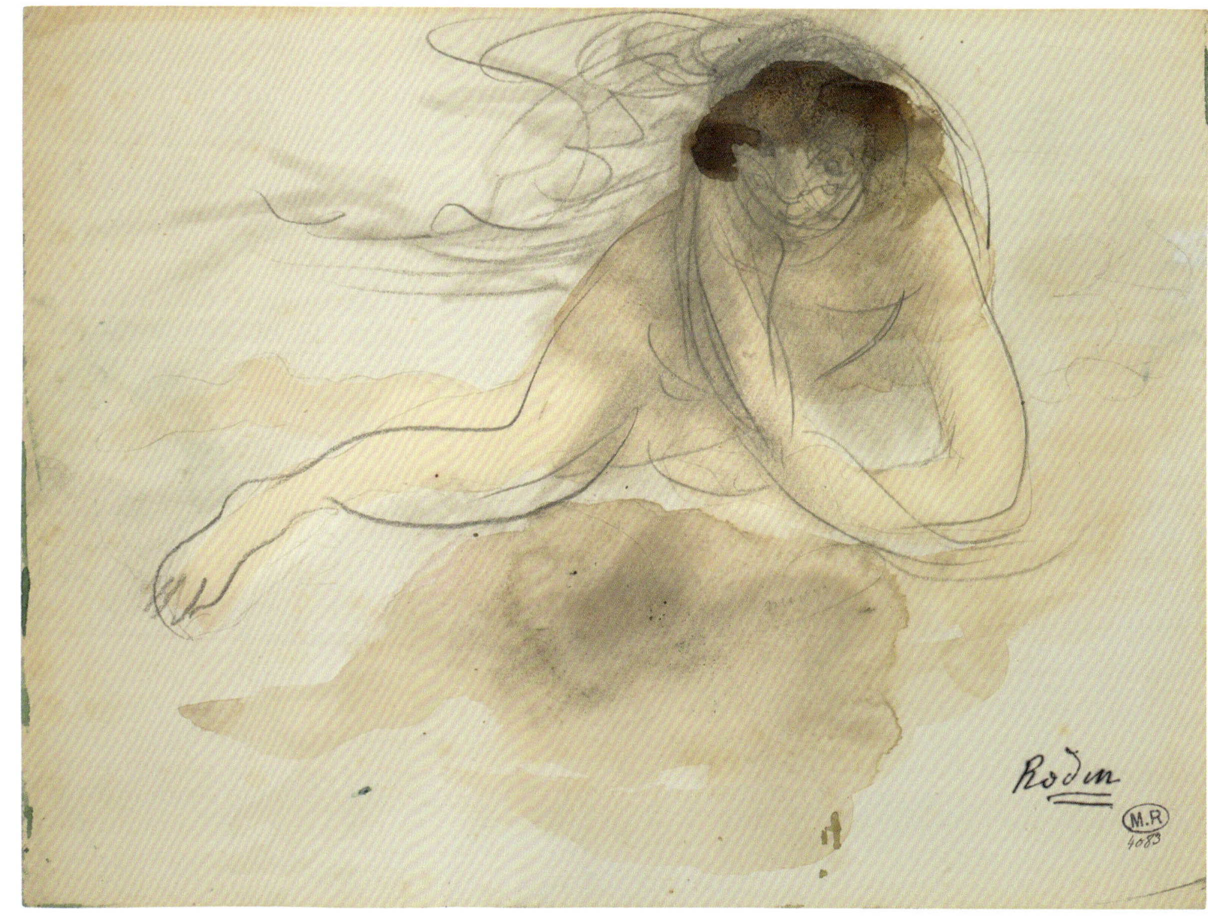

59
Auguste Rodin
Cloud
After 1896
Graphite with stump and
watercolour on paper
H 24.9 cm, W 32.6 cm
Musée Rodin, D. 4083
Rodin donation, 1916

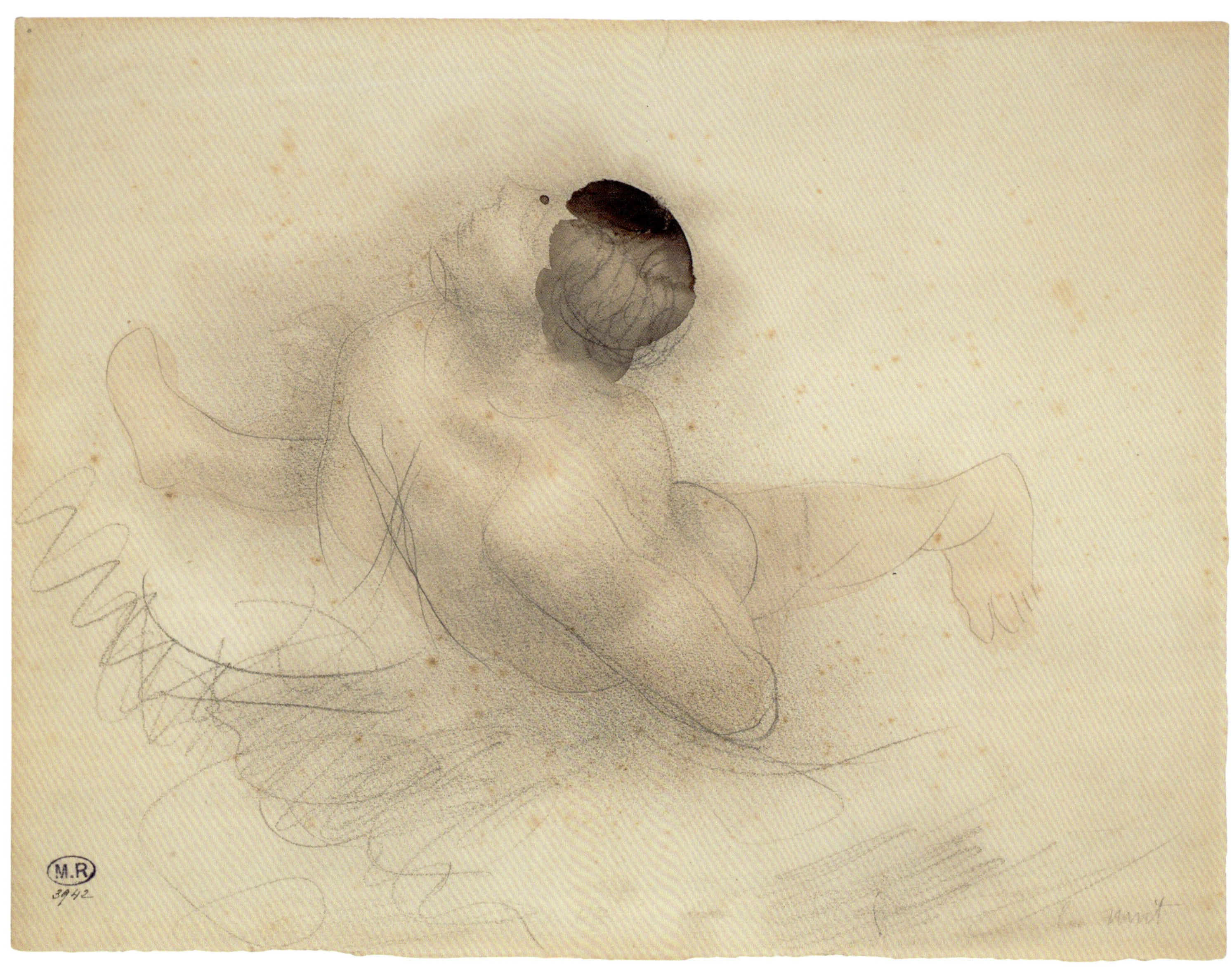

Fig. 26
Auguste Rodin
The Night
After 1898?
Graphite with stump and
watercolour on paper vellum
H 25.3 cm, W 32.5 cm
Musée Rodin, D. 3942
Rodin donation, 1916

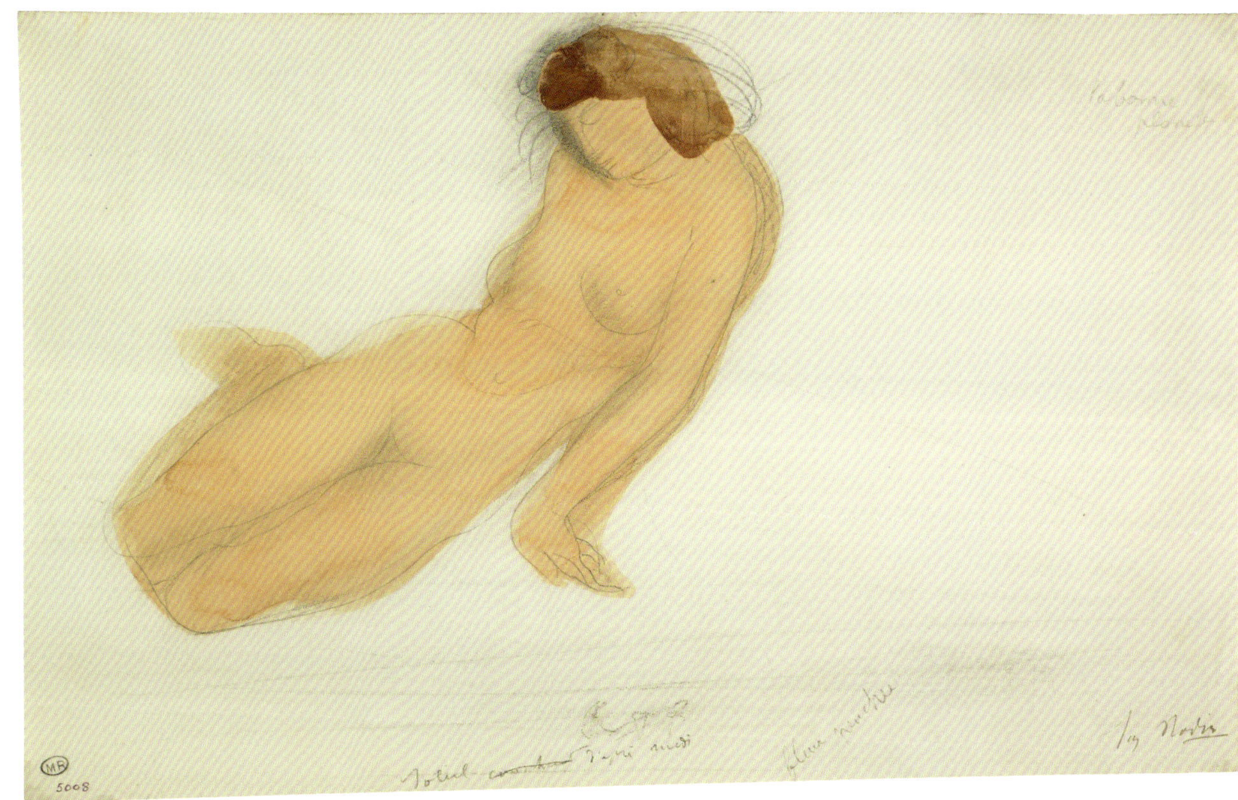

Fig. 27
Auguste Rodin
The Good Planet
After 1896
Graphite with stump and watercolour on watermarked paper
H 31.3 cm, W 48.3 cm
Musée Rodin, D. 5008
Rodin donation, 1916

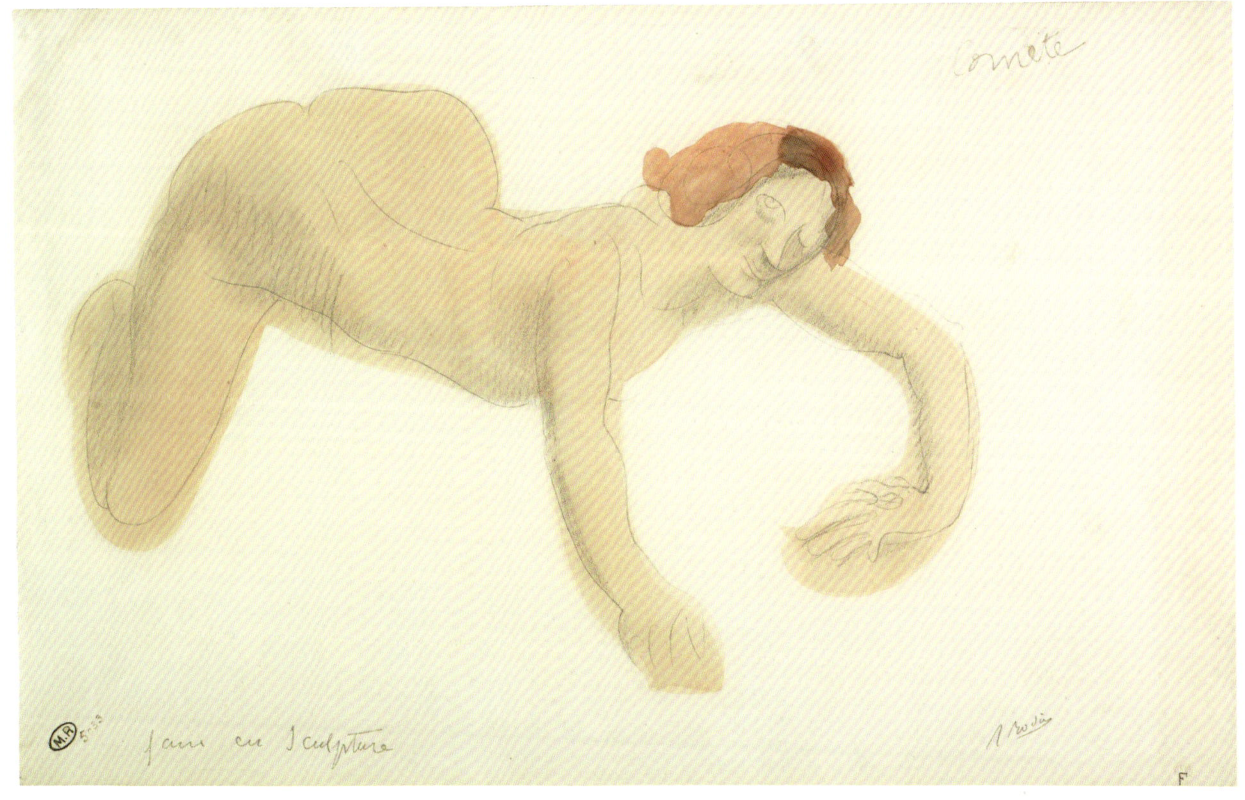

60
Auguste Rodin
Comet
After 1898?
Graphite with stump and watercolour on watermarked paper
H 32 cm, W 49.7 cm
Musée Rodin, D. 5033
Rodin donation, 1916

The fragment

These are the damaged statues, found in the ruins; and they are no less masterpieces for being incomplete.

Auguste Rodin, quoted by G. Duranteau, 'La sculpture et l'art d'après Rodin', *La Gaulois du Dimanche*, 4 June 1907

When the Parthenon sculptures arrived in England, Lord Elgin asked Antonio Canova to restore them and replace the missing parts. The sculptor refused, saying that the fragments were the touchstone of authenticity for ancient Greek sculpture. Like Canova, Rodin found sincerity and inspiration in the fragment that had been shaped by time.

In the mid-1890s, Rodin's passion for antiquity took him in a new direction and he began to assemble a vast collection of over 6,000 antiquities, many of which were fragments. He considered the fragment to be complete, so to speak, and it inspired him to become the first modern sculptor to make the headless, limbless torso into a genre of art in its own right.

Fig. 28
Anonymous
Rodin's antiquities under the peristyle of the Pavillon de l'Alma in Meudon
1906–1917
Gelatin silver print
H 13.9 cm, W 8.8 cm
Musée Rodin, Ph. 2709
Rodin Donation, 1916

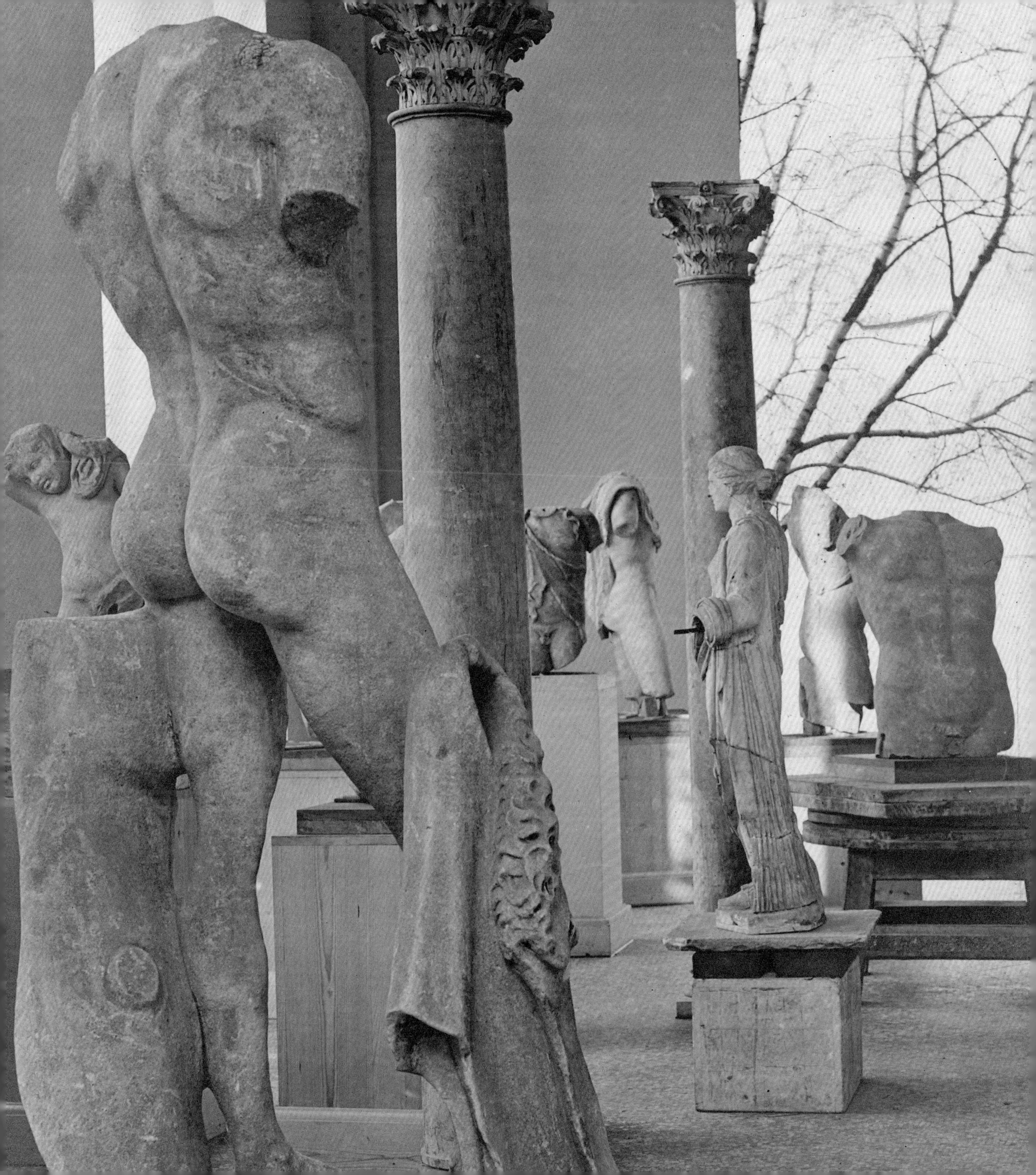

This now battered torso (Cat. 61) is the principal fragment of a figure representing the messenger god Hermes, who heralded the chariot of Athena on the West Pediment of the Parthenon. The composition here represented the contest between Athena and Poseidon to become the patron deity of Athens. Rodin would have admired the subtle torsion in the body of the god, whose head, now missing, once looked back over his shoulder. This unprepossessing ruin tends to be overlooked in the popular reception of the Parthenon sculptures, but seen through the eyes of Rodin it is reinvigorated. In 1904 Rodin asked his sculpture assistant Henri Lebossé to enlarge the group *I Am Beautiful* (see Cat. 44). Rodin found the enlargement of the *Falling Man* (Cat. 62), which was cut into fragments for technical reasons, pleasing, and kept it with the name *Torso of Louis XIV*. The severed neck, arms and thighs, and the power of the torso reduced to a fragment recall the ancient broken fragment of Hermes from the Parthenon.

OPPOSITE
62
Auguste Rodin
Torso of the *Falling Man* from *The Gates of Hell*, also known as *Torso of Louis XIV*
1904
Patinated plaster
H 116 cm, W 71.4 cm, D 50.7 cm
Musée Rodin, S. 3440

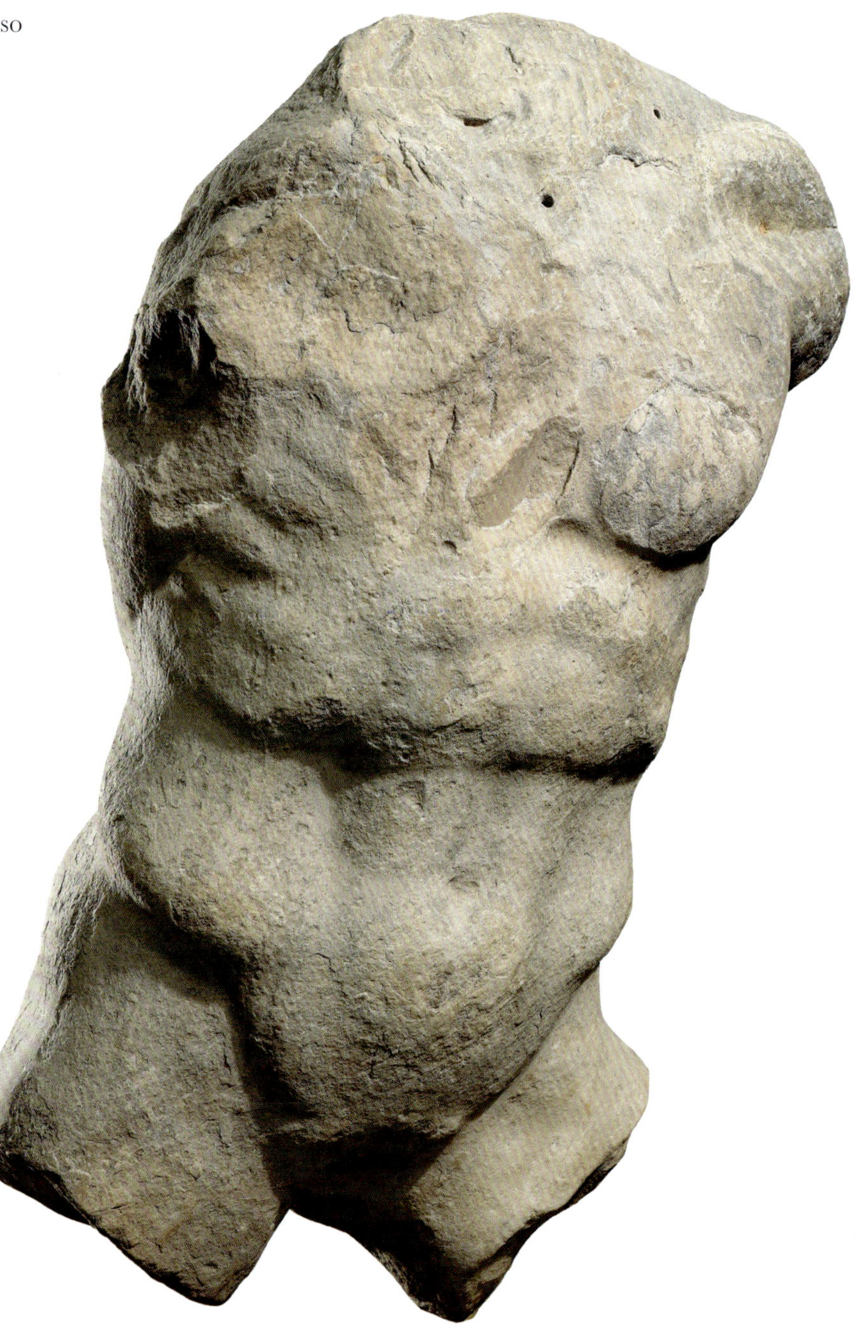

61
Torso of the messenger god Hermes
Figure H from the West Pediment of the Parthenon
Greek
About 438–432 BC
Marble
H 115 cm, W 74 cm, D 74 cm
British Museum, 1816,0610.100

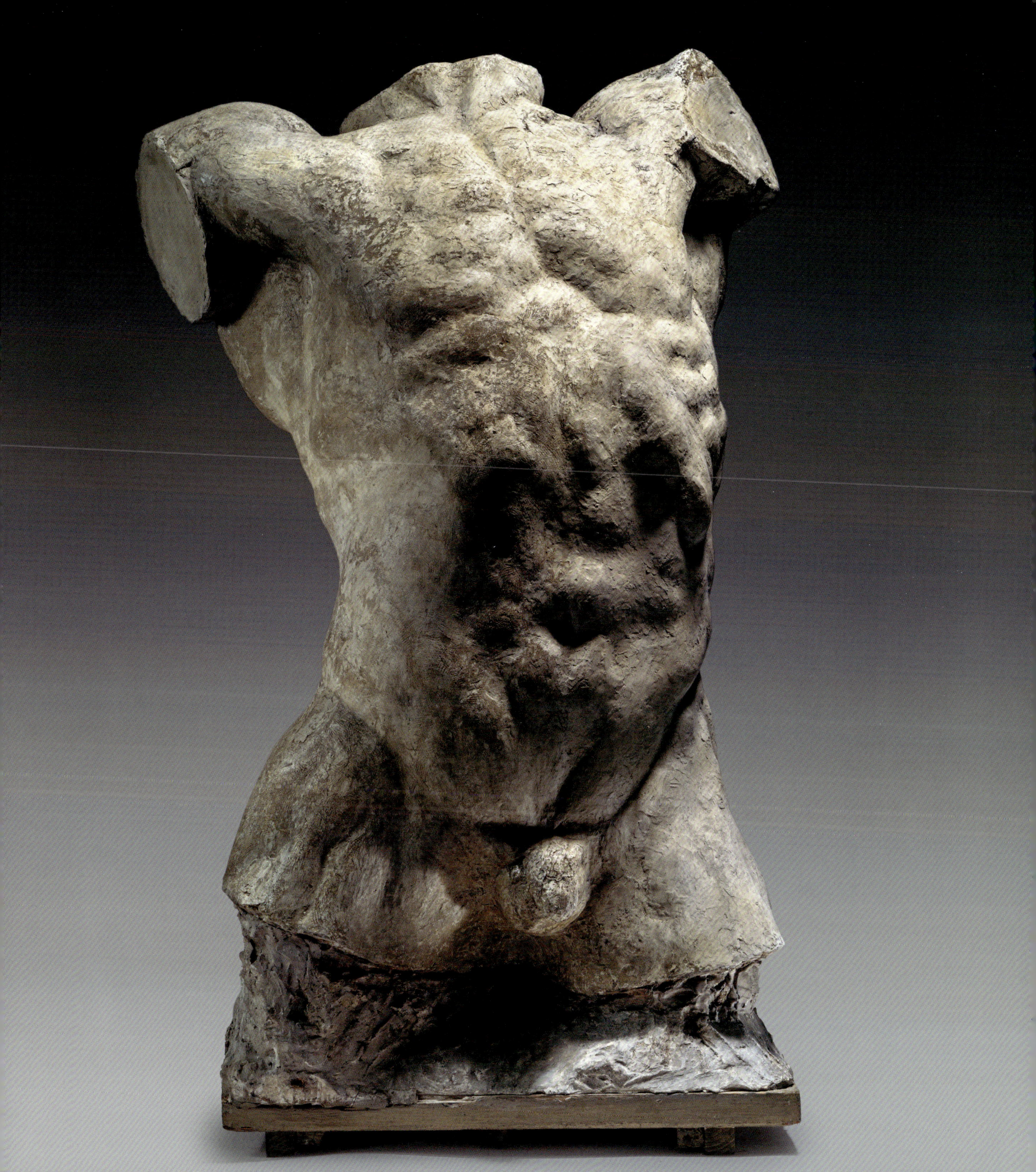

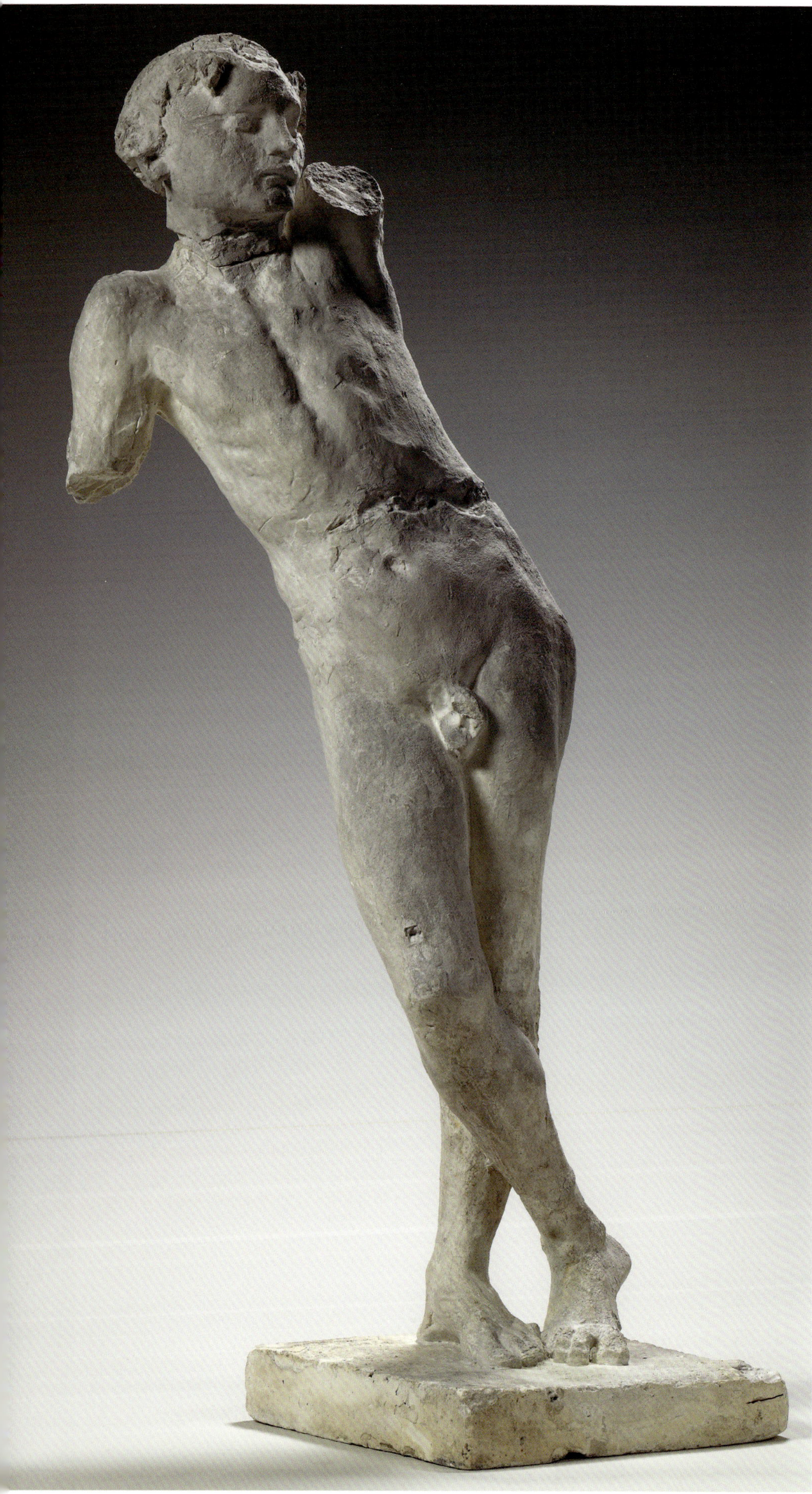

63
Funerary Spirit, also known as
The Spirit of Eternal Repose
1898
Plaster
H 94.5 cm, W. 36.8 cm, D 33.7 cm
Musée Rodin, S. 752
Rodin donation, 1916

Rodin presented this sculpture for the first time in Brussels in 1899, without the arms. He then exhibited it in 1900 at the Pavillon de l'Alma, with a left arm folded back from the head, and placed it on top of a tall composite column. He also reused it by enlarging it in the *Monument to Puvis de Chavannes*, which was commissioned in 1899. The work was directly inspired by the Roman copy of an ancient Greek statue known as *Pothos* (desire) in the Louvre, as well as other ancient models. The sinuous movement of the body and the position of the head are reminiscent of the Lapith from South Metope XVI of the Parthenon (Cat. 64).

Rodin rejoiced in the fragment, but he would also have been intrigued by two fragments of the same sculpture finding each other after a long separation. An instance of this is the joining together of two fragments of a metope from the Parthenon: the torso had come to the British Museum with the Elgin collection, while the head was acquired later, in 1854, from the Duke of Devonshire.

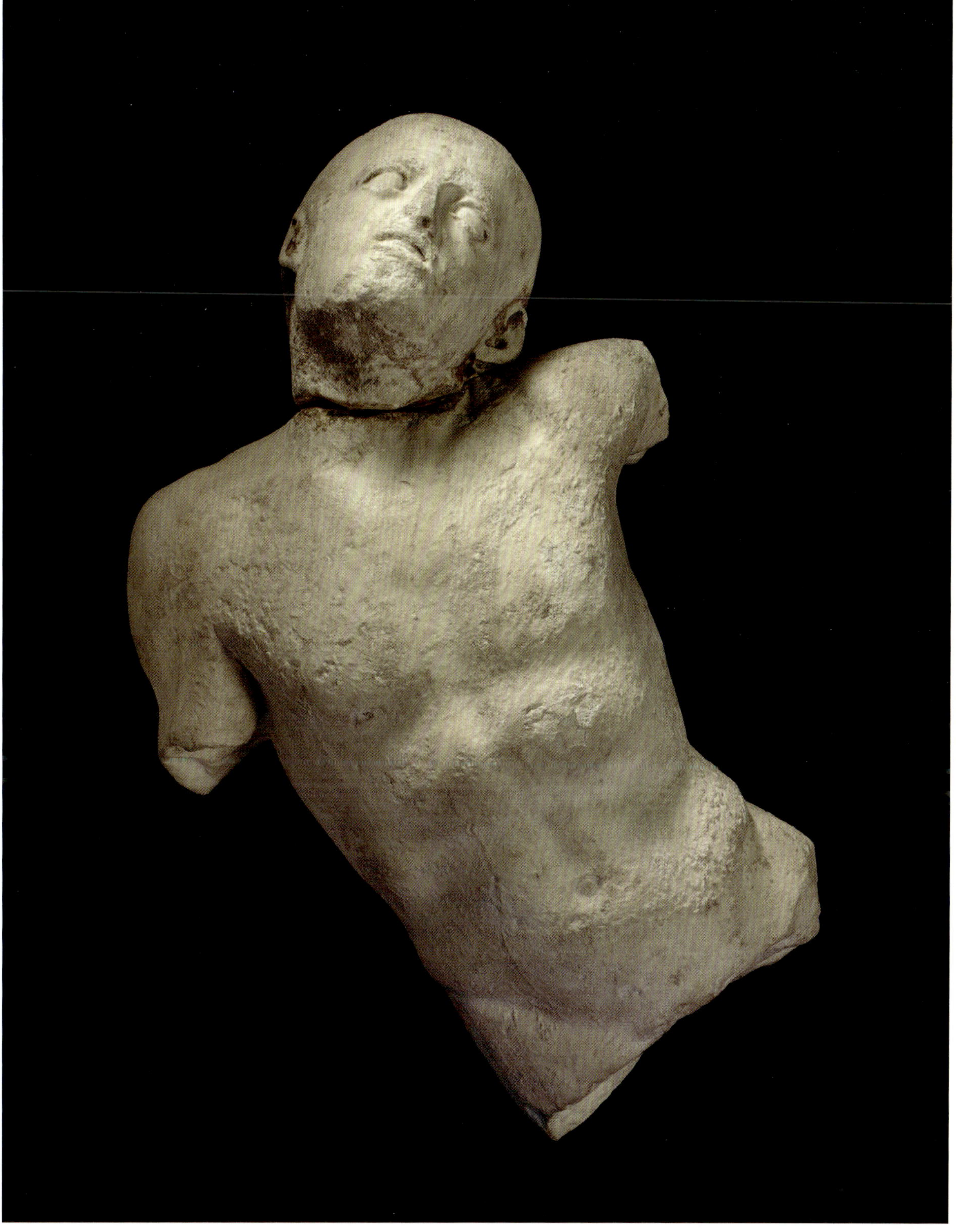

64
Head and torso of a Lapith
South Metope XVI of the Parthenon
Greek
About 447–438 BC
Marble
H 61.5 cm, W 41.5 cm, D 23 cm
British Museum, 1854,0513.1 and 1816,0610.323
Donated by William George Spencer Cavendish, 6th Duke of Devonshire

At home I have fragments of gods for my daily enjoyment.… Contemplating them brings me the happiness of these solemn hours from which the ancient world always speaks to me …

Auguste Rodin, *Art: Conversations with Paul Gsell*, 1911

Rodin's Museum of Antiquities

At the end of 1900 Rodin built his 'Museum of Antiquities' at Meudon to house his collection. It was at this same time – a period when he was having many of his sculptures enlarged – that he also began to acquire fragments of monumental Graeco-Roman statues. On 20 August 1905, he acquired from the antiquarian Elie Geladakis a headless Roman statue of Hercules (Cat. 65), one of his favourite ancient pieces, which he displayed under the peristyle around the Pavillon de l'Alma and then in his Museum of Antiquities. At night, Rodin would play with the effects of lamplight to show his visitors all the details of the statue's modelling, and caress its eroded surface to experience the essence of the sculpture (Fig. 30).

In summer, the sculptor would move the torsos of Venus (Cat. 66) and some satyrs (Cat. 67; Fig. 31) out into the garden and place them on funerary altars. Each day as he went walking, he would rediscover them in natural daylight, which, he felt, brought to mind the light of Greece: 'This Faun is, is he not, like the god of this rural spot. The daylight takes pleasure in caressing his amorous hips. These ancient artists were great only because they adored earthly existence and expressed their joy in life unreservedly.' (Auguste Rodin, quoted by Paul Gsell, 1907).

Rodin's garden was a vast studio open to the sky, where antiquities were as much inspiration for meditation as they were objects of experimentation. A plain scarf could be used to conceal from sight those parts that Rodin judged to be less than perfect (Fig. 29). A simple leg fragment (Cat. 69) had the evocative force and power of a monumental statue. The statue of *Seated Agrippina*, 'the Muse of Contemplation' (Cat. 68), formed a pendant to Rodin's *Cybele*. 'Between the tall columns of the Pavillon de l'Alma, the ancient and the new were brought together, an ancient masterpiece and an adaptation of ancient beauty by Rodin.… In the studios and in the gardens too, the juxtaposition of Rodin's masterpieces demonstrated that they belonged to the same tradition' (Frisch and Shipley, 1939).

Greek art was of course not neglected, and in 1913 a large fragment of a stele (Cat. 30) greeted visitors in the colonnade at the Pavillon de l'Alma. Rodin associated 'these tombstones' with unattainable fragments of the Parthenon. Some marble funerary vessels (*lekythoi*; see Cat. 28) came into view along the pathways, often perched on a plaster pedestal or on tall columns, like Rodin's sculptures at the exhibition of 1900 in the Pavillon de l'Alma. With a single glance, the visitor could assimilate works of antiquity and those of Rodin, as if modelled by the same artist. Like a Pygmalion to these creatures, Rodin was able to bring to life modest Roman fragments and return them to 'their former beauty'.

Fig. 29
François Vizzavona (1876–1961)
Rodin's collection of antiquities in the Tweed Studio in Meudon
December 1906
Gelatin silver print
H 12.9 cm, W 17.9 cm
Musée Rodin, Ph. 6135

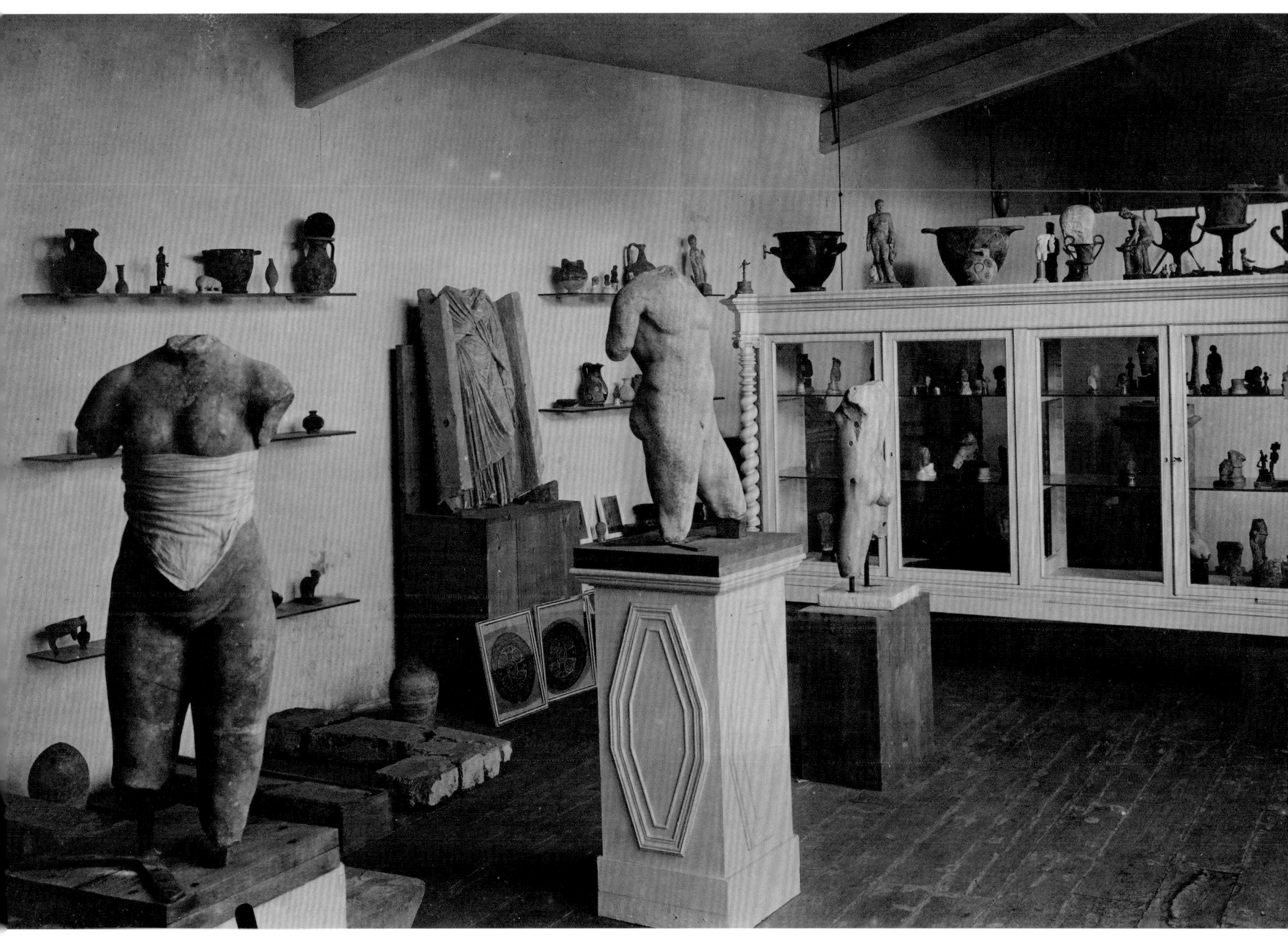

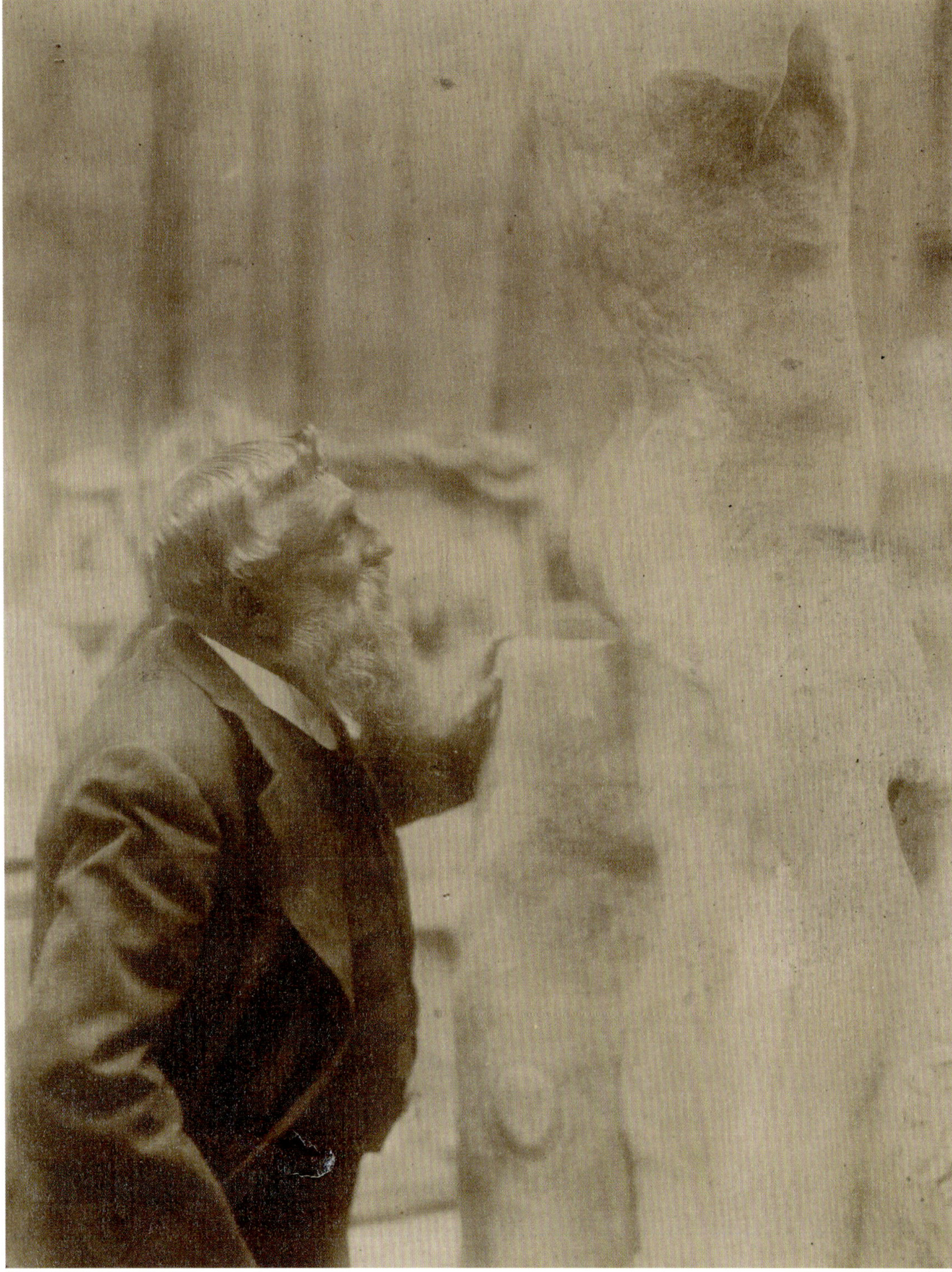

LEFT
Fig. 30
Cl. Gerschell (1866–1942?)
Rodin caressing his marble statue of Hercules
Around 1908
Gelatin silver print
H 22.5 cm, W 16.8 cm
Musée Rodin, Ph. 873
Rodin Donation, 1916

OPPOSITE
65
Youthful Hercules with bow and lion-skin
Roman
AD 117–161
Marble
H 183 cm, W 103 cm, D 55 cm
Musée Rodin, Co. 1107
Rodin donation, 1916

At certain times, he simply stands before his relics, meditating.… How his fingers tremble when he touches these old stones!

Gustave Coquiot, *Rodin à l'Hôtel de Biron et à Meudon*, 1917

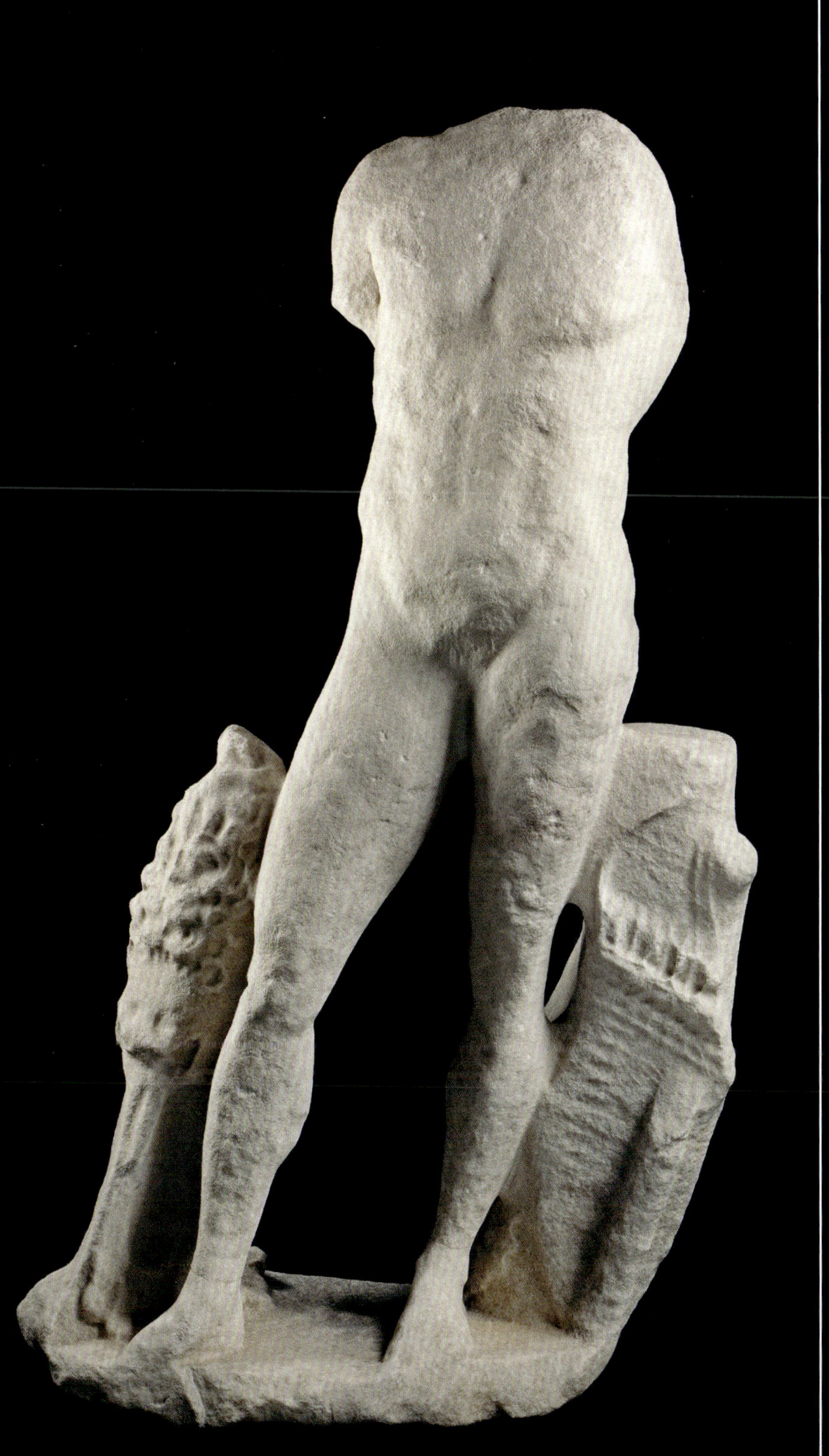

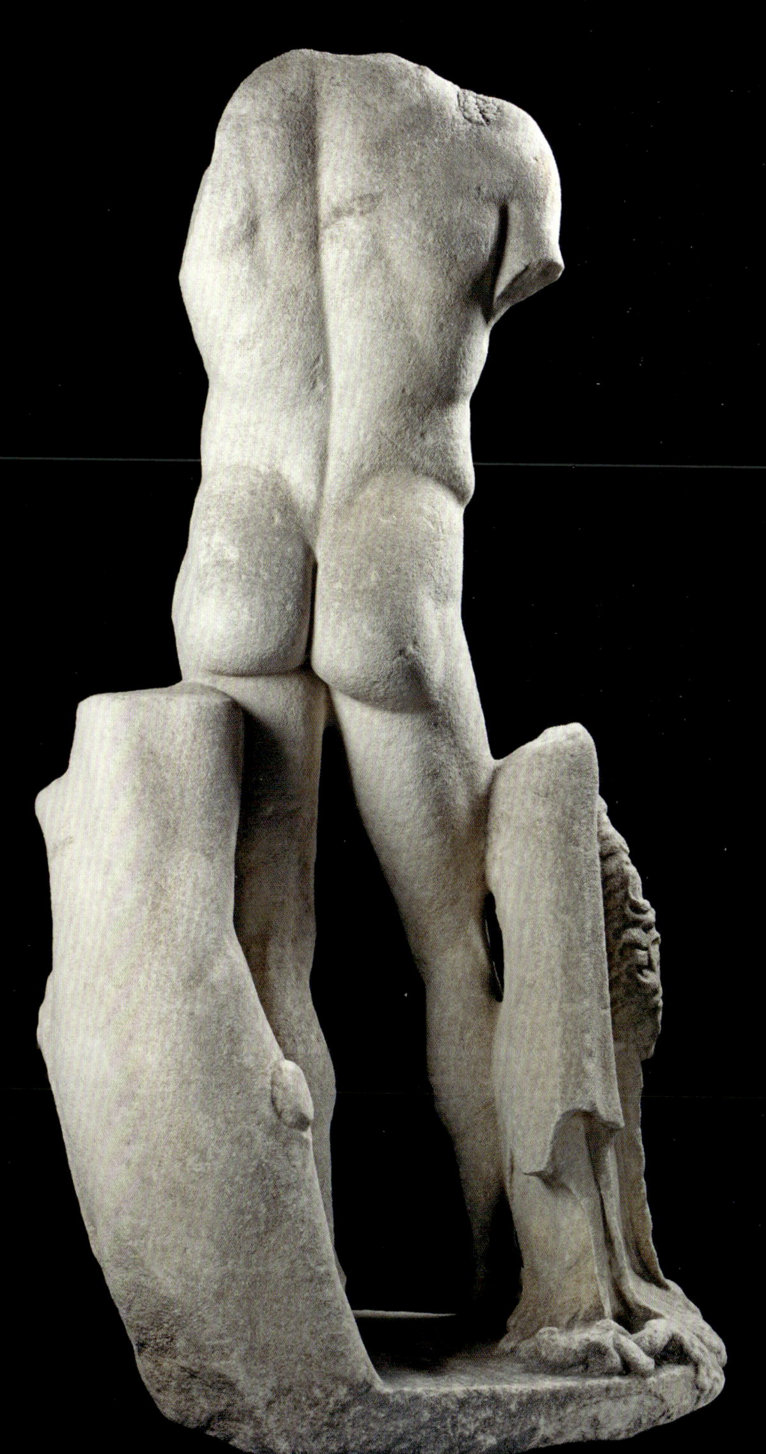

This is real flesh! … It must have been moulded by kisses and caresses! … One almost expects, when feeling this torso, to find it warm.

Auguste Rodin, *Art: Conversations with Paul Gsell*, 1911

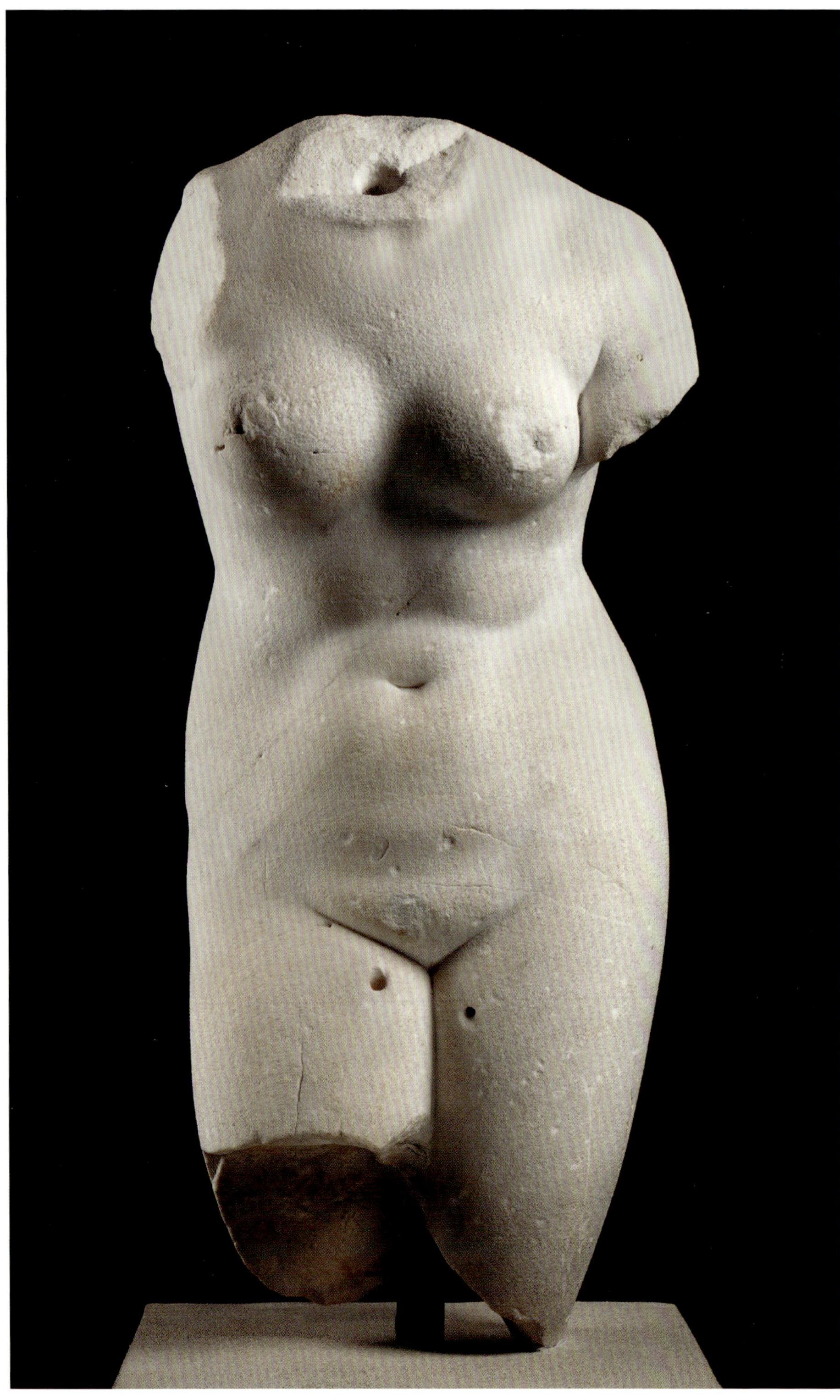

66
Torso of Aphrodite of the Capitoline type (*Venus pudica*)
Roman
AD 50–125
Marble
H 86 cm, W 37.5 cm, D 31 cm
Musée Rodin, Co. 472
Rodin donation, 1916

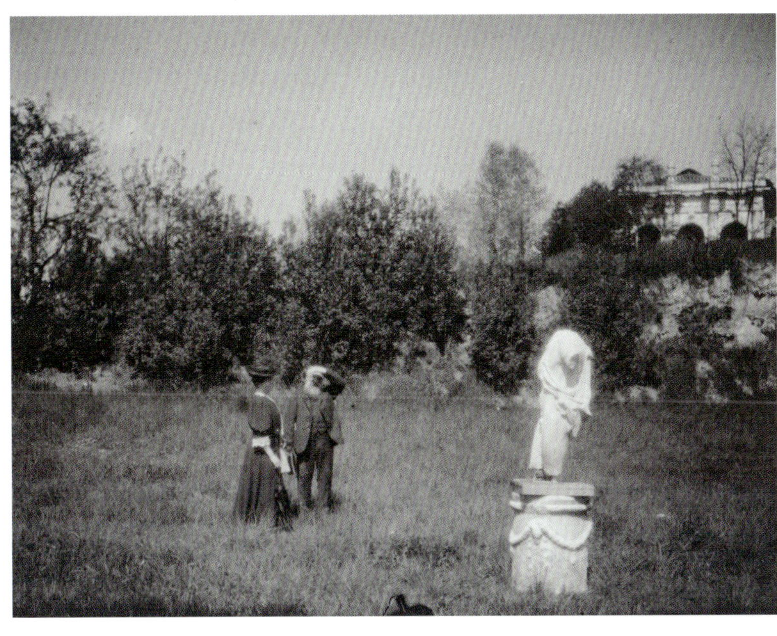

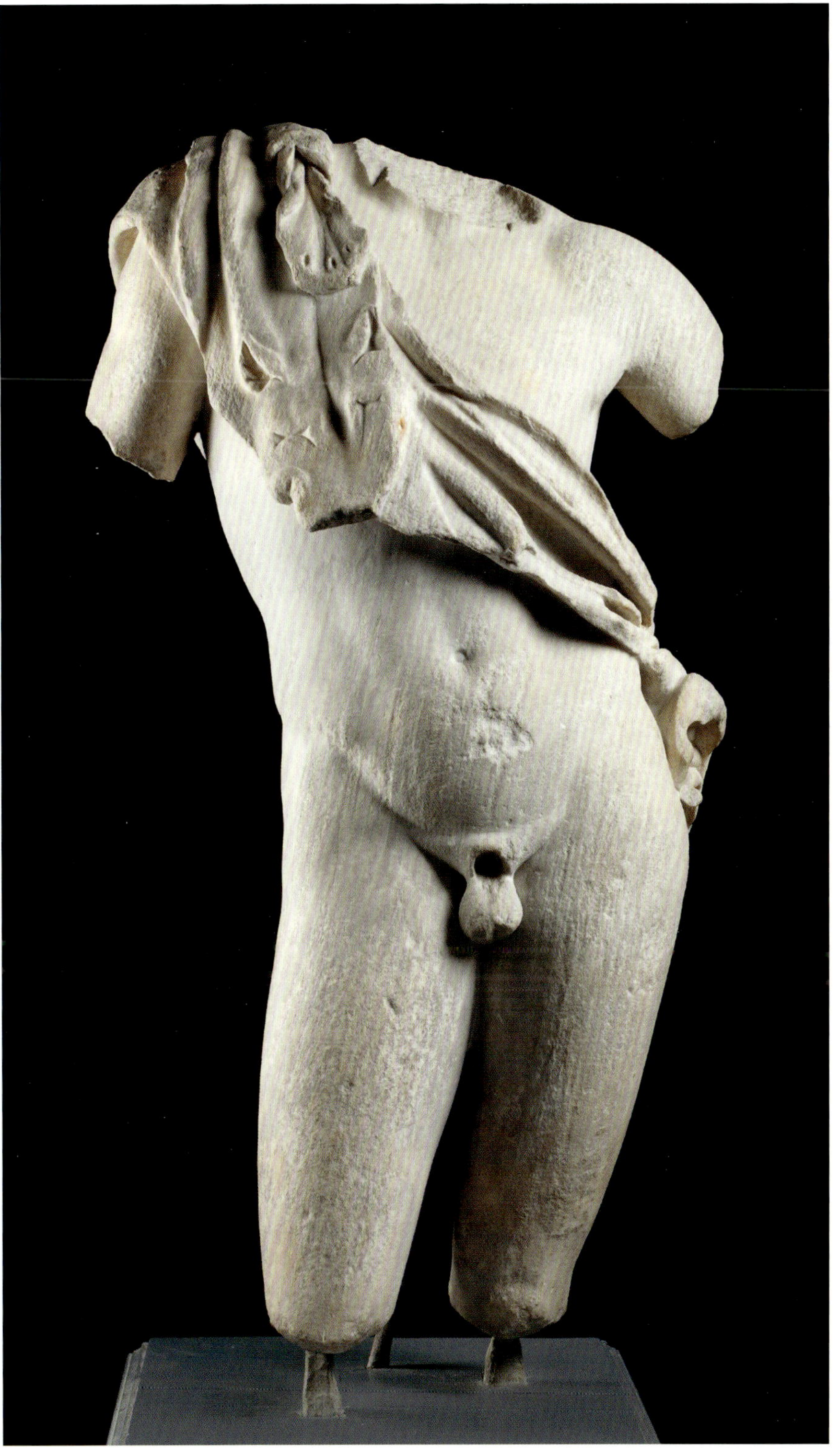

ABOVE
Fig. 31
Anonymous
Rodin and Kate Simpson in front of the torso of a Satyr in the garden at Meudon
Around 1908
Platinum print
H 8.4 cm, W 10.7 cm
Musée Rodin, Ph. 2101
Rodin donation, 1916

RIGHT
67
Torso of a Satyr
Roman
AD 100–125
Marble
H 105 cm, W 54 cm, D 36.5 cm
Musée Rodin, Co. 492
Rodin donation, 1916

68
Headless statue of the so-called
Seated Agrippina type
Roman
AD 96–192
Marble
H 93 cm, W 128 cm, D 51 cm
Musée Rodin, Co. 471
Rodin donation, 1916

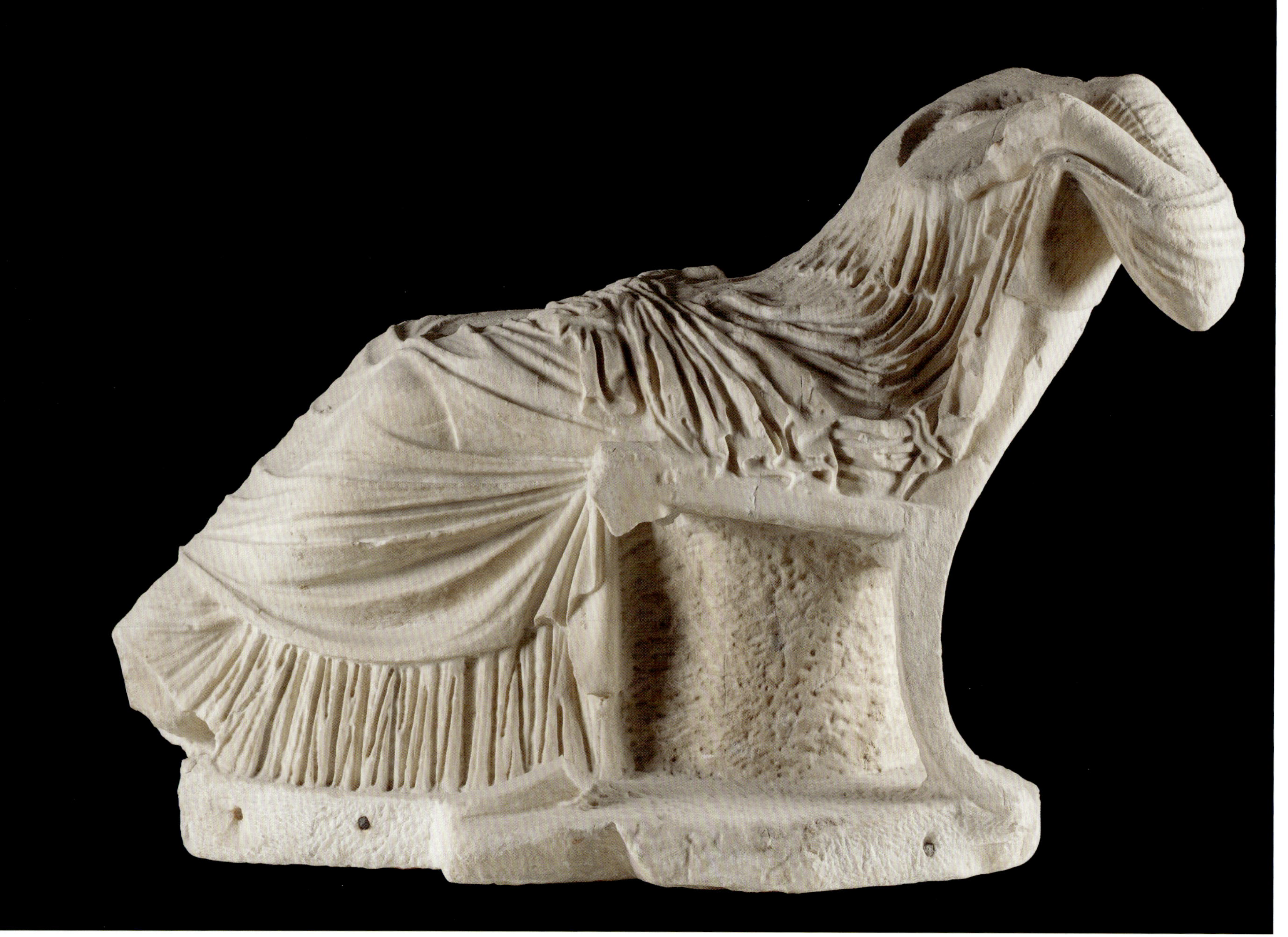

69
Right leg and trophy from
a colossal statue
Roman
AD 100–125
Marble
H 115 cm, W 71.5 cm, D 47 cm
Musée Rodin, Co. 498
Rodin donation, 1916

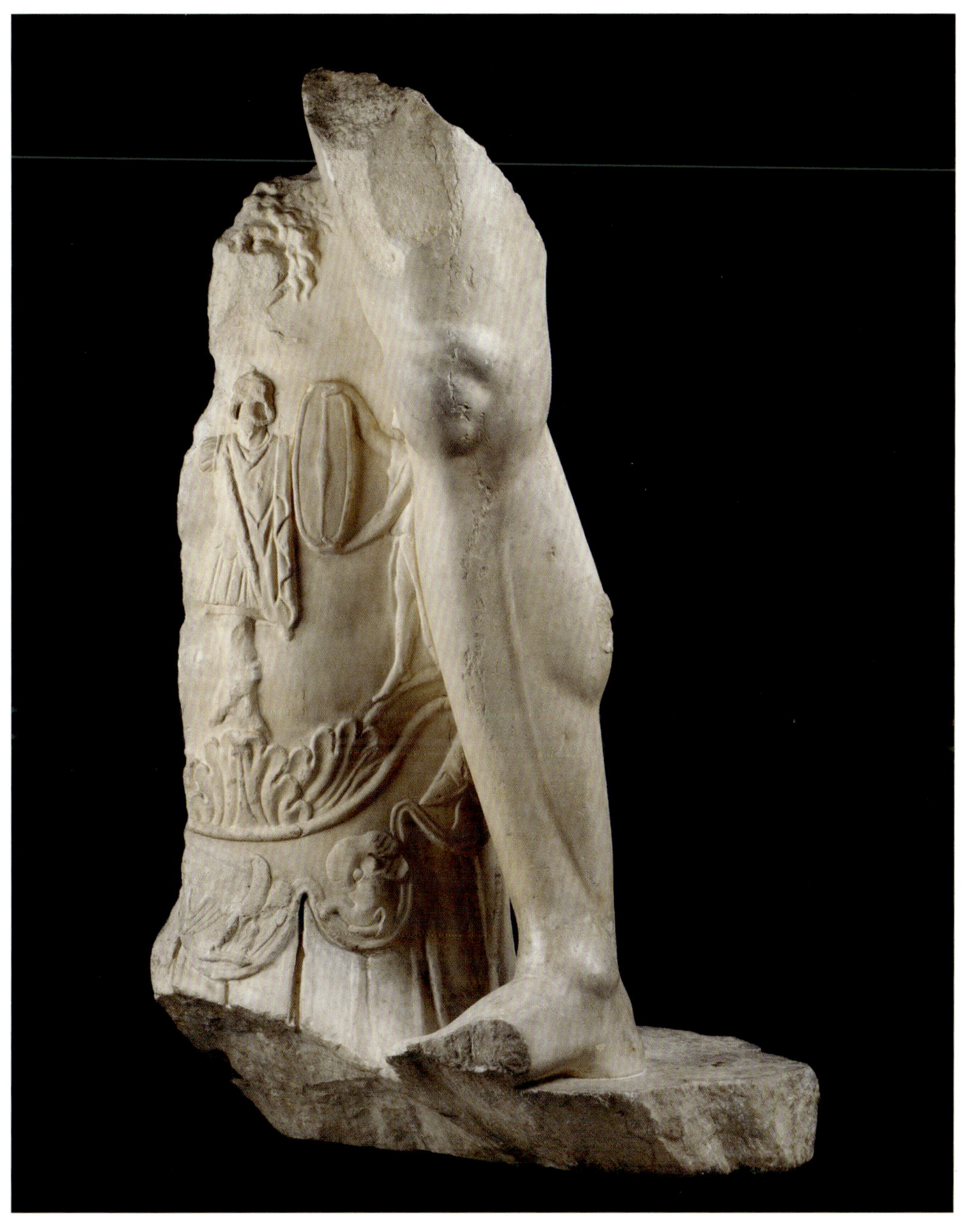

Rodin reverted again and again in his figures to this turning-inward-upon-oneself, this tense listening to inner depths.... Never before has a human body been so concentrated about itself, been made by its own spirit to bend so.... The neck ... holds the listening head above the distant sounds of life's tumult.

Rainer Maria Rilke, *Auguste Rodin*, 1902

70
Auguste Rodin
The Inner Voice or *Meditation*
without arms, large version
1896
Plaster
H 147 cm, W 76 cm, D 55 cm
Musée Rodin, S. 5415

The figure of *Meditation* is derived from a damned woman depicted on the right of the tympanum of *The Gates of Hell*, and bears all the imprint of Michelangelo's example of withdrawal of self and expression of inner torment. Rodin reused the figure in the *Monument to Victor Hugo*, which was commissioned in 1889 for the Panthéon in Paris. The figure was then enlarged to triple its size in 1895 and was given the name *The Inner Voice* – one of the muses that inspired Victor Hugo. Her arms were removed and the cuts to the knees are traces of the figure having once been part of the *Monument*. Rodin exhibited it in this state in 1896 at the Salon of the National Society of Fine Arts in Paris. He wrote in a letter to the Prince of Sweden in 1897 that 'The study of Nature is complete, and I have made every effort to render art as complete as possible. I consider that this plaster is one of my best finished works, the most advanced.'

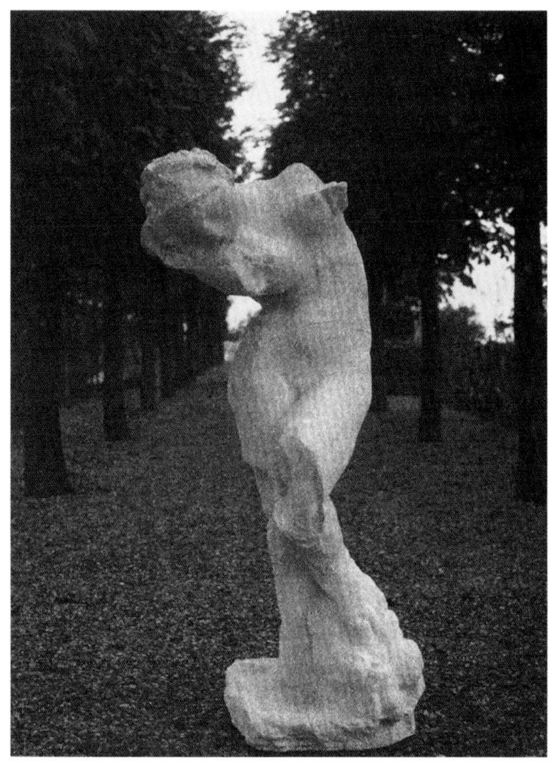

Fig. 32
Stephen Haweis (1878–1969)
and Henry Coles (1875–?)
Meditation
1903–1904
Carbon print
H 22.5 cm, W 16.5 cm
Musée Rodin, Ph. 1295
Rodin donation, 1916

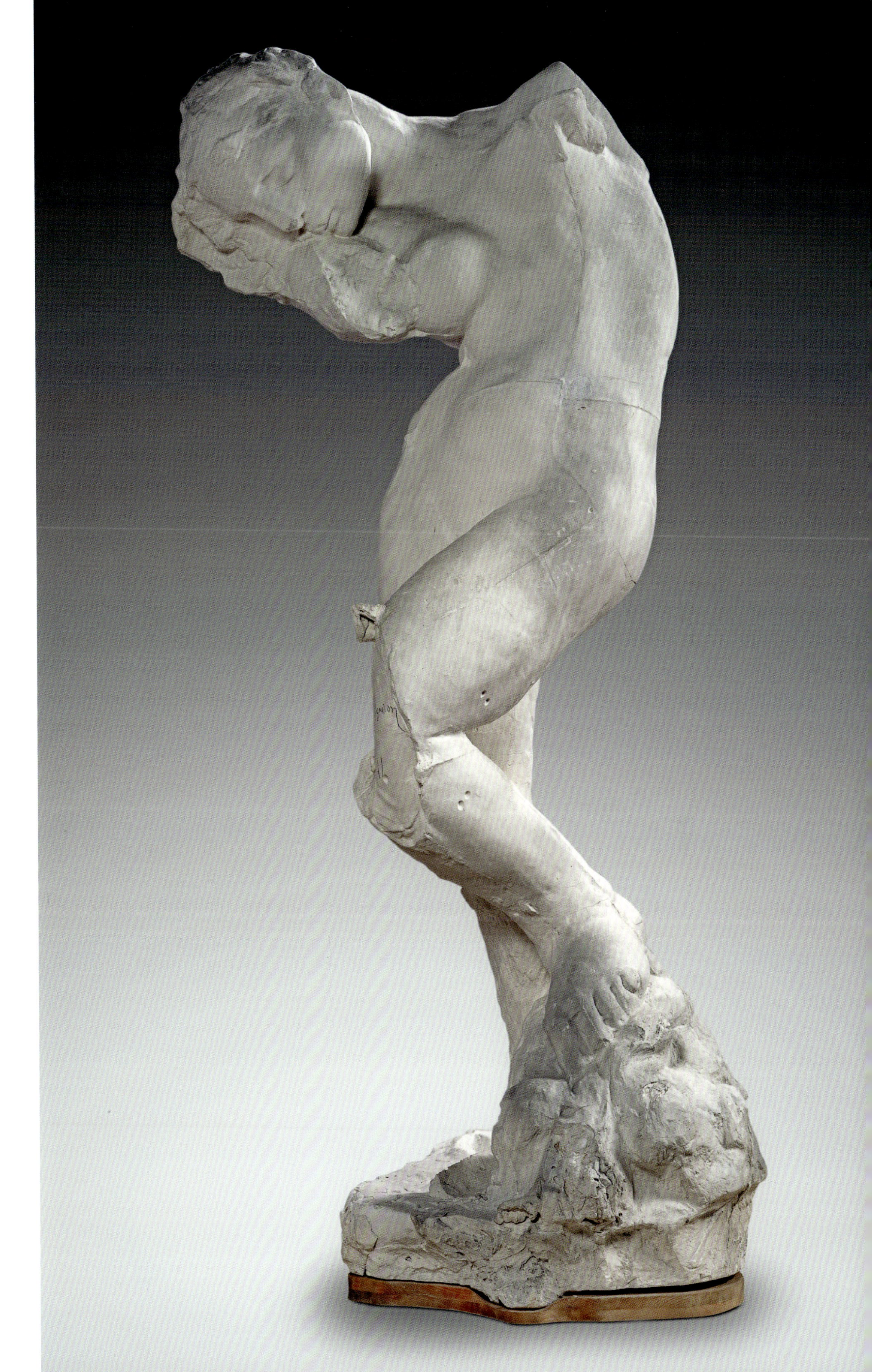

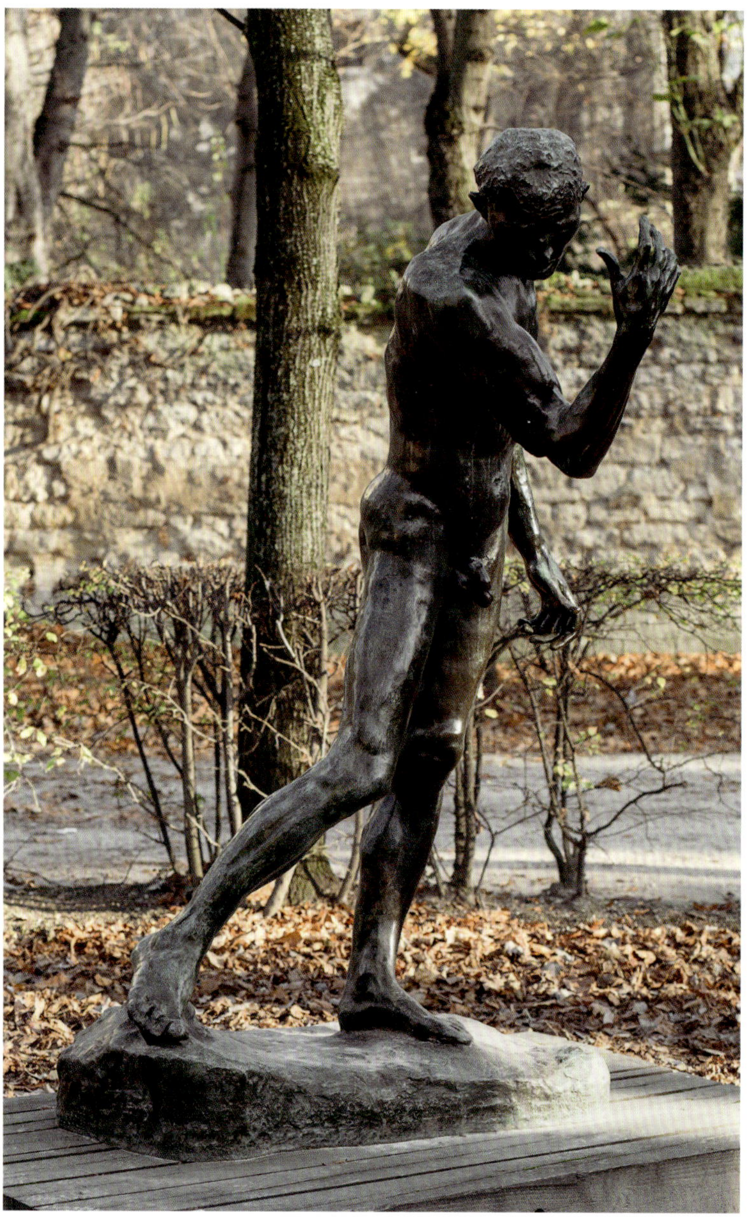

Pierre de Wissant is one of the group of figures of *Monument to the Burghers of Calais*, which Rodin received the commission for from the city of Calais in 1885 (see also Cat. 102). The monument commemorated the heroism of the six men who, in 1347, during the Hundred Years' War, agreed to sacrifice their lives by handing over the keys of the besieged city to King Edward III of England. Rodin first modelled the monumental statue of Pierre de Wissant naked. He then had it cast, and made a clothed version; it was first exhibited in this state in 1887. But it is the naked figure in plaster, a preparatory work without the head or hands, elements that Rodin worked on separately, that he chose to introduce his exhibition in the Pavillon de l'Alma in Paris in 1900, as a manifesto for a new sculpture (Cat. 73). On 8 July 1907, Rodin bought the statue of Apollo Ludovisi from the antiquarian Elie Geladakis (Cat. 74). The statue originally came from the gardens of the Villa Ludovisi in Rome and Geladakis had acquired it in the sale of the collection of Léon de Somzée on 27 May 1907. Rodin displayed this Apollo at Meudon in the peristyle of the Pavillon de l'Alma, which he had rebuilt in the garden. There it was an echo of the statue of Pierre de Wissant, without head or hands, which had been the first sculpture that visitors encountered in the exhibition in 1900.

71
Auguste Rodin
Pierre de Wissant,
monumental nude
1886
Bronze; lost-wax cast by Fonderie de Coubertin, 1977
H 196 cm, W 113 cm, D 95 cm
Musée Rodin, S. 626

72
Auguste Rodin
Pierre de Wissant, monumental, also known as *The Passer-By* or *Burgher Volunteering*
1887
Bronze; lost-wax cast by Fonderie de Coubertin, 1988
H 214 cm, W 106 cm, D 118 cm
Musée Rodin, S. 6139

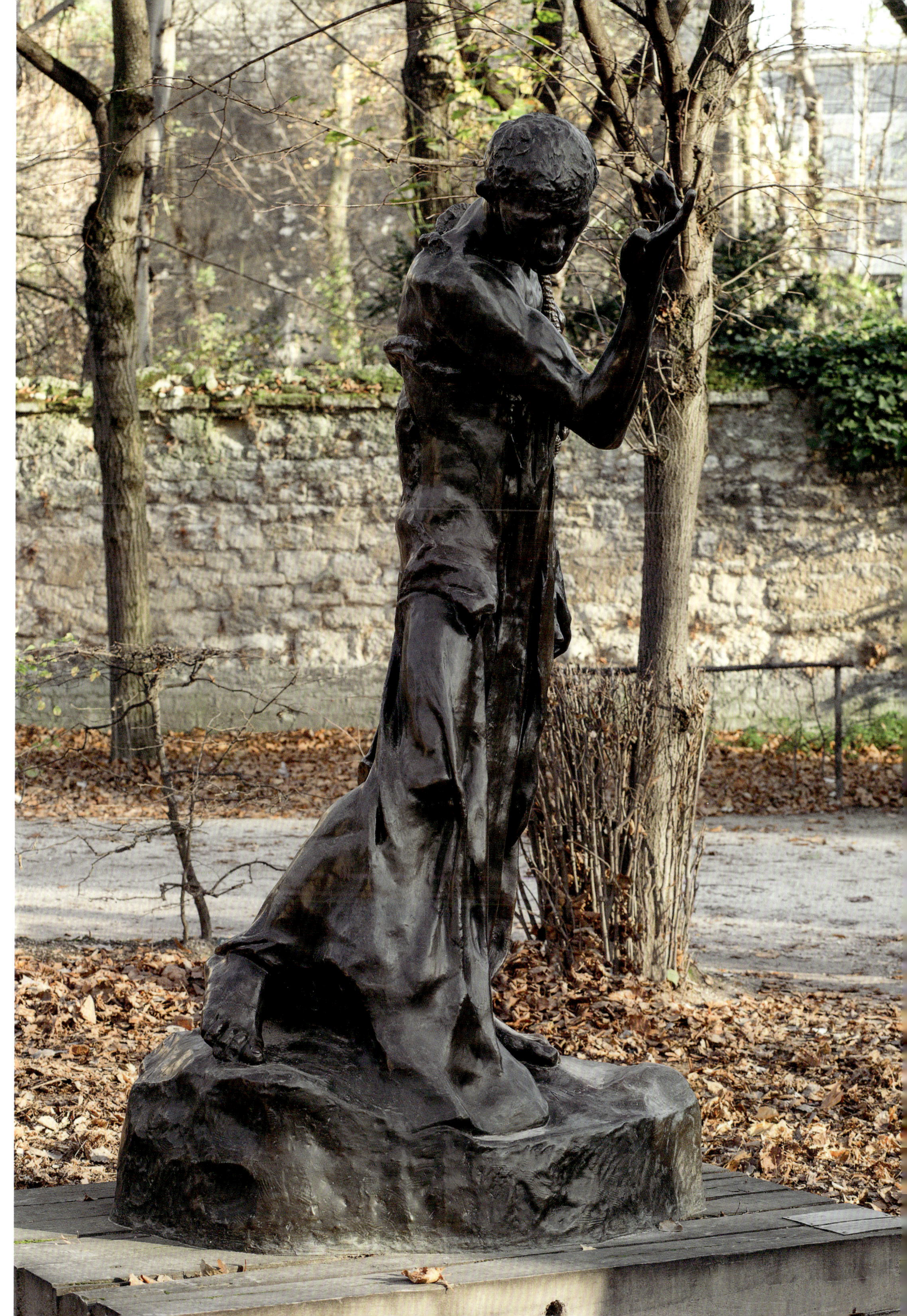

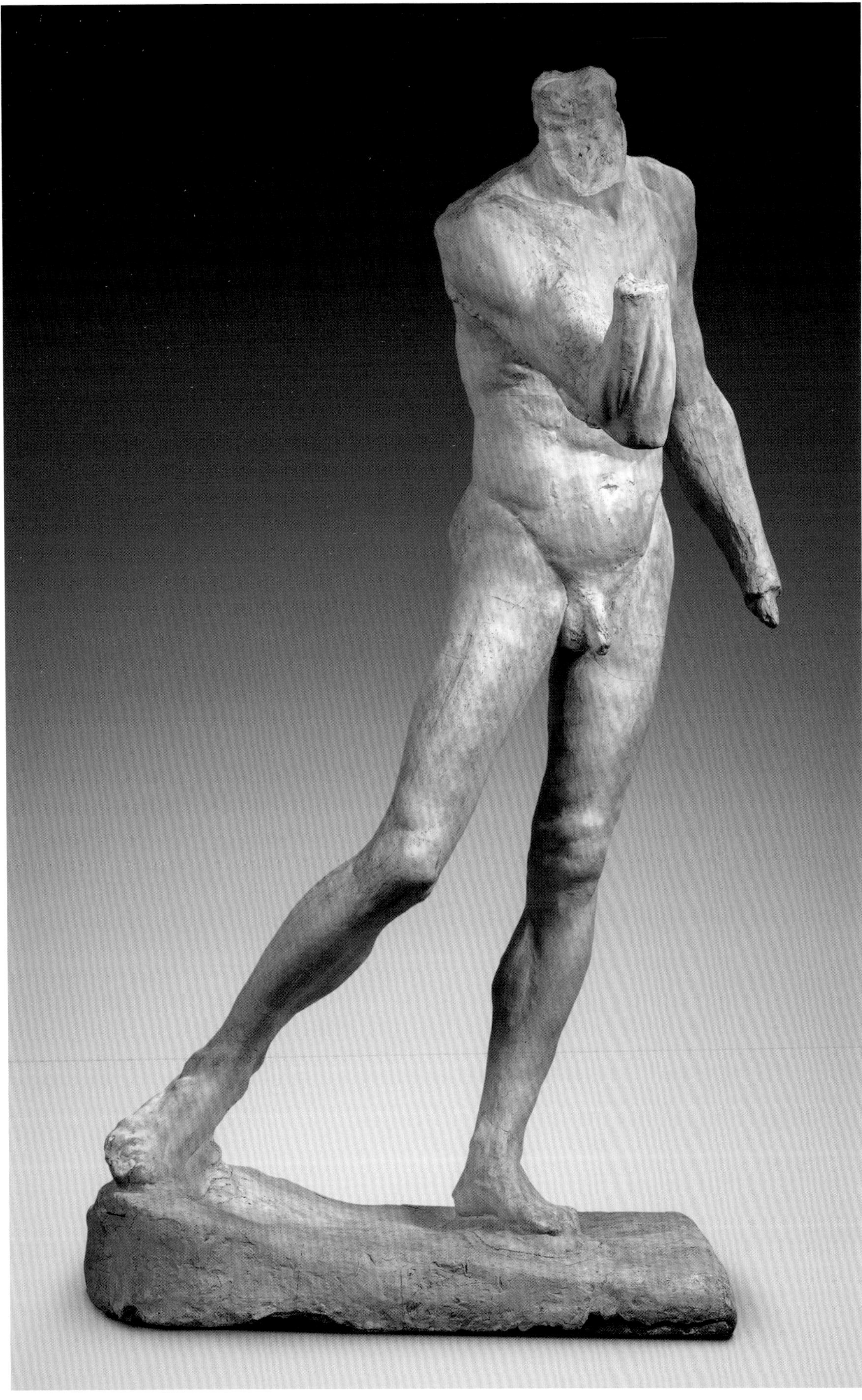

73
Auguste Rodin
Nude Pierre de Wissant, without head or hands, large version
1886
Plaster
H 190 cm, W 100 cm, D 82 cm
Musée Rodin, S. 448
Rodin donation, 1916

74
The so-called Apollo Ludovisi
Roman
First–second century AD, copy of a lost Greek original of the mid- to late fourth century BC
Marble
H 170 cm, W 67 cm, D 46 cm
Musée Rodin, Co. 1139
Rodin donation, 1916

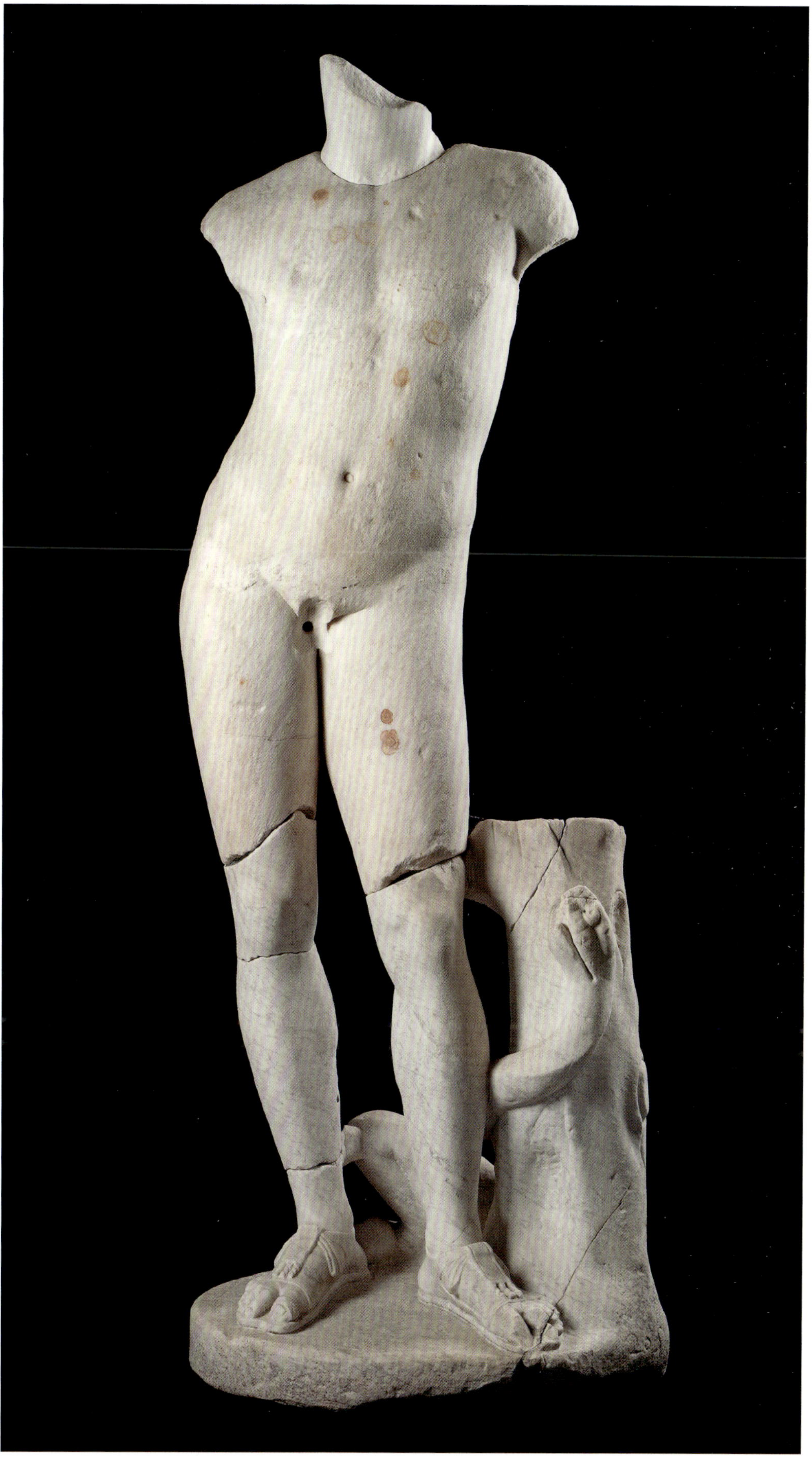

I often evoke the floral souls that you have raised up out of antique vases.

Letter from Rainer Maria Rilke to Rodin, 8 March 1908

Ancient artefacts, modern meanings

Throughout his career Rodin playfully used the technique of assemblage, bringing together different objects, whole or fragmentary. From the 1890s he became increasingly experimental, creating strangely poetic new compositions. As he began to collect antiquities, he would sometimes integrate them with his own figures, often from *The Gates of Hell*, sometimes making a plaster version of an ancient piece to incorporate it into his own creation. He usually modelled these maquettes in plaster or clay in his studio, but he was occasionally commissioned to translate them into marble or bronze.

The series of works presented here is intended to show one of many examples of Rodin's creative process in all its complexity, and illustrates his art of metamorphoses, largely inspired by his readings of the Roman authors Ovid and Apuleius. Changing from one form to another, the figure is given a new life and context by its association with a different figure or object. Although this was not a new technique, Rodin developed and enriched it by using different parts of the body from a range of his own works. In this example he used the figures of Venus, *The Sphinx*, *Obsession* and the *Head of a Slavic Woman* to create various compositions. Rodin played with what he called *abattis*, small models of heads, arms, legs and feet that he made separately before casting them in multiple plaster versions ready to be assembled in a work. These pieces are difficult to date precisely and do not follow a logical sequence. What we can say is that these figures were reworked and recomposed between 1895 and 1910.

Fig. 33
Jean Limet (1855–1941)
Rodin working in the peristyle of the Pavillon de l'Alma, Meudon
Around 1912
Albumen print
H 22.3 cm, W 17 cm
Musée Rodin, Ph. 47
Rodin donation, 1916

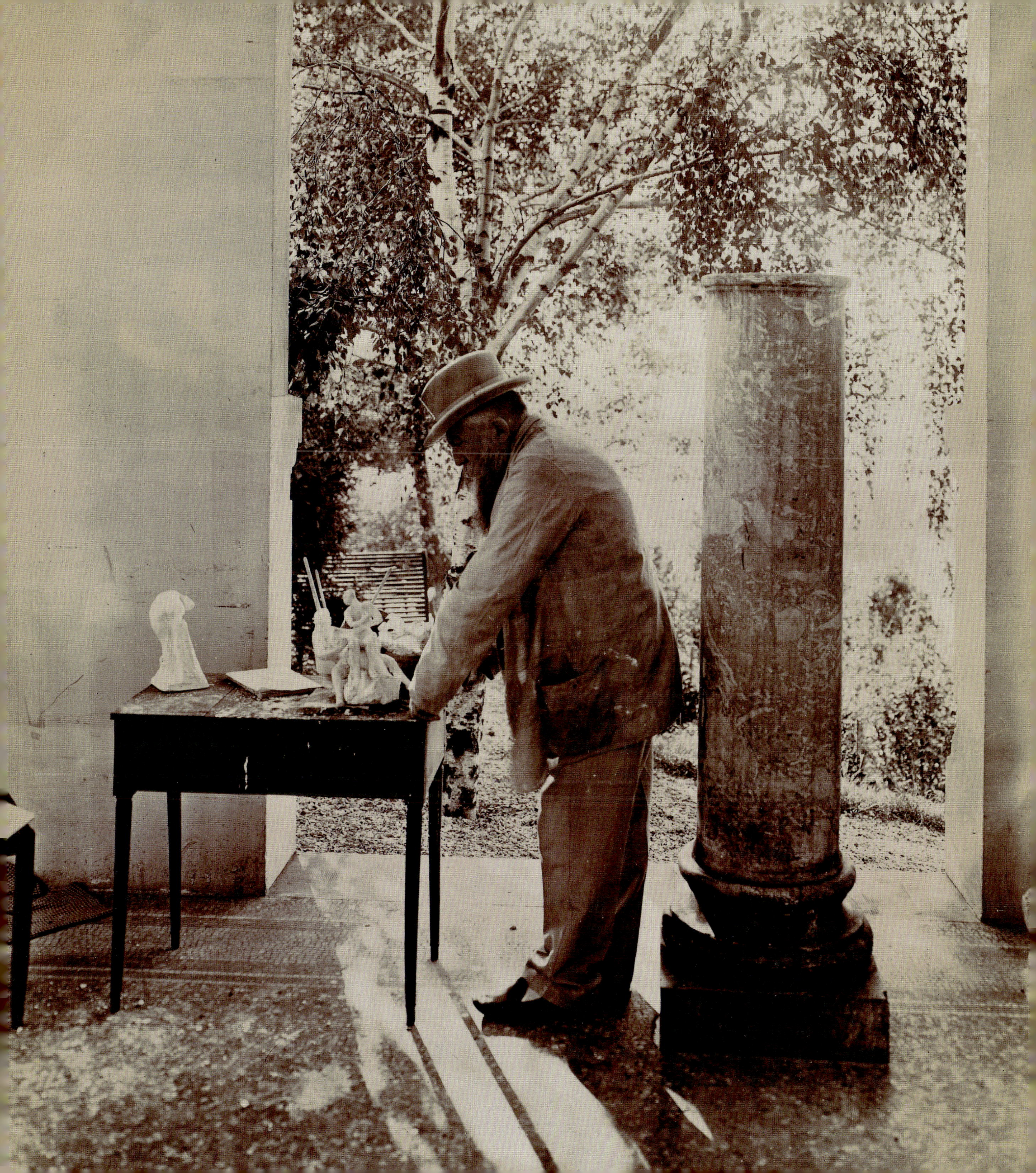

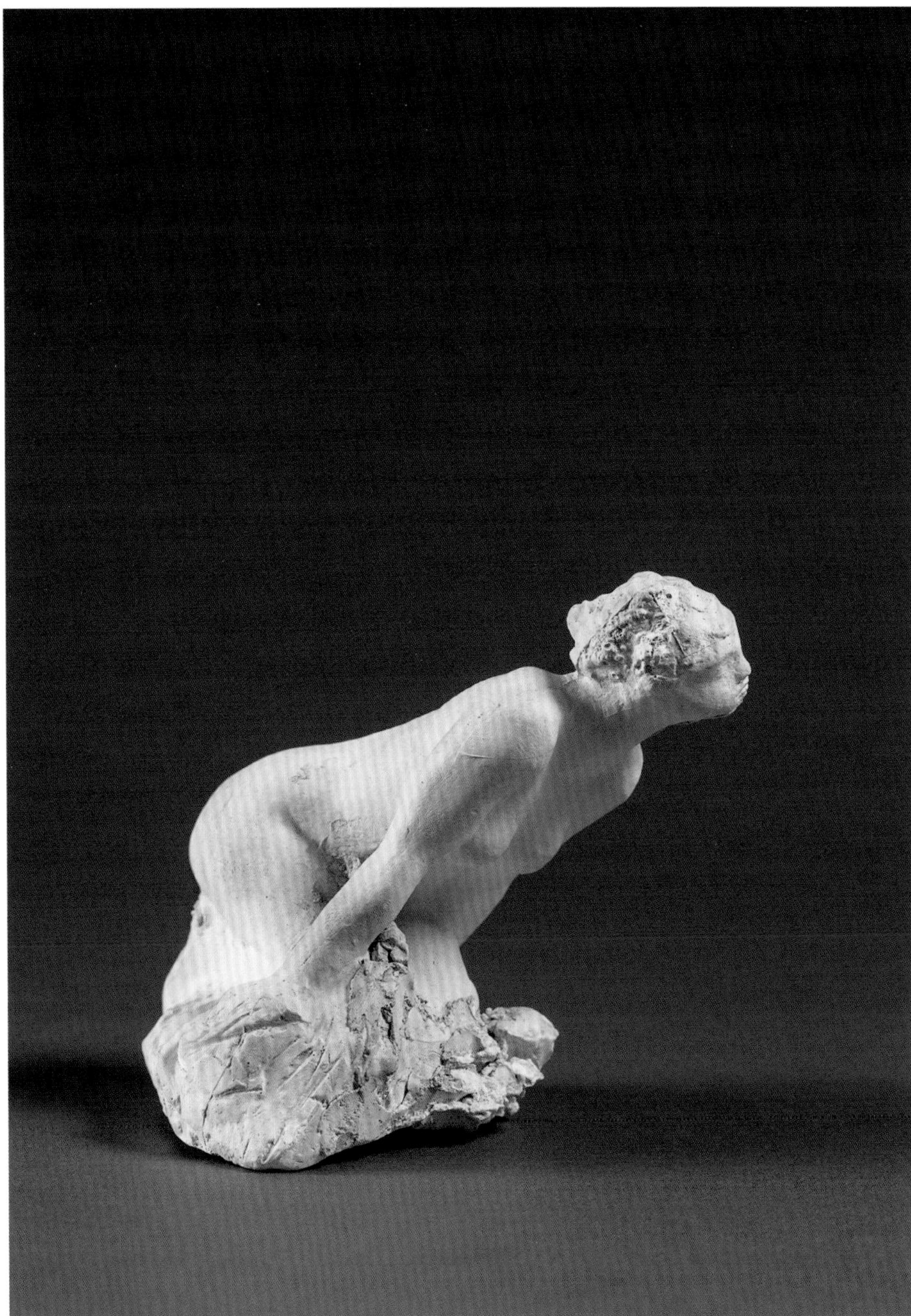

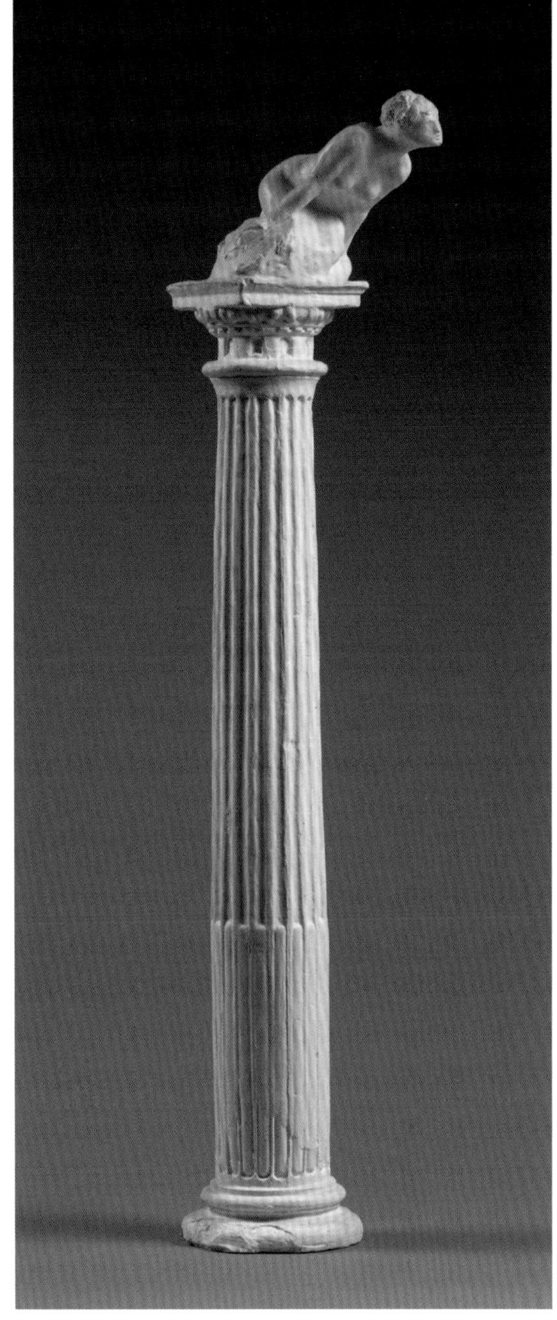

The figure of the crouching Sphinx originated in the right door panel of *The Gates of Hell*. Rodin first exhibited it under the name *The Sphinx* or *Sphinge* at the Galerie Georges Petit in Paris in 1889 as a pendant to *The Succubus*, which it resembles. The sculptor then straightened the back of the original figure into an animal posture, with head raised (Cat. 75). In 1900, in the exhibition of all his sculpture in the Pavillon de l'Alma, he presented it on top of a fluted column with a decorated capital (Cat. 76).

75
Auguste Rodin
The Sphinx
Around 1886
Plaster
H 16.2 cm, W 12.5 cm, D 16.5 cm
Musée Rodin, S. 822
Rodin donation, 1916

76
Auguste Rodin
The Sphinx, on a column
1900
Plaster
H 91.5 cm, W 15.5 cm, D 23 cm
Musée Rodin, S. 2478
Rodin donation, 1916

The Sphinx and its individual elements (the so-called *abattis*), including head and arms, were used in numerous compositions. Before 1903 it was combined with an ancient vase (Cat. 77) to become a woman in a pool, a term used by Rodin's assistant Louis-Dominique Matthet when carving the marble. Subsequently, after Rodin's death, it was known as *Little Water Fairy*. The sculptor also turned the figure upright for assembly with a vertical figure and added *abattis* to form the group the *Birth of Venus*, which would later be translated into marble (1906–1907, Madrid, Thyssen-Bornemisza Museum; Fig. 36). The vertical back of *The Sphinx* is reminiscent of the simplified, annotated drawing *Rock* (Fig. 35), with its fragmented vision of the body that can also be seen in the *Torso of a Woman* at the Victoria and Albert Museum.

Another maquette, most probably preparatory to the group, shows the figure of the *Birth of Venus* without arms, simply assembled with the *Head of a Slavic Woman* (Cat. 84). An old photograph shows it without its *abattis* (Fig. 37). *Abattis* of this head, like that of the female sphinx, were cast in large numbers ready to be assembled with other figures, though some were placed individually on their own support (Cat. 85).

The ancient theme of the birth of Venus appears very early in Rodin's work in a retouched photograph of an assemblage annotated 'Birth of Venus emerging from the waves' (Fig. 34).

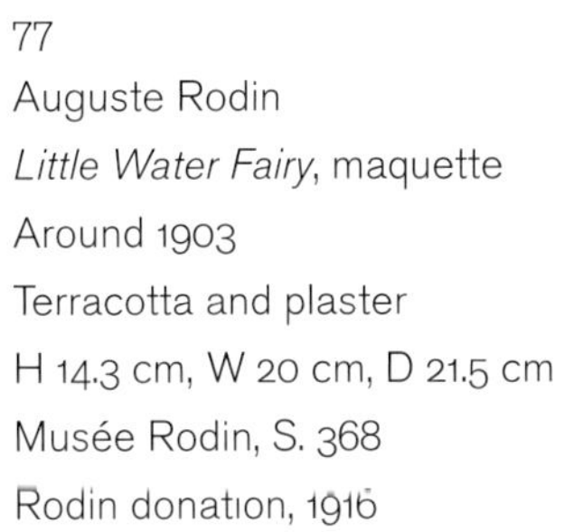

77
Auguste Rodin
Little Water Fairy, maquette
Around 1903
Terracotta and plaster
H 14.3 cm, W 20 cm, D 21.5 cm
Musée Rodin, S. 368
Rodin donation, 1916

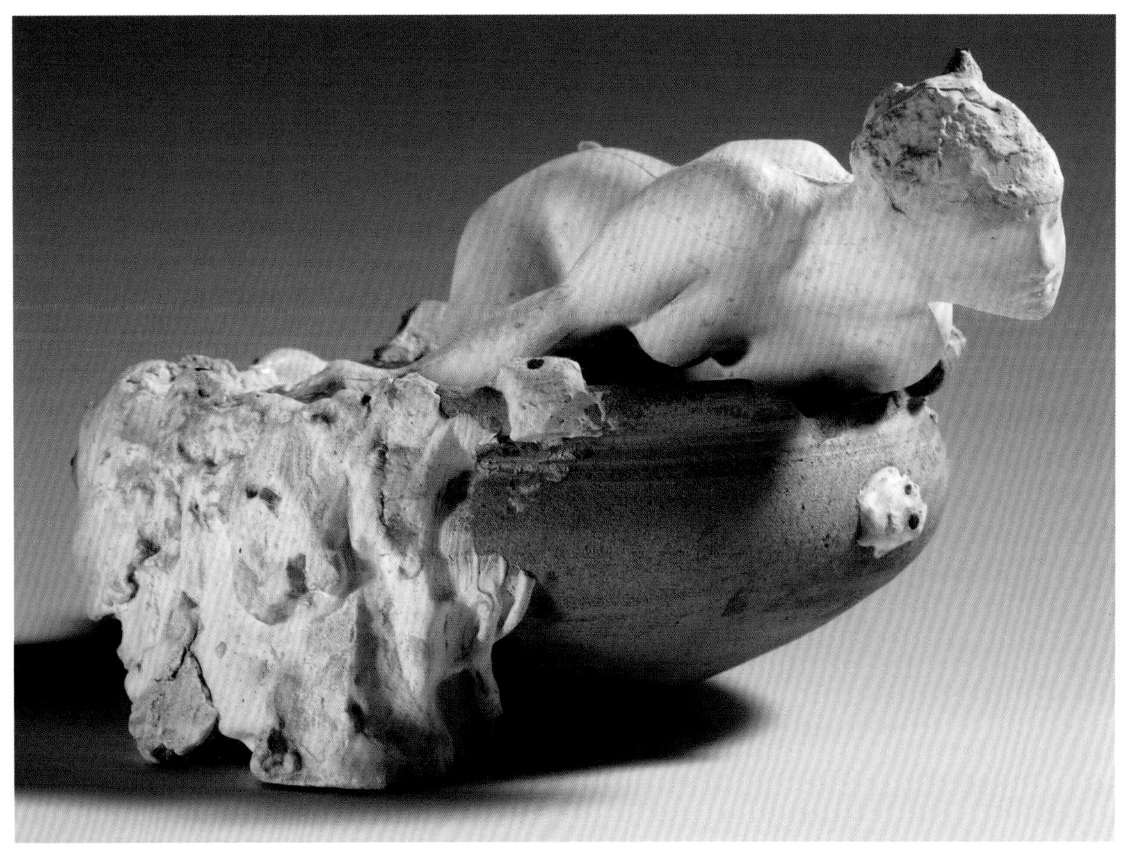

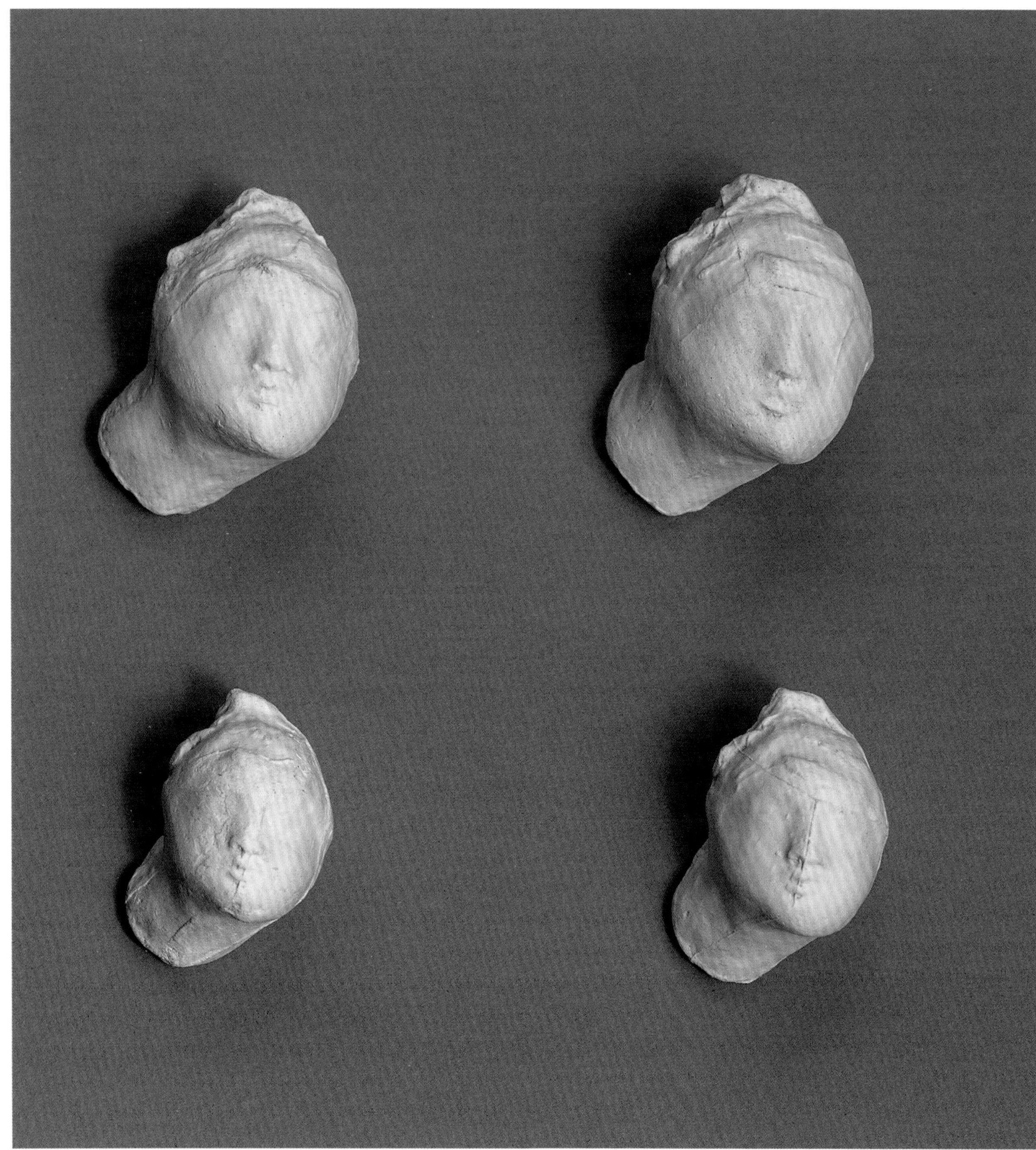

78
Auguste Rodin
Head of *The Sphinx*
After 1886
Plaster
H 5.5 cm, W 3.5 cm, D 5.3 cm
Musée Rodin, S. 4256
Rodin donation, 1916

79
Auguste Rodin
Head of *The Sphinx*
After 1886
Plaster
H 5.8 cm, W 3.9 cm, D 5.6 cm
Musée Rodin, S. 4247
Rodin donation, 1916

80
Auguste Rodin
Head of *The Sphinx*
After 1886
Plaster
H 4.5 cm, W 2.8 cm, D 4.2 cm
Musée Rodin, S. 6146
Rodin donation, 1916

81
Auguste Rodin
Head of *The Sphinx*
After 1886
Plaster
H 5.5 cm, W. 3.5 cm, D 5.3 cm
Musée Rodin, S. 4248
Rodin donation, 1916

He returned to the theme again in the first decade of the twentieth century in both drawing and sculpture, particularly through annotations, but also in a diverse range of representations. Venus is a section of body, made rigid and placed diagonally to represent the movement of her sudden emergence from the water. The assemblage seen in Fig. 38 can be compared with the drawing Cat. 90 annotated 'birth of Venus'. More obscurely, the annotation 'birth of Venus' appears on the neck of a plaster *Head of Pierre de Wissant*, though it is difficult to know what the artist's intention here may have been (Cat. 89).

Arms no larger than my little finger, but so full of life that they make your heart beat faster … filled with such an abundance of wisdom … hundreds of them there, not one like any other.

Rainer Maria Rilke, Letter to Clara Westhoff Rilke, 1902

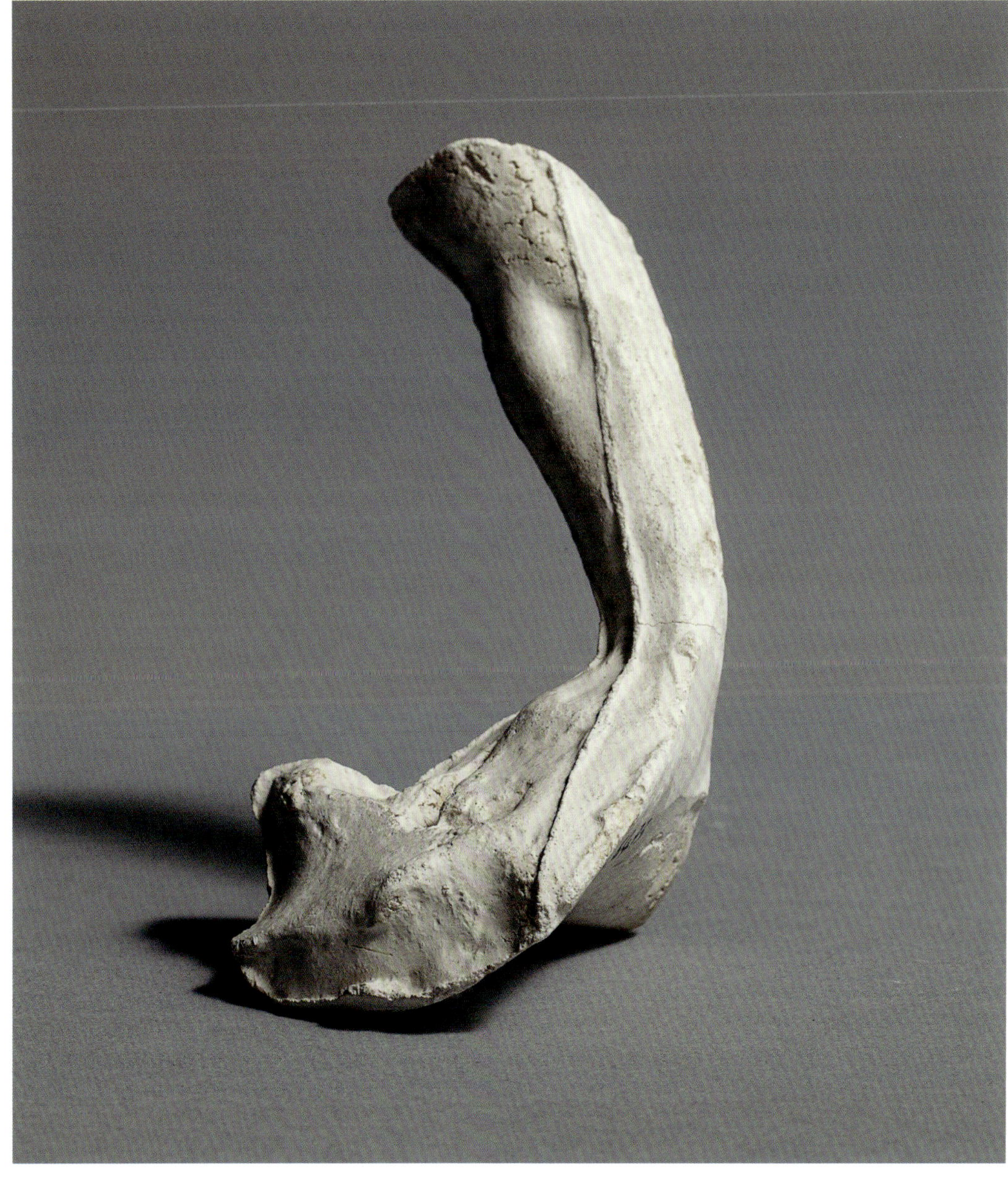

82
Auguste Rodin
Left Arm, hand against a mound (*The Sphinx*?)
After 1886
Plaster
H 9.4 cm, W 4.6 cm, D 4.4 cm
Musée Rodin, S. 6473
Rodin donation, 1916

The recurring sculpted figure of the *Birth of Venus* appears again in an assemblage with an ancient vase in the shape of a basket known as a *kalathos* (Cat. 93), which was also combined with the plaster figure of *Obsession* (Cat. 94). The figure of *Obsession* was elsewhere placed on a wooden board and attached to an inclined marble plaque, perhaps for a marble relief project (Cat. 95). Rodin wrote on it in pencil 'flash/of drawings'.

Rodin would have seen in the Louvre ancient vases from Canosa, in southern Italy, which had separately made figures attached, and he also had photographs of them (Fig. 39). He began exploring the technique of creating assemblages of his own figures with an ancient vase in 1895, when he started to collect ceramics. Rodin chose a figure and a vase that would form a harmonious group, and joined the two elements together with plaster, with a sudden, rapid action. The body thus emerged from the mouth of the vase defying gravity, often at the very edge of imbalance. But Rodin could only preserve the ancient vase by having several casts made and then assembling these plaster versions with his own, usually female, figures. In this way, for instance, he produced variations using a cup from Boeotia in Greece (Cat. 92) in no fewer than three compositions: the *Birth of Venus* (Fig. 38), *Galatea* (Cat. 91) and *Flowers in a Vase* (Musée Rodin, S. 3700). The original material, texture and function of the vase were changed, leaving only its shape in a new material that was integrated as an object into Rodin's sculpture. The revered antiquity of the piece from his collection thus became incorporated as an element of his work. The small female figures, posed in complete freedom, took ownership of the vase with familiarity, sheltering in it or resting on it. The technique was a laboratory for infinite experimentation and ideas.

Between 1895 and 1910, Rodin became obsessed by the image of the vase, which was simply another cast that he assimilated to the female form. Working from a model, he captured poses in his drawings that he then simplified in order to blend them with the contours of a vase, sometimes adding a pencil sketch of the painted decoration from an ancient Greek vase on the body of the woman (*Woman as Vase*, Fig. 40). These woman-vases were frequently enhanced with a wash of terracotta watercolour. Woman-vase, woman becomes vase, woman in a vase. Using scissors, Rodin would cut out his coloured drawings of women and assemble them together, gluing them to a sheet of paper, in the same way as with his sculpture (Fig. 41).

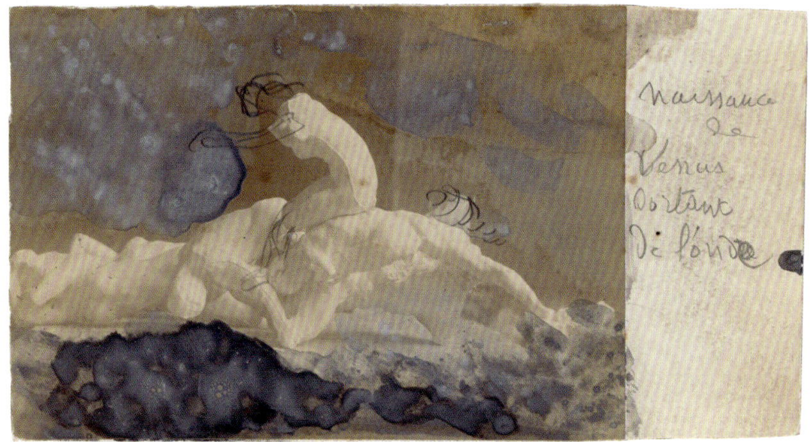

ABOVE
Fig. 34
Auguste Rodin
Birth of Venus Emerging from the Waves
Before 1889
Albumen print
H 10 cm, W 14.3 cm
Musée Rodin, Ph. 1053
Rodin donation, 1916

OPPOSITE
83
Auguste Rodin
Birth of Venus
1903
Plaster
H 40 cm, W 29.5 cm, D 18 cm
Musée Rodin, S. 2630
Rodin donation, 1916

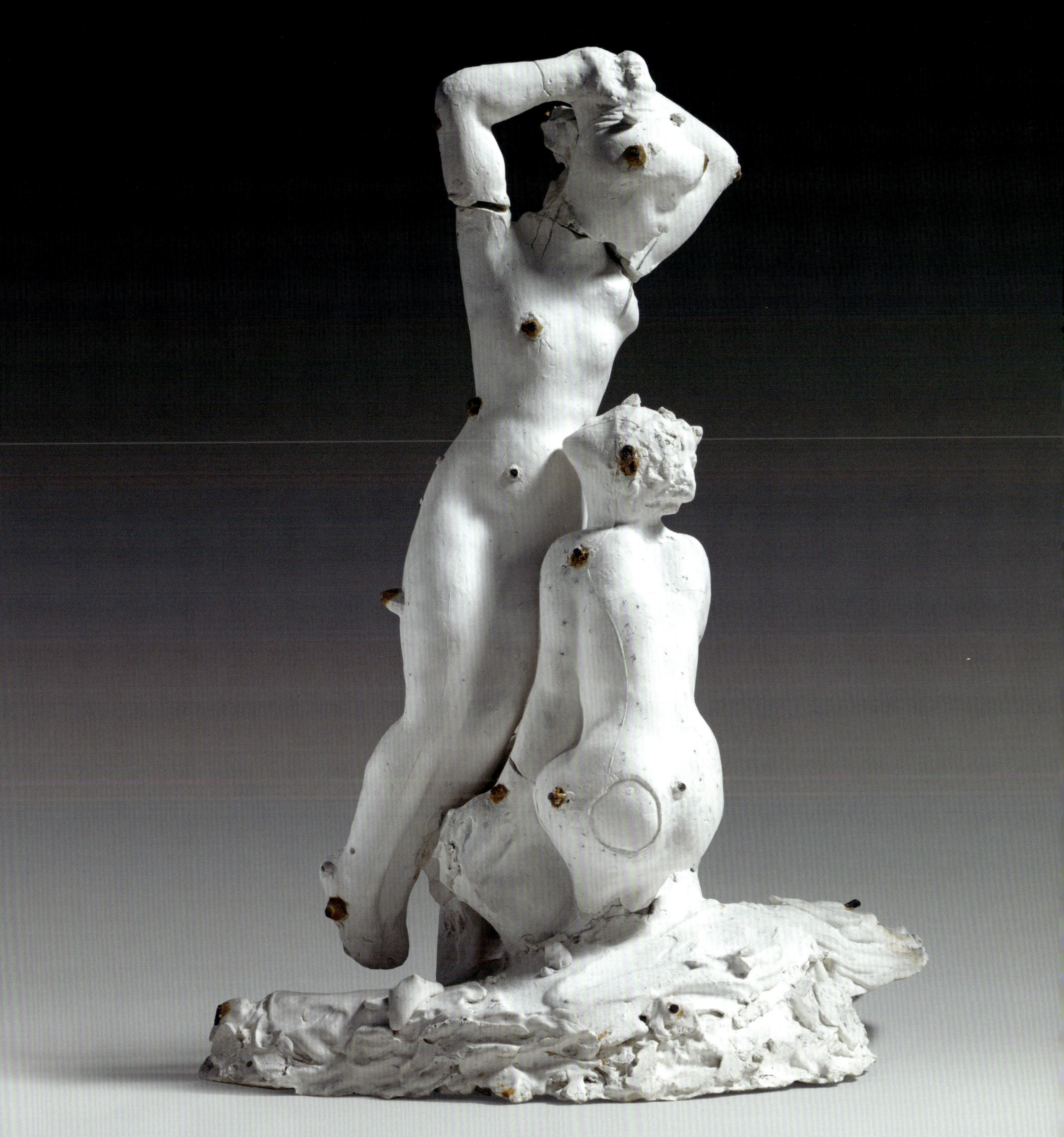

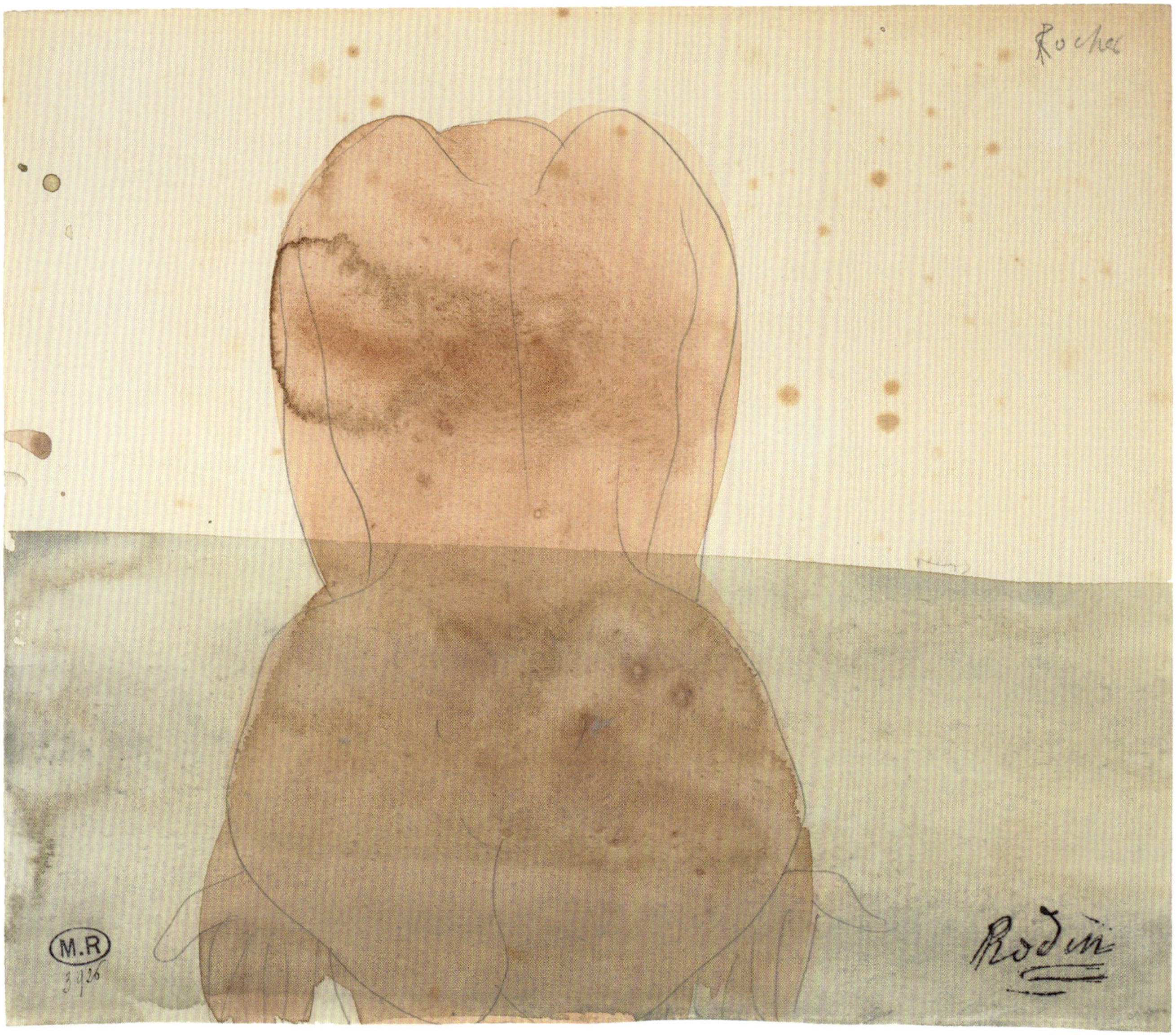

Fig. 35
Auguste Rodin
Rock
Around 1900
Graphite and watercolour
H 21.9 cm, W 24.7 cm
Musée Rodin, D. 3926
Rodin donation, 1916

Fig. 36
Jacques-Ernest Bulloz
(1858–1942)
Birth of Venus, in marble
1907?
Gelatin silver print
H 37.5 cm, W 27.2 cm
Musée Rodin, Ph. 5779

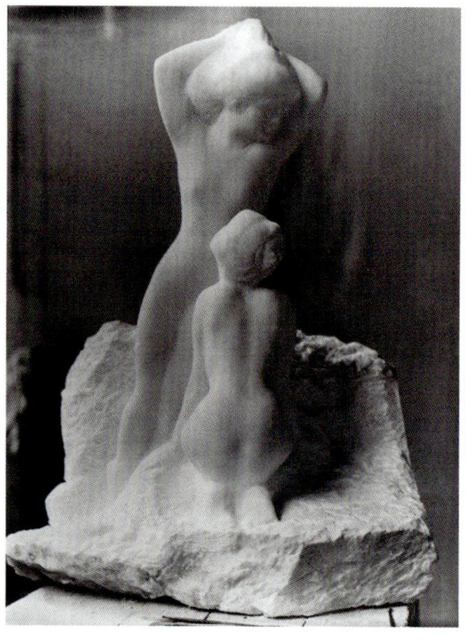

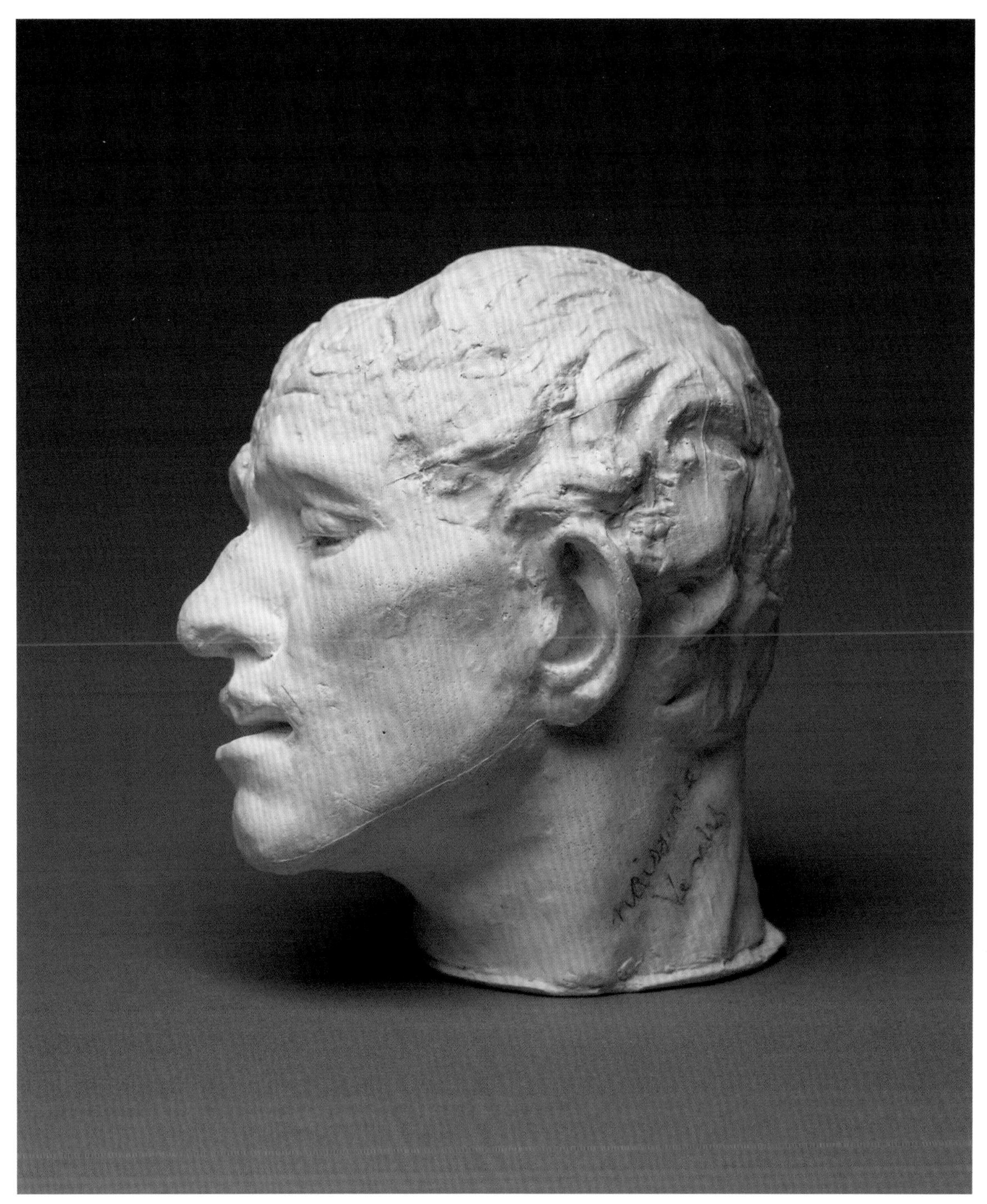

89
Auguste Rodin
Head of Pierre de Wissant, reduced
Before 1900
Plaster
H 10.5 cm, W 8 cm, D 9.4 cm
Musée Rodin, S. 4271
Rodin donation, 1916

90
Auguste Rodin
Birth of Venus
Around 1900
Graphite with stump and watercolour on paper
H 32.5 cm, W 25.2 cm
Musée Rodin, D. 3913
Rodin donation, 1916

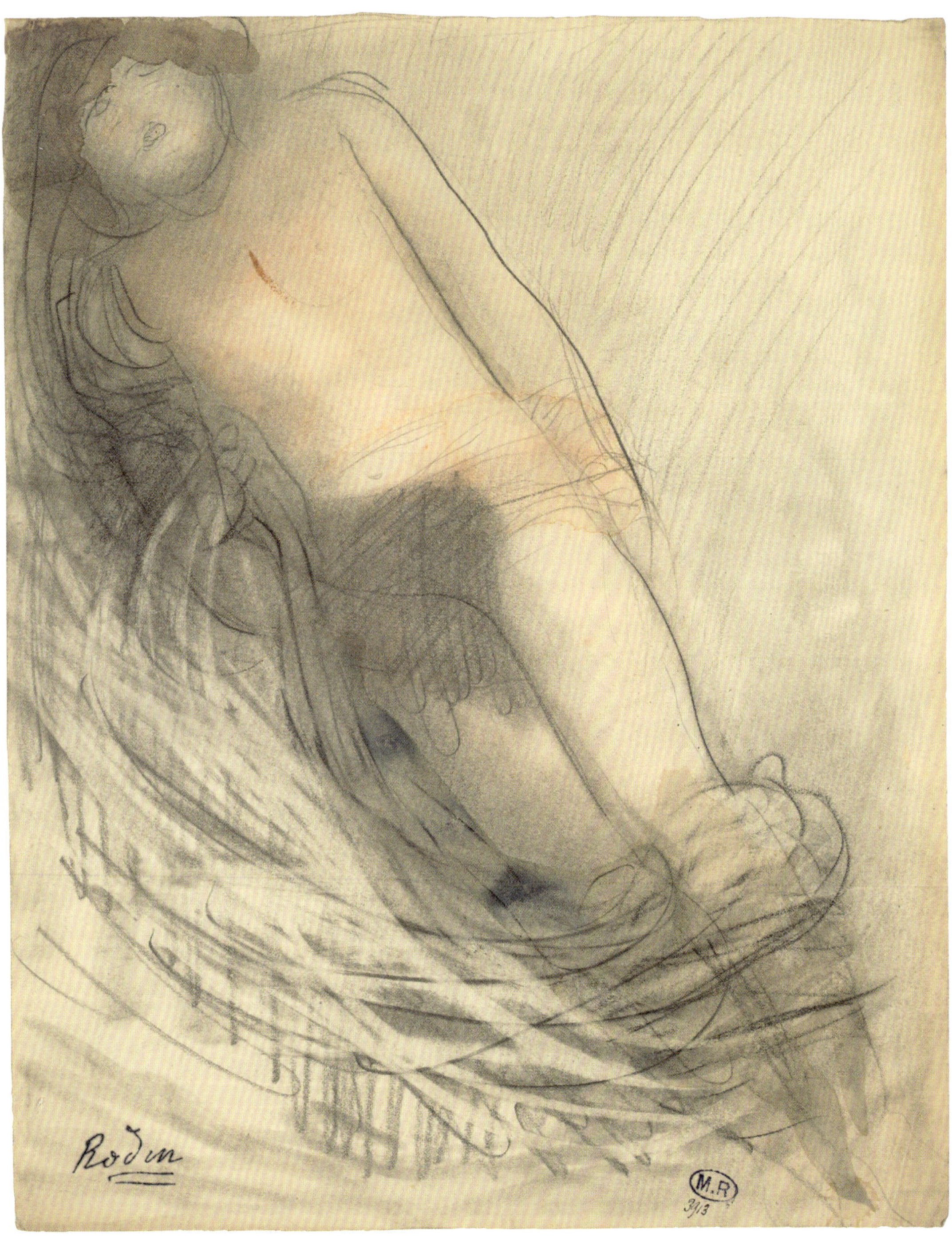

OPPOSITE ABOVE LEFT
Fig. 38
Auguste Rodin
Standing female from the *Birth of Venus* in a cast of a Boeotian cup
After 1895
Plaster
H 35 cm, W 21.4 cm, D 23.4 cm
Musée Rodin, S. 3612
Rodin donation, 1916

OPPOSITE ABOVE RIGHT
91
Auguste Rodin
Galatea cut to the thighs in a cast of a Boeotian cup
After 1895
Plaster
H 23.7 cm, W 32 cm, D 28 cm
Musée Rodin, S. 3721
Rodin donation, 1916

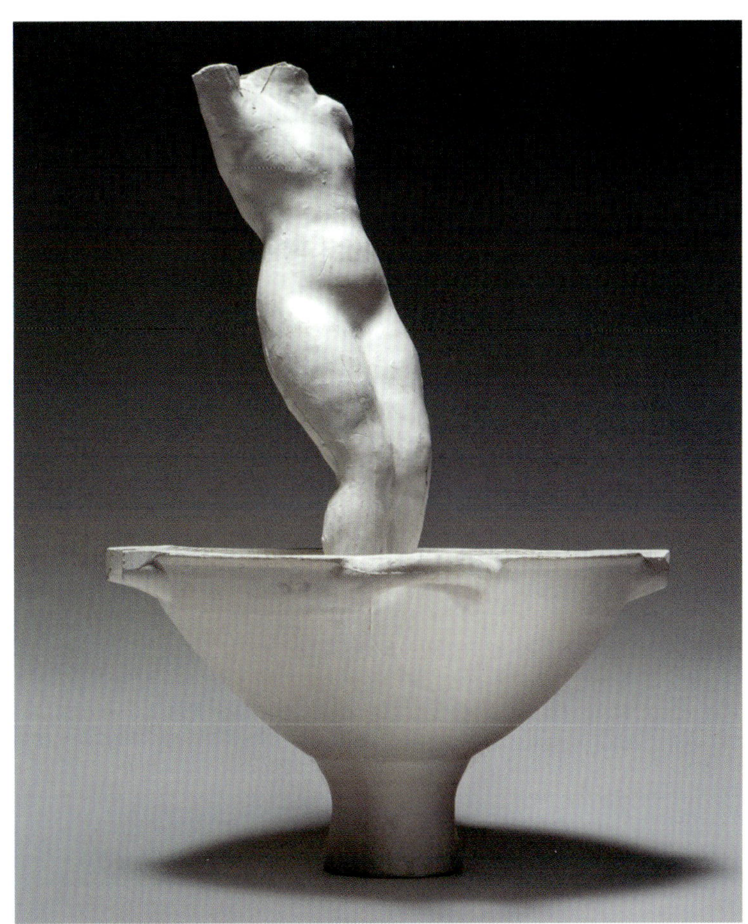

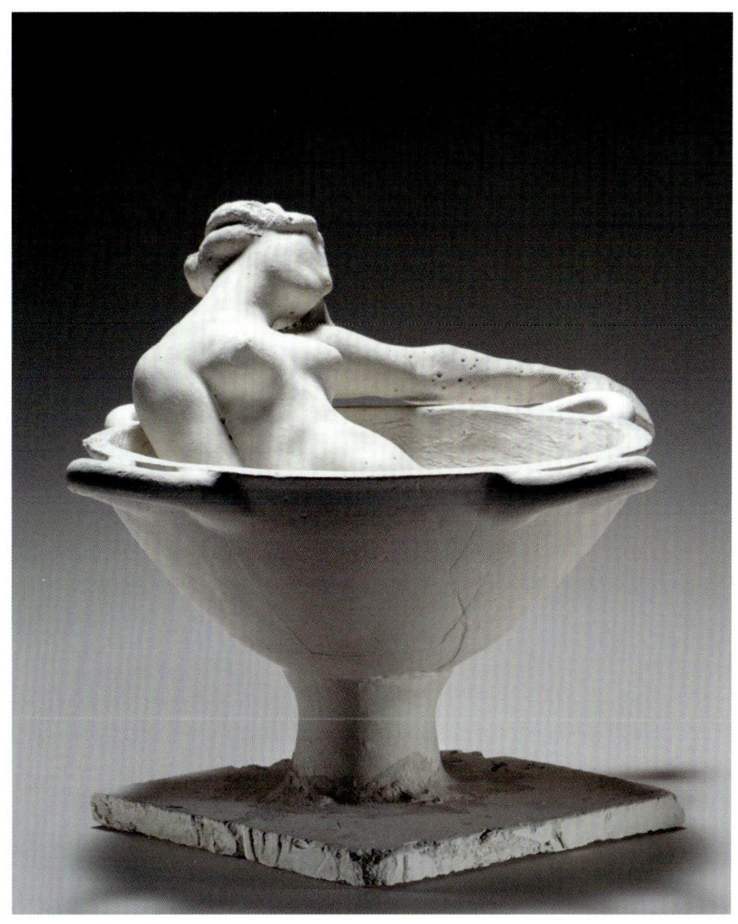

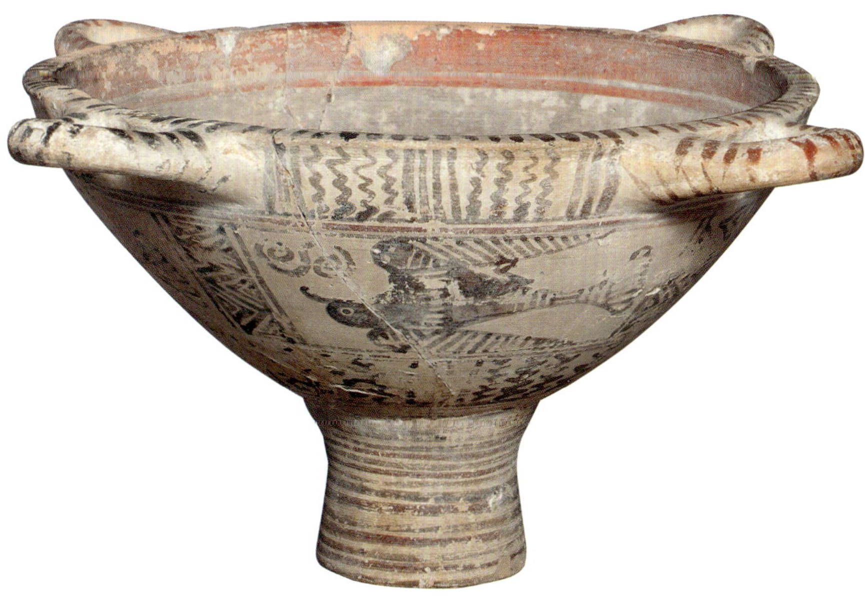

92
Boeotian cup
Greek
550–530 BC
Terracotta
H 13.8 cm, W 27.9 cm, D 21 cm
Musée Rodin, Co. 1373
Rodin donation, 1916

BELOW LEFT
93
Auguste Rodin
Standing female from the *Birth of Venus* in an ancient Greek vase (*kalathos*)
After 1895
Plaster and terracotta
H 30.7 cm, W 15.8 cm, D 22.6 cm
Musée Rodin, S. 3716
Rodin donation, 1916

BELOW RIGHT
94
Auguste Rodin
Obsession in an ancient Greek vase (*kalathos*)
After 1896
Plaster and terracotta
H 26.5 cm, W 16.4 cm, D 16.4 cm
Musée Rodin, S. 377
Rodin donation, 1916

RIGHT
Fig. 39
Anonymous
A Canosan vase in the Louvre Museum
Albumen print
H 17.8 cm, W 14 cm
Musée Rodin, Ph. 9171
Rodin donation, 1916

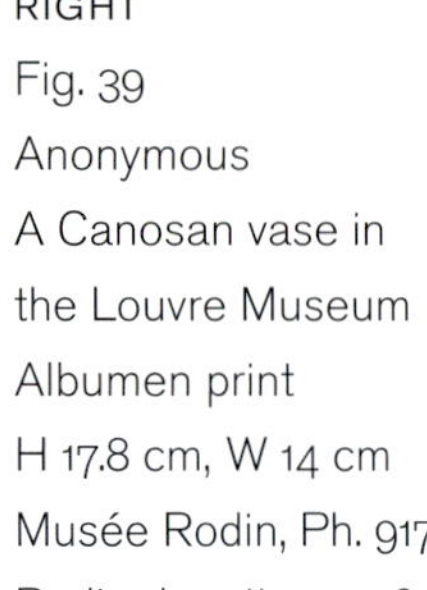

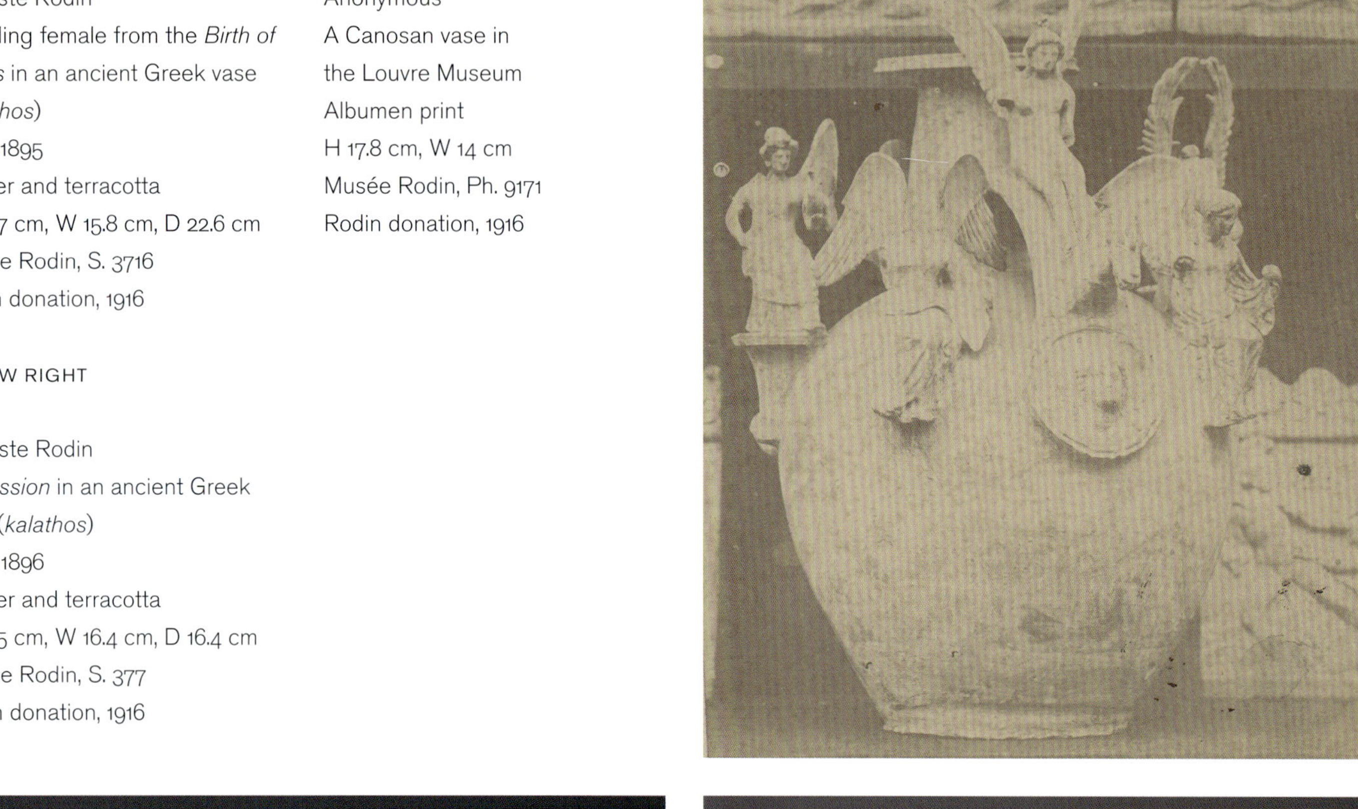

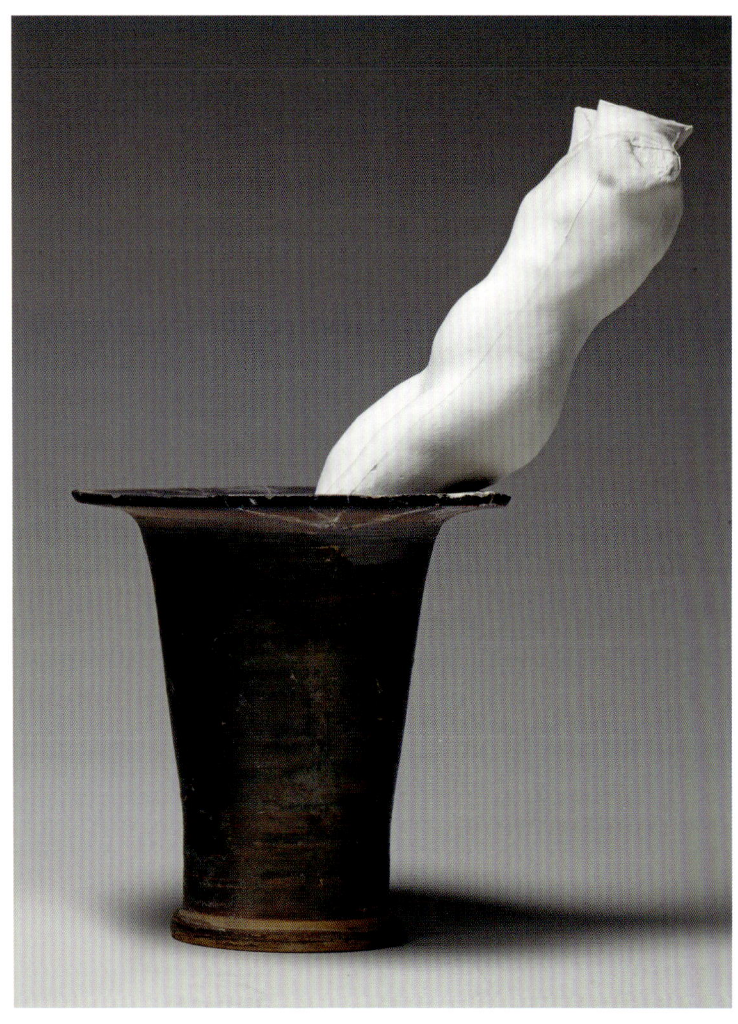

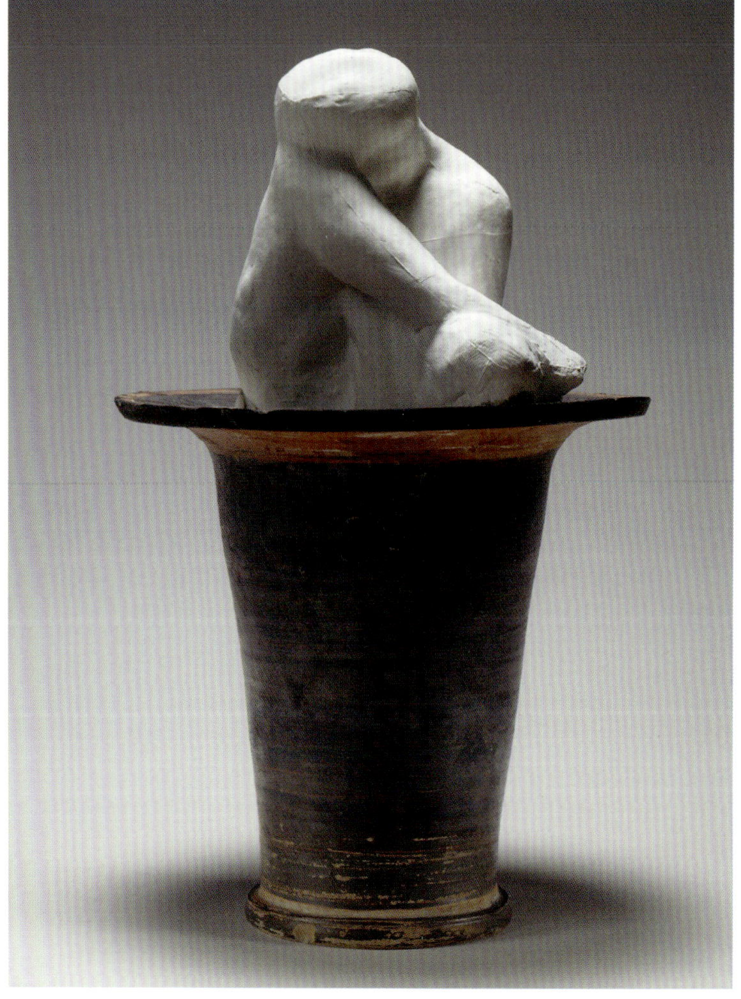

RIGHT
Fig. 40
Auguste Rodin
Woman as Vase
About 1902?
Graphite and watercolour
on watermarked paper
H 49.2 cm, W 32.3 cm
Musée Rodin, D. 4771
Rodin donation, 1916

FAR RIGHT
Fig. 41
Auguste Rodin
Two nude women half reclining
About 1896
Graphite with stump and
watercolour cut-out, paper vellum
H 32.7 cm, W 26.2 cm
Musée Rodin, D. 5192
Rodin donation, 1916

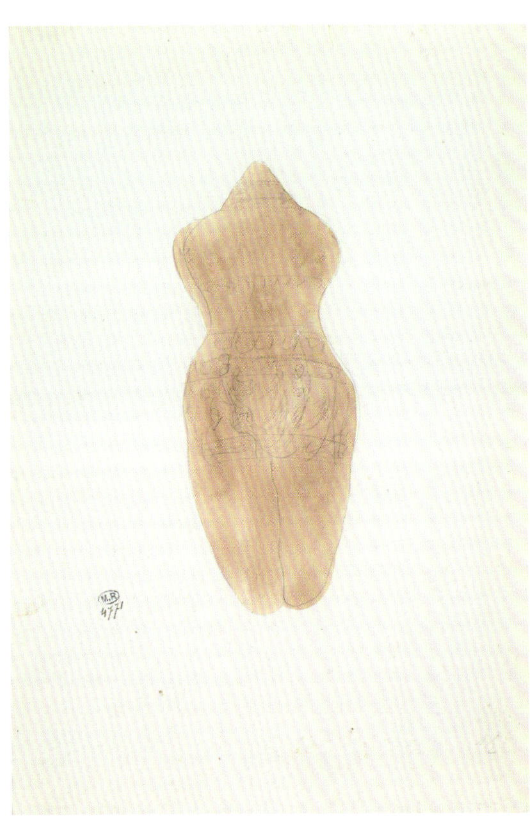

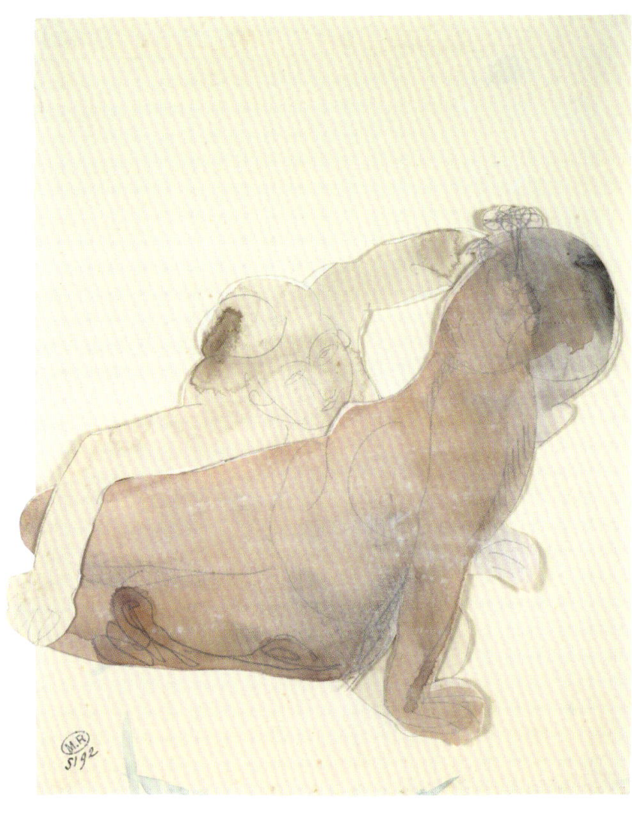

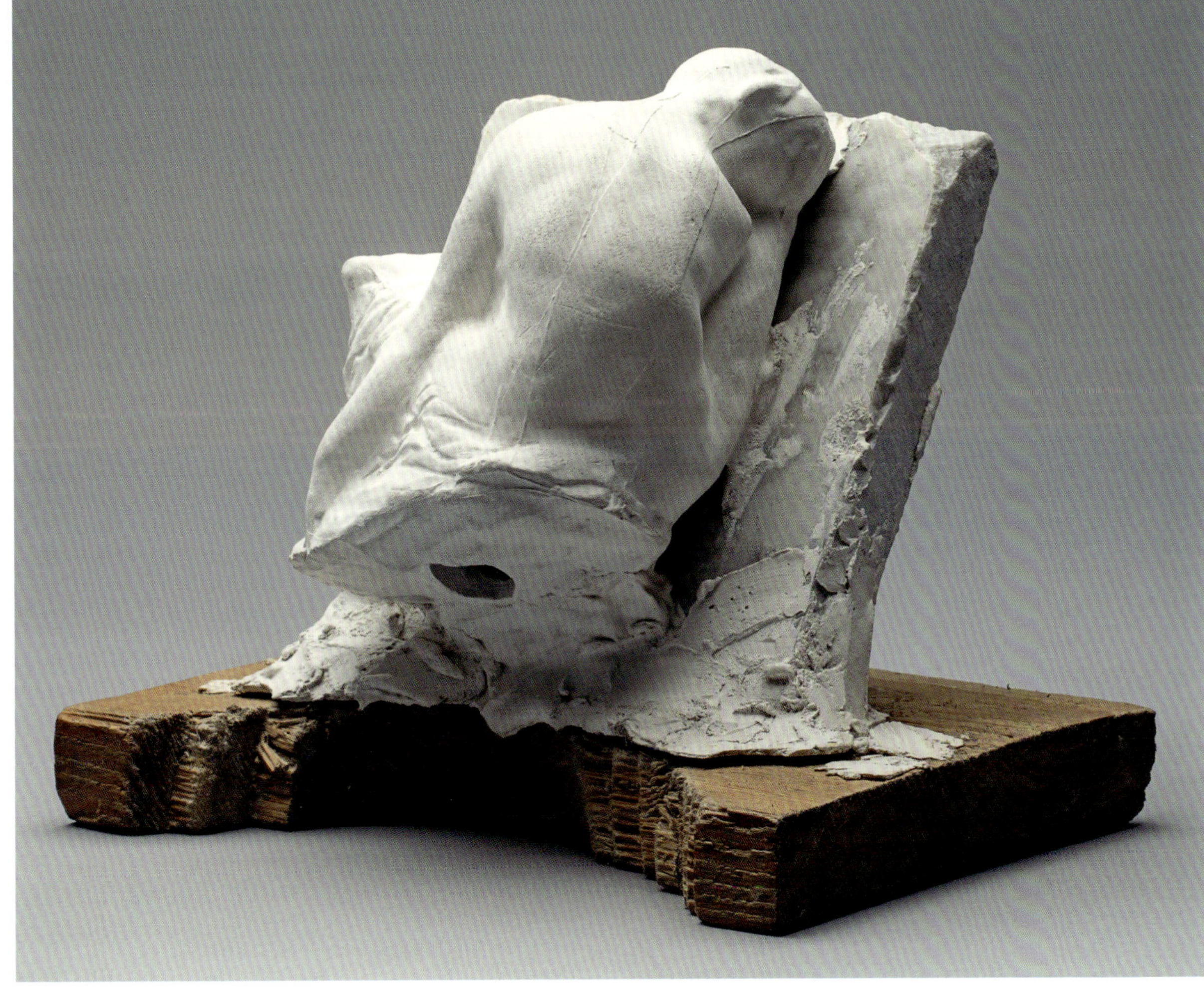

LEFT
95
Auguste Rodin
Obsession, high relief
1896
Plaster, with a wood and
marble base
H 16 cm, W 14.5 cm, D 13.3 cm
Musée Rodin, S. 2600
Rodin donation, 1916

In 1903 Rodin was unanimously elected President of the International Society of Sculptors, Painters and Gravers, founded by the painter James McNeill Whistler in 1898, and in 1905 he received a commission for a memorial to Whistler. The monument was not completed by the time of Rodin's death, but Rodin had chosen to evoke the theme of a muse climbing the mountain of glory, placing allegory at the centre of the composition. The return to the antique and the observation of nature were at the heart of his preoccupations. Using as his model the painter Gwen John (1876–1939), with whom he was having an affair, he captures the female body in all its vivacious life force. The drapery hanging from the hips around the lower half of the body evokes the statue of the *Venus de Milo*, which Rodin passionately admired and which he wrote an article about in 1910. On the raised left knee, Rodin placed a cast of a Roman funerary altar from his collection, another example of incorporating a pre-existing ancient object into his work.

96
Auguste Rodin
Draped Muse from the *Monument to Whistler*, fourth state, large version
1914–1918
Plaster and plasticine
H 238 cm, W 115 cm, D 128 cm
Musée Rodin, S. 2452
Rodin donation, 1916

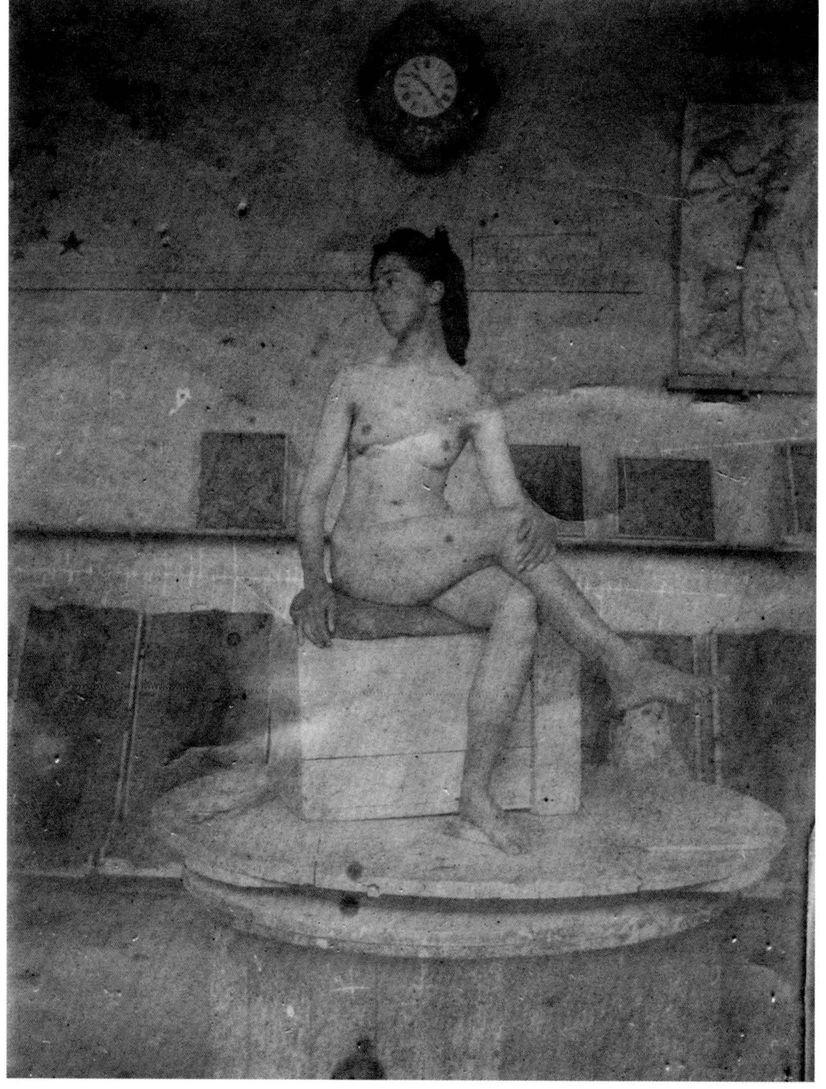

Fig. 42
Anonymous
Gwen John modelling in a studio, with casts of the Parthenon frieze on the wall behind
About 1907–1911
Photographic print
National Library of Wales, Cardiff, MS 23510D, item 25

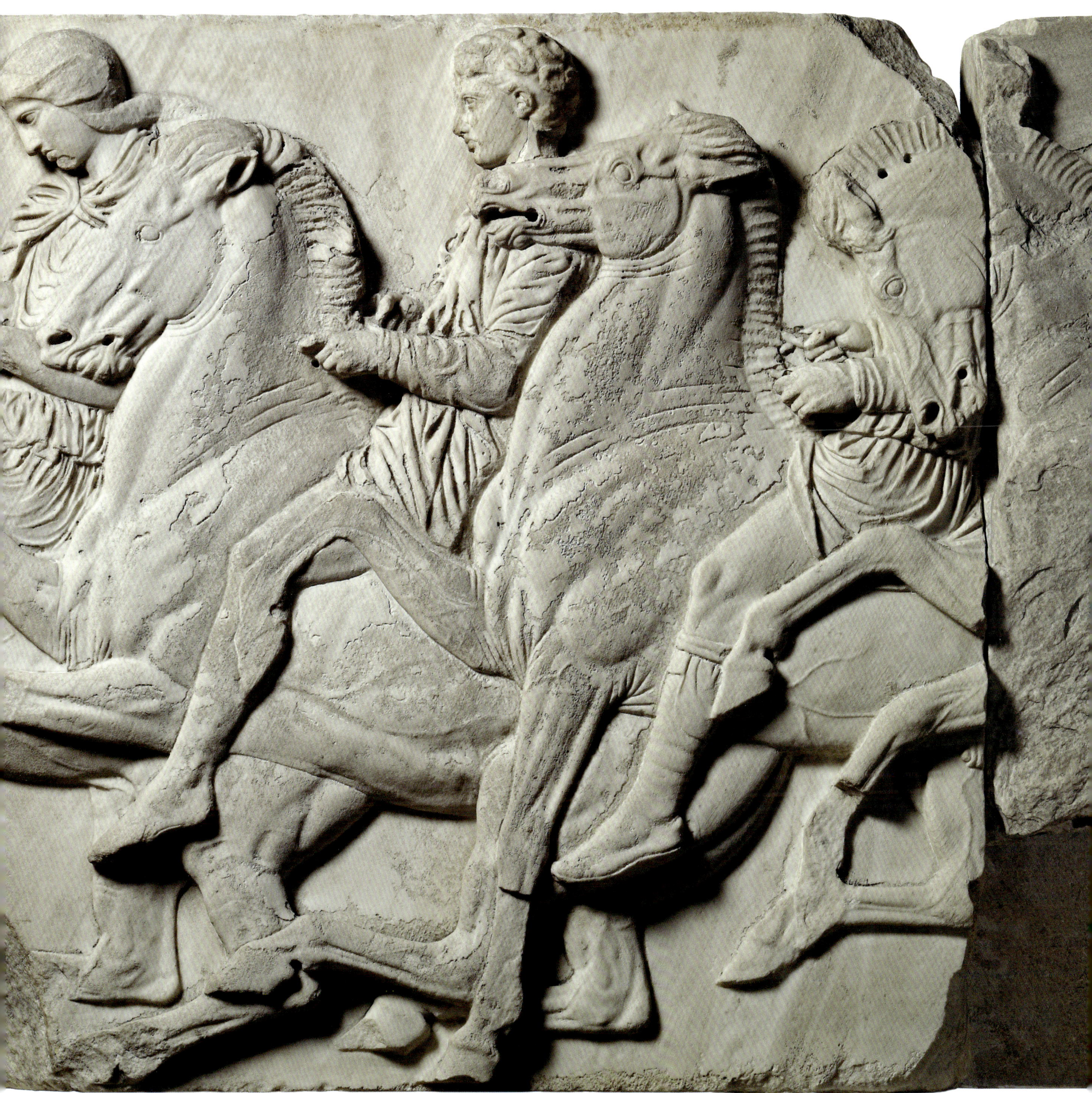

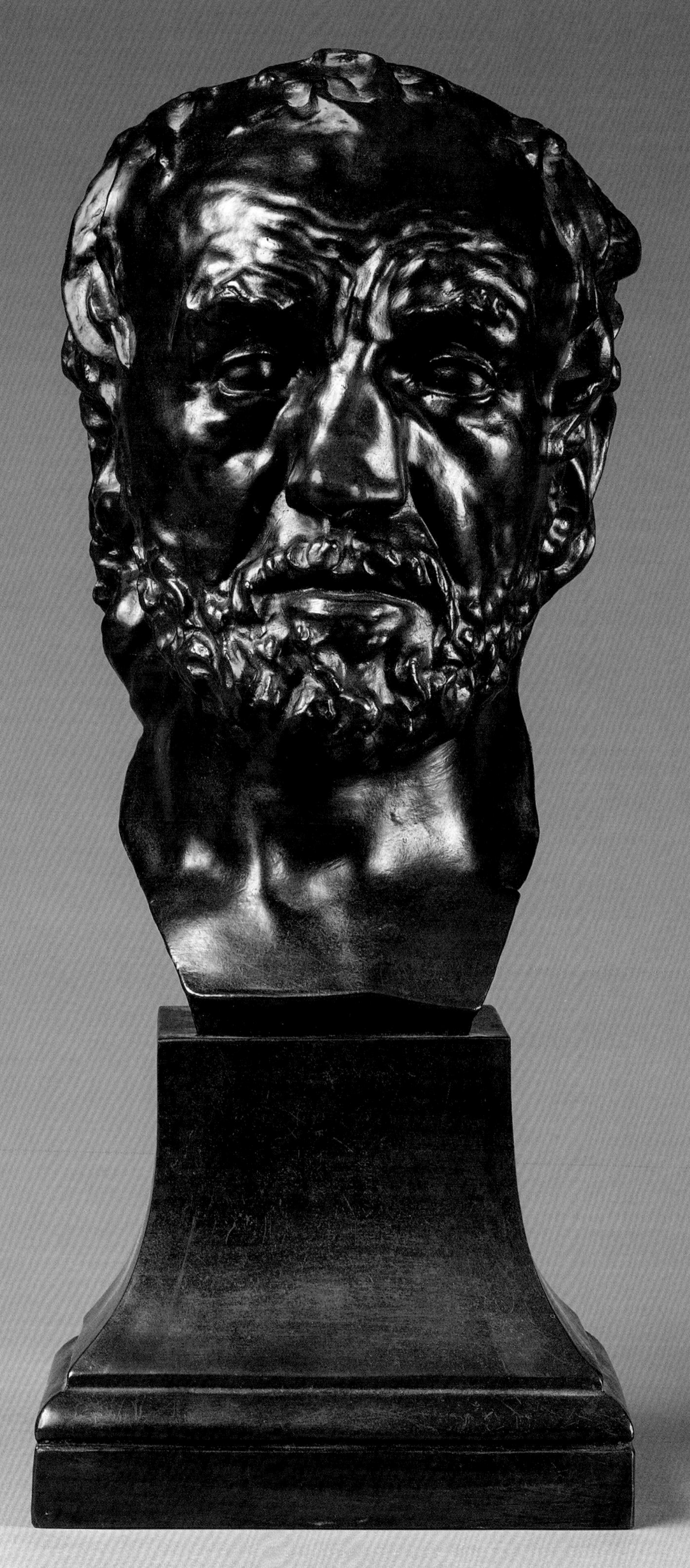

The head of an ageing and ugly man, whose broken nose only tends to accentuate the tormented expression of the face; it was the immense concentration of life in these features.... Life had not simply touched this facc, it had wrought it through and through, like some inexorable hands thrusting it into destiny and holding it there as in the rush of swirling, cleansing waters.

Rainer Maria Rilke, *Auguste Rodin*, 1902

Rodin is here experimenting with the conventions of portraiture in the western tradition. The head of the *Man with the Broken Nose* subverts the portrait type of an ancient Greek intellectual. A fuller version in marble, with the hair bound with a narrow ribbon, brings to mind the portraits of such distinguished figures as the philosopher Aristotle or the playwright Sophokles (Fig. 45). But the face, modelled on a working man named Bibi, does not wear the sage-like expression of the ancient portraits that inspired it. We seem to be confronted not by a man who is commanded by reason, but by one whose crumpled brow and broken nose suggest a temperament that is not altogether under control, and who has a tendency to violence and base instinct. It is curious that Rodin creates such a hybrid, but it is typical of his originality.

The first version of this work was the victim of an accident. In the depths of winter the temperature in the studio dropped below freezing, causing the front part of the head to separate from the back. As if it had become an archaeological relic, Rodin, ever ahead of his time, submitted it to the Salon of 1864, like a treasured fragment. The art establishment was not ready for a subject such as this, and it was refused. It was not until ten years later that it was finally accepted. It was a great success in particular in London with the artists Alphonse Legros and Frederic Leighton, and the collector Constantine Ionides.

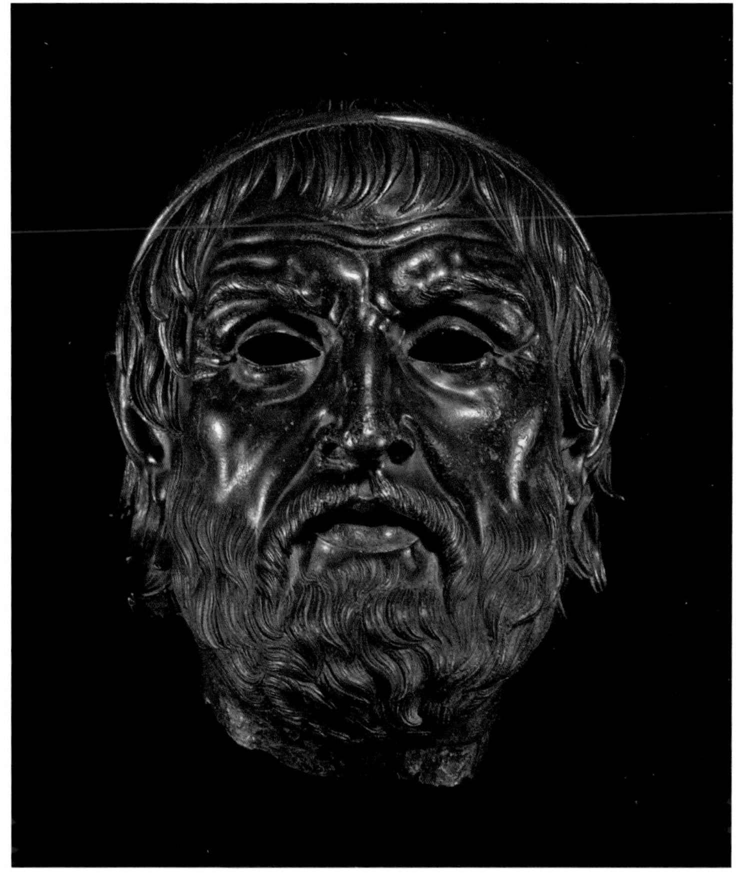

OPPOSITE
97
Auguste Rodin
Man with the Broken Nose (mask with upper chest and square pedestal cast at the same time, known as type I, fourth model)
About 1890?
Bronze; lost-wax cast by Fonderie de Coubertin, 1975
H 46.5 cm, W 18.9 cm, D 16 cm
Musée Rodin, S. 755

ABOVE
Fig. 45
Head from a statue, perhaps of the playwright Sophokles
Greek
200–100 BC
Bronze
H. 29.21 cm
British Museum, 1760,0919.1
Donated by Brownlow Cecil, 9th Earl of Exeter

98
Head of the horse of Selene
Figure O from the East Pediment
of the Parthenon
Greek
About 438–432 BC
Marble
H 62.6 cm, W 83.3 cm, D 33.3 cm
British Museum, 1816,0610.98

The generation of the sculptors of the Parthenon made new advances in the representation of emotion, not only in human subjects but also in animals. This horse's head is especially expressive. The mouth gapes, the nostrils flair, the veins stand out, the eyes bulge, the ears prick back – the whole composition communicates the stress and fatigue of the horse, one of four pulling the chariot of Selene, the moon-goddess, into the western horizon of the night's sky at break of dawn. The sculptor has captured the essence not just of one horse's condition, but rather has created a universal image that defines the very essence of equine exhaustion.

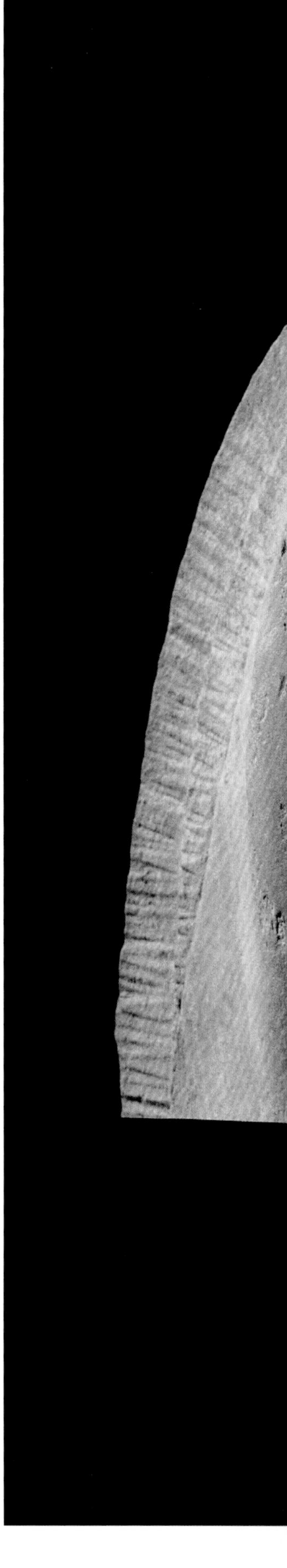

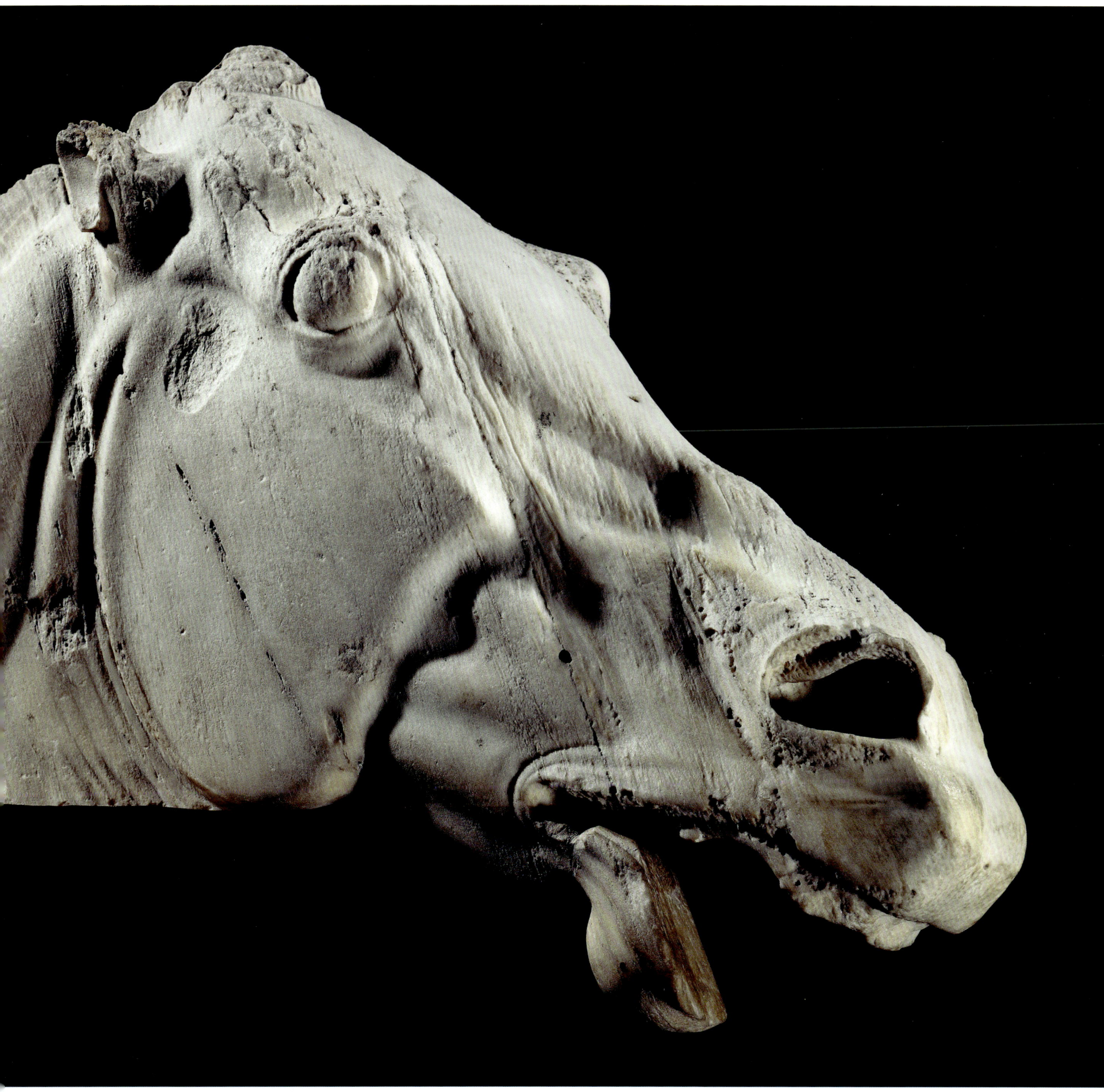

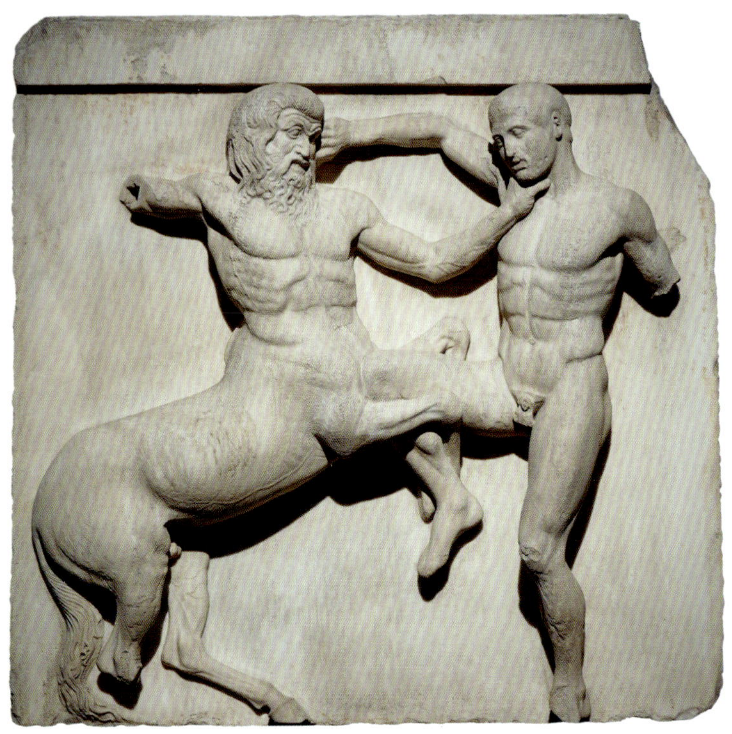

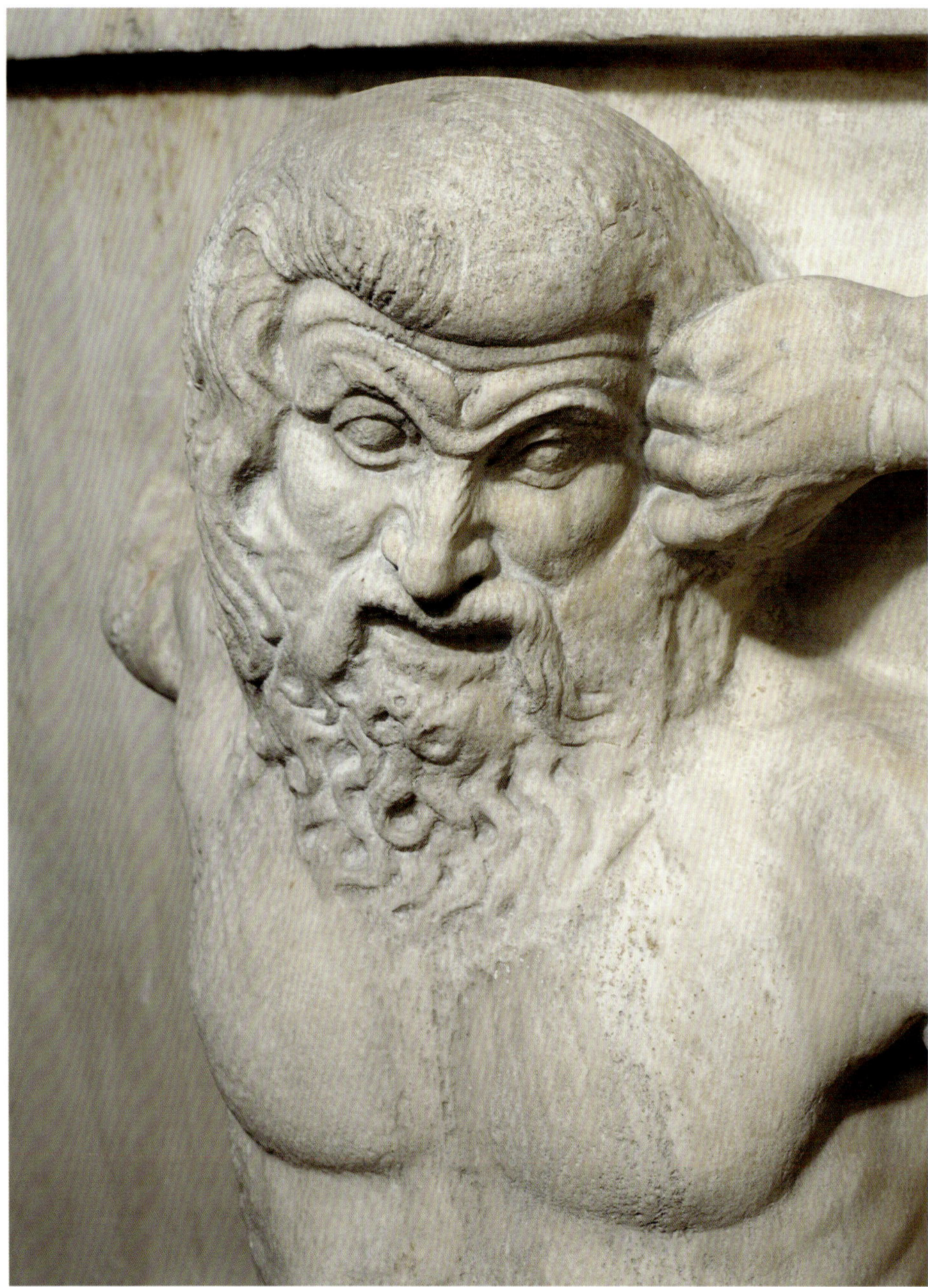

99
Centaur and Lapith locked in combat
South Metope XXXI from the Parthenon
Greek
About 447–438 BC
Marble
H 134 cm, W 132 cm, D 37 cm
British Museum, 1816,0610.15

The most expressive facial features of the Parthenon sculptures are found in the metopes. The south metopes show a battle at the marriage feast of King Perithoos, in which the pain of combat is represented by grimacing centaurs – part-man, part-horse – and wincing human Lapiths. This is one of the most dramatic and complete of all the south metopes and is utterly convincing and shocking in its violence. As the Lapith grips the wig-like hair of the centaur, the creature bares his teeth. Chaos and Reason are locked in mortal combat and the outcome is as yet undecided.

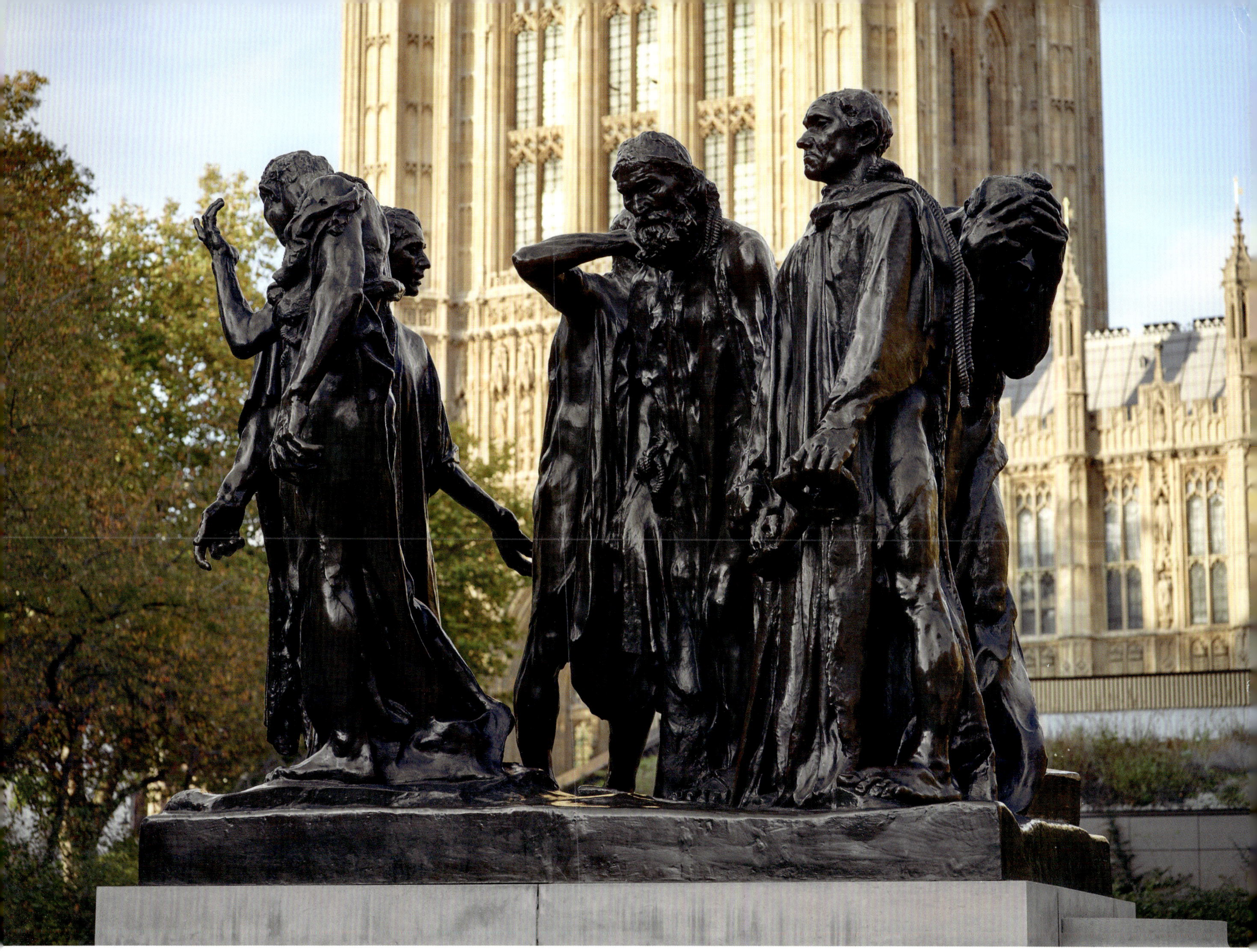

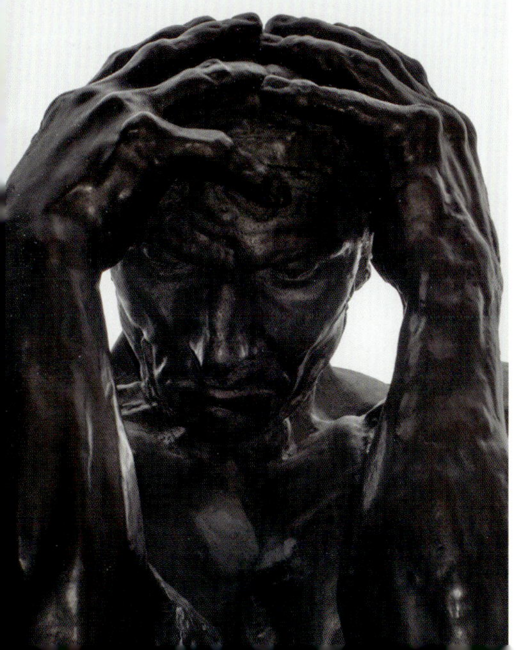
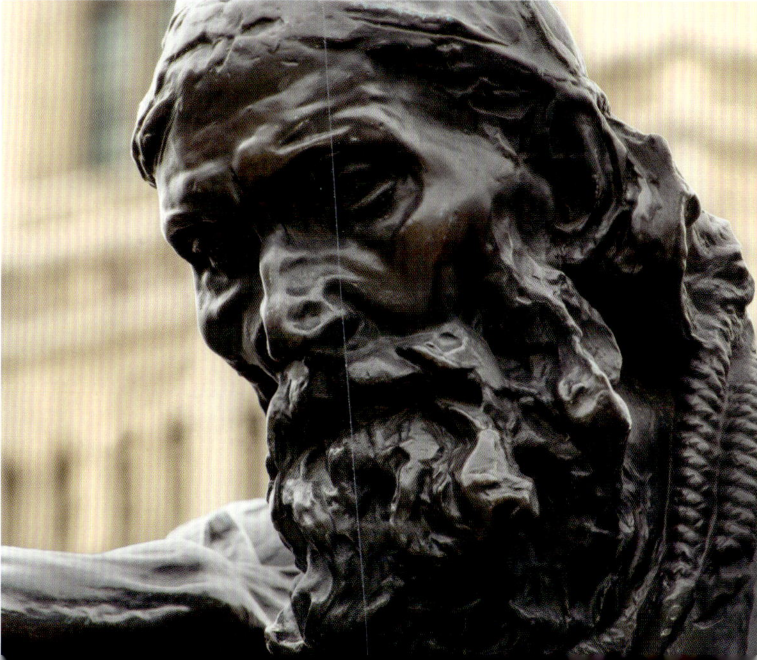
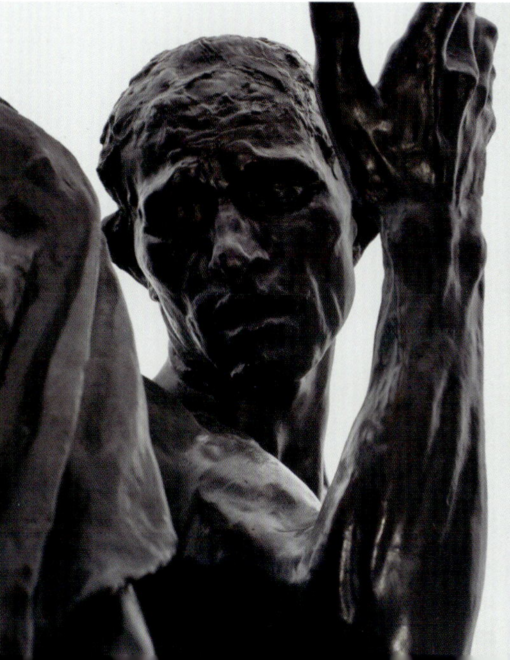

103
Cattle drove
Block XLVI (figs 133–136) from
the Parthenon South Frieze
Greek
About 438–432 BC
Marble
H 101 cm, W 122.5 cm, D 20 cm
British Museum, 1816,0610.86

The Parthenon frieze is an enchanted utopia from which overt signs of war and death are largely absent. Everybody is at the prime of their lives. It is only with the cattle and sheep that death enters the story; the cattle especially must go silently to the altar, and willingly, if there is to be a good omen from the sacrifice. These were not merely meat on the hoof, but they have status as *oikistai*, that is to say, as members of the household and therefore participants in the civic purpose of the festival. It is one of the most lyrical of all passages in the frieze procession. A wave of emotion is drawn in the line of the backs of the beasts, which runs even at first, then dips and rises to a high point before the wave falls, as if about to break on the shore, to run even again (Fig. 47).

BELOW
Fig. 47
Cattle drove of the Parthenon
South Frieze
Modified photograph emphasizing
the rise and fall of the backs
of the cattle

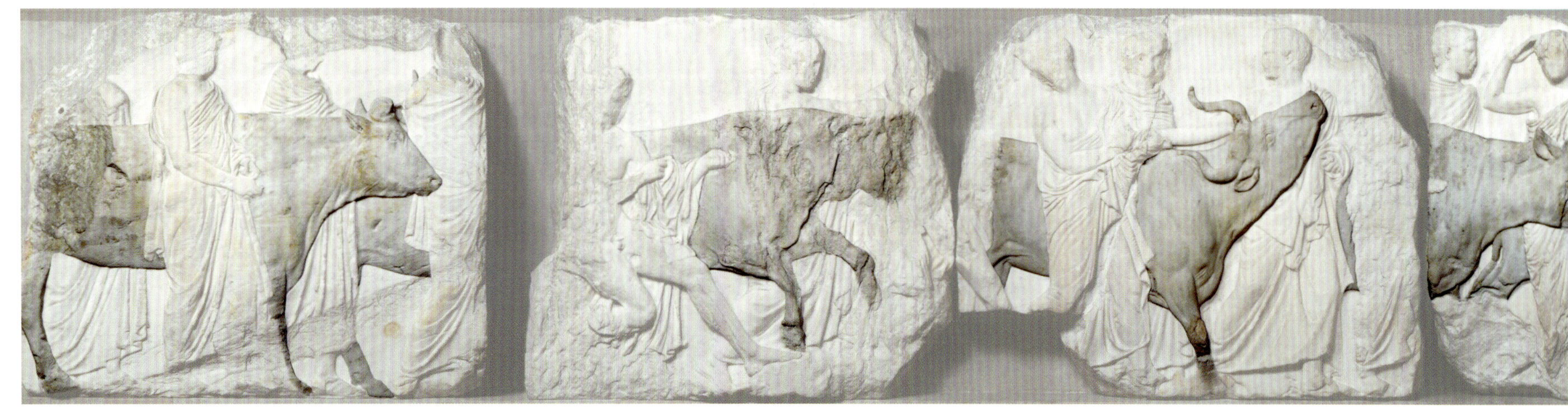

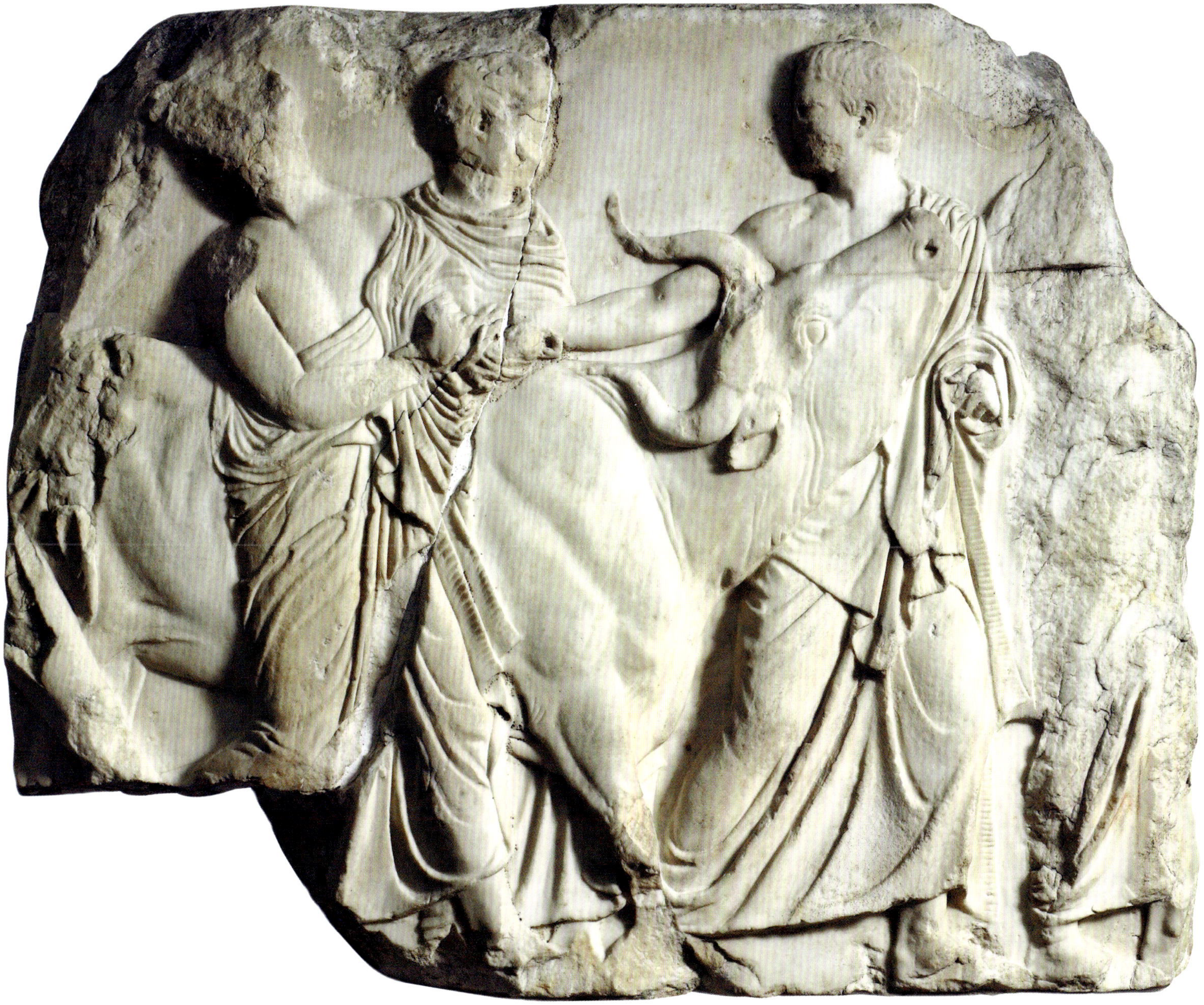

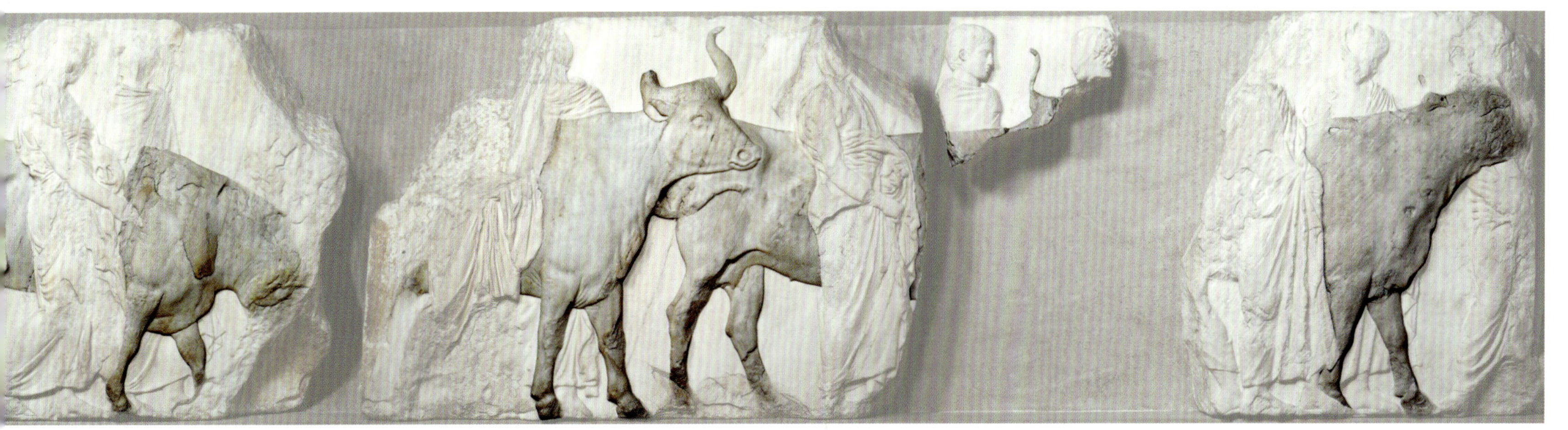

Motion

It's the artist who tells the truth and the photographer who lies. For in reality, time does not stand still.

Auguste Rodin, *Art: Conversations with Paul Gsell*, 1911

Like the artists of ancient Greece, Rodin rose to the challenge of representing motion in art. Rodin would have been excited by the different ways that the Parthenon sculptors simulated motion, including compositions that seem to pass energy from one figure to another, developing the narrative and forward movement.

The invention of the car and aeroplane during Rodin's lifetime dramatically changed people's perception of speed and time. The advent of photography and cinema also changed the representation of movement forever. However, for Rodin 'It's the artist who tells the truth and the photographer who lies. For in reality, time does not stand still.' Rodin claimed that a photograph merely froze an action in mid-air, arresting the energy artificially. Although he admired and used photography, he insisted that sculpture and drawing alone could capture the essence of movement.

Fig. 48
Stephen Haweis (1878–1969) and Henry Coles (1875–?)
The Walking Man in the garden at Meudon
Around 1903–1904
Carbon print
H 22.8 cm, W 16.3 cm
Musée Rodin, Ph. 4455
Rodin donation, 1916

104
Cavalcade
Blocks XLI–XLIII (figs 112–121)
from the Parthenon North Frieze
Greek
About 438–432 BC
Marble
H 101 cm, W 122.5 cm approx. each block, D 17–21 cm
British Museum, 1816,0610.40, 41 and 42

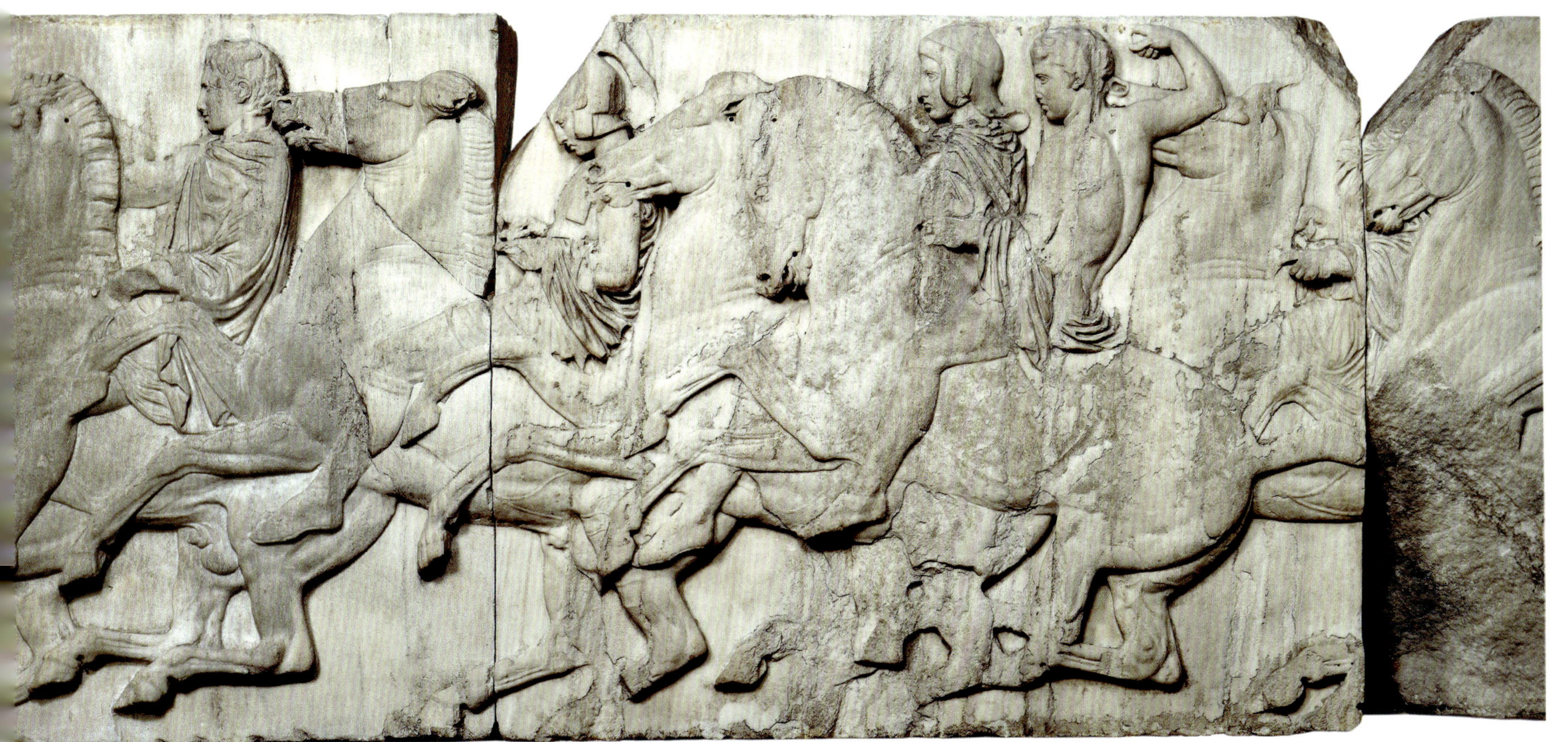

105
Speeding chariot
Block XXXI (figs 78–79) from the Parthenon South Frieze
Greek
About 438–432 BC
Marble
H 101 cm, W 122 cm, D 22 cm
British Museum, 1816,0610.81

Here we see a remarkable example of the sculptor's ability to carve in shallow relief, never more than five centimetres deep, the illusion of four fiery horses. The chariot was the fastest form of transport known to the ancient world. In the chariot race of the Parthenon frieze, the feeling of speed is communicated through the rush of air in the flickering manes of the horses, the flying crest of the foot soldier and the billowing cloak of his driver.

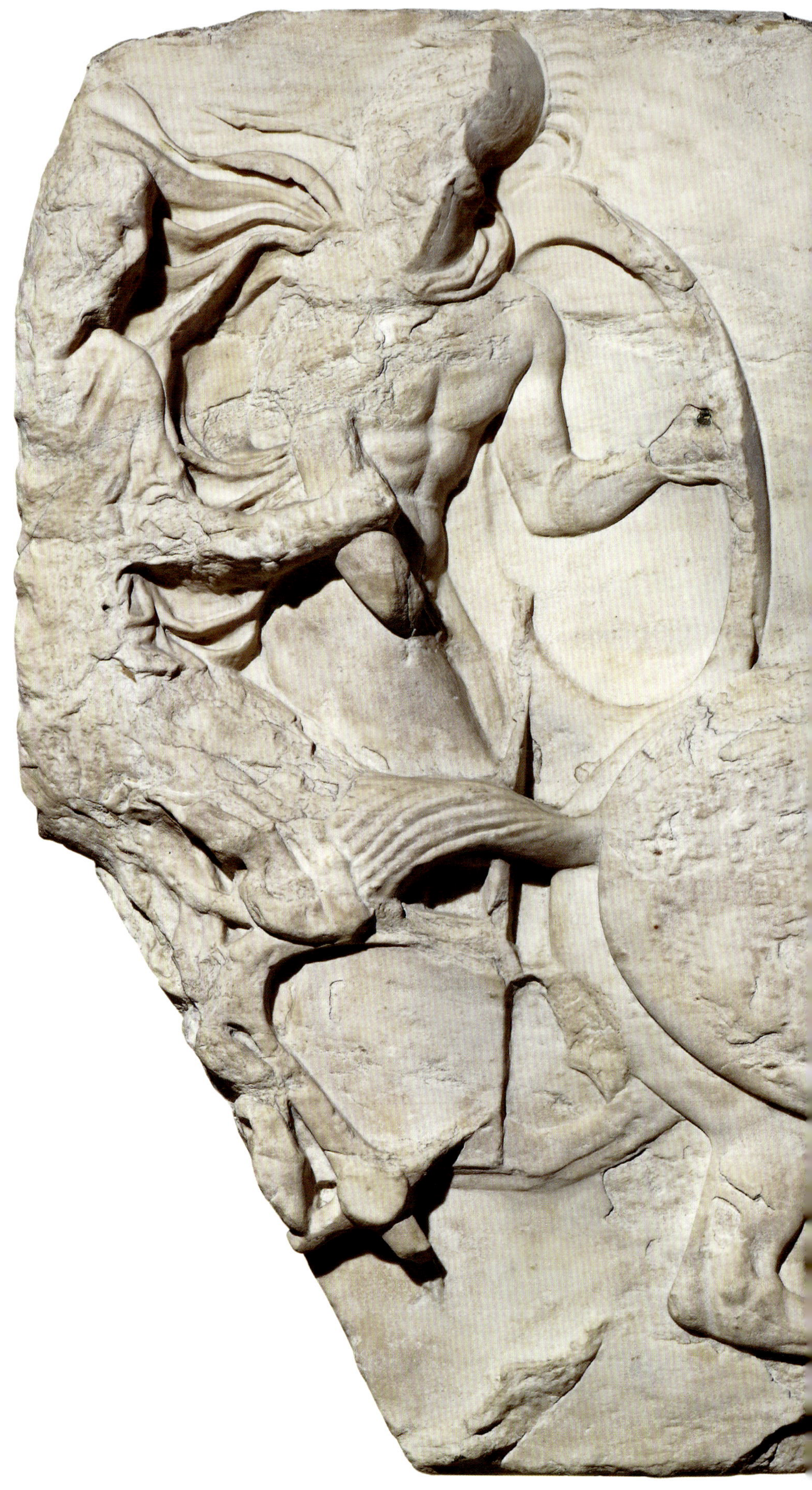

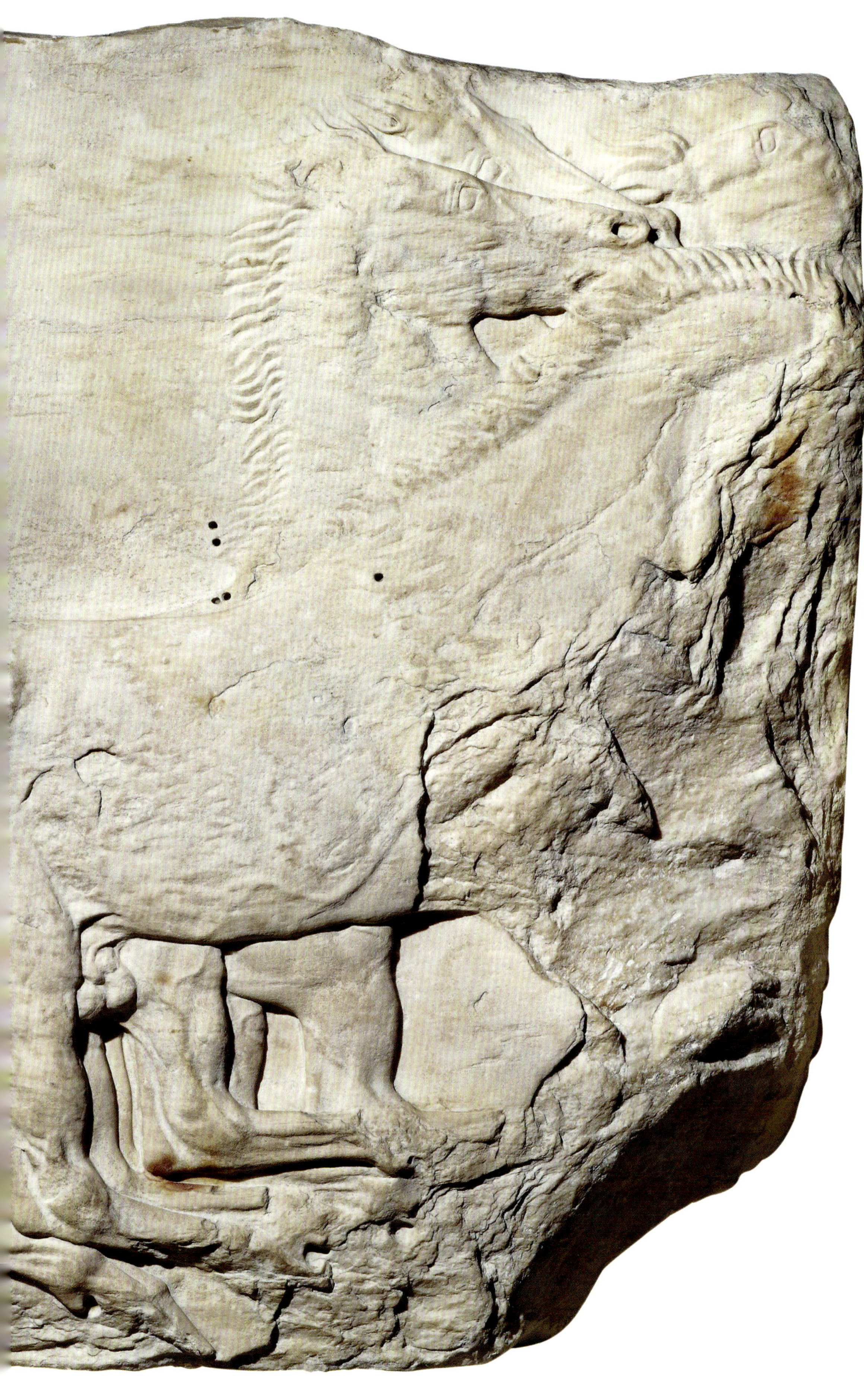

106
Iris
Figure N from the West
Pediment of the Parthenon
Greek
About 438–432 BC
Marble
H 135 cm, W 87 cm, D 72 cm
British Museum, 1816,0610.96

Iris, messenger of the gods and goddess of the heavenly ether, is cold, hard marble carved into warm flesh and flowing drapery, and then by peculiar alchemy is changed into air, her natural element. This miracle of transformation sees the youthful goddess suspended weightless above the holy rock of the Acropolis. Her bronze wings (now missing) once soared above her as she prepared to touch down from flight. The rush of air against her body moulds the flimsy tunic against breast, belly and thighs, and forces it to flap out to the sides.

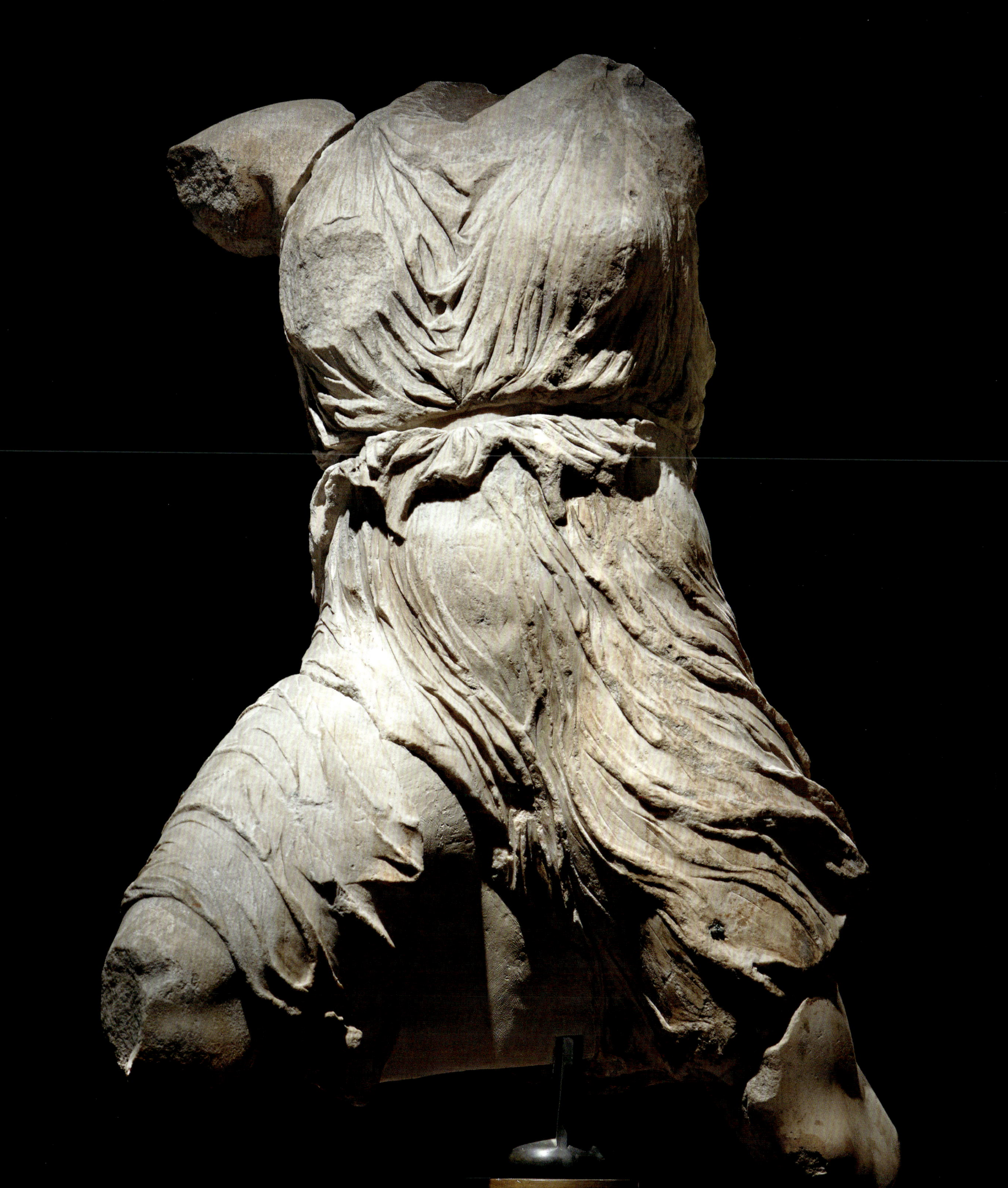

OPPOSITE
107
Auguste Rodin
Iris, Messenger of the Gods
1895
Bronze; sand cast by Alexis
Rudier (?), before 1916
H 83 cm, W 93 cm, D 42 cm
Musée Rodin, S. 1068
Rodin donation, 1916

This figure was first known as 'Study of a Woman with Legs Apart' when it was enlarged by Henri Lebossé in 1894. Rodin then used it in the second maquette of the *Monument to Victor Hugo*. Here it is shown in its final form, which was exhibited in 1898. Upright and headless, the figure does not touch the earth. Like the Parthenon goddess of the air (Cat. 106), she appears to defy gravity. Rodin worked from a model, perhaps a dancer, lying on her back to achieve this pose. By placing the figure upright, he confronts the viewer with a dynamic, liberated figure revelling in an astonishing leap.

OVERLEAF
108
Auguste Rodin
Illusion: Sister of Icarus
1894–1896
Marble; carved by Alexandre
Pézieux
H 62.5 cm, W 95 cm, D 53.5 cm
Musée Rodin, S. 1385

Supernatural beings are capable of transcending the natural forces of the world and they can command the elements in ways humans cannot. To attempt to emulate or compete with the gods is to invoke divine retribution. The aspirations of Icarus to fly resulted in failure and punishment. It is a weakness of human beings to envy the gods their powers of flight. Steeped in the Classics as Rodin was, his interpretation of Greek myth sometimes took a surprising turn. The master craftsman Daedalus' fledgling Icarus did not have a sister until Rodin invented her. Wings flapping hopelessly behind her, Icarus' sister literally nose-dives to earth after her unsuccessful attempt at flight.

Rodin reused the figure of *The Martyr*, which itself came from *The Gates of Hell*. He gave the figure wings, turned it and balanced it on its nose. Exhibited at the Salon of the National Society of Fine Arts in 1896, it took the title of *Illusion: Sister of Icarus*. Around 1900, Rodin was exploring the theme of the fall, ubiquitous throughout his work, through ancient mythology.

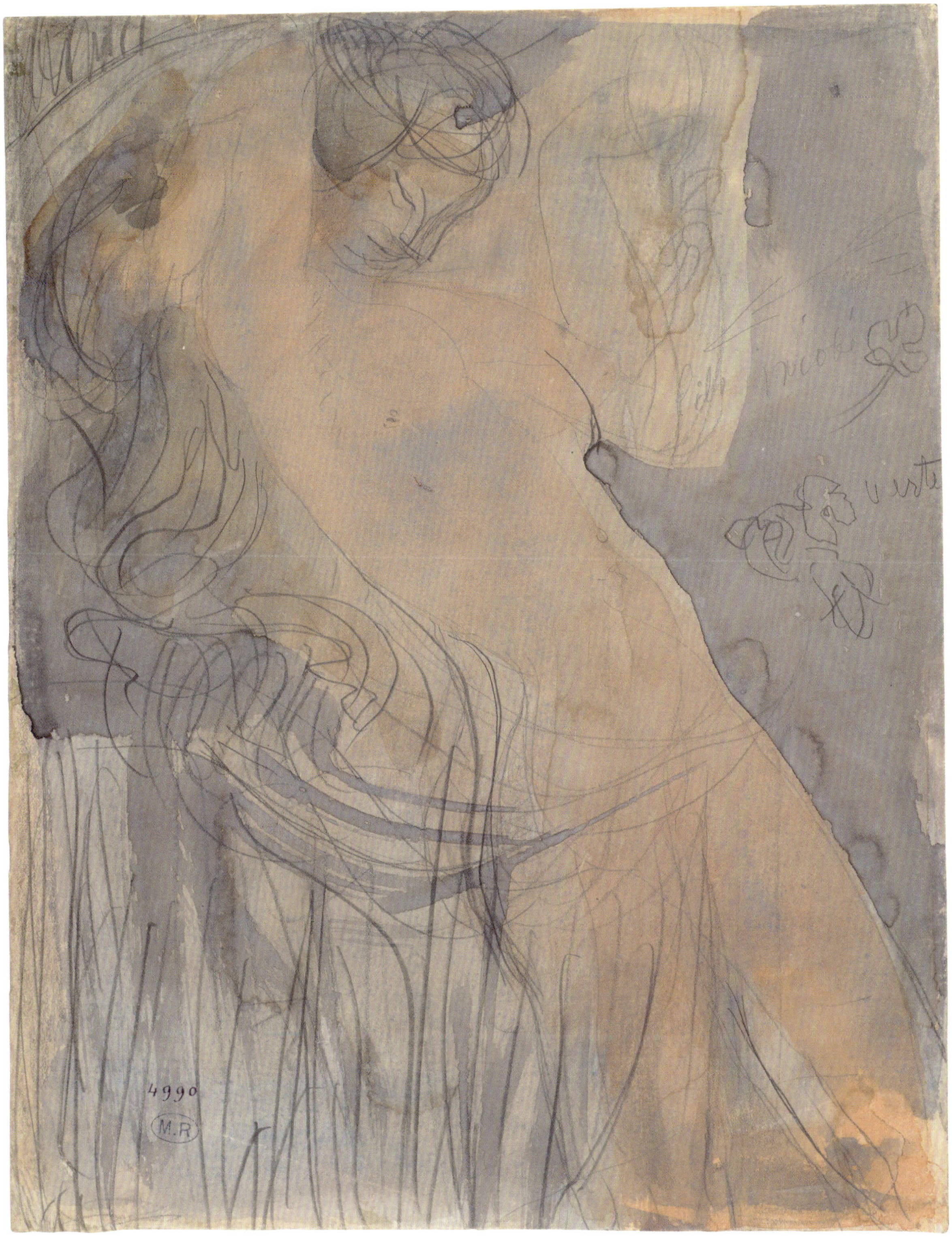

Rodin wrote on this drawing 'fils Niobé / verte', with an arrow and flowers. He associated this female figure with long hair and drapery with the drama of the Phrygian queen, Niobe, witnessing the death of her children. His desperate *Niobé* seems to dance with her veils, as did the famous dancer Isadora Duncan, one of Rodin's friends and models.

110
Auguste Rodin
Flying Figure, large version
About 1900
Bronze, lost-wax cast by Montagutelli, 1913
H 52 cm, W 77.5 cm, D 31.6 cm
Musée Rodin, S. 786
Rodin donation, 1916

This fragmentary female figure stretching her right leg horizontally and revealing her sex derives from the pair *Avarice and Lust,* created in 1887. On the back of the statue is the clean cut made in the clay when separating the two figures, probably shortly after their creation. The detached figure was then placed vertically, enlarged and cast in bronze for the first time in 1913, becoming an autonomous work. This flying figure, full of energy, is similar to Rodin's sculpture of *Iris* (Cat. 107).

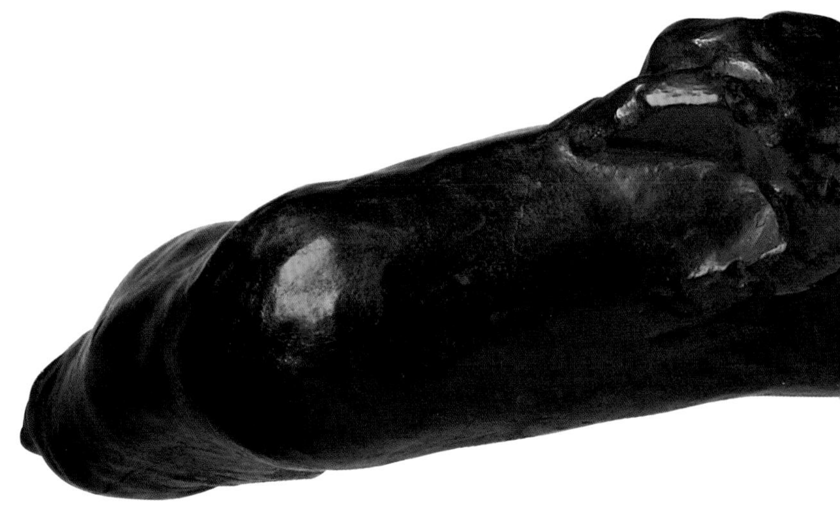

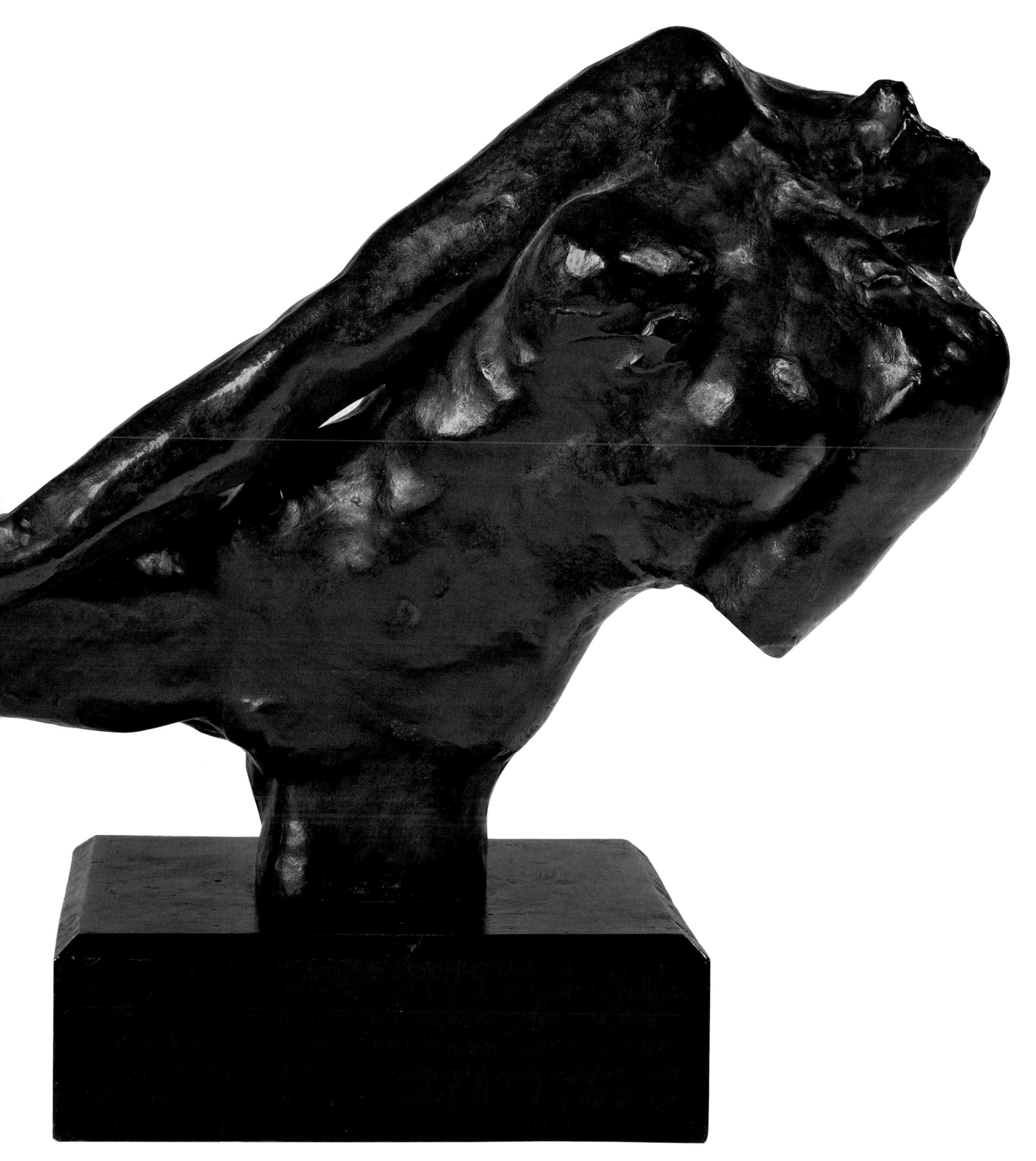

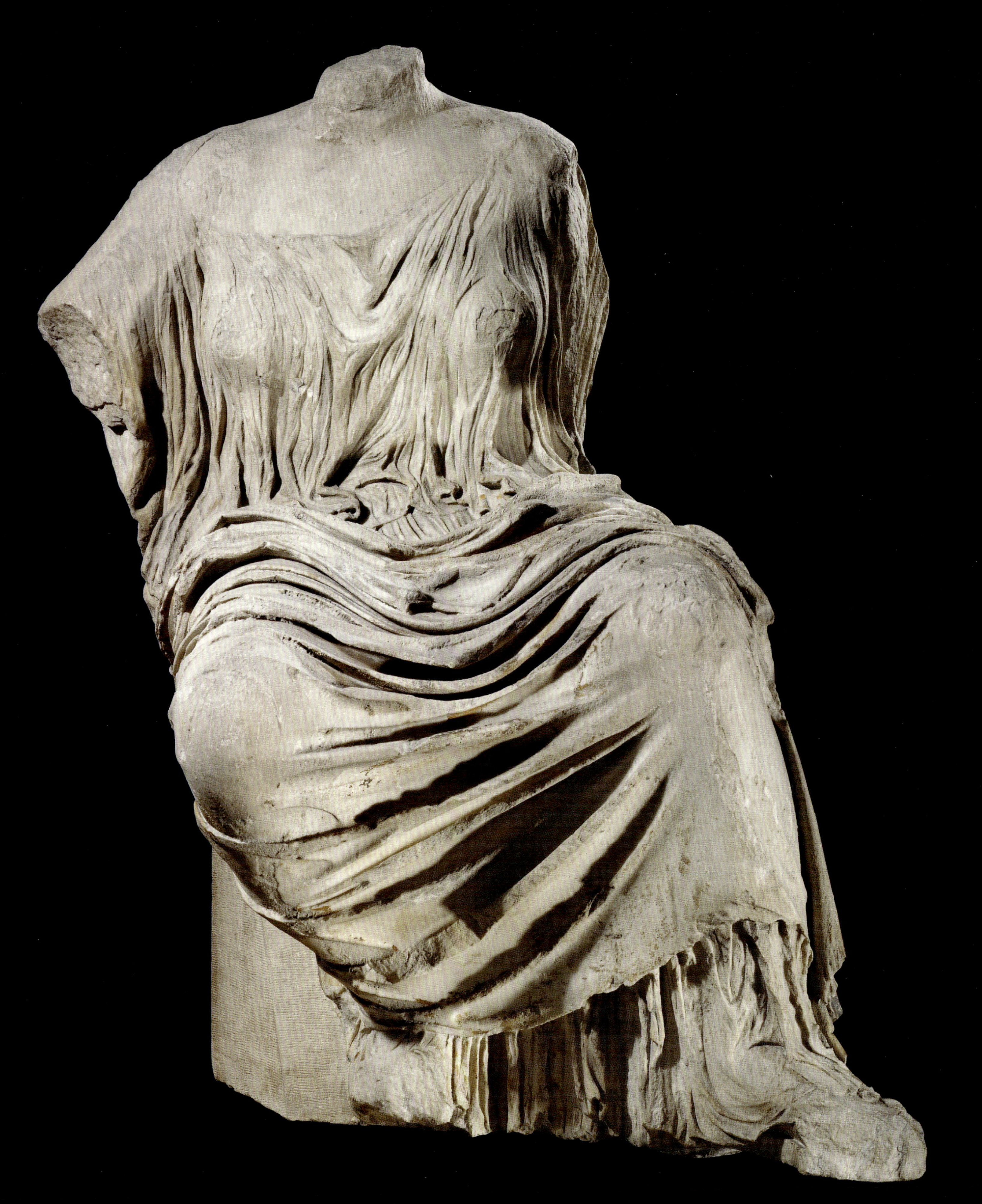

111
Rising Goddess
Figure K from the East Pediment of the Parthenon
Greek
About 438–432 BC
Marble
H 141 cm, L 110 cm, D 88 cm
British Museum, 1816,0610.405

The head and arms of this figure of a goddess are missing, but Rodin would have read her unsettled state of mind in the positioning of her body and the expressiveness of her drapery. The fine folds of a tunic cascade over her breasts to meet the wave-like folds of a heavier garment flowing over her lap. On the point of rising, her foot is positioned beneath her in order to serve as a lever with which to push herself up. The drapery over her knees is stretched smooth, while that between her lower legs forms a stack of taut parallel folds. This study in arrested movement achieves its purpose by assembling a number of visual points of reference for the eye of the viewer that convincingly express the essence of the action.

Rodin and his contemporaries were fascinated by the phenomenon of motion that is suddenly halted by the process of its representation in art. This arrested energy is not so much the act of stopping itself, but rather its artistic representation and the capacity of a work of art to capture the moment.

It is not my Walking Man in himself that interests me but rather the thought of how far he has come and how far he has yet to cover. This art which, through suggestion, purposely extends beyond the figure sculpted, rendering it integral to a whole that is pieced together step by step by the imagination is, I believe, a fertile innovation.

Auguste Rodin, quoted by Paul Gsell, 'Propos de Rodin sur l'art et les artistes', *La Revue*, 1 November 1907

112
Auguste Rodin
The Walking Man
1907
Bronze; sand cast Alexis Rudier, 1913
H 213.5 cm, W 71.7 cm, D 156.5 cm
Musée Rodin, S. 998
Rodin Donation, 1916

Rodin breathed new life into the legacy of Pheidias. Not since antiquity had this ancient master been so admired by another artist. Through the Parthenon sculptures Rodin discovered the power of the fragment to convey the form and meaning of a complete work. This would influence successive generations of artists. Rodin presents *The Walking Man* as an archaeological ruin still full of vigour and purpose. With great daring, seemingly flying in the face of all convention, Rodin omits the head and arms of his subject, in keeping with the Parthenon sculptures. It was not until 1907, at the French National Fine Arts Society Salon, that Rodin exhibited a version of *The Walking Man* in plaster, enlarged by Henri Lebossé between 1905 and 1906 and later cast in bronze. While resembling the ruins of antiquity, stripped to its bare essentials *The Walking Man* seems to anticipate the abstraction of form in modern art.

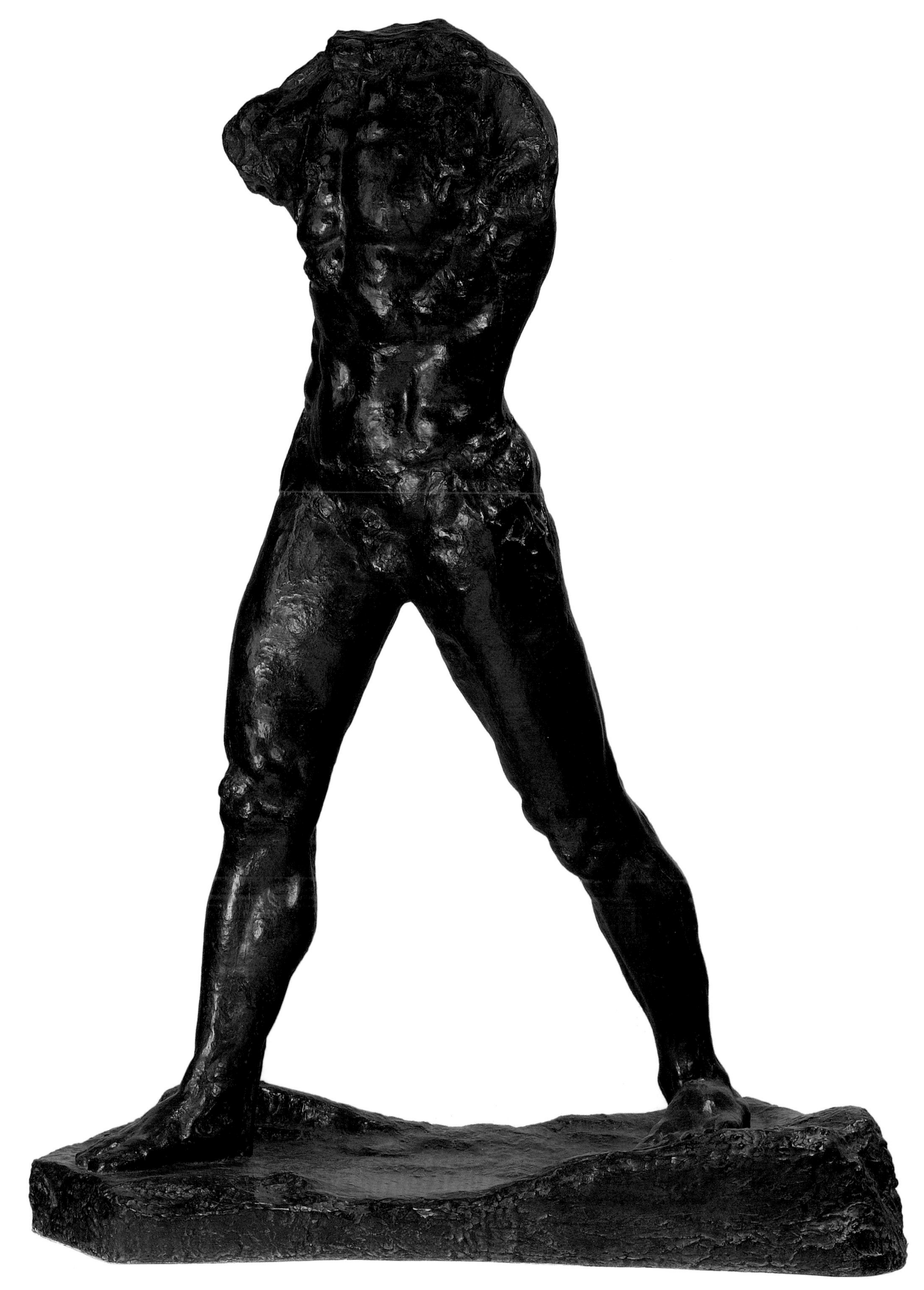

Chronology of Auguste Rodin

1840
Born in Paris on 12 November, son of a local police inspector.

1854–57
Studies drawing and sculpture at the Petite École. Regularly visits the Greek and Roman rooms at the Louvre and the Imperial Library.

1857–62
Fails the entrance exam for the prestigious École des Beaux-Arts three times.

1858
Works for a number of different decorative artists.

1862
Briefly enters the Congregation of the Blessed Sacrement as a novice following the death of his beloved sister Maria.

1864
Meets Rose Beuret (1844–1917), who becomes his lifelong partner. Begins working in the studio of the prominent sculptor Albert-Ernest Carrier-Belleuse (1824–1887), gaining insight into the running of a large workshop.

1865
The original plaster version of *Man with the Broken Nose* is rejected by the Salon.

1866
Birth of his illegitimate son Auguste-Eugène Beuret (1866–1934), future draughtsman and engraver.

1870
Drafted into the Garde Nationale, but is discharged for being short-sighted.

1871–72
Works for Albert-Ernest Carrier-Belleuse in Belgium. Their collaboration ends when Rodin is discovered showing his works under his own name.

1873
Collaborates with the Belgian sculptor Antoine-Joseph Van Rasbourgh (1831–1902), making sculptural decoration on public buildings.

1875
A marble version of *Man with the Broken Nose* is exhibited at the Salon. Travels to Italy to study Renaissance art, especially that of Michelangelo.

1876
Exhibits at the Centennial International Exhibition in Philadelphia, USA.

1877
Exhibits *The Age of Bronze* at the Salon in Paris, but is accused of having made a life cast. Returns to France and works again as an ornamental sculptor due to financial hardship.

1879–82
Designs ceramics for the Sèvres porcelain factory (run by Albert-Ernest Carrier-Belleuse).

1880
The French government purchases a cast of *The Age of Bronze*. Receives his first major commission to design gates (*The Gates of Hell*) for a future museum of decorative arts. Moves into his first studio at the Dépôt des Marbres, which he keeps for the rest of his life.

1881
Makes his first visit to London (after 22 July–before 1 September) and the British Museum.

1882
Visits London (end of May) with his pupil Gustav Natorp (1836–1908) and the painter Henri Gervex (1852–1929). Cast of the mask of *Man with the Broken Nose* is exhibited at the Grosvenor Gallery in London and purchased by the artist Frederic, Lord Leighton (1830–1896).

1883
Meets the sculptor Camille Claudel (1864–1943), who becomes his protégée, studio assistant and lover. In London (end of May) and exhibits some of his works at the Egyptian Hall in Piccadilly (organized by the Dudley gallery). Draws Assyrian sculptures in the British Museum.

1885
The city of Calais commissions *Monument to the Burghers of Calais*, which is unveiled ten years later.

1886
In London (26 May–June). Gives two of his prints of Victor Hugo to the British Museum. Travels to Peterborough to see Camille Claudel, who is staying with her friend Jessie Lipscomb (1861–1952).

1888
The French government commissions a marble version of *The Kiss* for the Paris Exposition Universelle of 1889.

1889
Becomes one of the founder members of the Société Nationale des Beaux-Arts. 'Monet–Rodin' exhibition is held at the Galerie Georges Petit, Paris.

1891
The Société des Gens de Lettres commissions Rodin to design a monument to Honoré Balzac (1799–1850).

1892
Relationship with Camille Claudel begins to deteriorate.

1893
Succeeds the sculptor Jules Dalou (1838–1902) as Vice-President of the Société Nationale des Beaux-Arts and President of the Sculpture section.

1895
Purchases the Villa des Brillants in Meudon, outside Paris, which he has rented since 1893. He begins collecting antiquities.

1898
Rodin's relationship with Camille Claudel ends. The Société des Gens de Lettres refuses the plaster of *Balzac*.

1899
First solo exhibition in Brussels, then Rotterdam, Amsterdam and The Hague.

1900
Appointed Knight of the Order of Leopold of Belgium. Organizes his first solo exhibition in France, to coincide with the Exposition Universelle, in a pavilion specially built for the occasion on the Place de l'Alma, Paris. It is then dismantled and reconstructed in the grounds of the Villa des Brillants, Meudon, where it is converted into a studio.

1902
Major 'Rodin' exhibition in Prague, where he meets the poet Rainer Maria Rilke (1875–1926), whom he employs as a secretary from 15 September 1905 to 12 May 1906. In London (14–20 May) to attend a dinner in his honour at the Café Royal during the exhibition 'Paris à Londres'. *St John the Baptist* presented to the Victoria and Albert Museum after a public subscription.

1903
Nominated Commander of the Legion of Honour. Stays with the sculptor John Tweed (1869–1933) in London (around May–5 June). Discovers the so-called Warren Head in an exhibition at the Burlington Fine Arts Club. Visits the collector Edward Perry Warren (1860–1928) in Lewes, Sussex, who had commissioned a marble version of *The Kiss* in 1900. Elected president of the International Society of Sculptors, Painters and Gravers, succeeding its founder, James McNeill Whistler (1834–1903).

1904
The Thinker (large-scale plaster version) is first exhibited at the fourth annual exhibition of the International Society of Sculptors, Painters and Gravers, at the New Gallery, Regent Street, then at the Paris Salon (bronze version). In London (8–15 January) and attends a banquet in his honour on 12 January. Begins liaison with the Welsh painter Gwen John (1876–1939), model for the Muse in the *Monument to Whistler*.

1905
In London (19–around 28 February) for the fifth International Society exhibition. Appointed member of the Conseil Supérieur des Beaux-Arts. The University of Jena awards him an honorary doctorate. Publishes article against the proposed restoration of the Parthenon.

1906
In London (20 February–around 9 March). Exhibits work at the sixth International Society exhibition. Meets King Edward VII (who later visits him in Meudon on 6 March 1908). Awarded an honorary doctorate from the University of Glasgow and appointed member of the Prussian Academy of Arts, Berlin.

1907
Sojourn in England (24 June–around 5 July). Awarded an honorary doctorate by the University of Oxford. Visits the Ashmolean Museum. Stays with John Tweed in Chelsea. *The Walking Man* (large plaster version) is shown at the Salon de la Société Nationale des Beaux-Arts, Paris.

1908
Rilke tells Rodin about the Hôtel Biron, a derelict eighteenth-century mansion temporarily leased to artists and writers. Rodin uses the premises to receive admirers, journalists, art dealers and collectors. Major exhibitions of Rodin's drawings held in Vienna, Leipzig and Paris.

1909
The French government announces the sale of the Hôtel Biron. Rodin endeavours to save the mansion and plans the donation of his estate to the Nation.

1910
Named Grand Officier of the Legion of Honour.

1912
Solo exhibition in Tokyo, Japan. Inauguration of the Rodin Room at the Metropolitan Museum, New York.

1913
In London (25 May–around 12 June) to oversee the installation of a cast of the *Monument to the Burghers of Calais* purchased by Britain 1911. Exhibition at the Faculté de Médecine, Paris, where Rodin's antiquities are exhibited for the first time with his own work.

1914
Exhibits at major exhibition of French art in Grosvenor House, London. Leaves France with Rose Beuret and his friend, the writer Judith Cladel (1873–1958), and stays in London (29 June–3 July). Returns to London (19–24 July). On the outbreak of the First World War his works are stranded. A six-month loan to the Victoria and Albert Museum is arranged for his eighteen sculptures, after which Rodin decides to donate them to the museum in honour of the British and French soldiers fighting in the war. Travels to Rome. Visits Cheltenham in Gloucestershire (5–around 25 September) and stays in London for the last time (around 25 September–7 October).

1915
Monument to the Burghers of Calais is unveiled in Victoria Gardens, outside the Houses of Parliament, London. Exhibition at the Royal Scottish Academy, Edinburgh, of sixteen of the eighteen sculptures that Rodin donated to Britain.

1916
A stroke leaves him with permanent neurological damage. He offers to donate his work, his collection and the Villa des Brillants to the French nation on condition that the Hôtel Biron is converted into a Rodin museum.

1917
Marries Rose Beuret on 29 January in Meudon, two weeks before her death on 14 February. Dies on 17 November and is buried on 24 November beside Rose in Meudon. A large-scale cast of *The Thinker* is erected on their grave.

1919
The Musée Rodin opens in Paris to the public on 4 August, and in Meudon in 1948.

Further reading

Anonymous, 'A great French Sculptor in London. M. Rodin's confession of faith', *The St James's Gazette*, London, 16 May 1902

Anonymous, 'Mr Rodin in London', *The Daily Chronicle*, 2 March 1903

Anonymous, 'A French Phidias, Rodin's impressions of London', *The Tribune*, London, 2 March 1906

Anonymous, 'Les Arts–Le musée Rodin', *Le Cri de Paris*, 7 May 1916

Nicole Barbier, *Marbres de Rodin: Collection du musée*, Paris: Éditions du Musée Rodin, 1987

Charles Baudelaire, *The Complete Verse*, vol. 1, translated and introduction by Francis Scarfe, London: Anvil Press Poetry, 1986

Alain Beausire, Hélène Pinet, Florence Cadouot and Frédérique Vincent, *Correspondance de Rodin 1860–1917*, 4 vols, Paris: Éditions du Musée Rodin, 1985–1992

François Blanchetière (ed.), *L'enfer selon Rodin*, Paris, Éditions Norma, 2016

Ch. Bouras, 'Restoration work on the Parthenon and changing attitudes towards the conservation of monuments', in P. Tournikiotis (ed.), *The Parthenon and Its Impact in Modern Times*, Athens: Melissa Publishing House, 1994, pp. 310–339

Antoine Bourdelle, 'Les Dessins du sculpteur Rodin', *La Grande Revue*, January 1908, 166–172

Paul Hippolyte Boussac, 'La vie contemporaine contre la restauration du Parthénon', *La Plume*, 1 June 1905, pp. 515–549

Theodore Bowie and Diether Thimme (eds), *The Carrey Drawings of the Parthenon Sculptures*, Bloomington and London: Indiana University Press, 1971

Ruth Butler, *Rodin: The Shape of Genius*, New Haven and London: Yale University Press, 1993

Gulru Çakmak, 'Gérôme, Rodin, and Sculpture's Interior', Nonsite.org, 2014

Roger de Chateleux, '"Hard work makes the artist" says Rodin, greatest sculptor since Michelangelo', *The World Magazine*, 26 May 1907

M. Choiseul-Gouffier, *Voyage pittoresque de la Grèce*, 3 vols, Paris, 1782–1822

Cicero, *Brutus. Orator*, translated by G. L. Hendricks and H. M. Hubbell, Loeb edition, Cambridge, Mass. and London: Harvard University Press, 1939

Judith Cladel, *Auguste Rodin. Pris sur la vie*, Paris: Éditions de la Plume, 1903

Judith Cladel, *Rodin, sa vie glorieuse, sa vie inconnue*, Paris: Bernard Grasset, 1936

Christoph W. Clairmont, *Fauvel: The First Archaeologist in Athens and His Philhellenic Correspondents*, Zurich: Akanthus, 2007

Frédéric de Clarac, *Musée de sculpture antique et moderne ou, Description historique du Louvre et de toutes ses parties …*, vol. II, Paris: Imprimerie royale, 1841

Bernard Yves Cochain, *Pierre Louis Rouillard (1820–1881), Sculpteur animalier, Professeur de sculpture et d'anatomie*, Advanced research dissertation École du Louvre, under the tutelage of Anne Pingeot, 1997

Maxime Collignon, *Le Parthénon: l'histoire, l'architecture et la sculpture*, Paris: Hachette et Cie., 1912

Jeremy Cooper, *Nineteenth-Century Romantic Bronzes: French, English and American Bronzes 1830–1915*, Newton Abbot: David & Charles, 1975

Gustave Coquiot, *Le Vrai Rodin*, Paris: Jules Tallendier, 1913

Gustave Coquiot, *Rodin à l'hôtel de Biron et à Meudon*, Paris, Librairie Ollendorff, 1917

Frederick Cummings, 'B. R. Haydon and his School', *Journal of the Warburg and Courtauld Institutes* 26, 1963, pp. 367–380

Frederick Cummings, 'Phidias in Bloomsbury: B. R. Haydon's drawings of the Elgin Marbles', *The Burlington Magazine* 106, 1964, pp. 323–328

Claire Cullen Davison, *Pheidias: The Sculptures & Ancient Sources*, 3 vols, edited by Geoffrey B. Waywell, London: Bulletin of the Institute of Classical Studies, Supplement 105, 2009

Paul Delaroche, Henriquel Dupont and Charles Lenormant, *Bas-reliefs du Parthénon et du temple de Phigalie disposés suivant l'ordre de la composition originale et gravés par les procédés de M. Achille Collas*, Paris, Didier et Cie., 1834

Richard Dorment, *Alfred Gilbert: Sculptor and Goldsmith*, New Haven and London: Yale University Press, 1986

Henri-Charles-Étienne Dujardin-Beaumetz, *Entretiens avec Rodin*, Paris: Paul Dupont, 1913

G. Duranteau, 'La sculpture et l'art d'après Rodin', *Le Gaulois du Dimanche*, 4 June 1907

Albert Elsen, *Rodin's Gates of Hell*, Minneapolis: University of Minnesota Press, 1960

Élie Faure, 'Au pied du Parthénon', *Le Musée: revue d'art antique*, vol. III, 1906, 373–377, reprinted in *Formes et forces*, Paris: H. Floury, 1907

Antoine Michel Filhol, *Galerie du Musée Napoléon*, Paris: Imprimerie de Gillé fils, 1804–1828

J. G. Frazer, *Pausanias's Description of Greece*, London: Macmillan & Co., 1898

Victor Frisch and Joseph T. Shipley, *Auguste Rodin, A Biography*, New York: Frederick A. Stokes Co., 1939

Bénédicte Garnier, *L'Antique est ma jeunesse. Une collection de sculpteur*; English edition: *Antiquity is My Youth: A Sculptor's Collection*, Paris: Éditions du Musée Rodin, 2002

Bénédicte Garnier, 'The sculptor, the collector and the archaeologist: Auguste Rodin, Edward Perry Warren and John Marshall', in Claudine Mitchell (ed.), *Rodin: The Zola of Sculpture*, London: Ashgate Publishing, 2004, pp. 121–133

Bénédicte Garnier, *Rodin Intime: La Villa des Brillants à Meudon*, Paris: Éditions du Chêne, 2015

J. W. von Goethe, *Italian Journey*, translated by W. H. Auden and Elizabeth Mayer, London: Collins, 1962; original German edition *Italienische Reise*, 1816–1817

E. Grumach (ed.), *Goethe und die Antike: Eine Sammlung*, 2 vols, Berlin: De Gruyter, 1949

Paul Gsell, 'Propos de Rodin sur l'art et les artistes', *La Revue* 21, 1 November 1907, pp. 95–107

Paul Gsell, 'Chez Rodin', *L'Art et les Artistes*, special issue, *Rodin, l'homme et l'oeuvre*, February 1914, pp. 393–415

Ernst-Gerhard Güse, *Auguste Rodin: Drawings and Watercolours*, London: Thames & Hudson, 1985

Ruth Guilding, *Owning the Past: Why the English Collected Antique Sculpture, 1640–1840*, New Haven and London: Yale University Press, 2014

E. B. Harrison, 'Motifs of the City-Siege on the Shield of the Athena Parthenos', *American Journal of Archaeology* 85, 1981, pp. 281–317

E. B. Harrison, 'Pheidias', in Olga Palagia and J. J. Pollitt (eds), *Personal Styles in Greek Sculpture*, Cambridge: Cambridge University Press, 1996, pp. 16–65

Jacques Hittorff, *Restitution du temple d'Empédocle à Sélinonte, ou l'architecture polychrôme chez les Grecs*, Paris: Librairie de Firmin Didot Frères, 1851

Ian Jenkins, '"G. F. Watts' Teachers": George Frederic Watts and the Elgin Marbles', *Apollo* 120, 1984, pp. 176–181

Ian Jenkins, 'Acquisition and Supply of Casts of the Parthenon Sculptures by the British Museum, 1835–1939', *Annual of the British School at Athens* 85, 1990, pp. 89–114

Ian Jenkins, 'La vente des vases Durand (Paris 1836) et leur reception en Grande-Bretagne', in Annie-France Laurens and Krzysztof Pomian (eds), *L'Anticomanie. La collection d'antiquités aux 18e et 19e siècles*, Paris: Éditions de l'École des Hautes Études en Sciences Sociales, 1992, pp. 269–278; republished in B. B. Rasmussen et al. (eds), *Peter Oluf Brøndsted (1780–1842): A Danish Classicist in His European Context*, Copenhagen: Royal Academy of Sciences, 2007, pp. 162–170

Ian Jenkins, *Archaeologists and Aesthetes in the Sculpture Galleries of the British Museum 1800–1939*, London: British Museum Press, 1992

Ian Jenkins, '"Athens Rising near the Pole" – London, Athens and the Idea of Freedom', in Celina Fox (ed.), *London – World City 1800–1840*, New Haven and London: Yale University Press 1992, pp. 143–154

Ian Jenkins, *The Parthenon Frieze*, London: British Museum Press, 1994

Ian Jenkins, 'The South Frieze of the Parthenon: Problems in Arrangement', *American Journal of Archaeology* 99, 1995, pp. 445–456

Ian Jenkins, '"Gods without Altars": The Belvedere in Paris', in Matthias Winner et al. (eds), *Il Cortile delle Statue: Der Statuenhof des Belvedere im Vatikan*, Mainz: Philipp von Zabern, 1998, pp. 459–474

Ian Jenkins, 'The Parthenon frieze and Perikles' cavalry of a thousand', in Judith M. Barringer and Jeffrey M. Hurwit (eds), *Periklean Athens and Its Legacy. Problems and Perspective*, Austin: University of Texas Press, 2005, pp. 147–161

Ian Jenkins, *Greek Architecture and Its Sculpture*, London: British Museum Press, 2006

Ian Jenkins, *The Parthenon Sculptures in the British Museum*, London: British Museum Press, 2007

Ian Jenkins and Kim Sloan (eds), *Vases and Volcanoes: Sir William Hamilton and His Collection*, London: British Museum Press, 1996

Stephen Jones et al., *Frederic, Lord Leighton, Eminent Victorian Artist*, exhibition catalogue, London: Royal Academy, 1996

Claudie Judrin, *Inventaire des dessins*, 4 vols, Paris: Éditions du Musée Rodin, 1984–1992

Jason M. Kelly, *The Society of Dilettanti: Archaeology and Identity in the British Enlightenment*, New Haven and London: Yale University Press, 2010

Léon de Laborde, *Le Parthénon: documents pour servir à une restauration*, Paris: Le Leux, 1848

Catherine Lampert, *Rodin: Sculpture and Drawings*, New Haven and London: Yale University Press, 1987

Catherine Lampert (ed.), *Rodin*, London: Royal Academy Publications, 2006

Kenneth D. S. Lapatin, *Chryselephantine Statuary in the Ancient Mediterranean World*, New York and Oxford: Oxford University Press, 2001

Colin Lemoine and Véronique Mattiussi (eds), *Rodin / Bourdelle. Correspondance*, Paris: Gallimard, 2013

Antoinette Le Normand-Romain, *Rodin et le bronze. Catalogue des oeuvres conservées au musée Rodin*, 2 vols, Paris: Éditions du Musée Rodin / Éditions des musées nationaux, 2007

Athena S. Leoussi, *Nationalism and Classicism: The Classical Body as National Symbol in Nineteenth-Century England and France*, Basingstoke: Macmillan, and New York: St Martin's Press, 1998

J. D. Le Roy, *Les ruines des plus beaux monuments de la Grèce…*, Paris: Louis-François Delatour, 1758

Jean Marcadé and Christiane Pinatel, 'Les avatars de la plaque des Ergastines du Louvre au XIXe siècle', in Ernest Berger (ed), *Die Parthenon-Kongress Basel. Referate und Berichte, April 1982*, 2 vols, Mainz: Philipp von Zabern, 1984, pp. 336–342 and 455–458.

Jean-Luc Martinez, 'La collection de moulages: un musée pédagogique', in Simon Texier (ed.), *L'Institut d'art et d'archéologie Paris 1932*, Paris: Picard, 2005, pp. 93–104

Georges-Marie Matthijs, *Julien Dillens, sculpteur, 1849–1904*, Brussels: Palais des Académies, 1955

Camille Mauclair, *Auguste Rodin. The Man – His Ideas – His Works*, London: Duckworth, and New York: E. P. Dutton, 1905

Ivan Meštrović, 'Quelques souvenirs sur Rodin', in *Ivan Meštrović chez Rodin, l'expression croate*, Paris: Nicolas Chaudun/Éditions du Musée Rodin, 2012

Adolf Michaelis, *Der Parthenon*, Leipzig: Breitkopf und Härtel, 1870–1871

Aubin-Louis Millin, *Monuments antiques, inédits ou nouvellement expliqués*, Vol. 2, Paris: Laroche, 1806

Octave Mirbeau, *Correspondance avec Auguste Rodin*, edited by Pierre Michel and Jean-François Nivet, Paris: Du Lérot, 1988

Octave Mirbeau et al., *Auguste Rodin et son oeuvre*, Paris: Éditions de 'La Plume', 1900

Eugène Müntz, *Guide de l'École nationale des Beaux-Arts*, Paris: Maison Quantin, n.d.

Leonée and Richard Ormond, *Lord Leighton*, New Haven and London: Yale University Press, 1975

Maxime Paz, *La formation d'Auguste Rodin (1854–1865) ou Les petits arrangements avec la mémoire*, Master's dissertation, University of Paris I Panthéon-Sorbonne, under the tutelage of Pierre Wat, 2013

Pascale Picard et al., *Rodin: La Lumiere de l'antique*, Paris: Éditions Gallimard, 2013

Sander Pierron, *Étude d'art: François Rude et Auguste Rodin à Bruxelles*, Brussels: Xavier Havermans, 1903

Plutarch, *Lives: Pericles*, translated by Bernadotte Perrin, Loeb edition, Cambridge, Mass. and London: Harvard University Press, 1915

J. J. Pollitt, *The Ancient View of Greek Art: Criticism, History, and Terminology*, New Haven and London: Yale University Press, 1974

Elizabeth Prettejohn, *The Modernity of Ancient Sculpture: Greek Sculpture and Modern Art From Winckelmann to Picasso*, London: I. B. Tauris, 2012

Benedict Read, *Victorian Sculpture*, New Haven and London: Yale University Press, 1982

Salomon Reinach, *Répertoire des reliefs grecs et romains*, Vol. I, *Les ensembles*, Paris: E. Leroux, 1909

Salomon Reinach, 'Courrier de l'art antique', *La Gazette des Beaux-Arts*, January 1910

Rainer Maria Rilke, *Auguste Rodin*, Berlin: Richard Muther and Julius Bard, 1903; translated into English by Jessie Lemont and Hans Trausil, New York, Sunwise Turn Inc., 1919; translated into French, by Maurice Betz, Paris: Éditions Émile-Paul Frères, 1928

Rainer Maria Rilke, *Rodin and Other Prose Pieces*, introduction by William Tucker, London: Quartet Books, 1996

Florence Rionnet, *L'atelier de moulage du musée du Louvre (1794–1928)*, Paris: Réunion des musées nationaux, 1996

Jacob Rothenberg, *Descensus Ad Terram: The Acquisition and Reception of the Elgin Marbles*, New York and London: Garland Publishing, 1977

Henry Rousseau, *Catalogue sommaire des moulages*, Brussels: Musées royaux du Cinquantenaire à Bruxelles, 1913

Diana Rowell, *Paris: The 'New Rome' of Napoleon I*, London: Bloomsbury, 2012

William St Clair, *Lord Elgin and the Marbles: The Controversial History of the Parthenon Sculptures*, Oxford: Oxford University Press, 3rd ed., 1998

A. H. Smith, *The Sculptures of the Parthenon*, London: British Museum, 1910

A. H. Smith, 'Lord Elgin and his Collection', *Journal of Hellenic Studies* 36, 1916, pp. 163–372

J. Spon and G. Wheler, *Voyage d'Italie, de Dalmatie, de Grèce, et du Levant, fait aux années 1675 & 1676*, 3 vols, Lyon: A.Cellier, 1678

James Stuart and Nicholas Revett, *The Antiquities of Athens measured and delineated*, 4 vols, London: J. Haberkorn, 1762–1816

P. Tournikiotis (ed.), *The Parthenon and Its Impact in Modern Times*, Athens: Melissa Publishing House, 1994

Jules-Antoine Vauthier and Pierre Lacour, *Monuments de sculpture anciens et modernes*, Paris: Bance, 1820–39

Antoine Héron de Villefosse and Etienne Michon, *Musée du Louvre, Département des Antiquités grecques et romaines, catalogue sommaire des marbres antiques*, Paris: Librairies-Imprimeries réunies, 1891–1901

E. Q. Visconti, *Mémoires sur des ouvrages de sculpture du Parthénon, et de quelques édifices de l'Acropole à Athènes…*, Paris: Pierre Dufart, 1818

Dyfri Williams, '"Of publick utility and publick property": Lord Elgin and the Parthenon Sculptures', in Athéna Tsingarida and Donna Kurtz (eds), *Appropriating Antiquity: Saisir l'Antique: Collections et collectionneurs d'antiques en Belgique et en Grande-Bretagne au XIXe siècle*, Brussels: Le Livre Timperman, 2002, pp. 103–164

Dyfri Williams, 'Lord Elgin's firman', *Journal of the History of Collections* 21, 2009, pp. 49–76

J. J. Winckelmann, *Geschichte der Kunst des Alterthums*, Dresden: Walther, 1764

R. Worsley, *Museum Worsleyanum; or, A collection of antique basso relievos, bustos, statues and gems…*, London, 1794–1824

Works by Rodin

Auguste Rodin, 'La tête Warren', *Le Musée: revue d'art antique* 1 (6), 1904, pp. 298–301

Auguste Rodin, 'Le Parthénon et les Cathédrales', *Le Musée: revue d'art antique* 2 (1), 1905, pp. 66–68

Auguste Rodin, 'Rodin en Grèce', *La Liberté*, 25 December 1906

Auguste Rodin, 'À la Vénus de Milo', *L'Art et les Artistes* no. 10, March 1910. Published in English as 'To the Venus De Milo', *Art and Progress*, 3, no. 2, December 1911, 409–413

Auguste Rodin, *L'Art: Entretiens réunis par Paul Gsell*, Paris: Bernard Grasset, 1911; 1986

Auguste Rodin, *Art: Conversations with Paul Gsell*, translated by Jacques de Caso and Patricia B. Sanders with an introduction by Jacques de Caso, Berkeley: University of California Press, 1984

Auguste Rodin, 'Pierre et marbre', *Paris Le Journal*, 1 January 1912

Auguste Rodin, *Les cathédrales de France*, Paris: Armand Colin, 1914

Image credits

The publisher would like to thank the copyright holders for granting permission to reproduce the images illustrated. Every attempt has been made to trace accurate ownership of copyrighted images in this book. Any errors or omissions will be corrected in subsequent editions provided notification is sent to the publisher.

Further information about the Museum and its collection can be found at britishmuseum.org

All images from the British Museum are © The Trustees of the British Museum unless otherwise stated below.

All images from the Musée Rodin are © Musée Rodin unless otherwise stated below.

Frontispiece and Cat. 5: © Musée Rodin (photo Jean de Calan)
Page 8: © Musée Rodin (photo: Eugene Druet)

The French romance for Greek marbles
Fig. 4: Guildhall Art Gallery, City of London
Fig. 5: Image courtesy of the Watts Gallery, Compton
Fig. 6: Photo © Christie's Images / Bridgeman Images
Fig. 7: © Tate, London 2018
Fig. 8: © National Museum Wales
Fig. 10: Image courtesy of the Athens City Museum
Fig. 11: Private Collection, image courtesy of Sotheby's
Fig. 14: Photo © RMN-Grand Palais (Musée du Louvre) / Jean-Gilles Berizzi
Fig. 15: Photo © Beaux-Arts de Paris, Dist. RMN-Grand Palais / image Beaux-arts de Paris
Fig. 16: © Léopold Mercier / Roger-Viollet

'My dream as a sculptor' – the thousand Parthenons of Auguste Rodin
Fig. 3: Photo © Beaux-Arts de Paris, Dist. RMN-Grand Palais / image Beaux-arts de Paris
Fig. 4: Photo © Beaux-Arts de Paris, Dist. RMN-Grand Palais / image Beaux-arts de Paris
Fig. 5: Photo © Beaux-Arts de Paris, Dist. RMN-Grand Palais / image Beaux-arts de Paris
Fig. 6: © Musée Rodin (photo Jean de Calan)
Fig. 12: © The Estate of Edward Steichen / ARS, NY and DACS, London 2018

Catalogue
The British Museum: a temple of the Muses
Cat. 1: © Musée Rodin (photo Christian Baraja)

Rodin's Parthenon
Fig. 3 © The Estate of Edward Steichen / ARS, NY and DACS, London 2018
Cat. 2: © Musée Rodin (photo Jean de Calan)
Cat. 3: © Musée Rodin (photo Jean de Calan)
Cat. 4: © Musée Rodin (photo Jean de Calan)
Cat. 5: © Musée Rodin (photo Jean de Calan)
Cat. 6: © Musée Rodin (photo Jean de Calan)
Cat. 7: © Musée Rodin (photo Jean de Calan)
Cat. 8: © Musée Rodin (photo Jean de Calan)
Cat. 9: © Musée Rodin (photo Jean de Calan)
Cat. 10: © Musée Rodin (photo Herve Lewandowski)
Cat. 11: © Musée Rodin (photo Jean de Calan)
Fig. 4: © Musée Rodin (photo Jean de Calan)
Fig. 5: © Musée Rodin (photo Jean de Calan)
Cat. 12: © Musée Rodin (photo Jean de Calan)
Cat. 13: © Musée Rodin (photo Herve Lewandowski)
Cat. 14: © Musée Rodin (photo Herve Lewandowski)
Cat. 15: © Musée Rodin (photo Herve Lewandowski)
Cat. 16: © Musée Rodin (photo Jean de Calan)
Cat. 17: © Musée Rodin (photo Jean de Calan)
Fig. 7: © Musée Rodin (photo Herve Lewandowski)
Cat. 18: © Musée Rodin (photo Jean de Calan)
Cat. 19: © Musée Rodin (photo Jean de Calan)
Cat. 20: © Musée Rodin (photo Jean de Calan)
Cat. 21: © Musée Rodin (photo Jean de Calan)
Cat. 22: © Musée Rodin (photo Jean de Calan)
Cat. 23: © Musée Rodin (photo Jean de Calan)
Cat. 24: © Musée Rodin (photo Jean de Calan)
Fig. 10: © Musée Rodin (photo Jean de Calan)
Cat. 25: © agence photographique du Musée Rodin – Pauline Hisbacq
Cat. 26: © Musée Rodin (photo Jean de Calan)
Cat. 27: © Musée Rodin (photo Christian Baraja)

Cat. 28: © agence photographique du Musée Rodin – Pauline Hisbacq
Cat. 29: © Musée Rodin (photo Angele Dequier)
Cat. 30: © agence photographique du Musée Rodin – Pauline Hisbacq
Cat. 31: © Musée Rodin (photo Christian Baraja)
Cat. 35: © Musée Rodin (photo Christian Baraja)
Cats 36–37: © Musée Rodin (photo Christian Baraja)

Art and nature

Cat. 38: © Musée Rodin (photo Christian Baraja)
Cat. 40: photo © The Trustees of the British Museum
Cat. 42: Photo © RMN-Grand Palais (Musée d'Orsay) / René-Gabriel Ojéda

The monument

Fig. 15: Photo (C) RMN-Grand Palais (Musée d'Orsay) / Droits réservés
Fig. 16: © Musée Rodin (photo Herve Lewandowski)
Cat. 43: © Musée Rodin (photo Beatrice Hatala)
Cat. 44: © Musée Rodin (photo Christian Baraja)
Cat. 45: © Musée Rodin (photo Christian Baraja)
Fig. 17: © Musée Rodin (photo Jean de Calan)
Fig. 18: © Musée Rodin (photo Jean de Calan)
Fig. 19: © Musée Rodin (photo Jean de Calan)
Cat. 46: © Musée Rodin (photo Jean de Calan)
Fig. 20: © Musée Rodin (photo Jean de Calan)
Cat. 47: © Musée Rodin (photo Herve Lewandowski)
Cat. 48: © Musée Rodin (photo Christian Baraja)
Cat. 49: © agence photographique du Musée Rodin - Jérome Manoukian
Fig. 21: Photo (C) Musée du Louvre, Dist. RMN-Grand Palais / Daniel Lebée / Carine Déambrosis
Cat. 51: © Musée Rodin (photo Christian Baraja)
Cat. 52: © Musée Rodin (photo Herve Lewandowski)
Cat. 54: © Musée Rodin (photo Christian Baraja)
Cat. 55: © Courtesy National Museums Liverpool
Cat. 56: © agence photographique du Musée Rodin – Pauline Hisbacq
Fig. 23: © agence photographique du Musée Rodin – Pauline Hisbacq
Cat. 57: © Musée Rodin (photo Herve Lewandowski)
Cat. 58: © National Museum Wales
Fig. 24: © Musée Rodin (photo Jean de Calan)
Fig. 25: © Musée Rodin (photo Jean de Calan)
Cat. 59: © Musée Rodin (photo Jean de Calan)
Fig. 26: © Musée Rodin (photo Jean de Calan)
Fig. 27: © Musée Rodin (photo Jean de Calan)
Cat. 60: © Musée Rodin (photo Jean de Calan)

The fragment

Cat. 62: © Musée Rodin (photo Christian Baraja)
Cat. 63: © Musée Rodin (photo Christian Baraja)
Cat. 65: © Musée Rodin (photo Angele Dequier)
Cat. 66: © Musée Rodin (photo Angele Dequier)
Cat. 67: © Musée Rodin (photo Angele Dequier)
Cat. 68: © Musée Rodin (photo Angele Dequier)
Cat. 69: © Musée Rodin (photo Angele Dequier)
Cat. 70: © Musée Rodin (photo Christian Baraja)
Cat. 71: © agence photographique du Musée Rodin – Jerome Manoukian
Cat. 72: © agence photographique du Musée Rodin – Jerome Manoukian
Cat. 73: © Musée Rodin (photo Christian Baraja)
Cat. 74: © Musée Rodin (photo Angele Dequier)
Cat. 75: © agence photographique du Musée Rodin – Pauline Hisbacq
Cat. 76: © agence photographique du Musée Rodin – Pauline Hisbacq
Cat. 77: © Musée Rodin (photo Christian Baraja)
Cats 78–81: © agence photographique du Musée Rodin – Pauline Hisbacq
Cat. 82: © agence photographique du Musée Rodin – Pauline Hisbacq
Cat. 83: © Musée Rodin (photo Christian Baraja)
Fig. 35: © Musée Rodin (photo Jean de Calan)
Cat. 84: © agence photographique du Musée Rodin – Pauline Hisbacq
Cat. 85: © agence photographique du Musée Rodin – Pauline Hisbacq
Cats 86–88: © agence photographique du Musée Rodin – Pauline Hisbacq
Cat. 89: © agence photographique du Musée Rodin – Pauline Hisbacq

Cat. 90: © Musée Rodin (photo Jean de Calan)
Fig. 38: © Musée Rodin (photo Christian Baraja)
Cat. 91: © Musée Rodin (photo Angele Dequier)
Cat. 92: © Musée Rodin (photo Angele Dequier)
Cat. 93: © Musée Rodin (photo Christian Baraja)
Cat. 94: © Musée Rodin (photo Christian Baraja)
Fig. 40: © Musée Rodin (photo Jean de Calan)
Fig. 41: © Musée Rodin (photo Jean de Calan)
Cat. 95: © agence photographique du Musée Rodin – Pauline Hisbacq
Fig. 42: By permission of Llyfrgell Genedlaethol Cymru/ National Library of Wales
Cat. 96: © Musée Rodin (photo Adam Rzepka)

Emotion

Cat. 97: © agence photographique du Musée Rodin – Pauline Hisbacq
Cat. 100: © Musée Rodin (photo Christian Baraja)
Cat. 101: © Musée Rodin (photo Christian Baraja)
Cat. 102: Image © The Trustees of the British Museum
Fig. 47: Illustration by Kate Morton, British Museum

Motion

Cat. 107: © Musée Rodin (photo Herve Lewandowski)
Cat. 108: © Musée Rodin (photo Christian Baraja)
Fig. 49: © Musée Rodin (photo Christian Baraja)
Cat. 109: © Musée Rodin (photo Jean de Calan)
Fig. 50: © Musée Rodin (photo Christian Baraja)
Cat. 110: © Musée Rodin (photo Christian Baraja)
Cat. 112: © Musée Rodin (photo Adam Rzepka)

List of lenders

Apart from those from the British Museum, the objects included in the exhibition *Rodin and the art of ancient Greece* have been kindly loaned by a number of public collections and institutions. The British Museum would like to thank all the lenders for their generosity, in particular the Musée Rodin in Paris, who have lent over 90 works of art. The exhibition has been made possible by the provision of insurance through the Government Indemnity Scheme. The British Museum would like to thank HM Government for providing Government Indemnity, and the Department for Digital, Culture, Media and Sport and Arts Council England for arranging the indemnity.

Musée Rodin, Paris
Amgueddfa Cymru – National Museum Wales, Cardiff
Musée d'Orsay, Paris
National Museums, Liverpool
The Royal Parks

Acknowledgments

The authors of this catalogue thank the many individuals who have contributed in so many different ways to bring this exhibition about. There are inevitably omissions here but we are grateful to all. Tiphaine Ameil, Chloé Ariot, Sophie Biass-Fabiani, François Blanchetière, Sandra Boujot, Alexis Bross, Sonia Christon, Peter Dawson/Grade Design, Darrel Day, Audrey D'Hendecourt, Cyrielle Durox, Nicola Elvin, Joanna Fernandes, Mark Finch, Sara Forster, Clémence Goldberger, Claire Guitton, Peter Higgs, Pauline Hisbacq, Elaine Hunter, Susanna Ingram, Anais Izard, Sophie Joigneau, Maggie Kennedy-Creagh, Deklan Kilfeather, Verena Kotonski, Fanny Kurzenne, Christine Lancestremère, Ella Lewis-Collins, Marie Louis, Jill Maggs, Jérome Manoukian, Aurelia Masson-Berghoff, Freddie Matthews, Véronique Mattiussi, Marcel Molac, Kate Morton, Tomasina Munden, Jenny Nicholls, Robert Owen, Hélène Pinet, Michael Raymond, Jenny Suggitt, Tracey Sweek, Diane Tytgat, Sarah Vernon-Hunt, Alice Wallon and John Williams. Particular thanks go to Claudia Bloch (Senior Editorial Manager), Lucy More (Project Manager), Rebecca Penrose (Interpretation Officer), Victoria Ward (Senior Designer), and guiding spirits Lesley Fitton and David Souden.

Many individuals and outside organizations have supported the project in various ways, they include colleagues at the V&A, especially Alicia Robinson, Alison Smith at Tate Britain and Catherine Lampert, whose gracious support and encouragement has been hugely reassuring. Other lenders must also be thanked and they are Amgueddfa Cymru – National Museum Wales, Cardiff, the Musée d'Orsay, Paris, National Museums, Liverpool, and The Royal Parks. Our thanks also go to the outside designers Stephen Greenberg and Claus Voigtmann at Metaphor, Matt Bigg at Surface 3, David Robertson at DHA Designs, and Factory Settings for the build.

The director of the Musée Rodin especially wishes to thank Neil MacGregor for his encouragement of this project from its early stages.

Index of works by Rodin

Italic page numbers indicate illustrations

General index

Italic page numbers indicate illustrations